1.3. Archaeological sites, some mod⟨…⟩ ⟨…⟩ d in this
book. Names of settlements in the Cu⟨…⟩ s in the text
can be located on this map (or in fig. ⟨…⟩ ng below:

Inka Settlement Planning

INKA
SETTLEMENT
PLANNING

John Hyslop

 University of Texas Press, Austin

First Edition, 1990

This book has been supported by a grant from the National
Endowment for the Humanities, an independent federal agency.

∞ The paper used in this publication meets the minimum
requirements of American National Standard for Information
Sciences—Permanence of Paper for Printed Library Materials,
ANSI Z39.48-1984.

Library of Congress Cataloging-in-Publication Data

Hyslop, John, 1945–
    Inka settlement planning / John Hyslop. — 1st ed.
        p.   cm.
    Includes bibliographical references.
    ISBN 0-292-73852-8 (alk. paper)
    1. Incas—Architecture.   2. Land settlement patterns, Prehis-
toric—Andes Region.   3. Incas—Antiquities.   4. Andes Region—
Antiquities.   I. Title.
F3429.3.A65H97   1990
980'.01—dc20   89-39443
                                                                CIP

To Dr. C. A. Tripp,
a most original, perceptive,
and generous friend

Contents

Preface

Anyone who sees an Inka state settlement rarely forgets the experience. This book explores the design of such settlements. It may be of interest to the tourist visiting Machu Picchu, to the archaeologist studying an Inka fort or administrative center, and to those with a general interest in pre-Columbian architecture and native American civilization.

Why is the design of Inka settlements important? First, they are a major archaeological phenomenon spread over an area larger than that of any other pre-Columbian civilization. Second, their design informs us about how Inkas thought, and about ideas purveyed to their subjects. Third, the planning of Inka state installations tells us something about how the empire was organized, managed, and defended. Finally, the settlements are so complex that information from them influences the interpretation of most other Inka physical remains.

My research on Inka settlements began in 1974, when I surveyed the site Chucuito on the shore of Lake Titicaca during doctoral dissertation fieldwork. That interest expanded between 1978 and 1981, when I surveyed a number of segments of the Inka road system throughout the Andes (Hyslop 1984) and had the opportunity to visit a number of large Inka installations distant from Cuzco, the Inka capital in southern Peru.

In 1979 I began research at Inkawasi, an Inka garrison in Peru (Hyslop 1985). Mapping and interpreting Inkawasi raised many questions about Inka site planning. I decided then that knowledge about Inka site design could be advanced by a comparative study. My realization that most Inka state settlements were not in the Cuzco area, but spread throughout the Andes, led me in 1986 and 1987 to carry out survey and mapping at more than a dozen Inka settlements from Ecuador to Chile. Meanwhile, frequent visits to Cuzco and environs from 1973 on familiarized me with many of the sites in the Inka heartland.

This book discusses a range of Inka settlements in the Cuzco area and throughout Tawantinsuyu. It includes more aerial photographs and detailed site plans than any previous Inka study. It includes new and ignored information, particularly from state settlements in Argentina and Ecuador. The site descriptions here are nearly always based on my field notes as well as on the published works of others.

This book is a companion for my *The Inka Road System*, published in 1984. Both books deal with the physical infrastructure of the Inka state. Both compare evidence within a pan-Andean perspective. Each has greater relevance when accompanied by the other. This book is, however, potentially more controversial because it attempts to ascribe Andean meaning to archaeological features and patterns. The emphasis here on the symbolic aspects of Inka archaeological remains is only touched on in *The Inka Road System*.

The words *city* and *urban* are usually avoided in this book because of the diverse meanings that have accrued to them in specialized literature. Instead, I most often used the more general terms "state settlement" and "state installation," meaning a group of buildings and associated features where people lived or worked while engaged in activities related to the Inka Empire.

All maps, line drawings, and photographs are by me unless credited completely or partially to another source. Abbreviations used in the credit lines represent the following institutions: AMNH, American Museum of Natural History, New York; S.A.N., Servicio Aerofotográfico Nacional, Lima.

Acknowledgments

My surveying and mapping at Inka settlements took place in 1986 and the first part of 1987. It was sponsored in the United States by the Institute of Andean Research, New York City. I thank its president, Dr. John V. Murra, and secretary, Dr. Craig Morris, for their support of the project and efforts on its behalf. Paul Beelitz, the institute's administrator, managed bureaucratic tasks with concern and efficiency.

My fieldwork was funded by grants from the National Endowment for the Humanities, a federal agency which supports the study of such fields as history, philosophy, literature, languages, and archaeology; the Stella and Charles Guttman Foundation, Inc.; Dr. C. A. Tripp; and Mr. Leon Pomerance.

In South America numerous scholars and students accompanied me to the field and provided a base for my survey. In Argentina, Dr. Juan Schobinger extended great hospitality and facilitated the trip to La Rioja Province for the Chilecito survey. Prof. J. Roberto Bárcena made possible a return excursion to Ranchillos in Mendoza. Through Dr. Schobinger's initiative, it was possible to organize the expedition to Nevados de Aconquija. Mr. Antonio Beorchia and Prof. Bárcena also accompanied that expedition, contributing much to its success. Our estimable guide on that journey was Mr. Juan Carlos Reales.

I thank archaeologist Víctor Núñez Regueiro, director of the Institute of Archaeology of the National University of Tucumán, for providing me with a base from which I was able to visit sites in Catamarca province. Prof. Eduardo Arias, also of the institute, was most helpful with local arrangements and I thank him for accompanying Dr. Alberto Rex González and me on a field trip to the Santa María and Vallecito areas. I thank Rex González for stimulating conversations concerning Inka and Argentine archaeology. Mr. Mario Guerra was my excellent assistant on one lengthy trip into Catamarca.

My gratitude is extended to Mr. Pío "Pibe" Pablo Díaz, director of the Archaeological Museum of Cachi, Salta Province. Pibe not only made possible a return to the sites La Paya, Cortaderas, and Potrero de Payogasta, but took valuable time to accompany me to the Quebrada de Humahuaca in Jujuy Province to inspect several other settlements.

In Bolivia I am grateful to Mr. Edmundo Claure, the archaeologist of Samaipata, for the time and concern he invested in my visit. In Cochabamba, I owe much to the archaeologists of the university's Archaeological Museum, Mr. David Pereira and Mr. Ramón Sanzetenea, who made possible a return to Incallacta.

Gratitude is extended to Dr. Ramiro Matos of Lima, Peru, who was most generous in sharing his ideas and information about Pumpu and arranging for me to visit the site. I thank Mr. Alfredo Altamirano for assisting my activities at Pumpu and for doing the ink renderings of several of the plans published here. I am grateful to Mr. Elias Mujica of Lima, who accompanied me to the department of Puno, where we visited Pucará and returned to Chucuito to record map data.

In Ecuador I wish to acknowledge the help and advice of Dr. Antonio Fresco, director of research of the Archaeological Museum of the Central Bank of Ecuador. He arranged for students to accompany me to the sites Callo and Pambamarca. In Cuenca I was pleased to visit Dr. Jaime Idrovo and Mr. Jorge Guaman, who were generous with their time and ideas concerning the remarkable Tomebamba excavations.

Conversations with numerous other scholars in the Andes aided in the development of my ideas about Inka settlement planning. I thank Chileans Mr. Hans Niemeyer, Mr. Carlos Aldunate, Mr. Rubén Stehberg, and Dr. Mario Rivera. Argentine scholars who have stimulated my thinking are Dr. Ana María Lorandi, Dr. Rodolfo Raffino, and Mrs. Teresa Piossek Prebisch. In Bolivia I thank Dr. Hernando Sanabria Fernández, Dr. Hugo Daniel Ruiz, and Mr. Oswaldo Rivera Sundt. Several Peruvian scholars have aided me considerably with problems addressed in this book. I particularly thank Dr. Luis Guillermo Lumbreras, Dr. María Rostworowski de Diez Canseco, and Mr. Santiago Agurto Calvo.

I am most grateful to N.E.H. for the grant that enabled me to prepare this manuscript. Ms. Elizabeth Arndt supervised the grant with efficiency and concern. Work began on the manuscript in April 1987, and was concluded in June 1988. The Institute of Andean Research was able to supply additional stipend funds from a donation by Mr. Leon Pomerance. A donation from Dr. C. A. Tripp was used to cover photographic, copying, drafting, and editing expenses. Dr. Tripp also donated computer and printer facilities and supplied valuable computer advice.

During the writing of the manuscript, I frequently used the facilities of the New York Public Library, which I thank for its customary fine service. I also thank the Bobst Library of New York University, which was often useful. Dr. Craig Morris of the American Museum of Natural History kindly made available the collections of Adolph Bandelier paintings and drawings and the Shippee Johnson photographs. I wish to thank Mr. Edward Franquemont for data and observations about the stones of Chinchero. Mr. Alfredo Altamirano drafted figures 3.3, 3.8, 3.9, 3.10, 3.23, 5.8, 6.22, 6.26, and 7.13. Mr. Edward Bahnimptewa drafted figures 1.2, 1.3, 2.3, 2.14, and 6.8. Mr. Delfin Zúñiga drafted figures 5.7, 7.10, and 7.18. I am grateful to Dr. Anthony Aveni for comments on chapter 8. The interest shown in this project by Dr. R. Tom Zuidema has been most gratifying.

I was most fortunate to acquire the deft editing services of Ms. Adriana von Hagen, who did much to polish the rough draft of this book. I also thank my parents, Mr. and Mrs. Robert Hyslop, for proofreading. Special gratitude goes to Dr. Fritz Fluckiger, who not only proofread the manuscript with great care, but made useful organizational suggestions. Although the research and ideas of many people are integrated into this book, I assume final responsibility for its content.

Inka Settlement Planning

1.1. *Tawantinsuyu, the Inka Empire. Its capital was Cuzco, a city now in southern Peru. At its greatest extent, Tawantinsuyu controlled the region from the Colombian-Ecuadorian border to a point south of Santiago, Chile. The eastern boundary of the Inka Empire in Ecuador, Peru, and Bolivia has not yet been precisely defined. It bordered on, and occasionally extended into, the Amazonian lowlands. The Andes were the backbone of Inka territory. The desert strip along the Pacific coast from the southern Ecuadorian border to north-central Chile is punctuated with irrigated river valleys. Inka settlements in northwest Argentina are located along irrigated valleys in arid territory to the east of the high Andes. Key: 1. Inka border, relatively accurate; 2. poorly defined Inka border; 3. modern international boundary between republics.*

1
Introduction

During the eighty years of its existence prior to the European invasion of the Andes in A.D. 1532, the Inka state had been expanding over 5,500 kilometers of some of the world's most rugged terrain (fig. 1.1). In most areas, the Inkas left buildings and public works constructed according to ideas developed in the south-central Andes, the area around Cuzco, the Inka capital.

The imperial activities of the Inkas were short-lived, but during their brief dominion they created planned settlements in a greater region than had any other native American civilization. This book will explore and interpret Inka architectural planning as seen throughout the Inka state.

Numerous publications have emerged in recent years defining aspects of Inka architecture. Because they are based primarily on abundant historical and archaeological data from the Cuzco region (fig. 1.2), they have added considerably to knowledge about how Inkas constructed buildings and compounds. They have not concentrated on aspects of Inka architecture apart from buildings, nor have they drawn many data from the great number of Inka settlements outside of the Cuzco area.

This book discusses how settlements were designed and how their locations were selected. It also analyzes a number of architectural features that are not buildings, but that are clearly part of the Inka settlement concept. Thus, rocks and outcrops (chap. 4), water systems (chap. 5), and terracing (chap. 10) are treated at some length. Because much existing Inka architecture forms part of forts and garrisons, an entire chapter (6) is devoted to aspects of military planning.

Distribution of Planned Inka Settlements
It would be easy simply to state that evidence for Inka architectural planning is found in all regions of the territory known to have been under the control of the Inkas (endpapers, fig. 1.3). For a number of reasons, this is not the case. For example, little or no Inka architecture is

3

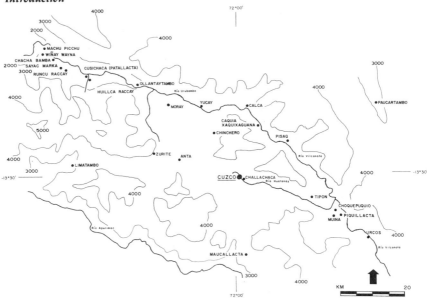

1.2. The area around Cuzco, the Inka capital, now in the southern highlands of Peru. From this region the small Inka kingdom expanded in the fifteenth century after Christ into pre-Columbian America's largest state.

found on the north coast of Peru, and few Inka buildings have been recorded in south-central Bolivia. Numerous other regions, some several hundred kilometers in extension, have no identified Inka buildings.

One reason for their absence in a given area is destruction during the last 450 years of Spanish colonial and republican rule. The destruction is a combination of natural and artificial factors. The apparent lack of Inka architecture in a region may also be attributed to a lack of research by archaeologists. In other words, many Inka sites remain to be discovered or described. It is now clear, however, that in some regions the Inkas constructed very few buildings or sites with architectural characteristics typical of their home territory.

In general, few areas of the Andes have failed to produce evidence of Inka architecture when archaeological preservation in a region is good, and when the area has been surveyed. This does not mean, however, that the domain of Tawantinsuyu is littered with the remains of Inka administrative centers, forts, and so forth. Often the Inka remains in an area are not particularly noteworthy. If conquered towns and villages could be used for the required Inka activities, little might be built in the Inka style, or only a few Inka structures would be constructed within or on the edge of pre-existing settlements (chap. 9).

4

The main concern of this work is Inka architectural planning. It is difficult (but not impossible) to extract information about site planning from isolated Inka buildings. Sites that contribute considerable information to this theme are those where the architecture is primarily Inka and where local (non-Inka) architecture is limited. Unfortunately, the planning of a number of the larger Inka centers, such as Quito (Porras G. 1983), Hatun Xauxa (D'Altroy 1981), Cajamarca (Tello 1941; Ravines 1976), Ríobamba and Chuquiabo (M. Portugal 1956), cannot be studied easily, since they lie beneath modern cities. The known distribution of large, intact Inka settlements by no means indicates high-priority areas of the Inka state. Factors other than the state's political priorities dictate whether and if one will find good examples of Inka planning in a region. For example, planned settlements are usually found in regions where the infrastructure of pre-existing settlements could not be used by the Inkas. Thus military installations are among some of the best examples of Inka architectural planning, since they were built where the Inka state could not utilize pre-existing building complexes.

Characteristics of Inka Architecture

In the last seventy years many publications have described individual Inka buildings and sites in relative detail. In 1946 Rowe published observations about Inka domestic and public architecture, and commented on town planning (1946: 222–229). The definition of basic aspects of Inka architecture based on a comparative examination of many sites did not occur until the 1970s. Using settlements located primarily in the Cuzco region, works by Kendall (1974, 1976, 1985), Gasparini and Margolies (1977, 1980), Bouchard (1976a, 1976b, 1983), and, to a lesser degree, Hemming and Ranney (1982) have defined and clarified fundamental components of Inka architecture. They concentrate primarily on basic structural forms and characteristics of building shapes, doors, niches, floors, roofs, and so forth. These publications also discuss construction materials and briefly consider the question of the architecture's origins.

Before launching into aspects of Inka architectural planning, it is useful to review the most relevant information about Inka architecture. The following discussion should give readers a "feel" for the nature of Inka buildings and introduce them to the growing vocabulary used by specialists.

The Rectangular Building

The fundamental Inka architectural unit is a rectangular structure, generally without internal subdivisions. These single-room buildings were

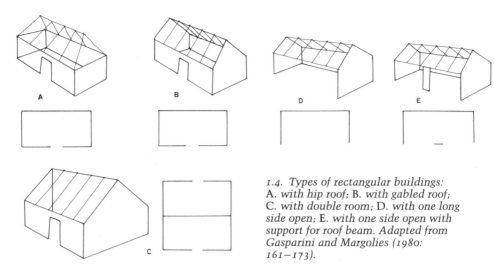

1.4. Types of rectangular buildings:
A. *with hip roof;* B. *with gabled roof;*
C. *with double room;* D. *with one long
side open;* E. *with one side open with
support for roof beam. Adapted from
Gasparini and Margolies (1980:
161–173).*

of many different sizes, yet small enough to be roofed with wooden beams.[1] The simplest of these structures had stone or adobe walls of uniform height, covered by a hip roof composed of wood poles covered with thatch (fig. 1.4, A). Several variations of this basic unit existed. Sometimes roofs were gabled (fig. 1.4, B). It was not unusual for two rectangular buildings to share a long wall, with that division becoming the support for a gabled roof (fig. 1.4, C). In this case, the single-room structure became a double-room building, but the individual-unit concept remained, since there were rarely any doors between the two rooms. Another variant of the single-room building was the rectangular structures with one long open side (fig. 1.4, D). If the open side was too long to be spanned by a wooden beam, a column or pillar would be placed in the open side to help support the roof beams (fig. 1.4, E). There were double open-sided structures that, like the double-room building, shared a long wall. Less commonly, two rectangular buildings might share an end wall. The single-room structures often had numerous specialized features, such as roof pegs, door ties, drain holes, and internal platforms, features described by Kendall (1976). The individual rectangular structures should not be considered single-family dwellings, particularly the open-sided type, which were open to the elements. Nor is there any certainty that the rectangular units used in Inka public architecture evolved from pre-Inka family dwelling units in the Cuzco area.

Form only sometimes indicates function in Inka architecture. That is, the shape of a building, or its name, usually provides little information for understanding how a building was used, or what it may have meant. In the case of single-room rectangular structures, some may have served as dwellings, but others may have served for various types of administrative or religious activities, and even for storage. In the words of Gasparini and Margolies (1980: 134): "The rectangular plan dominates almost all Inca building. From humble rural houses to the halls of the most sacred temple, the Qori Kancha, Inca architecture showed no special interest in seeking a variety of alternative shapes. Likewise, in both peasant houses and temples and 'palaces,' the rectangular plan was the basis of a single chamber [that is, not subdivided]."

Circular and Curved Buildings

Occasionally, curved walls were used, particularly in retaining walls as a response to irregular terrain. Curved walls in buildings were far less common. When present, they appear to have been in response to topography, or introduced in very important buildings as an element of prestige. Examples are the western wall of the Sun Temple in Cuzco, or the Torreón building at Machu Picchu. In some cases, curved or circular buildings may have adapted their shape from a local non-Inka architectural form. Examples are the round *chulpa* (burial towers) of fine Cuzco masonry in the Lake Titicaca area (Hyslop 1976), or the great oval building at Ingapirca (fig. 1.5).

1.5. Oval building of fine Cuzco masonry at Ingapirca, Ecuador. The curved shape was occasionally used in Inka buildings of high prestige. Here, it may have been derived from the oval house shape of the Cañari ethnic group, which inhabited the area around Ingapirca.

7

In the Cuzco area, round structures built by Inkas were rare. Two round buildings stood in the main plaza in Cuzco. The foundation of another round structure may be seen on the top of Saqsawaman (chap. 2) to the north of Cuzco. More round structures are found in and near Inka administrative centers outside of the Cuzco area than within it. In the central Andes, as well as some parts of Inka territory in eastern Bolivia and northwestern Argentina, silos, or *qollqa*, are frequently round.[2] When they are not *qollqa*, simple round buildings found within Inka administrative centers are generally thought to be dwellings built according to local (non-Inka) architectural tradition.

Two-Story Buildings

One story was most common in Inka buildings, but second stories were occasionally constructed from wood beams set within the walls, or on shelves built into the walls. The entrances to these second stories appear to have always been from the outside, by steps or from high terrain if the building was built on a steep slope. Many administrative centers and military installations had at least one two-story building (figs. 1.6, 1.7).

First (ground level) floors were flat, covered with packed earth, gravel, or even stone. The walls of buildings were usually battered inward but, according to Kendall (1976: 29), were generally no more than fifteen degrees off the vertical. Wall thickness did not diminish with height, unless a second story was used or a ledge created for a roof or floor support. Several factors appear to have influenced wall thickness, which varied from 65 centimeters to 1 meter in the Cuzco and Urubamba area (Kendall 1976: 30). Such factors include the building size, its importance, and structural considerations (e.g., the dividing wall of double-unit structures is generally quite thick, as it supports the roof).

Wall Apertures

In the Inka heartland, wall apertures were generally trapezoidal in form. Doors, which could be multiple, were usually placed on one long side of a rectangular unit and were generally symmetrically placed. If a door was placed in the end or lateral wall it was generally narrower than the front door(s) and asymmetrically located, often next to the perpendicular long wall. Kendall (1976: 33, 35) found that the base width of doors did not generally exceed 1.65 meters. Windows and niches were generally placed 1.25 meters above ground level and rarely had a base width over 60 centimeters. Lintels were stone or wood—often wrapped in braided fiber. Windows could be located high on a division wall or in the gables. Windows and niches were tall, up to body height, or very small, such as niches in water catchments or "baths."

1.6. A large two-story Inka building, the Pilco Kayma, located on the Island of the Sun in Lake Titicaca, Bolivia. Corbeled stone vaults formed the ceiling of the first floor. The second story has nearly disappeared. Corbeled stone ceilings are found in the Lake Titicaca region, where they were introduced into Inka architecture.

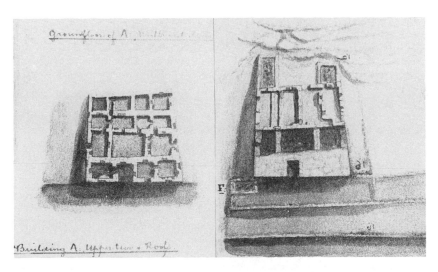

1.7. Plans of the ground floor (left) and the second story (right) of Pilco Kayma made by A. Bandelier in 1895. Courtesy Department of Anthropology, AMNH.

9

Especially elegant and no doubt prestigious was the use of double and triple jambs, generally on the exterior of buildings. Although not used throughout the Inka domain, the double-jamb doorway and niches of fine masonry are synonymous with Inka architecture (figs. 1.8, 1.9). Double and triple jambs are a form of ornamentation in Inka architecture, as were, no doubt, some wall apertures.

Square or rectangular wall apertures are found almost to the exclusion of the trapezoidal form in Inka buildings south of Lake Titicaca. The square or rectangular form mixes with trapezoidal shapes in apertures of buildings on the south coast of Peru.

Ornamentation

By western standards, Inka ornamentation was limited. There was more than can be seen today. Walls were sometimes painted or adorned with metal plaques. Carved and natural rock outcrops with considerable symbolism adorned architectural assemblages, and the landscape was often "sculpted" by the ingenious placement of terraces with well-laid walls and decorative niches. Landscape remodeling should be considered an integral part of an Inka settlement's architecture.

1.8. Trapezoidal window and double-jamb doorway at Colcampata, Cuzco, Peru.

Occasionally, small animals or simple geometric patterns were sculpted on Iṇka stonework. These are rare, and their depiction may have increased in Inka masonry laid in early Spanish colonial times. Another aspect of site ornamentation certainly included canals, reservoirs, stone tanks, or fountains. The complexity and symbolism of Inka waterworks is such that they must be considered an integral part of site architecture.

Construction Materials

No review of imperial Inka architecture would be complete without some comments on construction materials. The most common building material was fieldstones generally set in mortar. A variant of this was semiworked blocks set in mortar (fig. 1.10). Often, combinations of the two would be used, with semiworked blocks forming critical sections such as corners or edges. At times it is difficult to see if stones have been worked, or if they have simply been laid with a flat side out. The walls of rough stone appear different in various sites, since the nature and quality of the stone varies from area to area. In many cases, walls of rough or semiworked stone were covered with a stucco-like mud or clay

1.9. Double-jamb niches in a building at Huaytará, Peru. This Inka structure, one of the finest ever constructed, has been converted into a church.

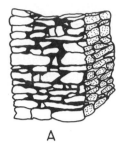 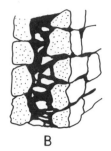

A   B

1.10. Two types of Inka stone wall construction: A. composed of fieldstones set in mortar; the mortar could be made of earth, clay, sand, and organic materials; B. composed of semiworked blocks with central fill. Redrawn from Bouchard (1983: 33).

surface and then painted. In most structures it is often difficult to tell if such surfacing was used uniformly, since it may have been washed away by rains. Frequently, the only indication of such a surface is its remains inside niches or under lintels, where erosion has not taken place. Wall surfaces were painted black, red,[3] white, and yellow/ochre, and sometimes the paint was applied with horizontal color changes.

Many buildings in the Cuzco region were built partly of adobe. Moorehead (1978: 65) writes that "the craftsmanship of Inca stonework has been glorified to such an extent as to give the general impression that the Incas built only in stone." She goes on to note that the Inkas used adobe bricks in some of their finest as well as their common buildings. The adobe bricks were frequently made of earth with grass (fig. 1.11). Inka adobes are generally rectangular, but with irregularities in flatness and in the angularity of the corners. English bond was frequently the laying technique. Adobes were generally laid over stone foundations over one meter in height, probably to protect against rain and groundwater. Thus adobes often form the upper parts of walls where windows and niches are located and were also common in gables and second stories. As with some Inka stone walls, adobe walls were often covered with a mud-clay surface. The coating apparently was aesthetic and protective, covering the bricks, mortar, lintels, and sometimes the stone beneath and bestowing a relatively smooth and uniform surface (Moorehead 1978: 67).

Fine Masonry

Fine Inka masonry is the most famous aspect of Inka architecture. Superbly cut and shaped stones, fitted together with remarkable precision and without mortar, continue to amaze tourists and archaeologists alike. One must not assume, however, that fine masonry always accompanies Inka architectural complexes. In fact, it occurs only infrequently in certain regions and in special constructions outside the Cuzco area. Fine Inka masonry is but one of many features sometimes integrated into Inka settlement plans.

There has been much conjecture about how such stones were moved, shaped, and fitted together. One need not refer to mystical technologies, stone-eating liquids, or long-lost cutting tools to explain how such stones were cut. The production of fine masonry continued into the historical era and people saw, or remembered, how they were produced. The chronicler Bernabé Cobo (1964II: 261–262, Bk. 14, chap. 12) wrote:

> The thing that impresses us most when studying one of these buildings is the question of what tools or machines can have brought these stones from the quarries, worked them, and placed them where they are without iron tools or wheeled devices. . . . Thus one is justifiably amazed at the vast number of people needed [to build] these structures. . . .
>
> The tools that they used for cutting and working stones were hard black cobbles from the streams. They employed these more by pounding than cutting. They transported stones to where they

1.11. An example of Inka adobe wall construction. This building has 2-meter-high stone walls. The upper parts of the central wall and gables are adobe bricks. It is located at Inkahuasi on the edge of the high grasslands in the upper Pisco Valley, Peru.

were needed by pulling them. Having no hoists, wheels, or lifting devices, they made a sloping ramp up against the building and lifted the stones by rolling them up this. As the building rose, they raised the ramp proportionately.

Cobo also noted that to fit the stones together it was necessary to place them and then lift them many times so as to grind the surfaces to a perfect fit. The priest Joseph de Acosta (1985: 297, Bk. 6, chap. 14) also noted that the exact fitting of the stones required that they be checked many times. Both Cobo and Acosta mention only the use of stone tools to work stone. A study by Gordon (1985) demonstrates that sometimes bronze tools were used, particularly if depressions were cut with plane surfaces and angles.

1.12. *Polygonal (cellular) masonry at the site of Limatambo, west of Cuzco.*

1.13. *Polygonal (encased) masonry in the street of Hatun Rumiyoc in Cuzco.*

1.14. *Coursed (sedimentary) masonry in a building of the Intiwatana sector of Pisaq, Urubamba Valley, Peru.*

1.15. *Coursed (sedimentary) masonry at the site of Callo, south of Quito, Ecuador.*

Historian Gutiérrez de Santa Clara (1963III: 252, chap. 63) wrote one of the more detailed descriptions of how the stones of a fine masonry wall were lifted into place:

> to place one big stone over another, they worked it first and, before raising it, first put much earth at the foot of, and level with, the first placed stone. And then they put some large, thick posts of pine over the packed earth and there raised the stone with much effort. In this manner, the stone being raised, they fit it well into that below it. And as the building grew, they placed more well-packed and trampled earth at the feet of the fitted stones and laid larger beams over which they raised the other stones, which were excessively large. After this was done they took away the beams and all the earth and thus the wall appeared completed without any mortar.

In short, the stones were moved up over wood beams on earth ramps.[4] They were shaped with other stones, mainly by pounding, and laid in place by careful fitting and adjusting.[5] Large rocks were hauled considerable distances by large numbers of people with fiber, vine, and leather ropes. If there was any "secret" to the production of fine Inka masonry, it was the social organization necessary to maintain the great numbers of people creating such energy-consuming monuments.

Fine masonry may be classified in two categories: polygonal, and coursed or rectangular (Rowe 1944: 24–26, 1946: 225–227; Harth-Terré 1964). Agurto (1987: 144–175) has created a more detailed typology. He divides polygonal masonry into two categories: cellular, with small stones (fig. 1.12); and cyclopean, with very large stones (fig. 2.12). Coursed or rectangular masonry is classified as encased (*engastado*), with large semirectangular blocks whose shape is often interrupted to accommodate the corners of other blocks (fig. 1.13), and sedimentary, with rigidly rectangular blocks in horizontal or nearly horizontal rows (figs. 1.14, 1.15).

The polygonal varieties have individually fitted irregularly shaped blocks (cellular and cyclopean). They are most commonly used in terrace walls and river canalization, only rarely in buildings. The coursed or rectangular masonry is composed of rectangle-shaped blocks. The encased variety often has larger stones than the sedimentary variety, and is most commonly found in important perimeter walls and in the corners and wall apertures of buildings often constructed of rougher stones. Sedimentary blocks are used in important buildings and perimeter walls, but rarely in retaining walls or riverbank canalization.

When truly enormous stones are used in walls, they are polygonal (cyclopean), and are usually used in terracelike walls with much earth fill behind them. The cyclopean masonry is relatively rare. Some cyclopean stones exceed 6 meters in height and have a weight exceeding 100 tons.

The cellular, cyclopean, and encased masonry was more difficult to fit than sedimentary masonry, since each stone was cut and ground to the unique shape of its neighbors. They formed stronger walls, however, and thus were frequently used in terrace walls supporting the earth fill. Technical reasons do not always explain why one sort of masonry was used, or why variations within the various categories are common. Agurto (1987: 164) suggests that some of the stylistic variations in fine masonry may be associated with the social groups who occupied or built the walls and buildings. Other variations may be related to the size and type of stone and to the aesthetic preferences of the builders.

One notable variation in much fine masonry involves the joints between the stones. They are generally sunk below the rounded or bulging exterior surface of the blocks. In certain cases, coursed masonry has joints that have almost no sinking, producing a nearly smooth or flat wall (figs. 2.7, 2.10). Such walls are often (but not always) found in important buildings. It is true that many Inka stones are so well fitted that one cannot insert the proverbial knife-blade between them. As with Inka walls of rougher stones, fine masonry walls are battered toward the interior. The stones used at the base may be larger than those higher up, but not vice versa.

One curious aspect of some fine masonry blocks is protuberances, usually near the base. According to Rowe (1946: 226), these facilitated the use of levers, which lowered the blocks in place or raised the blocks while the joint was being prepared. Agurto (1987: 168) suggests that they were used as ties for transporting the stones. Some stones have cavities near their base, possibly used in the same way as the protuberances. It is strange, however, that in some cases the protuberances were not removed. Their presence is disconcerting to those who prefer a uniform Inka wall with no irregularities. Perhaps the earth ramps used to raise the stones covered some blocks that had protuberances. When the ramps were removed, the masons had moved on to other works. Gasparini and Margolies (1980: 331) suggest that the real purpose of these protuberances may not yet be understood.

Kancha

If the basic unit of Inka architecture is the rectangular building, the basic composite form of this unit is the *kancha*. In Cuzco, the ideal *kancha* was a rectangular enclosure with three or more rectangular

1.16. Reconstruction of a kancha *in Cuzco. From Agurto C. (1980: 146).*

structures placed symmetrically around the side of the compound (fig. 1.16) with a patio in the center. In practice, the size of the *kancha* could vary tremendously, from part of a large city block in Cuzco to a much smaller enclosure. The number of buildings within a *kancha* varied considerably also—up to eight or more structures (fig. 1.17). *Kancha* were often set side by side within larger architectural units. Often *kancha* have only one entrance in their enclosure wall. Gasparini and Margolies (1980: 186) suggest that grouping three or four rectangular structures around a patio reflects the *kancha* distributive pattern, whether or not there is an enclosure wall.

Bouchard (1976*b*) discusses how *kancha* could be set together to form complex, repetitive blocks of structures. When grouped together, several *kancha* could form a unit, or "block," within an Inka settlement plan. That unit might be rectangular or irregularly shaped. Often surrounded by walls, streets, or corridors, it would have several doors or entry points that did not have the public character of streets. A most notable example of this is found at Ollantaytambo, where the individual units or blocks of an orthogonal pattern are formed with two *kancha* (fig. 1.17, *B*).

Identifying a *kancha* in Inka architecture does not necessarily tell us about the activities carried out within it. It is clear that *kancha* were the architectural basis for simple dwellings, just as they could compose the basis for a palace or temple. It would seem that rooms within a *kancha* should have similar functions, but that is improbable, because sometimes *kancha* are composed of rectangular rooms, some with doors and others that are of the open-sided type. Much of the central sector of Cuzco was composed of *kancha*, and these groupings around patios served a variety of purposes: residences for kings and persons of royal lineage (*panaqa*), special production areas, and temples.

17

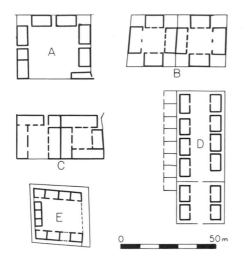

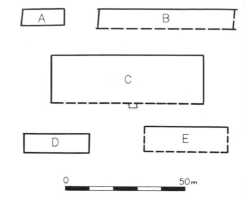

1.17. Plans of several kancha: A. *Tomebamba (Ecuador); B. Ollantaytambo (Peru); C. Incallacta (Bolivia); D. Shincal (Argentina); E. La Puerta (Chile). Redrawn from, A, Uhle (1923); B, Gasparini and Margolies (1980: 189); C, González and Cravotto (1977: fig. 7); D, Raffino et al. (1983–1985: 438); E, Niemeyer (1986: 239).*

1.18. Plans of different kallanka: A. Tomebamba (Ecuador); B. Huánuco Pampa (Peru); C. Incallacta (Bolivia); D. Potrero de Payogasta (Argentina); E. Chinchero (Peru). The locations of the doors in the* kallanka *of Tomebamba (A) and Potrero de Payogasta (D) cannot be ascertained, since only foundations remain of the side walls. Redrawn from, A, Uhle (1923); B, Morris and Thompson (1985: 83); C, Nordenskiöld (1913); D, Hyslop (1984: 117); E, Alcina F. (1976: 40).*

Kallanka

Another basic Inka building was the *kallanka*. Like *kancha, kallanka* defines an architectural form but tells us little about the activities associated with such constructions. *Kallanka* are long, often gabled, rectangular halls (fig. 1.18). Generally placed on Inka plazas, their doors opened onto the plaza. Usually these halls had one unsubdivided open space. At way stations along the Inka roads, these halls appear to have been used as residences for temporary occupants such as soldiers, quarters for the rotating supply of workers, or housing for anyone on state business. In Cuzco and some other places, *kallanka* were built on a much grander scale and used for ceremonies and festivals (P. Pizarro 1978: 160, chap. 2).

No *kallanka* remain in present-day Cuzco. Only a few examples of *kallanka* are found in the Cuzco-Urubamba region. Gasparini and Margolies (1980: 201) suggest that this may be because these settlements were not exposed to the transit of large masses of people. *Kallanka* are therefore best known and defined from examples outside of the Inka heartland (fig. 1.19). Several problems surround the definition of the *kallanka*. For example, no one has yet defined how large a rectangular Inka building must be to be called a *kallanka*. The word *kallanka* as used to define a form of building is of recent origin. A more appropriate term might be sought. The first Spaniards in the Andes called such halls *galpones*.

Origins of Inka Architecture

Much remains to be learned about the origins of Inka architecture, and some published commentary is merely speculative. It is now clear, however, that all aspects of Inka architecture did not have a common origin. That is, the Inkas drew ideas from diverse sources and traditions. One reason for this is that the Inkas did not have extremely ancient roots in the Cuzco area (Rostworowski 1988: 33).

Many characteristics of Inka architecture still defy analysis as to their origins. One example is the rectangular building. Rowe (1944: 24) suggested that it developed from the homes of peasants. Research in the last generation has demonstrated that house units in the Cuzco area (before the imperial Inka period) were not necessarily rectangular (Kendall 1985: 249; Arminda Gibaja, personal communication, 1987). Moreover,

1.19. The remains of a long hall, or kallanka, *on the south side of the plaza at Pumpu, Peru.*

the houses of the Chancas, Wankas, and Aymaras—their neighbors—were also irregularly shaped or round. Thus it is still not clear from where this most fundamental unit of Inka architecture came, or whether it was "invented," and thus had no prototype.

Archaeologists tend to consider that all cultural remains have antecedents. Such is not always the case. There are proven examples of the invention of relatively complex items that only faintly resemble earlier things. Some characteristics of Inka architecture may be the same. Unfortunately, the archaeology of the period just prior to the growth of the Inka state is still so poorly understood that it is often premature to claim which aspects of Inka architecture were invented and which have clear-cut prototypes.

It has been suggested that the Inka *kancha* derived from an architectural tradition on the north Peruvian coast (Rowe 1946: 229). Rectangular enclosure walls were common on the north coast during the several centuries preceding the rise of the Inka state. Indeed, *kancha* have rectangular enclosure walls, but their internal design is far different from the architecture found within the coastal enclosures. It is also generally assumed that the design of Cuzco, with its *kancha*, was established before Inka contact with the north coast became significant. In short, there is little solid proof to suggest that the origins of the *kancha* are to be found on the north coast.

A more attractive explanation is offered by Kendall (1976: 92, 1985: 352), who sees important origins of Inka architecture "in the local cultures of Cuzco and in those with Wari influence which penetrated the area to Lucre and Urubamba, with its influences in the Middle Horizon and the Late Intermediate Period." She points out that rectangular forms or enclosures and the grid pattern are present in the pre-Inka Wari and Lucre tradition in the neighborhood of Cuzco. Of course, if Inka rectangular enclosures go back to Wari models, it is clear that the Inkas modified the Wari enclosure considerably. For example, the extremely high walls of Wari enclosures are generally not found in Inka enclosure walls.

The Wari architectural tradition continued in the Cuzco area after the decline of the Wari culture. One particularly interesting demonstration of this is Choquepuquio, 28 kilometers southeast of Cuzco. The site lies only 4 kilometers from the great site of Piquillacta, which was apparently abandoned with the fall of the Wari culture around the eleventh century after Christ. Choquepuquio has tall fieldstone enclosure walls very similar to those of Wari Piquillacta (fig. 1.20). The site's pottery indicates it was inhabited for several hundred years up to and during the Inka imperial period.

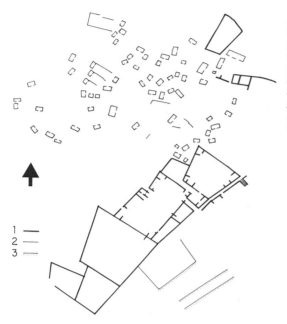

1.20. *Choquepuquio near Cuzco, Peru. The thick lines (1) indicate Lucre walls built before the expansion of the Inka state. The narrow lines (2) depict Inka buildings. Some terracing (3) is found on the southeast. Redrawn from Gibaja (1983: 43).*

Choquepuquio (Gibaja 1983) has a sector of monumental walled enclosures that clearly derive from the Wari architectural style (fig. 1.21). The walls are from 1 to 1.2 meters thick and up to 6.5 meters high. Unlike at Wari Piquillacta, some of the walls have niches, some of which are apparently trapezoidal. Besides the large walled enclosures one finds approximately sixty-nine rectangular Inka structures, which contain Inka pottery; Lucre and Killke pottery (Rivera D. 1978; McEwan 1984), both pre-imperial Inka, is found in the high walled enclosures.

Arminda Gibaja, the archaeologist who studied Choquepuquio, observes that there are similarities, but also differences, between the enclosures at the site and typical Inka *kancha*. The rooms inside the enclosures are not built like Inka *kancha*, but they are placed against the walls, as might be those of the Inkas. The large enclosures have other traits that typify Inka architecture: pegs (of wood) probably serving as roof ties; mud/clay plaster on the walls; holes for closings on the doors, and trapezoidal niches.

In summary, the Wari culture introduced the walled enclosure to the Cuzco region. The enclosures continued in use for several hundred years, as at Choquepuquio, until the expansion of the Inka state, which would distribute the architectural form throughout the Andes.

Other characteristics of Inka architecture appear to have come from the south, the Lake Titicaca region. Here, several hundred years prior to the Inka expansion, the Tiwanaku culture (A.D. 500–1100) developed stoneworking to extraordinary heights. In general, early historical sources tell us little about the origins of Inka architecture, but they do provide some relevant information. The chroniclers Cieza de León and Cobo report that the Inka Pachakuti visited Tiwanaku and commanded that Cuzco be built in a similar manner. The written sources do not say which architectural attributes were carried from Tiwanaku to Cuzco, or how they were conveyed, however.

Gasparini and Margolies (1980: 7–25) have published a detailed analysis of the Tiwanaku influence on Inka architecture. They write that the "Tiwanaku architectural influence manifests itself in Inca works through two channels of transmission: first, through the introduction of high-quality stoneworking, and second, through the acceptance by the Incas of some elements of form and aesthetics that, although reworked into a new expression, allow one to identify their origin" (p. 7).

At the site of Tiwanaku one finds stone building blocks as finely cut as the best in Cuzco. For example, good examples of rectangular, coursed blocks are found at the base of the Akapana mound (fig. 1.22). They are virtually indistinguishable from blocks in the Inka Sun Temple, the Qori Kancha.

How did Tiwanaku stoneworking technology arrive in Cuzco? One early Spanish inspection report, the *visita* of Diez de San Miguel in 1567 (1964), includes interviews with Aymara (Lupaqa) lords living on the southwestern side of Lake Titicaca. Several indicated that hundreds of their subjects were sent to Cuzco as part of the rotational Inka labor system, the *mita*, to make "walls and houses." Gasparini and Margolies (1980: 11) conclude that the masonry experts of the Lake Titicaca area

1.21. *A tall enclosure wall with niches at Choquepuquio. It was associated with Killke and Lucre (pre-imperial Inka) pottery.*

1.22. *Fine masonry blocks at the base of the Acapana at Tiwanaku, Bolivia.*

were primarily responsible for much of the technical expertise found in some of the most typical buildings of Cuzco.

The claim that Inka stoneworking technology derives from Tiwanaku confronts one basic problem. Several centuries elapsed between the construction of the Tiwanaku monuments and the development of fine Inka stonework. How was the stoneworking technology maintained in these centuries when, apparently, no fine stonework was produced anywhere in the Andes? Gasparini and Margolies (1980: 12) suggest that people from the lake region had "models in plain sight" and could therefore be expected to "satisfy the exigencies" of the Inkas. In other words, fine Inka stonework represents a revival or rebirth of Tiwanaku masonry. The Inkas also imitated Tiwanaku pottery, so the validity of this interpretation must be considered, however improbable it may sound.[6]

There is, however, evidence that quarried and worked stone continued in the lake region during the centuries after Tiwanaku. An example is found at the site of Tanka Tanka (Hyslop 1976: 333–340; 1977a) only 70 kilometers to the west of Tiwanaku. Both its surface pottery and surrounding large walls are characteristic of the period between Tiwanaku and Inka. It has several kilometers of walls surrounding much of an inhabited area that may have been as large as that of Tiwanaku itself. The walls are of a soft rock, and therefore poorly conserved, and now stand from 2 to 6 meters high. Their worked stones range from about 1 to 2.5 meters in diameter (fig. 1.23). The stonework is somewhat similar to Inka polygonal masonry. The stones are not perfectly joined, although they have a generally smoothed surface and fit together.[7] In summary, the techniques of quarrying, cutting, smoothing, and fitting stone were probably not lost in the post-Tiwanaku–pre-Inka period in the Lupaqa area southwest of Lake Titicaca.

1.23. Two examples of masonry walls surrounding the site of Tanka Tanka near the Peruvian-Bolivian border south of Lake Titicaca. The walls were built after the decline of the Tiwanaku culture and before the rise of the Inka Empire. They demonstrate that worked masonry continued to be used during this period.

In Cuzco, interesting excavations took place under the present-day Hotel Libertador between Romeritos and San Agustín streets. A number of walls associated with Killke pottery were found beneath Inka and Spanish colonial remains. Some walls were made of rough unworked stones or cobbles (González C. 1984), but others were worked. Some of the stones had their exposed surfaces lightly worked but were laid in clay mortar. Similarly worked Killke-associated stones of andesite have also been found in nearby excavations in the Sun Temple, Qori Kancha. Here they were used in retaining walls, a type of wall not found in the Hotel Libertador excavations. Although evidence is still limited, it would seem that people in Cuzco were making walls with stones other than rough fieldstones before the development of the empire. Additional excavations in Cuzco are necessary to clarify the matter, but worked building stone in Cuzco may have preceded Pachakuti's visit to Tiwanaku in the fifteenth century.

One final point concerning the early arrival of fine masonry in Cuzco deserves comment. Several of the Inka origin myths and state histories point to the Lake Titicaca region as the origin for the Inkas. Valcárcel's study (1939: 218–221) of Inka myths about the origin of the world, of humankind, and of the Inka state describes successive waves of migration from the high Titicaca plateau to the Cuzco region. Thus one might speculate that fine Inka stonework is connected with ideas about Inka origins, and that Inkas prior to the rise of the empire may have built walls of worked stone, a technology brought from their place of origin. This conclusion is speculative. If correct, fine masonry may have been important to the Inkas because of its link to ideas about their origin.

Apparently, Tiwanaku's fine stonework made a greater impression on the Inkas than other building techniques of the lake region. At Tiwanaku the techniques for containing earth platforms are different from those used by the Inkas. The Inkas' minor borrowing from Tiwanaku in terms of architectural planning and organization could be explained by the extremely poor architectural preservation at the site, apparently in ruins even in Inka times. Only stonework, earthen platforms, and mounds remain. Given the vast spread of surface pottery in areas where there is no visible architecture, it is probable that most of Tiwanaku was built of adobe or earthen structures, which eroded in the centuries between the decline of the Tiwanaku culture and the rise of the Inka. Thus the Inkas would not have known many details of Tiwanaku's urban plan. Moreover, the Inkas built little in Tiwanaku, although they held the ancient remains in great veneration. The only archaeological trace of their influence is a limited amount of Inka pottery (Rydén 1947: 49, 76–77; Bennett 1934: 458–459).

There are a number of ornamental aspects of Tiwanaku architecture that appear to have passed into the Inka repertory. One of the chief features is the double-jamb doorway, whose long history in the high plateau goes back to before the birth of Christ. It was used prominently in Tiwanaku doors and niches. The Inkas incorporated the double jamb into some of their wall apertures, and in a few cases even built doors with a stepped design by the lintel (typical of Tiwanaku) in some buildings in the Lake Titicaca region and in Cuzco.

There is no clear evidence for the origins of the trapezoidal form so common in Inka architecture. Trapezoidal doorways were used by a number of pre-Inka cultures, and they are still common in some parts of the Andes. Thus it is doubtful that the trapezoidal form is an Inka invention. Whatever tradition inspired it, the Inkas gave that form fame and prestige and made it into a hallmark of their architecture. Contrary to popular belief, Inka plazas were rarely built in the form of a true trapezoid (chap. 8).

Many questions remain concerning the roots of Inka architecture. One of the most important is to what degree did the pre-imperial (Killke) occupation in Cuzco influence the later Inka urban design? Another question is to what degree did the Killke occupation influence elements of the imperial Cuzco architecture? Someday research may resolve these questions.

Chronological Considerations during the Inka Period

There is now general agreement that sometime in the early fifteenth century a small kingdom in the Cuzco region began its transformation into an empire (Lumbreras 1974: 214, 215). There is considerable debate about the meaning and interpretation of the lists of early Inka kings,[8] but it is probable that only the last ones, Pachakuti, Thupa Yupanki, Wayna Qhapaq, and Waskar, were real individuals who governed in succession during the ninety or so years prior to the Spanish conquest which began in A.D. 1532. After a lengthy and scholarly discussion, Rowe (1945), drawing heavily on the information in the sixteenth-century Cabello chronicle, assigns specific dates to the reigns of the last Inkas. These dates have been used rather dogmatically by dozens of scholars in the last generation,[9] few of whom have heeded Rowe's warning that the dates are "plausible" rather than exact.

The approximate date for the beginning of Pachakuti's rule is A.D. 1438. The beginnings of the Inka Empire and the remodeling of Cuzco into a cosmopolitan capital have been attributed to his reign (Rostworowski 1953). Apparently, the architecture of Inka Cuzco coalesced as a style in the mid-fifteenth century or slightly before. During the following three generations it was distributed throughout the Andes.

Historical sources are not generally reliable for information about pre-imperial Cuzco, since Pachakuti appears to have remodeled not only Cuzco but its history.[10] The archaeology of the Cuzco area tells us that prior to the empire there were small towns only a couple of hundred meters long, and that the pottery was a style known as Killke (Rivera Dorado 1978) and Qotakalli (Barreda 1982). Classic Inka pottery developed at least in part from its Killke predecessor.

Classic Inka architecture ended within a few years of the Spanish conquest, but Inka masons and architects continued to construct some buildings in the Cuzco-Urubamba region and the nearby jungle for at least a generation (Kendall 1974: 81, 86, 1985: 349–354). This so-called neo-Inka architecture is found in sites such as Vilcabamba, Ollantaytambo, Yucay, and Cuzco.[11] Fine neo-Inka masonry walls in Cuzco are usually vertical, not battered, and the larger stones are not necessarily placed in the lower courses.

Classic Inka architecture therefore developed for a little less than a century. Gasparini and Margolies do not discuss to what degree, if any, Inka architecture developed or evolved, apparently feeling that there is no dependable information. Kendall (1974: 60–93), on the other hand, addresses the subject at length.

Kendall's means of dating architectural characteristics is based on historical evidence that can, in certain cases, assign the construction of certain sites or buildings to one or two Inka kings.[12] She isolates constructions assigned to Pachakuti from those built by Thupa Yupanki or Wayna Qhapaq and attempts to identify common traits. Although some scholars may consider Kendall's conclusions (1976: 85–86) somewhat tentative,[13] it is nevertheless worthwhile to note some of her observations.

Contrary to Gasparini and Margolies (1980: 25) and Agurto C. (1987: 164), who consider that the variations of fine masonry have no chronological implications, Kendall thinks that the fine, flat-surfaced rectangular coursed masonry is early, dating generally to the time of Pachakuti. She also writes that rectangular masonry with rough, sunken joints and small nearly square stones was produced very late in the Inka period.

During the reign of Pachakuti and the early years of Thupa Yupanki's influence (ca. A.D. 1438–1471), there is considerable standardization in the form and secondary traits of important buildings. Platforms with steps are closely integrated with the surrounding architecture. There is a simplicity in the buildings and patios, and buildings are constructed with one type of masonry. During the reign of Thupa Yupanki (ca. A.D. 1471–1493) buildings became more complex. Niches were elaborated with various jambs, or double rows. This was part of a general tendency toward ornamentation and complexity, seen in the occasional use of columns, the combination of various types of masonry in one structure, and the isolating of platforms (*ushnu*) in large plazas. During the reign of Wayna Qhapaq (ca. A.D. 1493–1525) fewer buildings were built in the Cuzco area and energies were concentrated on constructions in Ecuador, where tendencies initiated under Thupa Yupanki continued. Smaller masonry blocks were used, and the utilization of adobe increased.

In general, Kendall's observations on chronology suggest that there were some changes in classic Inka architecture, but that they were elaborations rather than dramatic alterations.

The Evidence for Planning

Inka administrative centers, royal estates, sanctuaries, and military installations appear to have been planned; that is, there were Inka experts (Cobo 1964II: 260, Bk. 14, chap. 12) who decided where the settlement would be, how the space would be allocated, and where specific buildings and compounds would be placed. Support for this proposition is relatively abundant. Morris, the authority on the Inka administrative center Huánuco Pampa, writes (1980a: 11) that it was built "in accordance to an elaborate pre-conceived plan." Numerous chroniclers write that Cuzco in the time of Pachakuti was rebuilt from a master plan (chap. 2).[14]

Planning was no doubt aided by the use of models and paintings. A clay model was constructed of Cuzco (Betanzos 1968: 30, 48, chaps. 10, 16). Sarmiento de Gamboa (1965: 244, chap. 39) describes models used to reorganize conquered territories. Models continued to be used into the Spanish colonial period. Garcilaso (1987: 124, Bk. 2, chap. 26) describes a large model of Cuzco made for the arrival of Inspector Damián de la Bandera:

> I saw the model of Cuzco and part of the surrounding areas in clay, pebbles, and sticks. It was done to scale with the squares, large and small; the streets, broad and narrow; the districts and houses, even the most obscure; and the three streams that flow through the city, marvelously executed. The countryside with high hills and low, flats and ravines, rivers and streams with their twists and turns were all wonderfully rendered, and the best cosmographer in the world could not have done it better.

Garcilaso also says that the Inkas were capable of modeling or painting entire geographical regions. Confirmation for the use of geographical models has been found by Rostworowski (1979–1980: 188) in sources concerning litigation over coca lands in the Chillón Valley near Lima.

The local authorities of the two contending groups brought models of the disputed part of the valley to the Audience of Lima to demonstrate their claims. Sarmiento (1965: 244, chap. 39) describes geographical clay models used by an Inka king for the reorganization of people and settlements (chap. 6 here).

Unfortunately, no Inka-period clay models or paintings have survived. If the model Garcilaso saw in early Spanish colonial times was representative of models made during Inka times, his description suggests that the modeling and scaling were reasonably accurate. This is contradicted by an article by Pardo (1936), who describes several stone and pottery architectural models displayed in the Archaeological Museum of the University of Cuzco. In general, these artifacts appear to represent individual structures or compounds. If, as Pardo claims, some represent known Inka buildings, one must note that their scaling is as inaccurate as some of their portrayals of architectural details. Most of the stone models are less than 10 centimeters wide, and some may not be Inka. Rowe (1946: 224) claims that these "give a fair idea of the aids with which Inca architects worked." In fact, such artifacts may never have served for architectural planning, but may have had some ceremonial purpose, as suggested by their small size and Pardo's observation that a fragment of one such stone was found in a burial.

A subjective argument for the planning of Inka settlements is that they look planned. Whoever scrutinizes aerial photographs or maps of Inka sites cannot doubt that established ideas were used, in part because of their intricacy and, to the Western observer, their "strange" and varying geometric designs. Chapter 2 will examine the layout of the Inka capital, Cuzco, since many of the features and concepts used there were applied in the design of other settlements.

2
Cuzco

The city of Cuzco was the capital of the empire, where the laws
that were to be obeyed were given, with regard to religion as well
as government; from there the governors came to rule all of the
provinces, and those who concluded their term of office returned
there to give an account of what had happened. . . . The esteem
in which Cuzco was held continued to grow as strangers saw how
it was venerated by its residents and because of the mysteries
that these residents made people believe were in every hill,
spring, road, and canyon. (Cobo 1983: 242, Bk. II, chap. 35)

No study of Inka architectural planning can begin without first considering the design of Tawantinsuyu's capital, Cuzco. When it was first
seen by Europeans in A.D. 1533, it housed a considerable population—
probably more than 100,000. It was the largest "city" in South America.
The term "city" is used loosely here, since Cuzco was far different from
a city in the Western sense of the word.

Inka Cuzco was located in the same place as modern Cuzco, in the
south highlands of Peru. Although at an altitude of 3,395 meters above
sea level, it is only 13 degrees, 29 minutes south latitude (fig. 1.2). Thus
its considerable altitude makes for a cool climate, moderated by its location not far from the equator.

Cuzco is hailed by some of its present-day inhabitants as the "Archaeological Capital of the Americas." Nevertheless, given the importance of the city, there has been only a limited amount of archaeological
investigation there. For example, there is still no comprehensive scientific study of the Inka pottery from Cuzco. Much information concerning the identification and functions of certain buildings could be ac-
quired with simple and inexpensive excavations, but these have rarely
been carried out. Thus there is much debate concerning the layout of
Inka Cuzco, often based on conflicting or inexact early sources.

Defining and interpreting the design of Inka Cuzco is complicated by
numerous factors that altered the city's design. In 1534 the Spanish au-

thorities began the distribution of house lots and of space for public and religious buildings. This resulted in considerable modification of the buildings and changed the appearance of the main Inka plaza. The Inka attempt to retake the city from the Spanish in 1535 resulted in the burning and partial destruction of part of Cuzco. Our knowledge of Inka Cuzco's layout is also hindered by the lack of plans or maps of the capital before it was altered greatly by the Spanish.

The liquidation of the Inka state and the establishment of Spanish rule resulted in a decrease in Cuzco's population, which, with fluctuations, appears to have dropped below twenty thousand in the following three centuries (Azevedo 1982: 25–29). Social dislocation, unfavorable economic patterns, earthquakes, famine, and disease all kept Cuzco small. Only after 1950 did it reach a population equivalent to or greater than in Inka times. Cuzco's low population during the last four centuries has helped preserve the city and its street pattern, which often follows the Inka one. Limited urban development in colonial and republican times also saved many Inka buildings, which, in a more dynamic city, would have been leveled (fig. 2.1). Unfortunately, destruction of Inka remains in Cuzco continues,[1] sometimes with the knowledge of authorities.

Even given the factors that have destroyed Inka Cuzco as well as the general lack of detailed archaeological investigation, one can still argue that Cuzco is, or at least could be, the best understood of all prehistoric American cities. The existence of much of its Inka layout, at least in its central sector, combined with information in early written sources allows one to reconstruct and understand many aspects of the capital.

The Inka or Quechua language is toponymic; that is, place names usually mean something. Quechua speakers show a great interest in the meaning of names, since they often contain information about the nature or history of a place. Thus one might legitimately inquire about the meaning of the name "Cuzco." Unfortunately, there are many conflicting interpretations (Angles Vargas 1978: 25–27). Cuzco may mean "center" or "navel," or it could mean "landmark" or "pile of stones." Others have suggested that it signifies "rock." In short, the confusion about the original meaning of the word makes it clear that one had best not attempt to understand Cuzco simply from its name.

Preimperial Cuzco

The earliest historical information about Cuzco before the Inkas is conveyed to us in mythological oral histories written down early in the Spanish colonial period. Betanzos (1968: 11–12) writes:

2.1. Aerial view of Cuzco, Peru, to the southeast. This modern city was once the Inka capital. Indeed, Inka walls are still found in parts of the city. Courtesy Department of Library Services, AMNH, Neg. no. 334755 (photo by Shippee Johnson).

In ancient times in the province of Peru on the location that to-day is called the great city of Cuzco, before the existence of the lords Orejones, Inkas, and Capaccuna, who were called kings, there was a small village of up to thirty small thatched, poor houses. In them there were thirty Indians, and the chief and head of this village was called Alcaviza. This village was surrounded by a swamp of reeds and grasses, caused by springs of water from the mountains and the place that is now the fortress [Saqsa-waman]. This swamp was in the place where one now finds the plaza and the houses of Marquis Don Francisco Pizarro who later seized this city.

In a detailed survey of early written sources, Valcárcel (1939: 190–206) weighs the evidence for the pre-Inka inhabitants of the Cuzco area. He found reference to approximately a dozen small ethnic groups. For most, nothing is known except their name. A detailed analysis of the histori-cal data for pre-Inka Cuzco is by Rostworowski (1969–1970, 1988:

21–30). She notes that the name of old Cuzco may have been Acamama and that it was divided into four districts. The most important ethnicity around Cuzco was the Ayarmacas. They originally fought with the Inkas, but ceased to be a significant political force as the Inka state began to expand.

Much controversy surrounds the interpretation of Inka origin myths (Valcárcel 1939: 206–222), which speak of the arrival of a founder, Manco Qhapaq (or, in some cases, Wirakocha), from the south, usually the Lake Titicaca region or the area of Paccaritampu. He settled in Cuzco, dominated the valley, and established what for the Inkas is the beginning of their history. Analysis of these myths was a challenging subject for early Andeanists such as Uhle (1912), Latcham (1928), and Jijón y Caamaño (1934). From these detailed analyses it is appropriate here to extract only that which relates to Cuzco's architectural design. One particularly interesting account is by *khipu* officials (Collapiña, Supno et al. 1974: 29), who in 1542 recalled that one of Manco's first acts was to establish a Sun Temple on the site of the Sun Temple used in imperial times (now the church of Santo Domingo). Betanzos 1968: 14, chap. 5) says Manco Qhapaq established his house there. Sarmiento de Gamboa (1965: 236–237, chap. 31) also notes that a Sun Temple rested where the later one was built by Pachakuti.

It is difficult to tell if such accounts are purely mythical or carry some grain of truth. The discovery of Killke pottery and walls near Santo Domingo indicates that the location was inhabited prior to the development of the empire, but there is not yet sufficient evidence to say that the Sun Temple had preimperial origins.

In summary, the early legends suggest that Cuzco was inhabited by non-Inka people for centuries prior to the Inka Empire. The Inkas emigrated into the area and gradually became the dominant group. Bueno (1981: 12) postulates two phases of Cuzco's early existence: (1) a rough village of stone walls and thatched roofs prior to Manco Qhapaq; and (2) a village occupied by Manco Qhapaq (around the thirteenth century) and his successors. Historical sources suggest that some characteristics of imperial Cuzco were present before the empire, such as quadripartition and the importance of Qori Kancha's location. The histories also suggest that with the arrival of Manco Qhapaq the village of Cuzco changed. This two-phase interpretation of preimperial Cuzco remains to be confirmed archaeologically. Archaeologists have only established that Cuzco was a settlement prior to the rise of the empire.

The Rebuilding of Cuzco

Two relatively insightful early sources, Betanzos (1968: 46–50, chap. 16) and Sarmiento de Gamboa (1965: 235–237, chaps. 30–32) say that

King Pachakuti rebuilt Cuzco, suggesting that it was a deliberately planned city. As noted, Betanzos wrote that Pachakuti used clay models for his development project. He also states that Pachakuti personally measured and decided upon the locations of houses and lots after evacuating the inhabitants for five leagues (about 25 kilometers) around the city, a description suggesting that Cuzco was rebuilt from the ground up. Only Inkas were to live in the central sector, and even the original (non-Inka) inhabitants were required to move to a nearby district some two shots of an arquebus away. He adds that the building effort took fifty thousand people twenty years. Sarmiento's account does not suggest that Pachakuti's rebuilding was as drastic. It relates that Pachakuti "rebuilt" Cuzco, introduced fine masonry, built many agricultural terraces, and removed the original inhabitants from a zone of two leagues (about 10 kilometers) around the city, primarily to acquire more agricultural land.

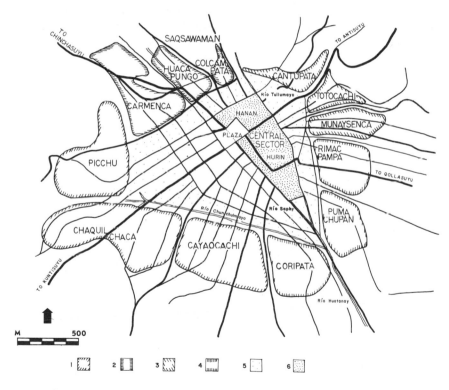

2.2. *Inka Cuzco's central sector and surrounding districts. Four main roads connected the city to the four parts* (suyu) *of the empire. The districts' locations are not precise.* Key: 1. *Kuntisuyu districts;* 2. *Chinchasuyu districts;* 3. *Antisuyu districts;* 4. *Qollasuyu districts;* 5. *intermediate zone;* 6. *central sector. Redrawn from Agurto C. (1980: 126).*

Only Betanzos suggests that the physical plan of Cuzco was created by Pachakuti. There is little doubt that Pachakuti was the major force behind the transformation of the Inka kingdom into an empire and that he revolutionized many aspects of Inka life, including religion and even history. Nevertheless, evidence that Pachakuti "designed" Cuzco from the ground up is still weak. Future archaeological work in Cuzco is necessary to shed light on this special problem. One provoking shred of evidence comes from the excavations at the Hotel Libertador, where a few preimperial (Killke pottery–associated) walls have generally the same orientation as the nearby fine masonry ones (González C. 1984). This suggests that the orientation of some buildings may have been the same in preimperial Cuzco as in the "rebuilt" Cuzco.

The Location

Cuzco is located in the upper part of a mountain valley, and three streams or rivers flow through it (fig. 2.2). Water is an important element in Inka architectural planning (chap. 5), and thus it is useful to understand the rivers of Cuzco. The Chunchulmayo runs from west to east, under present-day Avenida del Ejército. The Saphy (Huatanay) runs from northwest to southeast, passes between the main Inka plazas, and continues beneath Avenida del Sol. The Tullumayo also runs from northwest to southeast, a few hundred meters to the east of the Saphy under what is today Choquechaca. The Tullumayo and Saphy meet in the southern part of the central sector of Cuzco, forming the Huatanay River which runs 33 kilometers to the southeast before joining the Vilcanota River. Several early historical sources note that the Tullumayo and Saphy were canalized as part of the effort to drain the swampy terrain on which central Cuzco rests. Elegant remains of this canalization still exist south of central Cuzco, but are now covered within the city (Gasparini and Margolies 1980: 57, 59; Farrington 1983).

Early eyewitnesses disagree as to the limits of the capital. Traditionally, Cuzco has been described as the area between the Tullumayo and Saphy rivers, where one finds nearly all of the fine Inka masonry. The soldier Ruiz de Arce saw Cuzco before it was burned in 1553 and described it in just that manner (1955: 194): "The city is this way. It would have four thousand residential houses between the two rivers surrounding it and they are on a slope of a mountain, and at the head of the city in the same mountain there is a fort [Saqsawaman] with many rooms."

Cuzco also included areas where few architectural remains are now known, but that must be taken into account, since they are mentioned by early eyewitnesses. For example, one very early soldier's account

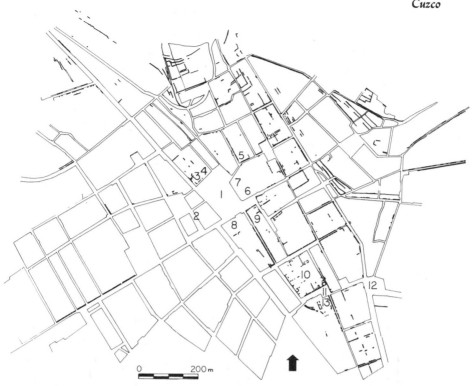

2.3. *Cuzco's Inka walls. The thin lines indicate modern streets and blocks. The thick lines depict existing Inka walls. Key: 1. Haukaypata Plaza; 2. Kusipata Plaza; 3. Qasana; 4. Cora Cora (probable location); 5. Waskar's compound; 6. Kiswarkancha (possible location); 7. Cuyusmanco (possible location); 8. Amarukancha; 9. Hatunkancha (aqllawasi); 10. Cusikancha; 11. Intipampa Plaza; 12. Limacpampa Plaza; 13. Qori Kancha. Redrawn from Agurto C. (1980: 111).*

(Sancho 1917: 194, chap. 17) described a much larger "city" than did his comrade Ruiz de Arce: "From the fortress [Saqsawaman] one sees around the city many houses out to a fourth of a league, half a league, and a league, and in the valley in the middle surrounded by mountains there are more than one hundred thousand houses. Many of them are for the pleasure and recreation of the lords of the past and of other chiefs of all the land."

Sancho's description of a city extending over many kilometers (a league is approximately 5 kilometers) is a more accurate view than one that limits the city to the area between the Saphy and Tullumayo rivers. For the purpose of this discussion, Cuzco will be defined as composed of two fundamentally different parts (fig. 2.2): (1) a central sector—the seat of royal Inkas and the main religious and political area—between the Tullumayo and Saphy; and (2) approximately a dozen residential districts that surrounded, generally at some distance, the central sector. This distinction is made by Agurto (1980) and Chávez Ballón (1970) and, to some degree, by Rowe (1967: 60, 65).

Good evidence for including the surrounding districts within the limits of Cuzco is that the central sector is only about 1,000 meters long by about 400 to 600 meters wide. Although it was full of buildings, it occupies a smaller area than that covered by some Inka centers in other parts of the Andes. In short, most of the large population described by eyewitnesses must have lived in the surrounding districts, since the central sector, covering some 40 hectares, is simply too small to make up the entire capital. Another reason for including the surrounding districts within the "limits" of Cuzco is that they housed important members of society such as "partial" Inkas, or "Inkas-by-privilege," and ethnic lords from various parts of the empire (see below, "Inkas and Others").

2.4. *The Plaza de Armas of modern Cuzco, once the Inka plaza Haukaypata. Adjoining it was the Kusipata Plaza, now partly covered over with buildings. It extended to, and possibly beyond, the small plaza in the background (top right). Courtesy Department of Library Services, AMNH, Neg. no. 334760 (photo by Shippee Johnson).*

A considerable amount is known about the central sector; far less is known of the "ring" of residential districts.

The Central Sector

Nearly all descriptions of central Cuzco—those for academics and tourists alike—are flawed because of an over-reliance on the famous but often inaccurate chronicle by Garcilaso de la Vega (1963II, III). Since he lived in Cuzco in the 1540s and 1550s, was the son of an Inka princess, and his chronicle was widely distributed, there has been a tendency to rely on his detailed descriptions, although more accurate information may be found in earlier, shorter sources. Here, Garcilaso will be used only if he can be defended or backed up by at least one other source.[2] Thus the following description will vary somewhat from most other published depictions of Cuzco's central sector (fig. 2.3).

The Dual Plaza

The most imposing architectural feature of central Cuzco was probably not any specific building, but rather a large plaza divided into two parts by the Saphy River. The easternmost part, called Haukaypata, was modified and became the main plaza (Plaza de Armas) of Spanish Cuzco (fig. 2.4). West of the Saphy River was the other plaza, called Kusipata. The exact size of Kusipata has never been determined, although it may have included the Plaza San Francisco. The Spanish soon modified it by placing some buildings within it. Two early depictions of Spanish colonial Cuzco show the dual plaza, but are far too schematic to depict aspects of Inka Cuzco with any accuracy. One (fig. 2.5) is in the book finished by Guaman Poma (1936: f. 1051) around 1614, and the other is the famous Monroy canvas painting portraying Cuzco in the earthquake of 1650 (fig. 2.6). All other early drawings of Cuzco are too fanciful to be of any use for understanding Inka Cuzco.[3] The Guaman Poma drawing depicts various Inka buildings that are not always situated properly in relation to the dual plaza.

The Haukaypata Plaza was covered with a deep layer (at least two and a half palms thick) of sand from the Pacific coast. It is the subject of a remarkable commentary by the Spanish magistrate Polo de Ondegardo (1916b: 109–110), who had the sand removed in 1559 after finding that it was considered sacred by the local residents, who buried gold and silver figurines and vessels in it. The "imported" sand was considered better than the local material and was used in the construction of the cathedral and bridges. Polo also relates that the original earthen surface of the plaza was venerated and carried to other parts of the empire.[4] The burying of offerings in the plaza becomes comprehensible when one

10 51

2.5. *An early seventeenth-century depiction of Cuzco (Guaman Poma 1936: f. 1051). It correctly locates the Haukaypata Plaza next to the Kusipata Plaza with the Huatanay (Saphy) River running between them. Named Inka buildings are not always located correctly in relationship to the dual plaza.*

considers the importance of the sea, the origin of all things, in Andean religion. Sherbondy (1982b: 16) notes that "by bringing the sea sand to Cuzco, the Inkas ritually situated the sea in the religious and political center of the Inka Empire."

If Cuzco had an architectural "center" it would be a spot near the middle of the two main plazas. Betanzos (1968: 33, chap. 9) wrote that Pachakuti placed a pointed stone covered with gold in the plaza, where the Spanish later put their *rollo* (gallows). The stone was highly revered, and a description of it before it was removed was made in 1534 by Pedro Pizarro, who was a young page when he arrived in Cuzco with Francisco Pizarro's soldiers. He was one of very few people who saw and wrote about Inka ceremonies in the plaza, which would soon be cut short by the Spanish. He wrote (1978: 89–91, chap. 15) that the mummies of the Inka kings were seated in a ring in the plaza, where they were fed by servants. In front of each mummy a fire was set in which the food was burned. Each mummy also had a metal or pottery vessel of corn beer (*chicha*), which was poured on the round stone "in the center of the plaza around which was a small basin drained by some tubes that they have made under the earth. This stone had a covering of gold, which fitted on it and covered it. And also they had made a type of little round house of woven reeds with which they covered it at night."

Pizarro goes on to describe how an image of the sun was also brought into the plaza and placed on a bench or seat (*escaño*). Unfortunately, he does not describe this seat in detail, but only says it was small, adorned with colorful feathers, and placed in the center of the plaza. The "sun" was offered food and drink, and the food was then burned. During this ceremony all observers sat quietly. Then, the food's ashes were thrown on the stone (here described as having the shape of a teat), where the *chicha* was also poured. Other ceremonies relating to this gold-covered stone are described by Segovia (Molina 1943: 30–31, 36), who notes that the drain of the stone ran underground to the house of the Sun, Thunder, and the Creator (the Sun Temple).

It is clear that this important stone was central to the Inka concept of *ushnu*, a topic addressed at length in the following chapter. The stone's symbolism was such that it, and the associated idea of a platform, would be represented in the architecture of many large Inka settlements throughout the domain of Tawantinsuyu.

Aveni (1981: 313–316) and Zuidema (1981a) have located the *ushnu* stone's position, identifying it with the location of the *rollo* in the

2.6. *A painting, commissioned by Alonso Cortés de Monroy, of the 1650 earth-quake in Cuzco. The view is to the southeast, over the two plazas, similar to that in fig. 2.4. Spanish colonial buildings divide the plazas but do not yet cover the Kusipata.*

Monroy painting. They demonstrate that its position agrees with a solar horizon observation known to have been made at the *ushnu* (Discurso 1906: 151). The *rollo* lies near the center of the dual plaza.

Compounds and Buildings on the Plaza

There were important Inka buildings or compounds on the northwest, northeast, and southeast sides of Haukaypata Plaza. These are usually identified on the basis of Garcilaso de la Vega's chronicle. Indeed, nearly every description of Cuzco written in the last two centuries is based on his observations. If one consults considerably earlier written sources describing the center of Cuzco, Garcilaso's descriptions sometimes seem inaccurate or fanciful. Particularly useful for defining the buildings about the plaza are the account of Pedro Pizarro (1978), a soldier who saw Cuzco before it burned and who described it in some detail, the *Founding Act of Cuzco* (Acta 1948), and the *First Book of the City Council of Cuzco* (*Libro Primero* 1965).

There is general agreement among the early accounts, even in Garcilaso, that two great compounds fronted the southeast side of the plaza. One was called Hatunkancha, to its west lay the Amarukancha. Hatunkancha is described as having only one door, facing on the plaza, and many houses. It contained an *aqllawasi* where "chosen women of the sun" lived and worked. It was also a refuge for Pizarro's invaders, who felt safe in it because of its high surrounding walls and restricted entry. Perhaps the most famous wall in Cuzco, that on the east side of Loreto Street (once Sun Street), formed part of Hatunkancha (fig. 2.7). Less is known about Amarukancha. Various early authors assign it to different Inka kings. Apparently the Amarukancha was not as enclosed as Hatunkancha. Garcilaso (1963II: 261–262, Bk. 7, chap. 10), whose identification of this compound is confirmed by earlier sources, may be right in noting that it had a great hall, or *galpón*, fronting on the plaza. Entering in the plaza in front of Amarukancha was a round building with a very tall, conical, thatched roof. Called *sunturwasi* or *cubo* by Garcilaso (1963II: 261, Bk. 7, chap. 10, 1963III: 60–61, Bk. 1, chap. 32), he claimed it had walls the height of four men.[5]

There were other *galpones*, or big halls, on the plaza. One on the northeast side of the plaza (on the location of the Triunfo Church) became the first Spanish church (Acta 1948: 90). That this large Inka hall became the church is substantiated by Garcilaso (1963II: 259, Bk. 7, chap. 9), who adds that it was the compound of King Wirakocha. The Anonymous Jesuit (1879: 148) also confirms that the first church was built over a large Inka building and assigns it to the creator deity Wirakocha. The association of that particular building with the name

2.7. *A fine masonry wall of the* aqllawasi *found on one side of Loreto Street, once called Sun Street, Inti Kuyllu. This street, with a short extension, connected the Haukaypata Plaza with the Sun Temple. Once one of Cuzco's most important streets, its average width was only 3.6 meters.*

Wirakocha, whether king or god (or both), may be inaccurate, since here one unreliable source confirms another. Molina (1943: 19) reports a Creator temple, Kiswarkancha, away from the plaza at a Spanish house lot, which I have been unable to locate.

The present topography of Cuzco's plaza and references in a document recording the allocation in 1534 of Spanish house lots (*Libro Primero* 1965: 32–36) make it clear that a terrace stood on the plaza's northeast side, and that buildings there rested on it. The house lot record notes another large hall on that terrace and some other buildings.[6]

The northwest side of Haukaypata Plaza also had at least one great hall, or *kallanka*. It fronted on the plaza as part of the Qasana compound, the palace of Wayna Qhapaq, later occupied by Francisco Pizarro (*Libro Primero* 1965: 33). One of its extraordinarily fine walls can still be seen, particularly from within the Roma Restaurant, where grotesque modern gilded statues have been placed in the fine trapezoidal niches.

41

Tourists are usually erroneously informed (due to Garcilaso's inaccuracy) that it was Pachakuti's palace. Several earlier, more dependable, sources indicate that the Qasana was Wayna Qhapaq's (Rowe 1979: 22, Ch-6:5; Sarmiento de Gamboa 1965: 260, chap. 58). Pedro Pizarro (1978: 161) describes two round buildings in front of the Qasana that extended somewhat into the plaza. These structures were of fine masonry with great thatch roofs resting on wood beams that, in Manco's siege of Cuzco, were ignited and took days to burn. Garcilaso (1963II: 261, Bk. 7, chap. 10) describes the Qasana as being large enough for the exercises of sixty horsemen. Elsewhere (Garcilaso 1963II: 198, Bk. 6, chap. 4) claims that it could have held three thousand people.

Fronting on the plaza to the east of Qasana was a complex of structures that must have been important, since they were given to Francisco Pizarro's brother, Gonzalo (*Libro Primero* 1965: 33). Not a trace of these buildings remains today. Next to them, farther to the east, on the north corner of the plaza, was a compound attributed to the Inka King Waskar. Little remains of it, and there are no written descriptions except the word *fortress* in the City Council's house lot record. This probably means it was set high on a terrace and surrounded by a strong wall. It must have been an important structure, since it was assigned to the second most important Spaniard then in Peru, Diego de Almagro.

The River Saphy flowed under the dual Inka plaza and, because it was canalized and covered, was not visible. For want of another informant here, it is interesting to note that Garcilaso (1963II: 262, Bk. 7, chap. 11) wrote that the river was covered with great wood beams which were surfaced with stone slabs. The Spanish used the wood for other purposes, building bridges over the river to connect the two sides.

What generalizations might be derived from this description of Inka Cuzco's main plaza(s) and its surrounding buildings? First, it is doubtful that any single construction dominated the plaza, as the church or cathedral does in the Spanish plaza. Second, the plaza itself, open to the southwest, must have been imposing, since it was very large. Third, the major buildings surrounding the plaza were *galpones*, or large halls, whose thatched roofs may have reached several stories into the sky. They were used for feasting, particularly during rainy weather. Architectural evidence for them has been almost completely destroyed, but historical evidence suggests that there were at least four of them: one on the northwest side (as part of the Qasana), and one on the southeast side (as part of the Amarukancha). On the northeast side there were two large halls on a terrace platform. Thus to observers the northeast side must have been the most impressive.

Other Activities and Buildings within Central Cuzco

The early historical sources name some other buildings on or near the plaza but evidence for their exact location is too limited, unreliable, or conflicting. "An Account of the Shrines" (Rowe 1979) allows one to identify several other buildings in and near Cuzco's central sector where important events took place. For example, the compound Cusikancha (Rowe 1979: 20–21, Ch-5:1) is described as a place maintained by Iñaca Panaqa and where Pachakuti was born.

A central institution of Inka social structure was the royal *panaqa*, or *ayllu*, social units tracing their descent to an alleged early ruler. Some or perhaps all of these maintained compounds, often incorrectly referred to as "palaces," within Cuzco's central sector. A number of these appear to have been placed in the blocks around and near the Plaza Haukaypata. A few compounds actually served as residences for Inka kings, and they can be called palaces. For example, the Qasana was Wayna Qhapaq's. In most cases it is difficult to assign these compounds to *panaqa*, or kings, since sources identifying them are vague, conflicting, or unsubstantiated. A good example is the compound of Amarukancha, which may have been associated with a *panaqa*, but which is given at least four different attributions by various early written sources.[7] Given the difficulty of associating most of the *panaqa* with specific compounds, the reader will be spared the weighing of dozens of references, which could only lead to tortured and uncertain conclusions.

Likewise, it is difficult to assign exact locations to the schools, jails, zoos, storage areas, temples, *tampu*, and botanical gardens alleged to have been in Cuzco (Chávez Ballón 1970: 7–9). It is clear that there were at least two smaller plazas, Limacpampa and Intipampa, to the northwest and northeast (but separated somewhat), respectively, of the Sun Temple, Qori Kancha. There is abundant historical evidence for extensive storage areas within Cuzco's central sector as well as nearby in Saqsawaman. All the earliest descriptions of Cuzco, by persons who saw it before it was burned in 1535, comment on the vast quantities of goods stored throughout the city (Pedro Pizarro 1978: 99–100, chap. 15). One somewhat representative description from 1535 (Estete 1924: 47) elaborates:

> Great vessels and devices for drinking, well made of gold and
> silver in great quantity, were found in this city. There were end-
> less feathers, and trappings for war. There was a great quantity of
> wool, and in houses, storerooms, and boxes everything that the
> land produces from lizards and insects to everything else of all

that was supplied to the lord and the temples. And there it was guarded by the hands of caretakers for necessities, soldiers, and lean years. Understand that in all this enters maize and the wine that they are used to making, and all the other things for sustenance.

Qori Kancha, the Gold Enclosure or Sun Temple

Cuzco had an extraordinary number of sacred places, shrines, and temples, but the most famous was the Qori Kancha, the Sun Temple (fig. 2.8). No Inka compound in Cuzco was mentioned more often by the earliest Europeans to see it (Hemming and Ranney 1982: 78–86) and none has been the subject of more detailed architectural commentary in this century (Lehmann-Nitsche 1928; Rowe 1944: 26–41; Kubler 1952: 10–12; Ladrón de G. 1967; Gasparini and Margolies 1980: 220–234).

The fame of the Qori Kancha and its gold was so great that an advance party of three Spaniards was sent in 1533 to Cuzco to loot the temple. Of primary concern were the gold plaques adorning the temple. For religious reasons, no Indians would help the Spaniards pry them loose. Mena in the following account (1967: 93) describes various rooms within the Qori Kancha:

> In another house they entered they found a seat of gold where they did their sacrifices. This seat was so big it weighed nineteen thousand pesos, and two men could fit in it. In another very big house they found many clay vessels covered with gold sheets that weighed a lot. They did not want to break them so as not to infuriate the Indians. In that house there were many women, and

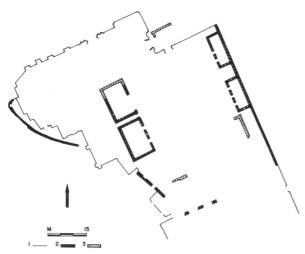

2.8. The Sun Temple, Qori Kancha, is only partially intact. Once decorated with gold plaques, it was looted by the first group of Spaniards to arrive in Cuzco. Covered in part by the Santo Domingo Church, four main rooms can still be seen. The famous fine masonry curved wall is found on the southwestern side. Key: 1. exterior wall of Santo Domingo Church; 2. Inka walls; 3. Inka foundations. Redrawn from Gasparini and Margolies (1980: 224).

there were two Indians mummified in a way. And next to them was a live woman with a mask of gold on her face. She was driving out the dust and flies with a fan. The mummies had in their hands a staff with valuable gold. The woman did not permit them to go inside unless they took off their shoes, so taking them off they went to see those dried-up bundles. They took many valuable pieces from them, but did not finish taking all because the lord Atawalpa had begged them not to, saying that they were of his father, Cuzco [the Inka], and that is why they did not dare take more.

This account was written in 1534 by a soldier who spoke directly with the three Spaniards who looted the temple. It is an unsophisticated description, but confirms later accounts that there was a great gold seat (probably for the sun image), women attendants, and important mummies within the rooms of the Qori Kancha. It also confirms that great respect—the removal of one's shoes—was required of those who entered it. This point comes up in another early description, that of the soldier Diego Trujillo (1948: 63–64), who entered Cuzco with Pizarro's band several months later. He wrote that the supreme priest, Villac Umo, stipulated that the Spanish could enter the temple only after fasting for a year, carrying a load on their backs, and removing their shoes. Needless to say, the Spaniards paid no attention and walked right in.

Virtually every early chronicler who passed through Cuzco in the following century described various aspects of the Qori Kancha. One of the most valuable descriptions is that by Pedro Pizarro (1978: 91–94, chap. 15), who marveled at its fine stone walls, which had been adorned with a band of gold (figs. 2.9, 2.10). Particularly important is his eyewitness description of the patio within Qori Kancha. It had a rock (*peña*) in the form of a bench or seat with a covering of gold. By day the sun image was placed in it, when it was not carried to the main plaza. By night the sun image was put in a small gold-adorned room or niche (*aposento*). Pizarro confirms the presence of women attendants (*mamaconas*), whose alleged virginity he disputed.

He also mentions a small garden in which gold corn plants were placed on important occasions. The size and contents of this garden were greatly exaggerated by imaginative chroniclers like Garcilaso. Pedro Pizarro relates that the golden garden was supplied by water carried in. Garcilaso (1963II: 116–118, Bk. 3, chaps. 23–24) devotes considerable time to a discussion of Qori Kancha's water system, saying it had six fountains. He claims to have seen only one, and when it dried up no one could be found who knew where the water came from. Later the

2.9. *Exterior of room on the northeast side of the Qori Kancha, Cuzco.*

2.10. *Interior of room on the southwest side of the Qori Kancha, Cuzco.*

leaking source was discovered and water was restored to Qori Kancha. Since no other informant tells of a special water supply for the temple, one might doubt Garcilaso were it not for the discovery of a double-drain fountain (fig. 5.2) near the base of the terrace to the west of Qori Kancha's curved wall. As noted in chapter 5, one aspect of Inka settlement planning is the association of special water systems with places of great ritual significance.

Cieza de León, who traveled in much of Tawantinsuyu in the 1540s, is one of the few later visitors to the temple whose capacity for careful description can be generally relied upon. He noted that the temple was as old as Cuzco itself and that it had been made more elegant by Pachakuti. Cieza describes two important niches (1976: 145, chap. 27): "There were two benches [niches] against that wall, which the rising sun fell upon, and the stones were very skillfully perforated, and the openings set with precious stones and emeralds. These benches were for the Lord-Incas, and if anyone else sat there, he was sentenced to death." Cieza does not specify whether the niches were for live or mummified Inkas.

Most early descriptions do not help determine how many principal rooms were in the temple. Cieza de León (1967: 92, chap. 27) writes that there were four, as does Las Casas (1958: 451), who was never in Cuzco but was in contact with early eyewitnesses. Gutiérrez (1963: 214, 252, chaps. 50, 64) mentions eight rooms. Much later Garcilaso records five rooms (1963II: 113, 115, Bk. 3, chaps. 21, 22), of which he claims to have seen only three standing with roofs. Both Garcilaso and Gutiérrez make the point that the Sun Temple was not just for solar worship, but that various rooms were dedicated to the worship of other celestial phenomena. The temple has been sufficiently destroyed to never know its exact form, or how many rooms it had. Gasparini and Margolies (1980: 224,

229) postulate seven. Although solar temples were built by the Inka state throughout its domain, none of the few that have been identified have an architectural form replicating the one in Cuzco.[8]

Since the earliest eyewitnesses are clear that many people, particularly women attendants, lived inside the Sun Temple, it is quite certain that there were buildings other than those of fine masonry today considered the Qori Kancha. These could have been on the south side of the *kancha,* where the boundary of the enclosure is uncertain, or on terraces to the west.

Another of Qori Kancha's roles was that of the geographical center of the Inka *zeque* system, a system of forty or forty-one radial lines with sacred shrines, or *waqa,* about which was organized the ritual system of Cuzco. Given the importance of the *zeque* system, it is discussed at greater length below and in chapters 5 and 7.

Zuidema (1982a: 212–215), working with Aveni, notes that Qori Kancha is aligned (west wall 66 degrees, 44 minutes; east wall 65 degrees, 15 minutes) to a sunrise on about May 25, an azimuth close to that of the Pleiades rise, and a day associated with the beginning of the Inka year, shortly before the June solstice. Whereas one might debate the exact meaning of the Qori Kancha's orientation, it is clear that the east wall (with the two decorated niches described by Cieza) of the two western rooms would have been bathed in nearly direct sunlight on the mornings of the days just before, during, and just after the June solstice.

Following the great earthquake of May 21, 1950, in which the Santo Domingo Church and cloister covering the Qori Kancha were significantly damaged, a restoration project exposed additional Inka walls and made some dubious "patches" in walls, imitating the Inka stonework. Gasparini and Margolies' review revealed details (1980: 222–228), noting that one especially fine, large niche was exposed on the inside of the great curved wall on the west end of the church. It may have held a particularly famous sacred stone called Subaraura, thought to have been the chief of the *pururaucas* who in Inka legend were stones turned into warriors who helped the Inkas defend Cuzco.

The central sector of Cuzco was divided into two main parts, *hanan* (upper) and *hurin* (lower) along the southern side of the plaza, with the *hanan* half in the north and the *hurin* half in the south. The two halves correspond to a dual or moiety division in Inka society and are fundamental for understanding Cuzco's design and the planning of other Inka settlements. This dual division or bipartition is discussed below and in chapters 5 and 7.

The Intermediate Zone

Uninhabited but generally cultivated land separated the central sector of Cuzco from its surrounding districts (fig. 2.2). One might include within this the particularly large area of terraces to the southwest of the Saphy River around Kusipata Plaza, which, if Garcilaso (1963II: 262, Bk. 7, chap. 11) is to be believed (and no other source confirms him), was being saved for the building projects of future monarchs. Assuming that the Kusipata Plaza reached to the west as far as the house of Garcilaso, one can make a rough estimate of the intermediate zone's expansion area (surrounding Kusipata) at about 48 hectares (Agurto 1980: 119). One argument supporting Garcilaso's claim that the area was reserved for future development is that the surrounding districts to the west are farther away from the central sector than are the others, thus creating the space needed for future expansion.

Since the exact locations of the dozen or more districts that surrounded the central sector are not known, it is difficult to determine the size of the intermediate zone. Agurto calculates the size of this surrounding belt (excluding the expansion area) at about 105 hectares.

One notable characteristic of the intermediate zone is that it was terraced. These terraces can be located today on the edges of the streets and in the yards of modern expanded Cuzco. A map created by the UNESCO survey project (Agurto 1980: 100) gives a very general idea of their location. Terraces were also present in the central sector and in areas occupied by the surrounding residential districts. In those inhabited areas they were not used for agriculture, but rather were occupied by buildings.

The Surrounding Districts

Because so few archaeological traces of these districts remain, their locations have been defined by toponyms rather than by physical remains (fig. 2.2). The confusion is augmented by the fact that some of the early historical sources describing Cuzco ignore these districts, probably because they generally had no fine Inka masonry, and were thus less impressive.[9] They were occupied mainly by people who were not Inka nobility. Many were from the provinces and probably returned home soon after the Spanish arrived. Nevertheless, there can be little doubt of the districts' existence, since eyewitnesses describe a valley full of houses surrounding Cuzco's central sector.

The issue is complicated, since the only detailed description of these districts is by Garcilaso de la Vega (1963II: 256–258), with whom, once again, there are some reasons to disagree. Rowe (1967: 65–66, 12) discards several names listed by Garcilaso and substitutes others. He is suspicious of some districts "probably settled" after the Spanish conquest. Agurto (1980: 130–136), following Chávez Ballón (1970), is less severe in his revisions of Garcilaso, discarding two district names (Quillipata and Pumacurco) from Garcilaso's list and including one new one (Coripata). Thus they arrive at twelve surrounding districts.

Given that the exact locations and names of the surrounding districts will be established only with additional archaeological and ethnohistorical research, it is useful to examine here the redrawing of Agurto's plan (fig. 2.2) depicting the central sector in relation to the intermediate area and surrounding districts. The Inka-period roads are also drawn, with the line thickness indicating their importance. The Inka concept of quadripartition can be seen in the surrounding districts, since three can be assigned to each of the four *suyu*, or divisions. The Chinchasuyu districts are Carmenca, Huacapungo, and Colcampata. The Antisuyu districts are Cantupata, Totocachi, and Munaysenca. The Qollasuyu districts are Rimacpampa, Pumachupan, and Coripata. The Kuntisuyu districts are Cayaocachi, Chaquilchaca, and Picchu.

It is difficult to say to what degree the surrounding districts were "designed" and to what degree their positions were defined by the topography. The depressions formed by streams are usually dividing lines between the districts, and the Ayahuayco, Chunchulmayo, and Tullumayo streams apparently divided many of the districts from the intermediate zone. On the other hand, planning seems apparent in the way the streets reach out from the central sector, a point discussed below.

Beyond the Ring of Districts

When Cuzco was "rebuilt" by Pachakuti, a considerable zone around the central sector was evacuated and turned into state agricultural lands and planned settlements. Agurto (1980: 120–121, plate p. 125) defines as part of Cuzco a suburban zone of some 540 hectares extending up to 5 kilometers from the center of Cuzco.

Proof that planned agricultural settlements were built around Cuzco has been supplied by Niles (1984), who has mapped and analyzed several of them. All are within two hours' walk to the east and south of the capital. All are built with rows of individual rectangular buildings facing downslope with single doors. The houses have foundations of fieldstones probably once topped with adobe. They are a specific and unique type of Inka town planning that has not yet been observed anywhere else in Tawantinsuyu. The towns have relatively small buildings, restricted in number (several dozen at most), and limited amounts of open space. They have little of the complexity of Cuzco-area settlements associated with more important occupants. It is uncertain whether these towns were inhabited by permanent Inka retainers or people from elsewhere, but their notable standardization indicates that their inhabitants had little social stratification (Niles 1984: 216). The planned agricultural communities appear to be dependencies of Cuzco, and thus should be considered a part of Cuzco's grand design.

There may always be debate as to how far out the city extended. One suggestion is that Cuzco ended where the *suyu* began. Sources vary, but some indicate that the *suyu* began some kilometers outside the central sector of Cuzco. In this case the surrounding districts would not be considered part of a *suyu* although each had a *suyu* affiliation. Cuzco might thus have terminated some distance beyond its densely populated areas. One support of the idea that the *suyu* begin some distance from the central sector of Cuzco is a plotting of settlements with *suyu* designations (Zuidema and Poole 1982). Cuzco may have had some characteristics of a modern federal district, or a political unit encompassing the capital and its surrounding territory without being a part of neighboring political or ethnic units. It would seem, however, that there is no agreement on this issue. One recent debate that sheds light on the question of Cuzco's boundaries and limits has to do with whether the city was designed in the shape of a puma.

A Puma Shape or Puma Metaphor?

Rowe (1967: 60) has published evidence and a drawing demonstrating that the central sector of Cuzco was in the shape of a puma: "The area between the rivers was laid out in the shape of a *puma*, the fortress [Saqsawaman] representing the *puma*'s head and the point where the rivers come together representing the tail. This point is still called 'the *puma*'s tail' [Puma Chupan] in Inca." Rowe bases his presentation on a suggestion from Chávez Ballón and by drawing on two historical sources, the earliest one by Betanzos (1968: 50, chap. 17) who writes: "After Inka Yupanki had organized the city of Cuzco in the manner you have heard, he gave names to all the places and patios, and to the whole city together he gave the name 'the lion's body,' saying that those neighbors and inhabitants of it were the members of such lion, and that his person was the head of it."

The word *lion* was commonly used by the Spaniards to mean puma. Some twenty years after Betanzos, Sarmiento de Gamboa (1965: 257–258, chap. 52) would write that Thupa Yupanki

> recalled that his father Pachakuti had called the city of Cuzco the lion city, and that the tail was where the two rivers that pass by the city come together, and that the body was the plaza and the populations around it, and that the head was missing, but that

some son of his would place it. And thus discussing this matter with the *orejones,* he said that the best head that he could place on it would be to make a fortress on a high eminence that the city has on its north side.

Andean scholars have generally accepted the concept of Cuzco's having a puma shape. Gasparini and Margolies (1980: 48) have presented two alternative puma shapes, with a lying or sitting puma with extended rather than crouching legs so as to encompass the space to the southwest of the Saphy River.

In an article on the symbolic use of felines by Inkas, Zuidema (1983a) refutes the idea that the actual shape of a puma could be imposed on Cuzco, and proposes that one must understand the references in a metaphorical sense. He presents an array of arguments suggesting why a puma was used as a metaphor by Betanzos, and by Inkas, to explain matters relating to social structure, royal succession, and borders. He then argues that Sarmiento's more direct comparison of Cuzco to the puma shape is spurious because he, as a later and less-sophisticated informant, had not understood the metaphorical nature of the puma as a city idea. Zuidema writes that Betanzos was describing a Cuzco much larger than its central sector, an area defined by the *zeque* system, the 41 lines and 328 *waqa,* or shrines that extend from Cuzco to within a perimeter of 15 to 25 kilometers. He argues for this interpretation, since the *zeque* system is the administrative instrument used by the Incas to describe the political organization of Cuzco. Zuidema's arguments are too many and too complex to present in their entirety here, but it is relevant to note that the metaphorical Cuzco may have corresponded not only to the limits of the *zeque* system, but to its hydrological area, which was more or less the same (Sherbondy 1982a, 1986). This included an area where some "Inkas-by-privilege" lived, and where the city's *ayllu* and *panaqa* had their closest lands and water. Zuidema's views indicate that Cuzco must be considered an area larger than even its central sector and ring of surrounding districts.

Thus Cuzco may be a puma only in a metaphorical sense. The debate concerning the "lion" in the city elucidates the important point that the boundaries of Cuzco may have varied depending on the criteria used to define limits.

Saqsawaman
The greatest architectural complex ever built by the Inkas is Saqsawaman, an immense religious-military construction on a hill to the north of Cuzco (fig. 2.11). Everyone who has ever seen it speaks of it in

2.11. *Aerial view of Saqsawaman, the religious-military complex built on a hill to the north of Cuzco. Three tiers of zigzag walls face on a plaza. Behind them (to the right) on the hilltop are the excavated remains of buildings, including the foundations of one round and one rectangular tower. The Suchuna sector is to the left. Courtesy S.A.N.*

2.12. *Three levels of polygonal masonry walls at Saqsawaman in Peru. Tens of thousands of laborers worked decades to construct Saqsawaman. It may never have been finished.*

the most superlative terms. Saqsawaman easily bears comparison with the most elaborate constructions of antiquity in both the New and the Old World (fig. 2.12). In many respects, it remains quite enigmatic. The earliest Spaniards saw it as a "fortress," no doubt because of its high walls, which appeared defensive to the European mind. Later and more sophisticated chroniclers such as Cieza de León (1967: 169–172, chap. 51) correct this simple view, noting that it was a "House of the Sun" with ceremonial and religious functions. If Saqsawaman had a military function, it was mainly symbolic. Its plaza could have served for ritual battles (Rostworowski 1988: 79). Some military gear was stored within the complex. Indeed, the earliest descriptions of Saqsawaman, particularly those written before its systematic dismembering to provide building stone for Spanish Cuzco, usually note two points: first, the impressive dimensions of the stones, and second, the large quantity of goods deposited in it.

There are many descriptions of Saqsawaman, but the earliest stand out as the most lucid, since the first eyewitnesses were able to bind their romantic eulogies to an accurate picture of the monument before its looting and destruction. Francisco Pizarro's secretary, Pedro Sancho, put down the following description (1917: 193–194, chap. 17) in 1534, which, because of its detail, deserves complete citation:

> there is a very beautiful fortress of earth and stone with big windows that look over the city and make it appear more beautiful. In it there are many chambers and a main round tower in the center made with four or five stories one on the other. The rooms and habitations inside are small, and the stones of which it is made are very well worked and so well placed next to each other

that it seems that they do not have mortar, and the stones are so
smooth that they seem to be prepared boards with the junctures
against each other like that used in Spain. There are so many
habitations, and the tower, that one person cannot see it all in
one day. And many Spaniards who have seen it who have been
in Lombardy and other foreign kingdoms say that they have
not seen another construction like this fortress, nor a more powerful castle. Five thousand Spaniards might be able to fit inside. It
cannot be attacked or undermined because it is located on an
outcrop. On the side facing the city there is only one wall on a
rugged mountain slope. On the other side, which is less steep,
there are three, one higher than the other. These walls are the
most beautiful thing that can be seen of all the constructions in
that land. This is because they are of such big stones that no one
who sees them would say that they have been placed there by the
hand of man. They are as big as pieces of mountains or crags, and
they are some thirty palms high and others as wide, and others of
twenty-five palms and others of fifteen, but none of them are so
small that three carts could carry them. These stones are not flat,
but very well worked and fit together. The Spaniards who see
them say that neither the bridge of Segovia nor other constructions of Hercules or the Romans are as magnificent as this. The
city of Tarragona has some works in its wall made in this way,
but they are not as strong or with such big stones. These walls
have curves so that if one attacks them one cannot go frontally
but rather obliquely with the exterior. These walls are of similar
stone, and from wall to wall there is so much earth fill that three
carts together can pass on top. The walls are made in the form of
three levels and one begins where the other ends, and another
begins where the last ended. This entire fortress was a great
storehouse of arms, clubs, lances, bows, arrows, axes, shields,
heavy jackets of quilted cotton, and other weapons of different
types. And there was clothing for soldiers, all collected here from
all areas of the land subject to the lords of Cuzco. There were
many pigments—blues, yellows, browns, and others for painting.
There was cloth and much tin and lead with other metals, and
much silver and some gold.

Sancho first describes the buildings on top of the hill, noting many
rooms with windows that look down on Cuzco. These structures have
been destroyed. Only some foundations remain, and these were un-

earthed only in this century (Valcárcel 1934–1935). Sancho also noted a tall tower. His compatriot Pedro Pizarro described (1978: 104, chap. 15) two tall buildings, as did Cieza de León, who observed that one was larger than the other (1967: 171, chap. 51).[10] Pizarro's description is similar to that of Sancho, but mentions a few extra details caught by his youthful eye, such as guards who looked after the stored materials, a large supply of tightly woven cane helmets (strong enough to protect any head from a strong blow), and a set of litters for carrying about the lords of the empire.

Saqsawaman's three massive terrace walls are so distracting that few descriptions exist of the area to the north side of the complex's large plaza, an area incompletely excavated by Valcárcel[11] and called Suchuna (1934–1935: vol. 2). The area is replete with aqueducts, cisterns, terraces, patios, stairs, and buildings. Valcárcel noted that its rock hill surrounded by walls had a military cast to it. He also felt that this area transformed the site into "another city." Perhaps there is some truth to this, since a major architectural feature of Saqsawaman is its grand plaza, and no major Inka "city" was complete without one or more plazas. One notable part of Suchuna is the so-called Throne of the Inka (fig. 4.2), which looks over the plaza and the three massive walls south of the plaza. This "throne" consists of a set of sculpted shelves in bedrock and is discussed in chapter 4.

Some of the stones used to make Saqsawaman are among the largest ever moved and worked by the Inkas (fig. 2.13). Reports vary about which king (usually Pachakuti, Thupa Yupanki, or even a predecessor) began the construction, and whether or not it was ever finished. Both Las Casas (1958: 194) and Cieza de León say it was never completed. Garcilaso (1963II: 289, Bk. 7, chap. 29) reports that it took fifty years to construct, but then adds it was really never finished. From the earliest Europeans to the most casual tourist or critical scholar, the nearly automatic question arises about how stones of such size were moved and put in place. Gutiérrez (1963: 252, chap. 63) states the unromantic obvious, that the stones were pulled into place with much human labor and great ropes of vine and hemp. Those ropes caught the eye of one of the earliest Spanish soldiers in Cuzco, Diego de Trujillo (1948: 63), who saw large buildings full of ropes, some as thick as a leg, with which stones were pulled to make buildings. Many of the great stones were quarried nearby, but at least some of them appear to have been hauled from a considerable distance (Hemming and Ranney 1982: 67; Protzen 1983; Kalafatovich 1970), a point confirmed by several early chroniclers. But the great "secret" of the construction of Saqsawaman is not the ropes, or

2.13. *Passageway between two levels of zigzag walls at Saqsawaman. The walls were once somewhat higher, but many stones were removed from the site to build Spanish colonial Cuzco.*

any mysterious technical practice,[12] but rather the rotating (*mita*) labor supply, which provided the enormous energies necessary to erect the walls and buildings. No one described this better than Cieza de León (1959: 153–154), whose bad fortune it was to view the great complex already in ruins:

> This work was conceived on such a vast scale that even if the monarchy had lasted until now, it would not have been completed.
>
> He [Pachakuti] ordered twenty thousand men sent in from the provinces, and that the villages supply men with the necessary food, and if one of them took sick, that another should be sent in his place and he could return to his home. These Indians were not permanently engaged in this work, but only for a limited time, and the others came and they left, so the work did not become onerous. Four thousand of them quarried and cut the stones; six thousand hauled them with great cables of leather and hemp; the others dug the ditch and laid the foundations, while still others cut poles and beams for the timbers. So that they would be contented, these people lived in separate groups, each with those of his own region, near the site where the building was to be erected. Even today most of the walls of the houses they occupied can be seen. Overseers went around watching what they did, and masters who were highly skilled in their work. Thus on a hill to the north of the city, at its highest point,

slightly more than the shot of an arquebus, this fortress was
built, which the native called "House of the Sun," and we
[Spanish] the "Fortress."

There is no evidence that Saqsawaman was ever used as a fortress,
except during the Inkas' siege of Cuzco (A.D. 1535), when it was occupied
by the Spanish. Thus the role of the monument within the design of
Cuzco remains somewhat unclear in detail even if one grants that it
served religious-ceremonial as well as storage purposes. Gasparini and
Margolies (1980: 285) weigh the idea that Saqsawaman was the major
monument of *hanan* Cuzco, "the most powerful division after the re-
forms and rebuilding of the city by Pachakuti." They discard this idea,
however, indicating that the concept of two kings reigning simultane-
ously in Cuzco is "poorly based modern speculation."[13] Whether or not
two kings ruled does not contradict the generally accepted dual division
of Inka Cuzco. It would seem preeminently reasonable for *hanan* Cuzco
to have its own House of the Sun, particularly since the old Sun Temple,
Qori Kancha, was clearly associated with, and located in, *hurin* Cuzco.
Because of the dual nature of Andean social organization, settlements
were divided and paired, now as in the past.

Perhaps a more significant question is whether Saqsawaman lies
within *hanan* Cuzco. Indeed, one could argue that Saqsawaman cannot
be placed within *hanan* Cuzco because it rests outside of the ring of peripheral districts. Nevertheless, the great complex is to the north, near
the origin of the waters that help define *hanan*, and really quite close to
central Cuzco. A leading expert on Saqsawaman, Valcárcel (1934–1935:
vol. 3: 4, 212) clearly thought the great complex should be considered
part of *hanan* Cuzco if not *the hanan* Cuzco. If one accepts Saqsawaman as a part of *hanan* Cuzco, it clearly puts the architectural weight of
the city on the *hanan* side and belies the Inka fiction that both halves
were equal. Saqsawaman breaks the symmetry of Cuzco's main plan of
a two-part central sector with peripheral districts. Thus it may not
have been part of the original urban plan. Finally, one must underline
Saqsawaman's uniqueness among all Inka building projects. It was the
largest monument ever attempted by the state in one place, and it is
risky to compare it to any other architectural accomplishment of the
Inkas or other Andean peoples.

The Roads of Cuzco

The Links to Regions beyond the City

Most early written descriptions of the Inka capital mention that four
main roads ran out of (or into) the city, and that each led to one of the

state's four great divisions, or *suyu* (fig. 2.2). Cieza de León (1959: 144, chap. 44) handled it this way:

> From this square four highways emerge; the one called Chinchay-suyu leads to the plains and the highlands as far as the provinces of Quito and Pasto; the second, known as Cunti-suyu, is the highway to the provinces under the jurisdiction of this city and Arequipa. The third, by name Anti-suyu, leads to the provinces on the slopes of the Andes and various settlements beyond the mountains. The last of these highways, called Collasuyu, is the route to Chile. Thus, just as in Spain the early inhabitants divided everything into provinces, so these Indians, to keep track of their wide-flung possessions, used the method of the highways.

Cieza's description of Cuzco's four main roads is typical of other earlier informants.[14] His observation that the Inkas understood or conceived of their domain through roads, and not through provinces, is particularly important. By this he meant that peoples and places were located and described in relation to main roads. In Andean society roads have a symbolic role that is considerably greater than in most Western cultures (Hyslop 1984: 340–343), and for that reason it is useful to look with special care at the road system within and leading out of the Inka capital.

The four main roads came together on the southern side of the Haukaypata Plaza. The road to Chinchasuyu left the plaza on the present-day street of Plateros. The road to Antisuyu passed in front of the Amarukancha and Hatunkancha and proceeded east on Triunfo and Hatun Rumiyoc streets. This road was also the dividing line between the *hanan* (upper) and *hurin* (lower) parts of the central sector of Cuzco. The road to Qollasuyu headed south on Loreto Street, once called Sun Street. Sources vary as to whether it continued southward or passed southeast through the plaza of Intipampa on through Limacpampa Plaza to the southeast; probably both were routes to Qollasuyu. The road to Kuntisuyu headed southwest from the plaza on Santa Clara Street. As the roads extend out from Haukaypata Plaza, two or three of them (Chinchasuyu, Antisuyu, and probably Qollasuyu) do not continue straight for any great distance. Within a few blocks of the plaza they curve to accommodate Cuzco's topography.

The frequent reference to four main roads leading from (or into) the city from the four *suyu* is accurate only in a general sense. The UNESCO survey (Agurto 1980: 94) reports remains of more than twenty roads connecting Cuzco to its hinterland. Clearly, the four roads to the *suyu* are only part of a rather massive road system in the Cuzco region.

Nevertheless, the four principal roads are of prime importance not only because they were the main arteries to very distant regions, but because they represented and linked the four *suyu* to Cuzco.

Roads to the Surrounding Districts

Chávez Ballón (1970: 9–10) writes that three streets ran from the central sector to each district and that they make a pattern like *zeque* lines. In fact, each district appears to have had from two to five streets, with three an average. (The idea that streets in some Inka settlements might represent *zeque* system spatial patterning is advanced in chapter 7.) Meanwhile, it may be useful to notice that the streets of Cuzco, while following an orthogonal pattern within the central sector, develop a radial pattern as they extend out and through the districts, (fig. 2.2). Agurto (1980: 133) mentions another correspondence between the physical plan of the surrounding districts and the *zeque* system. He notes that the degrees of arc defined by the *zeque* system's *suyu* are similar to the arcs defined by the districts of each *suyu*, with Kuntisuyu being the greatest and Qollasuyu being the smallest.

The Streets of the Central Sector: The Orthogonal Plan

The streets of central Cuzco were described as early as 1534 by Francisco Pizarro's scribe, Pedro Sancho (1917: 192, chap. 17), who noted: "[The houses] are built in an orderly way, and the straight streets are made in the form of a cross, all paved. Down their center passes a stone-lined water channel. A problem is the streets' narrowness, since only one horseman can ride on one side of the channel, and another [horseman] on the other side."

Sancho's observation that the streets were narrow can be confirmed by anyone who walks old Cuzco today. The UNESCO survey (Agurto 1980: 96) found that the main streets were between 4.4 and 5.6 meters wide, and that there were other streets and passageways from 1.6 to 3.2 meters in width. In a few streets the central gutter mentioned by Sancho is still intact. He neglected to mention that some of the streets, particularly those in the north, where the slope was rather steep, were stepped. This special feature of Inka streets and roads, suited to pedestrian traffic, was less useful to Spaniards with carts and to modern Peruvians with cars. In several cases the steps have been removed so as to permit vehicular traffic.

Sancho also noted an orthogonal pattern in central Cuzco when referring to "streets in the form of a cross" (fig. 2.3). Central Cuzco's layout is of particular interest to this study of Inka planning (chapter 7). Agurto (1980: 96, 142–144) summarizes important information about the generally rectangular units formed by the streets by noting that their dimensions varied. The units or "blocks" varied in width from about 30 to 45 meters and the lengths from about 45 to 70 meters. This is an important difference between some Inka layouts and those employed by the Spanish, whose blocks were of uniform size.

The rectangular units of Cuzco were defined by sets of longitudinal (northwest to southeast) and transverse (southwest to northeast) streets (Agurto 1980: 142–143). Agurto defines four longitudinal streets. One followed the Saphy River; to the east there was another street, generally parallel, passing along the east side of the plaza and through present-day Loreto Street and its continuation, Pampa del Castillo. Farther to the east was another street, now called San Agustín. The fourth and final longitudinal street ran beside the canalized Tullumayo River. It is probably a simplification to think that central Cuzco had only four generally parallel longitudinal streets. Others may have been lost in the many modifications made during the last 450 years.

Possible evidence for another street is found on the map (fig. 2.14) of the unit or block known as Cusikancha. Agurto (1980: 106) points out how Inka walls within the unit indicate that a longitudinal passageway probably passed through it. Whether one should define that passageway as a street is another question. The units or blocks formed by the streets comprised several *kancha* each, and passageways not only sometimes separated them but led into and between them. These accesses do not have the public character of a street, since they are already inside a greater unit. In Cuzco and other Inka settlements, it is important not to confuse streets with passageways inside of units formed by streets.

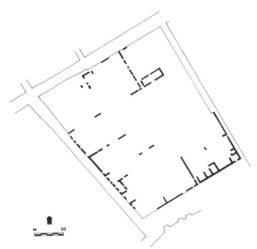

2.14. The "block" of Cuzco called Cusikancha. The thick black lines represent Inka walls. It is located to the northwest of the plaza of Intipampa and the Sun Temple. A survey within Cusikancha indicates that a street or passageway may have passed through it from northwest to southeast. Redrawn from Agurto C. (1980: 77).

There were at least five transverse streets running generally from southwest to northeast. The northernmost is today formed by Amargura, Concepción, Siete Borreguitos, and Quiscapata streets. Parallel and to the south was the street, partially intact, composed of Huaynapata, Ladrillos, and Atoc Saycuchi. To the south of it ran Mantas (south side of Haukaypata), Triunfo, and Hatun Rumiyoc. Farther south was the street composed of Afligidos, Maruri, and Cabrancancha. Finally, the southernmost transverse street included the plaza Intipampa and Zetas and Abracitos. The plan of the known Inka walls (fig. 2.3) suggests that there may have been some other transverse and longitudinal streets, but there is little evidence that they extended all the way from one side of the central sector to the other.

Astronomical Towers

Whereas roads united central Cuzco to its residential districts and points beyond, sight lines united the central sector to the nearby horizons and then the cosmos. Several of the early Spaniards in Cuzco described markers or pillars on hills about Cuzco, used to define points on the horizon when viewed from specific locations within or near Cuzco (Polo 1940: 133). Thus specific times of the year could be defined when the rising or setting sun was aligned with the point of observation and the marker.

Such markers were highly visible monuments, and thus are an integral part of the capital's architectural planning. Unfortunately, they were destroyed early in the Spanish period, since they were correctly identified as part of the Inka calendrical and ritual system. While none exist today, they are described in several early historical sources. The locations and astronomical role of some can be determined by archaeoastronomical reconstruction (Aveni 1981a; Zuidema 1981a, 1982b). Two sets of two towers each are mentioned in "An Account of the Shrines . . ." (Rowe 1979: 24–25, Ch-6: 9, 58–59, Cu-13: 3). Both marked sunsets on the western horizon. The monuments are called *mojones* (land markers), and in one case also described as *pilares* (pillars). Other *mojones* on the western horizon are described by two other sources (Discurso 1906: 152; Cieza de León 1962: 242, chap. 92). Both sources describe the markers as little towers (*torrecillas*). These same little towers are noted by other early residents of Cuzco. Betanzos (1968: 46, chap. 15) mentions, in addition, four other markers on the eastern horizon. He describes them as pyramids or stone columns the height of two men. Betanzos describes these monuments as part of his discussion of the rebuilding of Cuzco by Pachakuti, to whom he attributed the calendrical system, which used such markers to establish fixed dates. Sarmiento (1965: 236, chap. 30) describes the markers as four posts (*palos*), replaced by stone columns after their locations were well fixed, each with holes in the top through which the rays of the sun would pass (chap. 8). For him, there were two sets of four markers each, one set on the eastern and one on the western horizon. Somewhat similar information about four eastern and four western markers is related by Garcilaso (1963II: 72–73, Bk. 2, chap. 22), who claims to have seen them still standing in 1560, and Acosta (1985: 283, Bk. 6, chap. 3). Depending on the informant, these horizon markers were used to indicate important days in the agricultural and ritual cycle.

The well-documented use of stone tower markers on the horizons of Cuzco is evidence that astronomical concerns affected the city's appearance. They also give weight to the point that the limits of Inka Cuzco were not those of the central sector, but reached several kilometers beyond (at least to the horizon). In a symbolic sense, they linked the capital directly with the sun. The influence of astronomical concerns on the design of other Inka settlements is discussed in chapter 8.

The Population of Cuzco
The design of Cuzco becomes more comprehensible when one understands who lived in its various sectors. That is, it becomes possible to see why certain areas were separated from others.

Inkas and Others
The central sector was primarily occupied by Inkas of the royal lineages, or *panaqa* (royal *ayllu*). Betanzos's description (1968: 50, chap. 16) of the planning of Cuzco notes that central Cuzco's original inhabitants were moved to a surrounding district. The lineages were divided into two halves, or moieties, called *hanan* (upper) and *hurin* (lower). Those of *hurin* inhabited the southern part of the central sector, around the Sun Temple. Those of *hanan* occupied the northern part. The traditional division between the two halves is the southern side of the Haukaypata Plaza and Triunfo and Hatun Rumiyoc streets. It is interesting that this important spatial division or boundary was not emphasized architecturally in any special way. That is, the street dividing the two halves gives no indication by its construction that it is a special boundary or division. As will be discussed below, factors related to water rights outside of the central sector may have created the division, and thus it was not defined in any special way within the center of the city.

Ten *panaqa* or royal *ayllu* existed in Cuzco,[15] each associated in the formal Inka histories with one of ten kings. Five were of the *hanan* moiety and five of the *hurin* moiety. It is now generally recognized that these "kings" (at least the first seven) do not necessarily represent a succession of rulers, as is conveyed in some early chronicles, but rather symbolic founders of the basic paired divisions (five *panaqa* each) of Inka social organization (Zuidema 1964; Duviols 1979; Rostworowski 1983). A chief symbol of the ten royal *ayllu* was the mummies of the alleged kings, dug up in the sixteenth century and turned into religious objects (Sarmiento 1965: 236, chap. 31; Betanzos 1968: 54, chap. 17). It is important, therefore, not to think that the various "palaces" or compounds attributed to "early" Inka kings by some chronicles (and most tourist guides) were built in chronological succession. Compounds in Cuzco attributed to kings, with the exception of those of the last three or four kings, who were truly historical, are really compounds tended to by royal *panaqa*, with a "king" or a royal mummy as one of its symbols. As was noted earlier, the evidence is not sufficient to know which compounds belonged to which *panaqa*. In sum, the inhabitants of the central sector of Cuzco were Inkas associated with *panaqa*. Other people lived there who were not Inka such as retainers, guards, and chosen women, but little is known about where they lived and how many of them there were. Symbolically, the central sector of Cuzco was for Inkas.

The ring of districts around the central sector, and perhaps some other settlements within a few kilometers, were inhabited by non-Inkas. This included ten non-Inka *ayllu* (Betanzos 1968: 48, chap. 16; Sarmiento 1965: 214, chap. 11) said to live in Cayaocachi, and many provincial lords, their sons, and attendants, who came from distant regions to spend an obligatory period in Cuzco (Rowe 1967: 62, 69). One of the first Spanish soldiers in Cuzco, Ruiz de Arce (1955: 194), wrote that local lords of the empire had to reside in Cuzco four months and noted with surprise: "There was a lord who had his land 600 leagues from here [Cuzco] and he had to come and reside, as stated. Those lords who had their lands far away had the order that their people had to come and populate a settlement near Cuzco in order to serve and be in the court."

The surrounding districts were also populated by *mitmaq*, often specialized workers or artisans from various parts of the state. It is uncertain where the *mitayoq*, individuals doing their labor obligations or *mita*, stayed if required to come to Cuzco. Possibly they too were housed in the surrounding districts, with or near people from their region. This question will be an interesting one for future archaeological and historical research, since *mitayoq* were probably arriving in Cuzco continually. Pedro Pizarro reports (1978: 97–98, chap. 15) that he met a *mitayoq* from Cajamarca, 1,000 kilometers away, who had walked to Cuzco two times with a load of corn on his back. In short, the composition of the residential districts surrounding Cuzco's central sector was diverse, ranging from regional lords to workers, but it was all or primarily non-Inka. It turned Cuzco into a true anthropological hodgepodge and made it truly representative of the entire state.

The concept of Cuzco as a microcosm of the empire is quite solid, since several early historical sources confirm that people from all over the Inka state lived in Cuzco (Cieza de León 1962: 243, chap. 92). Garcilaso de la Vega (1963II: 258, Bk. 7, chap. 9) takes this grand idea a step farther and writes that the surrounding districts were divided according to the four *suyu* and that districts occupied the same general orientation in relationship to central Cuzco as did the four divisions, or *suyu*, of the empire. Thus lords who lived far away from Cuzco were required, when they came to Cuzco, to live in a district oriented in the same direction as their region to central Cuzco. Rowe (1967: 69) provides support for this concept, noting that "the Chachapoyas and Cañares, who came from the northern part of the empire, were settled in or near Carmenca, through which passed the main Inka road to the north." Thus the ethnic composition of Cuzco may have been a miniature replica of the empire, with even its spatial pattern repeated. Such a magnificent design is not confirmed absolutely, since Garcilaso is an untrustworthy informant. Nevertheless, the idea should be held in mind for the forthcoming analysis of the design of other Inka settlements.

Beyond the surrounding districts lived communities of people known as Inkas-by-privilege (Zuidema 1983*b*: 54–70), who occupied an area wider than that defined by the *zeque* system but who shared certain privileges. Guaman Poma (1980: 740 [754], 84–85 [84–85]) lists these people around Cuzco twice, and from his list, which enumerates groups by *suyu*, one notes that Chinchasuyu and Qollasuyu had most of the groups. They were the most populous *suyu* of the empire. Elite Inkas-by-privilege, with true Inkas, received important administrative positions (such as governor, road administrator, treasurer, and so forth). Mention is made here of this category of people to demonstrate an important point, namely, that all elements of Inka social structure did not necessarily live in, or at least originate from, Cuzco. In his discussion of Inkas-by-privilege Zuidema (1983*b*: 54) notes that many of these loyal subjects were sent as *mitmaq* to settlements in and around often-distant administrative centers.

The Size of Cuzco's Population

Just how extensive was Cuzco's population? The topic has been examined at length by Agurto (1980: 122–128), who estimates that there were from 15,000 to 20,000 people in the central sector, and about

50,000 people in the ring of surrounding districts. Beyond that, in a "suburban" area reaching up to 5 kilometers out from the center of Cuzco, he calculates from 50,000 to 110,000 people. Agurto takes into account the reports of the early eyewitnesses, land productivity, and modern population densities. His final estimate is a population of about 125,000 people within 5 kilometers of the center of Cuzco. There are many reasons why one might criticize this statistic, since it is primarily based on the vague and varied judgments of some of the first Europeans to see Cuzco. Nevertheless, barring the discovery of new data, it would be difficult to supersede Agurto's evaluations with a more certain estimate. He notes that his population estimate could grow when or if archaeological survey near Cuzco reveals yet-unknown inhabited areas.

Since it was so dependent on state activities, the population of Cuzco doubtlessly varied considerably from year to year and season to season. It is probable that Cuzco's population of Inkas, Inkas-by-privilege, and non-Inkas was considerably lower when major building projects requiring large numbers of laborers were not under way, when the king and his court were traveling, and when the regional lords were not in residence.

The Zeque *System*

Radiating out from the Qori Kancha were a set of 40 or 41 lines, or *zeques.* Located on them were approximately 328 *waqa,* or sacred places. The lines are grouped into the divisions already observed in the organization of Cuzco, such as two halves or four *suyu,* or quarters (fig. 2.15). The lines of each quarter are divided into three parts, ranked as *collana*

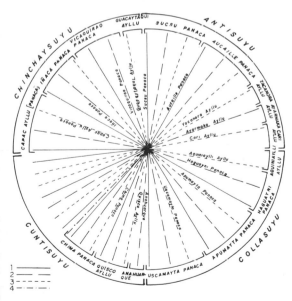

2.15. *Schematic diagram of the zeque system indicating which* panaqa *and* ayllu *were in charge of each line. The Kuntisuyu (Cuntisuyu) zeques occupied a larger arc than depicted. The Qollasuyu (Collasuyu) zeques occupied a considerably smaller arc. Nine lines of each suyu were divided into groups of three. Each group was called Collana, Payan, or Cayao. Individual lines in each group of three were similarly named. Key: 1. Collana zeque; 2. Payan zeque; 3. Cayao zeque; 4. subdivision within Kuntisuyu. From Sherbondy (1986: 74).*

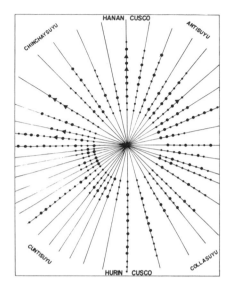

2.16. *Schematic diagram of the* zeque *system of Cuzco, indicating which* waqa *were related to water sources and main canals. The springs and canals, with their associated lands, are a critical factor making for the radial patterning in the design of the* zeque *system. Key:* 1. *simple* waqa; 2. *water source* waqa; 3. *main canal source* waqa. *From Sherbondy (1986: 72).*

(upper, Inka), *payan* (middle, Inka and non-Inka), and *cayao* (lower, non-Inka). The *waqa*, or sacred points of the system, are usually features in the landscape such as rocks, springs, and canals. It is noteworthy that one-third of them are water sources (fig. 2.16). Most of the lines were associated with *panaqa* and *ayllu*, responsible for rituals on their lines' respective *waqa*. *Panaqa* were always assigned to more important *zeque* than the *ayllu* (Zuidema 1964; Wachtel 1973). As Rowe (1979: 2) has noted in his introduction to a transcription describing the system, "[It is] probably the most important single document we have for the study of the topography of Inca Cuzco and its environs." It is also one of the best ways to learn how Inkas conceived of and organized space.

It would appear that the *zeque* system did not affect the architectural planning of Cuzco's central sector in any significant way. The lines radiating out from or near the Qori Kancha pass over central Cuzco and do not follow lines established by known architecture. There are *waqa* within the central sector, but most are outside of it. It is, however, plausible that the spatial form of the *zeque* system influenced the patterning of the residential districts around the central sector, since the *zeque* lines of each *suyu* in general pass over the districts of the same *suyu*. It is even more certain that topography, particularly that of the hydrological system, was a significant influence on the spatial design of the radial system.

Much research by Zuidema along with other colleagues such as Aveni, and a number of students, has demonstrated that the *zeque* system is no less than a grand scheme that spatially and temporally ordered many social and physical phenomena in a formal but flexible way.[16] Various scholars have defined the system differently. Sherbondy (1982*a*: 73) writes: "The Ceque System is an explicit model incorporating various Andean organizational principles to order aspects of the spatial, temporal and social reality of the capital of the Inca state, Cuzco, and by extension of the entire empire." Whereas the system was first studied in terms of social organization via kinship analysis (Zuidema 1964), it is now evident that the *zeque* system was much more complex than originally conceived. Additional analysis has enlarged our conception of the Inka calendar (Zuidema 1977*a*, 1982*a*), astronomy (Zuidema 1981*a*, 1981*b*, 1982*b*; Aveni 1981*a*), rituals (Zuidema 1982*c*, 1983*a*), social divisions and hierarchy (Zuidema 1977*b*, 1983*b*), and irrigation (Zuidema 1986*a*; Sherbondy 1982*a*, 1982*b*, 1986). One of the ideas explored in this volume (chap. 7) is that the spatial patterning of the *zeque* system also influenced architectural planning in other Inka settlements.

This is not the place to explore the diverse aspects of the *zeque* system, but rather to concentrate on aspects useful for understanding Inka settlement planning. Thus its spatial organization becomes particularly important. As was noted earlier, there is a clear use of bi-, tri-, and quadripartition within the organization of the system as expressed by the terms *hanan* and *hurin* (bi), *collana, payan, cayao* (tri), and *suyu* (quad). These concepts are fundamental to Inka social organization and influenced the planning of the capital and its environs.

A most notable aspect of the system is its radiality, formed by the lines pointing to a central location. Zuidema was the first to demonstrate that the space encompassed by the *zeque* of each *suyu* was somewhat different, with Kuntisuyu occupying the largest arc and Qollasuyu the smallest (fig. 7.16). In an article originally published in *Annales (ESC)* in 1978 Zuidema noted (1986*a*: 189) that the reasons for the lack of symmetry were hydrological. That is, the lines were anchored by *waqa* often associated with water sources and canals, and these could not be arranged into four equal spaces. It remained for Sherbondy to clarify the nature of the system's radiality. Her research led to the following important observations (1982*a*: 80):

> The intention of the radial organization of space in Cuzco was to assign discrete canal systems and irrigation districts to specific *panaqa* and *ayllu* in an ideal pattern of radial divisions of land into sectors of a circle based on a central point in Cuzco. Since there seems to have been a principle of locating the sources of major canals on specific *zeques* and assigning these *zeques* to specific *panaqas,* and *ayllu* as in the case in San Andrés de Machaca.[17]

Her discovery became clear when she realized that the *waqa* of a *zeque* often marked the sources of water for the principal canals, and that the *panaqa* or *ayllu* responsible for the *waqa* had rights to the canal and the land it enriched. Other *zeque* define the limits of irrigation districts. In short, the *panaqa* and *ayllu* of Inka Cuzco had as a base irrigation districts defined by *zeque waqa*. Hydrological factors also appear to have been important in defining the dual divisions of *hanan* and *hurin* as well as the four *suyu*. For example, the *hanan* and *hurin* designations have a clear topographic association with upper and lower land and water. Finally, the political importance of *panaqa* and *ayllu* appears to be reflected in the size and importance of their canals and lands, with the royal *panaqa* having better canals and lands than the *ayllu*. The ranking within the *panaqa* is also related to canals and land, since those with the genealogically most "ancient" founder were the least important. The most important canals and lands were held by Thupa Yupanki and Pachakuti, indicating that the system favored those who set it up (Sherbondy 1986: 46–51).[18] Thus the *zeque* system appears tied to the economic base of Inka Cuzco—its water and productive land.[19] It demonstrates that even in the Inka capital, as elsewhere in the Andes, "people and land are inextricably interrelated."

More will be said about the spatial organization of the *zeque* system in chapters 5 and 7. The principal point made here is that *zeque* organization clearly defined and ranked the groups who had access to land and water in the immediate vicinity of Cuzco.

In sum, the radiality of the *zeque* lines did not affect the architectural design of Cuzco, at least not within the central sector, where an orthogonal plan is evident. Beyond the central sector the waters and land of the city's residents were indicated and defined by the lines. One might also see a related radiality in the roads that fanned out from the central sector to the "ring" of residential districts surrounding Cuzco. Chapter 7 will discuss how a radiality was expressed in Inka settlement design elsewhere.

3
The Center

In 1532 Francisco Pizarro's soldiers fired shots from the top of a platform structure in the plaza of the Inka town Cajamarca (Xérez 1970: 67; Cieza de León 1984: 217, chap. 45; Mena 1967: 85, 86). Those volleys began the attack against King Atawalpa and resulted in his capture and the massacre of a large part of his court. The first inkling the Spanish had of the importance of this platform structure, called an *ushnu*, was Atawalpa's warning that they not ascend the platform. It is now recognized that Inka settlements from Ecuador to Argentina often have an *ushnu* platform set in or on the edge of their plazas. This chapter will explore how Inka architects integrated these platforms, and associated features, into their settlement layouts.

Ushnu *Defined*

Ushnu apparently signaled the centers of many planned Inka settlements. What, then, is an *ushnu?* The concept of *ushnu* is complex and varied. They sometimes served as thrones or reviewing stands (Gasparini and Margolies 1980: 264–280). They were not merely platforms, but also stones incorporating the concept of a basin with a drainage system. Only by delving into the religious and symbolic meaning of *ushnu* can it be understood why they are pivotal to Inka ceremony and their physical manifestation central to Inka architectural planning.

The multifaceted significance behind the concept *ushnu* has been explored by Zuidema (1980).[1] Here he first elaborates on how the *ushnu* was used in solar observations (chap. 8 here). He then notes the *ushnu* of Cuzco as a basin/drain associated with a pointed stone or a stone column (see also Discurso 1906: 151, 158; Albornoz 1967: 26; chap. 2 here). Clearly, in Cuzco's plaza there was a pointed stone with a drainage system. Liquids were poured therein as offerings to the Sun, whose image was placed on a nearby bench. A description uniting the concepts of stone, seat, and basin is found in the Discurso's description of the Citua feast (1906: 158):

> All the Indians of the area came together in the main plaza called Haukaypata and there, with much ceremony, they made their sacrifices on a pillar of stone with its shelf called *ushnu* in the middle of the plaza. [They sacrificed] llamas, valuable clothing, and many other things, and, at the foot of the bench they poured much corn beer. They said they were offering it to the Sun.

The idea of the *ushnu* is therefore closely bound to the idea of a seat, a trough, or a basin, and with a drain for libations.

If Cuzco's *ushnu* really was a relatively small bench with a stone and drainage basin—albeit of great ritual importance—how is it that massive platforms also became associated with *ushnu*? This concept was propagated by some of the later chroniclers such as Guaman Poma (1936: f. 398), who pictured an Inka king seated on a stepped platform called *usno* (*ushnu*) (fig. 3.1). One report (Molina 1943: 22) described the platforms as military reviewing stands.[2] Zuidema elucidates the question by citing Cristóbal de Albornoz (1967: 24), a priest engaged in eradicating idolatry who wrote in the latter part of the sixteenth century:

> There is another sacred place called *ushnu* on royal roads and in plazas of towns. They were in the shape of a ninepin and made of different kinds of stone or of gold and silver. To all [*ushnu*] they constructed buildings, made like towers of beautiful masonry, as I have been told, in many places such as Vilcas [Vilcas Waman], Pucará, Old Guanaco [Huánuco Pampa], and Tiwanaku. On the *ushnu* the lords sat to drink to the sun and made many sacrifices to it.

Albornoz presents the idea that a building was constructed to attend to or complement the *ushnu* and cites examples. Thus the platform structures often called *ushnu* are in fact only a more visible part of the material remains of *ushnu*.

Zuidema (1980: 344–351) goes on to suggest that in Cuzco there was a building, the Cuyusmanco, that was located on the side of the plaza and that formed an integral part of the *ushnu*. The exact location of the Cuyusmanco is not certain, but it is notable that some features of *ushnu* are found on the sides as well as within plazas. In Cuzco, however, there was no solid platform building associated with the stone *ushnu* in the plaza.

The Ushnu *Platform as a State Symbol*
There are no clearly identified *ushnu* platforms in the Cuzco region. Thus *ushnu* platforms are found in conquered or non-Inka territories. Consequently, the *ushnu* platform is related to conquered territories.

3.1. A drawing in Guaman Poma's sev-enteenth-century chronicle (1936: f. 398) depicting Manco Inka on his "throne" and "seat," an ushnu *platform, in Cuzco. Such platforms probably never existed in Cuzco but were built in more-distant Inka settlements.*

The reasons for this are not altogether clear, but it is important here to reflect on a commentary by Betanzos, who described (1968: 33, chap. 11) a fundamental difference between Cuzco's plaza (with its stone *ushnu*) and the Sun Temple (Qori Kancha). The temple was related and accessible only to the Inka nobility, while the plaza, in general, was used for rituals witnessed by common and non-Inka people.

Thus in conquered territories one finds *ushnu* platforms, uniting the idea of Inka nobility (since Inka kings sat on *ushnu*) to the great plazas, which are in turn associated with common and non-Inka peoples. Zuidema (1980: 352–357) explores the political significance of the *ushnu* idea and notes its close association with conquered areas. One of the activities of Inkas was the construction of *ushnu* in conquered territory (Santacruz Pachacuti 1879: 247, 273), and one of the *ushnu*'s functions was to provide a place for the Inka king to greet and receive conquered peoples. Thus Santacruz Pachacuti wrote of Wayna Qhapaq (1879: 299): "And after this was done, he was brought to the plaza of Haukaypata, where he had his *capac usno* [royal *ushnu*], like in Vilcas Waman, and he sits there, and so they say, all the great people and captains pay obedience to him, each with his own people."

The use of the *ushnu* for military reviews and ritual is another of its aspects. Cieza de León always referred to the *ushnu* stone in Cuzco's plaza as the "war stone." His description of it (1967: 80, chap. 23) matches that of others—a sugarloaf-shaped stone covered with gold. Troops were marshaled by the stone, and the most worthy soldiers were given commands there. As noted above, the *ushnu* platforms were also used for military purposes—as reviewing stands.

The concept of justice is also related to *ushnu*, as can be seen in a definition of the word. The early Inka language dictionary of González Holguín defines *ushnu* as stone and place of judgment (Zuidema 1980: 333, 352). The justice aspect of *ushnu* is also suggested in one regional historical source, Iñigo Ortiz de Zúñiga's inspection of Huánuco (in Shea 1966: 110). In the plaza of Huánuco Pampa the Inka governor gathered all the principal men and spoke to them about justice. The inference here is that governance or justice is in some way connected with the *ushnu* platform, which rests imposingly in the center of the plaza at Huánuco Pampa.

Finally, the *ushnu* platforms united Cuzco politically to provincial centers, and those centers to regions under their jurisdiction. This political strategy functioned through the institution of child sacrifice—*capac hucha*—which took place beside or at *ushnu* and connected the point of sacrifice with the child's origin by straight routes (Zuidema 1978, 1980: 354–356, 1981b, 1982c: 428–439).

The Origin of Ushnu

There is no clear evidence for *ushnu* origins. Thus this section will first consider the possible origins of *ushnu* platforms and comment on the origins of the *ushnu* as a rock-basin-drain complex.

Zuidema (1978: 160) has suggested that the *ushnu* as a platform may be an architectural form developed from the bench (where the sun image was placed) or the stone set in the plaza of Cuzco. Although his suggestion is insightful, it is difficult to prove. If such was the case, however, some *ushnu* platforms may have replaced stones and basins, or had them built into the platform.[3] This would explain the cases where archaeologists have observed platforms, but no stone, basin, or drain. Only when *ushnu* platforms are excavated to see if they are equipped with drains will more be known. This will not be easy, since many such platforms have been badly damaged by treasure seekers and zealous colonial priests.

Ushnu platforms may have originated outside of the Cuzco area. Agurto (1987: 70) argues for a connection with the ancient Andean coastal tradition of constructing buildings from solid masses. If Agurto is correct, the Inka contact with coastal cultures would have led to the adoption of solid structures. As Conklin (1986) has pointed out, Inka architecture in general does not emphasize solid buildings, and thus is fundamentally different from Andean coastal architecture. If solid buildings inspired *ushnu* platforms, then the absence of platforms in the Cuzco area becomes more understandable, since such platforms are generally found in settlements away from Cuzco built during the Inka state's expansion after the coast was conquered.

Another approach concerning the *ushnu* platform's origins is suggested by Lumbreras (personal communication, 1986), who believes that archaeological information from the centuries prior to Inka expansion is so limited, particularly in the southern highlands, that one cannot know the range of architectural forms used. Thus it is not known if *ushnu* platform prototypes existed before the Inkas.

Equally perplexing is the origin of the stone-basin-drain complex as described for the *ushnu* of Cuzco and Vilcas Waman. Little evidence exists for the use of these in the pre-Inka cultures of the Andean highlands. This lack of evidence may be due to our ignorance of pre-Inka architecture and settlement planning.

Only additional research will prove whether it is far-fetched to think that the Inka concern with "fluid communicators" (Moseley 1985: 46–48) derives from ancient practices dating even before the development of Chavín (800 B.C.). Certainly, the ritual use of water and concern with specialized canals and drains can be seen in much early Andean architecture (Williams 1985). Nevertheless, no prototypes of the Inka *ushnu* have yet been observed in the material remains of earlier Andean societies.

Finally, it has been suggested (Gasparini and Margolies 1980: 267) that the *intiwatana* stones,[4] often elaborately carved, found at high points at some sites in the Cuzco area—Machu Picchu, Tipón, and Pisaq having notable examples—could be types of *ushnu*. If so, they were transformed into the much more elaborate complexes with platforms outside of the Cuzco region. The *intiwatana* stones lack a close association with a plaza and are not necessarily centrally placed within a site's layout. In fact, they appear to be variants of the many types of "sacred" boulders and outcrops scattered throughout many Inka settlements (chap. 4).

The Distribution and Appearance of Ushnu

As discussed, *ushnu* may be identified by locating various related remains such as stones, seats, basins, drains, and platforms, which are in turn associated with plazas. At least in one case, that of Vilcas Waman (see below), all were found together. The apparent lack of platforms in the Cuzco heartland suggests that they are an architectural develop-

3.2. The ushnu *platform at Vilcas Waman. A stone for offerings and sacrifices once rested in the plaza before the platform. W. V. von Hagen; courtesy Adriana von Hagen.*

ment that began only after the Inka conquests, a point noted both by Kendall (1976: 86) and Zuidema (1980: 356).

Ushnu platforms are widely distributed throughout Tawantinsuyu. They are present within or on the edge of principal Inka plazas. Rarely do they appear associated with stones and basins, although it is possible that many of these were removed or destroyed by Catholic priests intent on eradicating idolatry. Albornoz (1967: 24), who specialized in such activity, even recommended destroying the platforms. In some places an *ushnu* stone may still be seen in an Inka plaza. The best examples of these appear in settlements where Spanish priests did not arrive.

The following review of archaeological evidence for *ushnu* is by no means complete. New evidence may emerge as new sites are surveyed and as old ones are revisited with a more discerning eye. Older maps or plans of Inka sites do not always indicate evidence of *ushnu,* since archaeologists may not have been aware of them. This is particularly true in the case of stones, basins, or drains in plazas—a most central and significant part of Inka settlements—which did not appear to archaeologists as "architectural evidence" worth placing on a site plan.

Vilcas Waman
The Inkas considered Vilcas Waman the geographical center of their great state (Cieza de León 1962: 236, chap. 89), since it was about equi-

distant from Quito in the north and Chile in the south. Vilcas was in Chanca territory, one of the first regions conquered by the Inkas during the formation of the empire.

Vilcas Waman has one of the best-described and generally intact *ushnu* complexes. Cieza de León, who saw it in the 1540s, wrote (1976: 126, 127, chap. 39):

> To one side of this plain [plaza], toward the rising sun, there was a shrine [*ushnu*] for the Lord-Incas, of stone, from which small terraces emerged, about six feet wide, where other enclosures came together, and at the center there was a bench where the Lord-Inca sat to pray, all of a single stone so large that it was eleven feet long and seven feet wide, with two seats cut for the aforesaid purpose. They say this stone used to be covered with jewels of gold and precious stones to adorn this place they so venerated and esteemed, and on another stone, not small, now in the middle of this square, like a baptismal font, was where they sacrificed animals and young children (so they say), whose blood was offered up to the gods. . . . In the middle of the great square there was another bench, like that of a theater, where the Lord-Inca sat to watch the dances and lay feasts.

Vilcas Waman's stepped platform and related stone seat is still intact (fig. 3.2). Nothing, however, remains of the sacrificial stone or basin,[5] or the other seat or bench in the plaza. Cieza may have understood that the stepped platform and the stone basin in the plaza were related, since he described the two together. Cieza does report (1962: 237, chap. 89) that a canal passed through the plaza, possible evidence for a drainage system. Cieza's description unites what we know of the *ushnu* in Cuzco (a stone with a basin-drainage and bench) with the *ushnu* of conquered territories—namely, a solid platform.

Possibly, the *ushnu* platform in Vilcas Waman was the most elegant (but not the largest) in Tawantinsuyu, serving as a prototype for platforms in other conquered areas. Two reasons support this. First, of all known *ushnu* platforms, Vilcas Waman's is one of the nearest to Cuzco.[6] Second, Vilcas Waman lies in one of the first territories conquered by the Inkas as they expanded out from the Cuzco area. Thus, it is possible that the *ushnu* platform in Vilcas Waman was one of the first ever built.[7]

Island of the Sun

A number of versions of the Inka origin myth point to the Lake Titicaca region as the origin of the Sun and the first Inkas. Some of the myths are quite explicit, indicating that they emerged from the lake or originated on the Island of the Sun. The Inkas thus developed the area around the Island of the Sun into one of their most sacred places. In most early historical sources the Lake Titicaca sanctuary ranks among the most significant and powerful in the empire, as famous as Pachacamac (chap. 9), on Peru's central coast.[8]

In 1894 and 1895, Adolph F. Bandelier carried out anthropological and archaeological investigations within the sanctuary and published his now classic study in 1910.[9] His interpretation of the Inka remains on the Islands of the Sun and the Moon, and the nearby Copacabana area, demonstrates that Inka intervention in the area was profound. The Inkas converted the Copacabana area and the islands into a religious zone, governed directly by Inkas, where most of the population was composed of Inkas from Cuzco or colonists, *mitmaq*, from many parts of the state (Ramos Gavilán 1976: 43–49, Bk. 1, chaps. 12, 13). Although no new "city" or large formal settlement was apparently constructed, buildings and building complexes were dedicated to the religious requirements of a major sanctuary. The most sacred and clearly

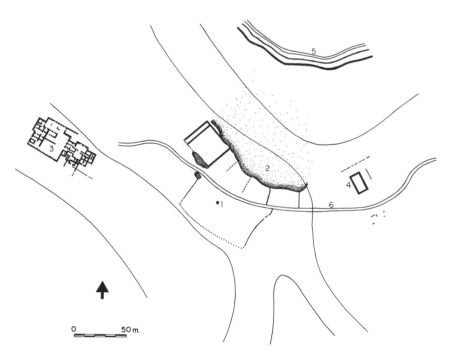

3.3. The main plaza and sacred rock on the Island of the Sun. A large flat rock rests near the center of the plaza, which also once had a basin. Key: 1. plaza; 2. sacred rock; 3. Chincana; 4. Sun Temple; 5. Lake Titicaca; 6. Inka road. Partially based on plan by A. Bandelier (1895) at the Department of Anthropology, AMNH.

3.4. View to the northwest over the main plaza of the Inka sanctuary in Lake Titicaca. The sacred rock protrudes on the right. The Inka road passes over the plaza.

most important part of the Titicaca religious complex was located at the northern end of the Island of the Sun. Here, a design existed that closely mirrors the *ushnu* complexes in Cuzco and Vilcas Waman.

The center of ritual activity was a large plaza lying in front of a great sacred rock (fig. 3.3). Indeed, it would have been difficult to find a more sacred rock in the entire Inka Empire (figs. 3.4, 3.5). This rock was especially significant, since Inka myths relate that from or behind it the Sun itself emerged. Some accounts claim that Manco Qhapaq, the legendary founder of all Inkas, emerged from the rock. Whatever the case, people who have viewed this outcrop from the sixteenth century up through the present might well think, as did the priest Ramos Gavilán (1976: 47, Bk. 1, chap. 13), that it exhibited no special characteristics and was not at all impressive.[10] In Inka times, however, the side of the rock facing the plaza was covered with gold plaques. The other side, which led down to the nearby lakeshore, was covered with fine cloth.

The plaza lying in front, or to the south, of the sacred rock had a number of characteristics similar to those of Cuzco. The most detailed early historical commentary on the area (Ramos Gavilán 1976: 47, 48, 93, Bk. 1, chaps. 13, 29) relates that the plaza was called Haukaypata (Aycaypata) and that it was covered with loose dirt, brought in from elsewhere, wherein gold figurines and pottery vessels were buried. Bernabé Cobo, who lived in the area at the same time as Ramos Ga-

3.5. *The sacred rock on the Island of the Sun. It was linked through mythology to the origin of the sun, or the first Inka. An unworked outcrop, it was once covered with gold plaques and fine cloth. A rectangular flat stone for offerings and sacrifices rests in the plaza.*

3.6. *The front of the Chincana, a complex of rooms to the west of the main plaza of the Lake Titicaca sanctuary.*

vilán, noted (1964: 193, Bk. 13, chap. 18): "A round basin-shaped stone can be seen in front of the outcrop and altar. It is admirably worked, the size of an average millstone, with a hole—which now holds the foot of a cross—into which *chicha* ran for the sun to drink."

Thus the Island of the Sun's main plaza was similar to that of Cuzco: it was covered with imported earth in which offerings were buried; there was a round basin for libations; and there was an "altar," about which there are no additional details.

Possibly, that "altar" is still in the plaza, although the basin has since disappeared.[11] This altar is a large, flat, square stone resting nearly in the center of the plaza (fig. 3.5). This was not mentioned by Bandelier (1910: 218) in his description of the plaza, which is otherwise quite detailed. He does, however, mention some "prismatic stones of andesite." He speculated that they might have formed part of a building or a wall. Today one sees a few such blocks found by the large square stone where children may have been sacrificed. The early sources agree that sacrifice indeed took place on the island. Bandelier (1910: 220–221, 225–226, 228) noted that valuable objects of metal and cloth as well as child burials were found nearby and associated them with sacrifices. Ramos Gavilán (1976: 23, chap. 6) writes that child sacrifices were done on a "somewhat wide, flat stone." The offering of *chicha*, valuable objects, as well as children—the *capac hucha*—is thus another similarity between the Titicaca *ushnu* and those at Cuzco and Vilcas Waman. Finally, as was the practice at the Sun Temple in Cuzco, "unofficial" visitors were not permitted to approach the plaza and rock, although they could observe it from a distance. Those approaching the rock, even the Inka himself, were required to walk barefoot.

The large plaza was not surrounded by buildings, although there were constructions a short distance both to the east and the west, as well as on one side of the sacred rock. Bandelier's careful analysis (1910: 216–225) of historical and archaeological evidence is one of the most insightful and complex parts of his study. To the west of the plaza lay a complex of rooms and patios called Chincana (fig. 3.6), apparently some sort of residence. The earliest report of it (Ramos Gavilán 1976: 48, chap. 13) calls it a *"dispensa* [larder?] of the Sun." To the east was a rectangular temple dedicated to the worship of the Sun, Thunder, and other gods (fig. 3.7). Today almost nothing remains of this building except a foundation.

In summary, the *ushnu* complex on the Island of the Sun shared the common convention of a basin and, apparently, a stone for sacrifices. There is no written or archaeological evidence for a platform structure. It is possible and logical that this was represented by the sacred stone itself, symbolizing the Sun and the Inkas.

Nevados de Aconquija

One of the most impressive settlements ever constructed by the Inkas in Argentina is Nevados de Aconquija, located at 27 degrees south latitude on Mount Aconquija, 4,200 meters above sea level. This site over-

3.7. *The Inka road entering near the main plaza of the Island of the Sun. The point where the road passes over the hill (top right) was called Intipunku ("gate of the Sun"). There, "unofficial" visitors could view the sacred rock but were not permitted to advance. The foundations of a rectangular Sun Temple (center left) are beside the road.*

looks the jungle of Tucumán and the pampas beyond and is the highest of all relatively large Inka sites. Because of its inaccessibility, few have visited it, and little destruction has taken place by treasure hunters or vandals. Little is known about the site's function in Inka times (Mansfeld 1948). Its location on an Inka border suggests a military role. Its dramatic *ushnu* complex indicates that ceremony and ritual were important.

Everything known about Nevados de Aconquija is from the archaeology, since the site is not mentioned in any early historical source.

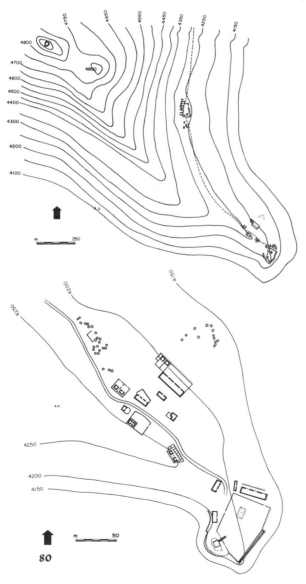

3.8. Plan of Nevados de Aconquija in Tucumán Province, Argentina. The site is composed of two parts, each with a plaza, separated by about 600 meters. An Inka road connects the two. To the west, at an altitude of 4,900 meters, one finds a cleared plaza, but no buildings. Adapted from author's notes and an unpublished plan of G. Rohmeder and E. Würschnidt supplied by J. Schobinger.

3.9. The southeastern part of Nevados de Aconquija. The plaza (lower left) has a three-level retaining wall sustaining its southeastern side. The ushnu *platform with steps leading into the plaza is on the southwestern side. A rectangular, paved area within the plaza once had an upright stone. Four or five* kallanka *are found in the sector, as are several small* kancha-*like patio groups. The circular foundations appear to be houses. Based on author's notes and a plan by O. Paulotti (1967: 335, 357).*

Paulotti has described Nevados de Aconquija in some detail (1958–1959, 1967). The site is divided into two parts, separated by about 600 meters (figs. 3.8, 3.9, 3.10).

The southeastern sector is the largest and has the most constructions. It also contains the site's primary plaza, where the *ushnu* is found. The plaza is walled, with doors both on the eastern and northern sides (fig. 3.11). Near the center of the plaza there is a "paved" rectangular area (fig. 3.12).[12] In the center of the rectangle stood a stone, described by Paulotti (1958–1959: 129–130) as a rough four-sided truncated pyramid with no polishing or incisions. The wide side had a maximum width of 26 centimeters, the narrow side a maximum width of 16 centimeters. Unfortunately, this stone had disappeared by the time I visited in 1986.

On the southwest side of the plaza there is a semi-artificial stepped platform (fig. 3.13). The side fronting the plaza is 32.5 meters in length. The platform stands at least 6 meters above the plaza, forms a square shape about 8 meters wide, and is reached from the plaza by a stairway of twenty-three or more steps. The external part of the platform is covered with worked (but not polished) stones, many of which have fallen, making it difficult to determine the original shape. It is also difficult to tell what portion of the platform is natural and what portion is artificial. Perhaps one-third is natural. A curved retention wall forms the back (southern and western sides) of the platform.

Long rectangular buildings are found on the northern and western sides of the plaza. One on the north is clearly a *kallanka*; their function, however, is unknown. The western and southern sides of the plaza have no structures except the platform, since they rest on dramatic precipices.

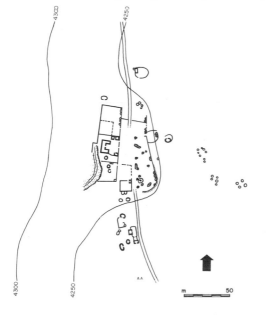

3.10. The northwestern part of Nevados de Aconquija. Enclosures are found on the western side of a plaza, which has numerous rockpiles, possibly recent. The one large outcrop in the plaza is surrounded by a circular stone platform. Based on author's notes and a plan by O. Paulotti (1967: 358).

81

3.11. View to the east over the main plaza at Nevados de Aconquija. Clouds cover the lowlands of Tucumán in the distance. The ushnu *platform is on the right.*

A monumental retention wall (fig. 6.10) with three levels sustains the eastern side of the plaza for 51 meters of its 70-meter length.

The northwestern part of Nevados de Aconquija also has a plaza, smaller and less developed than the plaza in the southeast (fig. 3.10). Its outstanding feature is a large rough stone set in its south-central part and surrounded by a ring of smaller stones (fig. 4.14). Attempts by vandals to uproot the stone have failed because of its massive proportions. It is difficult to say if this stone was part of an Inka *ushnu*, since no other aspects of the *ushnu* complex accompany it, such as a nearby platform.

In summary, the *ushnu* was represented by a stone placed near the center of the main plaza and a large platform structure on the side of the plaza facing the stone. There is no evidence for a basin. No scientific excavations have ever been carried out at Nevados de Aconquija, so it is impossible to know if there were offerings buried in the plaza, or if the *ushnu* stone and platform were connected with a drain.

Incallacta

Incallacta was one of the largest fortresses (fig. 6.18) ever built by the Inkas in the southern part of their state. It was one of a series of fortifications protecting the Inka frontier in the eastern Andes of Bolivia

3.12. *View from the top of the* ushnu *platform at Nevados de Aconquija. The rectangular stony area in the plaza (*where the person is standing*) once had an upright* ushnu *stone.*

from attack by marauding lowlanders. Incallacta provides evidence for an *ushnu* complex used in a military installation. One should not assume, therefore, that *ushnu* were used only in shrines, Cuzco, and administrative centers.

Previous descriptions of Incallacta (González and Cravotto 1977; Nordenskiöld 1915; Ellefsen 1973a, 1973b) have not identified the *ushnu*, in part because there is no obvious large platform structure. Nevertheless, a careful examination of Incallacta's main plaza reveals relatively certain evidence for an *ushnu*.

The plaza at Incallacta is irregularly shaped (fig. 3.14), but clearly divided into two parts by a massive terrace wall. Near the center of the upper plaza is a large stone (fig. 3.15) whose top surface has been flattened. On the northeast side of the plaza one finds an immense rectangular building, or *kallanka*, with twelve doors fronting on the plaza. On the exterior of the seventh door lies a small platform with a large unworked stone on it (fig. 1.18).[13]

The *ushnu* complex at Incallacta is represented by a platform with a stone on it set on the edge of the plaza, and by the large flattened stone within the plaza. This arrangement is similar to the plaza on the Island of the Sun, with its sacred stone on one side of the plaza and large flattened stone in the plaza.

3.13. The ushnu *platform at Nevados de Aconquija. Faced with rough stone masonry, approximately one-third of the platform is a natural outcrop.*

3.14. View to the south over the large kallanka *(A) to the left of the divided plaza at Incallacta in Bolivia. A small platform with unworked stones rests in front of the* kallanka *(B). Near the division between the two halves of the plaza is a large, flattened stone (C). The platform and flattened stone make up an* ushnu *complex.*

3.15. The large, flattened stone in the plaza at Incallacta.

Unfortunately, there are no early Spanish sources describing In-callacta, when the site may have been more intact. There is no histori-cal or archaeological evidence for a basin or drain, nor has the site been excavated. It will be recalled that another feature of an *ushnu* complex is a seat. As mentioned earlier, platforms may have developed from benches. In Cuzco the sun image was placed on a bench (*excaño*) in the plaza. At Incallacta, a sun image (the unworked stone) may also have been seated on a bench (the platform).

Platforms on Plaza Edges

As noted, there are few *ushnu* platforms located on the edge of Inka plazas. It is not possible to say why some platforms were placed on the edge of plazas, and others in the center. Two additional cases of plat-forms situated on the edge of a plaza are found at Pachacamac (Bueno 1982) (fig. 3.16) and at Tambo Colorado (Hyslop 1984: 108–111) (fig. 3.17) on Peru's central and south coast, respectively. Both have stairs leading from the plaza up to the platform, much like at Vilcas Waman and Nevados de Aconquija. One suspects that those stairs and platforms were aligned with a stone and basin in or near the center of their plazas, but no traces remain. Both Pachacamac and Tambo Colorado were close to large early Spanish communities, and it would not be surprising if sixteenth-century priests removed or destroyed the smaller, more central parts of these *ushnu* complexes.

Ushnu *Platforms within Plazas*

The prime archaeological evidence for an *ushnu* complex in many Inka sites is a raised platform in or near the center of a site's main plaza. Currently, it is possible to define two major zones where such platforms are relatively common: the central Peruvian Andes, and the Argentine provinces of Salta, Catamarca, and La Rioja.

In the Peruvian Andes north of Vilcas Waman centrally located platforms were a standard feature of site planning. Whereas the poor preservation of the Inka administrative center Hatun Xauxa makes it impossible to tell if its *ushnu* was located in or near the plaza's center (D'Altroy 1981: 493), it is clear that such was the case at the two leading administrative centers to the north, Pumpu (LeVine 1985: 173–221; Thompson 1968) and Huánuco Pampa (Shea 1966; Morris and Thompson 1985: 59–60). Although Cajamarca's *ushnu* platform no longer exists, historical reports (Mena 1967: 85, 86; Xérez 1970: 67) indicate that it also was in or near the plaza's center. The *ushnu* platforms at Pumpu

3.16. *The* ushnu *platform (foreground, center) at Pachacamac, Lurin, Peru. Located on the southeast side of the Inka plaza, it had a stairway leading into the plaza. It is a solid mass of Inka adobe bricks. Behind it (left) is the Painted Building, thought to be an* aqllawasi. *The Sun Temple is on the hill.*

and Huánuco Pampa deserve special comment, since they are among the largest still preserved, and because they form part of relatively well preserved sites, which allows one to study their relationship to site planning.

Huánuco Pampa and Pumpu

The *ushnu* platform at Huánuco is the largest ever built by the Inka state (fig. 3.18). It consists of a high (3.5 meters) platform resting on two lower ones. A broad staircase leads from the top of the south side of the platform to the lower platform. At least six stairways connected the lowest platform with the plaza. Of these, the staircase on the southeast corner (pointing east) was the broadest (Shea 1966: 111–116). The platform at Pumpu is clearly stepped (fig. 3.19), like Vilcas Waman. Unlike the platforms at Vilcas Waman and Huánuco Pampa, it is not made of fine Inka masonry. In both cases the platforms are aligned with a doorway on the eastern side of the plaza, which leads into an area of considerable ceremonial importance (figs. 3.20, 7.10). A stairway to the plaza on each platform points to this doorway. In both cases there is some evidence of a drain associated with the platform. That drain leads to the

*3.17. The **ushnu** platform at Tambo Colorado, Pisco, Peru. It rests on the southwestern side of the trapezium plaza. Its principal stairway leads into the plaza.*

3.18. The ushnu *platform at Huánuco Pampa, Huánuco, Peru. It is the most massive* ushnu *platform ever constructed by the Inkas. Unlike most others, its high upper platform is faced with fine Cuzco-style masonry.*

3.19. The ushnu *platform at Pumpu, Pasco, Peru. It appears to have had three levels. The staircase points toward the main door on the eastern side of the plaza.*

3.20. The main doorway leading into the largest enclosure on the eastern side of the plaza at Pumpu. Now badly damaged, it was aligned with the ushnu *platform in the plaza (*background*).*

principal doorway on the eastern side of the plaza. In neither case is there evidence of a basin or stone, which may have been removed or destroyed. They may have been located in either of two places: on top or on the side of the platforms,[14] or in the ceremonial sectors on the eastern side of the plazas where there is evidence for waterworks (chap. 5). The connection of the *ushnu* platforms by drains to an enclosed ceremonial sector suggests the pattern established in Cuzco. There, as noted in chapter 2, a drain connected the *ushnu* basin in the main plaza with the Sun Temple, Qori Kancha.

There is a hint that a drain may have been placed on the top of the Huánuco Pampa (Morris and Thompson 1985: 59) and Pumpu platforms. Unfortunately, treasure hunters have disturbed the tops of both structures and it is impossible to determine the original features.

Inkawasi

There is evidence of a small basinlike structure on the top of the *ushnu* platform (fig. 3.21) in the main plaza at Inkawasi in the Cañete Valley of Peru. The basin is illustrated in the early maps of the main plaza (Larrabure 1904; Harth-Terré 1933: fig. 5) and in at least one published

3.21. The heavily eroded ushnu *platform in the main plaza at Inkawasi, Cañete, Peru. It once had a basinlike structure on it. The stairs on its southern side (*left*) point southeast to the door of the sole large compound directly on the plaza.*

photograph (Strong and Willey 1943: plate 5b). It was destroyed, however, before I began my study of the site in 1979 (Hyslop 1985). Another, smaller, platform, which appears to be a subsidiary *ushnu*, is also found at Inkawasi, resting in the center of a smaller plaza (fig. 7.16). This platform had a hole in the center and was filled with small black rocks (Hyslop 1985: 120–122). The platform appears to have been constructed to receive liquids, as was, apparently, the case of the larger *ushnu* platform in the main plaza. These data are particularly important, since they suggest that sacrifice and libation pouring at centrally located platforms did not necessarily take place by rocks or basins near or in front of the platform, but might occur on top of the platform. This may partially explain why sites with platforms only occasionally have *ushnu* rocks or basins nearby. Finally, just as the platforms at Pumpu and Huánuco Pampa are aligned with important doorways and compounds on the side of their respective plazas, the same is the case in the main plaza at Inkawasi. The platform is set on a slightly raised road that passes through the center of the plaza (fig. 6.16). One stairway of the platform points south-south-east along the road leading into the principal entrance of the only major compound on the plaza.

3.22. The ushnu *platform at Shincal, Catamarca, Argentina. One of the best preserved in Tawantinsuyu, there is no evidence of features or structures on its top.*

Central Ushnu *Platforms in Southern Tawantinsuyu*

In Argentina, sites with *ushnu* platforms are generally less well preserved and somewhat smaller than at Pumpu and Huánuco Pampa. One of the most intact platforms is at the site Shincal (González 1966; Raffino et al. 1983–1985: 437–443). It measures approximately 16 meters square, about 2 meters in height, and has a stairway on its western side (fig. 3.22). The platform is set slightly off center in a large rectangular plaza (fig. 3.23). The sides of the Shincal *ushnu* platform extend above its solid mass, forming a wall less than a meter in height around the top. Shincal's layout is not well understood, since trees cover the site and not all structures in it have been mapped. No construction was detected on top of the Shincal platform.

Other *ushnu* platforms in northwest Argentina are less intact. At Potrero de Payogasta the platform in the plaza is so badly damaged that accurate measurements and orientations cannot be made of it (fig. 3.24). It appears to have measured about 7 to 9 meters square and about a meter and a half high. The available plans of the site are not particularly accurate (Difieri 1948; Raffino 1983: 105, 107; Hyslop 1985: 177).

The *ushnu* platform at the Argentine site Tambería del Inca, or Chile-

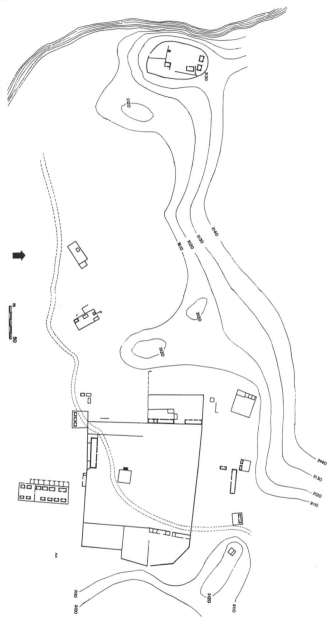

3.23. *Plan of Shincal in Catamarca, Argentina. The* ushnu *platform rests slightly off center in the large, rectangular plaza. Its stairway points to the east, unique among known* ushnu *platforms. Based on author's notes, a general plan by Raffino et al. (1983–1985: 438), and western sector by González (1966: 19); contours approximate.*

cito, is also semidestroyed, in part by treasure hunters and in part by the architect Greslebin (fig. 3.25). Greslebin's damage to the Chilecito *ushnu* is partially forgivable, since his work (Greslebin 1940) a half century ago produced the Tambería del Inca map (fig. 7.13), still the most accurate plan yet made of any Inka site in Argentina. The platform already had a large hole dug in it by treasure hunters prior to Greslebin's arrival in 1928. The structure is only 1.4 meters high, greater than the intact walls of any other building in the site. At the top, the rectangular structure measures approximately 9.8 by 11 meters.

Greslebin's drawing of the platform (1939: fig. 88) depicts foundations of a two-unit structure (9.8 by 2.8 meters) on the southern side of the top. It is impossible to tell whether these foundations represent rooms or open enclosures, yet this is one of the rare cases where any reliable record exists of some sort of construction on top of an *ushnu* platform. Greslebin's unpublished notes indicate that the structure had sloping exterior walls of cobbles, and thus he apparently misinterpreted the stairway on the east side. Greslebin excavated the northeast corner, and did not clear a sufficient part of the platform to have detected such items as basins or drains. He revealed that the structure was filled with

3.24. The heavily eroded ushnu *platform at Potrero de Payogasta, Salta, Argentina.*

cobbles. Digging to a depth of 2.6 meters, Greslebin found a pre-Inka habitation level with a layer of ash and a grinding stone. It did not escape Greslebin's architectural eye that the platform was in the "geometric center" of the site (figs. 7.13, 7.14) and that it was an "important mound."[15]

Although not well preserved, the *ushnu* platform at Chilecito shares several characteristics with larger, more intact platforms far to the north at Pumpu and Huánuco Pampa. Chilecito's platform and stairs are pointed toward the site's largest patio compounds on the eastern side of the rectangular plaza. The site's probable water supply, a gully converted into a canal, ran directly on the northern side of the platform, and the canal could have served to drain liquids to the east (chap. 5).

Ushnu platforms have not been discovered in Inka sites south of the Argentine province of La Rioja. Perhaps this is because farther south there are no sites that might be considered significant Inka centers. Large *tampu* such as Tocota (Berberian et al. 1977–1978) and Ranchillos

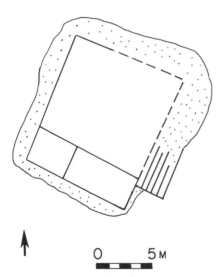

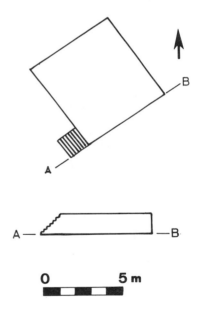

0 ____ 5 M

3.25. *The Chilecito* ushnu *platform once had two rectangular foundations on its top's southern side. Located in the center of a generally rectangular plaza, its stairway points to the east-southeast, where one finds three patio enclosures. The dashed line indicates an indistinct side. The dotted area is debris around the platform. Based on author's notes and an unpublished drawing by Greslebin (1939).*

0 ____ 5 m

3.26. *The small* ushnu *platform at Viña del Cerro in the Copiapó Valley in Chile. Redrawn from Niemeyer (1986: 243).*

(Aparicio 1940; Hyslop 1984: 197–199) on the Inka road leading south present no evidence of *ushnu* platforms.

In the Argentine province of Catamarca there are a number of other sites with small *ushnu* platforms. I examined the Punta de Balasto (Carrara et al. 1960) platform in 1986 and found it to measure about 5 by 6 meters, and no more than 1.4 meters in height. Its stairs point to the east. The site is in poor condition, since it is covered by sand from gully and river overflows. About all one can say about the Punta de Balasto platform is that it is located somewhat near the center of the site. Its exact location within what must have been a plaza is uncertain, since the perimeter of the plaza is not visible. A similar small *ushnu* platform in the province of Catamarca is found at Hualfín (Raffino et al. 1983–1985: 434). Finally, Lorandi reports (1983: 6) a badly damaged *ushnu* platform at the site of Chaquiago. At the time of writing, the province of Catamarca in Argentina has more reported *ushnu* platforms than any other zone of similar size in the Inka state.

Curiously, a number of relatively small *ushnu* platforms are reported from sites in Chile and Argentina, but almost none of such small dimensions (8 meters by 6 meters, or smaller) have been reported in Peru. Whether small platforms are characteristic of the southern part of the Inka state, or whether small platforms have not been reported from the north, is yet uncertain.

A small *ushnu* platform in Copiapó, Chile, deserves special comment. It is located at the site of Viña del Cerro (fig. 10.2), a major Inka foundry (Niemeyer, Cervellino, and Muñoz 1984; Niemeyer 1986). The platform with a stairway (fig. 3.26) is located in the eastern side of the site's rectangular plaza. Evidently, such a platform indicates that even specialized sites such as foundries could have *ushnu*. Niemeyer has mapped another small *ushnu* platform (Niemeyer, Schiappacase, and Solimano 1971) at the site of Poblado de Saguara in the Camarrones Valley of northern Chile.

Ushnu *Not on Plazas?*
Whether *ushnu* not associated with settlements and plazas were ever built remains unanswered. This was suggested by Albornoz (1967: 25) when he referred to *ushnu* as being "on the royal roads and in the plazas of the towns." My study of Inka roads (Hyslop 1984) produced no good candidates for roadside *ushnu*, but it is possible that evidence for such may have been overlooked. There is, however, one platform that was perhaps a roadside *ushnu*. It is a rectangular structure on the Inka road from Pumpu leading to the south. As the road first views Lake Junín, there is an isolated platform aligned with it.

A rubble and earth rectangular mound, similar to some *ushnu* platforms, is found on a hilltop overlooking the Mantaro Valley west of the Inka center Hatun Xauxa (D'Altroy 1981: 102, 408). A set of seventy-five storage structures almost encircle the hill. The mound has no direct association with a plaza, road, or habitation area. If the platform had *ushnu* properties, it is located in a context far different from most known *ushnu*.

Northern Ushnu

Archaeological evidence for *ushnu* in the northern part of Tawantinsuyu is somewhat problematic, especially in Ecuador, where the chief Inka administrative centers were destroyed by Spanish and modern cities built on them. The Inka city of Tomebamba is a case in point, since very little remains of the site. Nevertheless, the data are sufficient to have some idea of its *ushnu*.

Historical evidence exists (Cabello Valboa 1951: 365, Pt. 3, chap. 21) for an *ushnu* in the plaza of Tomebamba, the "second" Inka capital now covered by the modern city Cuenca (chap. 5). Beginning in 1919, Uhle (1923: 4, 5) excavated here and looked for a platform structure in a place called Usno beside Huayna Capac Avenue. Here (fig. 5.7) he found a "small artificial rise 1.2 meters high by 26 meters wide and 28 meters long." Uhle does not say explicitly that he excavated the platform, but states that he found no ancient remains on or in it. Fortunately, he does indicate where the platform rested, and one sees that it was located in the south-central part of Tomebamba's great plaza (fig. 5.7). Modern houses cover the alleged platform and nothing remains today of the structure seen by Uhle, although Ecuadorian archaeologists and I have searched for it.

Uhle (1923: 5) lamented not having located Tomebamba's "Sun Temple," but suggested that it may have rested on the eastern side of the main plaza, where there were "gardens of the sun." Uhle did not excavate there, but rather in large compounds to the north and south of the plaza. His observations, however, recall that the significant ceremonial areas of administrative settlements to the south—Pumpu and Huánuco Pampa—are on their respective plazas' eastern sides.

There is no certain evidence for other *ushnu* in Ecuador. Ecuador's most famous Inka site is Ingapirca (figs. 1.5, 9.15). The leading authority on the site, Antonio Fresco (1983: 196–200), does not interpret its large oval platform building (figs. 1.5, 9.16) as an *ushnu* platform, but rather as a sanctuary, perhaps related to the solar cult. His view makes sense for a number of reasons. Ingapirca's platform is closely linked to a set of rooms just to the south, quite unlike the generally "isolated" *ushnu* platforms elsewhere. The platform's oval shape is also unique (Gasparini and Margolies 1980: 298, 299). All known *ushnu* platforms are square or rectangular. Ingapirca's oval structure rests on the northwestern side of a small plaza or patio (30 meters north-south and 25 to 50 meters east-west). There is no other evidence for an *ushnu* complex in or on the edges of the plaza/patio. Ingapirca is discussed at greater length in chapter 9.

Better candidates for *ushnu* in northern Tawantinsuyu are found in sites, often of a military nature, north of Quito. The best studied of these is the Pucará de Rumicucho (Almeida 1984), located near the

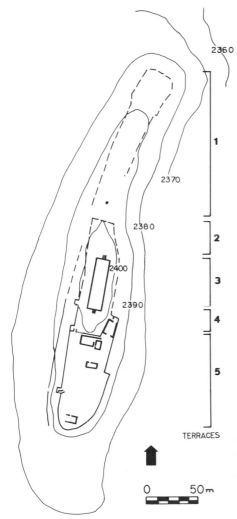

3.27. *Plan of Rumicucho, Pichincha, Ecuador, located nearly on the equator north of Quito. A large rectangular platform is found on the top center of the site. A large stone is found about 50 meters to the north of the platform. Redrawn combining plans from Almeida (1984: 28, 32).*

3.28. The northern stairway of Rumicucho's central platform points to a large un-worked boulder (foreground) in a patio.

town of San Antonio de Pichincha on the equator just north of Quito. The site may not have been a *pucará*, or fortress, since it could not have been easily defended on the low hill where it rests. Excavations reveal that a whole series of different activities (e.g., herding, weaving) took place here. The excavations also reveal that the site was constructed in Inka times, although there is also local cultural influence. The Inka builders of Rumicucho may have been aware that they were constructing a settlement on the equator, which might have been of considerable interest to a culture whose solar cult was one of its major religious manifestations.

Rumicucho consists of a series of walled terraces surrounding a hill rising 24 meters above a plain (fig. 3.27). On the top (third terrace) there is a large (16 by 54 meters) rectangular structure, probably an *ushnu* platform. The platform measures less than 1.5 meters high in its reconstructed form, and has steps on its northern and southern sides. Excavations on the platform did not reveal any buildings (Almeida 1984: 29, 44). There is, however, a report of a circular stone paving in the platform's center, since destroyed by pot hunters who dug a large hole at its location.

The steps on the northern side point to the first and second terraces. There is little evidence of constructions on the first terrace; if the site had a plaza it would have been located there. In the center of this terrace is a large, unworked stone 1.1 to 1.3 meters in diameter (fig. 3.28), which was brought into the site (Almeida 1984: 29). The steps on the southern side of the platform lead to a patio (fourth terrace), which in turn leads to the site's most architecturally complex sector (fifth terrace).

Rumicucho thus has evidence for an *ushnu* complex. A centrally located large platform is oriented toward a large stone located in a plaza. The layout of Rumicucho is, nevertheless, different from that of other sites farther south with centrally located *ushnu* platforms. The site is not arranged around a large plaza. Rumicucho's compactness may have to do with the exigencies of military architecture, since Inka sites of a clear military nature in the same region repeat its layout. This variant of Inka architectural planning is discussed in chapter 6 (Pambamarca). Since many Inka forts in the Pichincha and Imbabura provinces of Ecuador have centrally located platforms, it is possible that there may be even more *ushnu* there than in the Inka settlements of Catamarca in Argentina, where quite a number of *ushnu* are known.

The Centrality of Ushnu

The various political, religious, and military uses of *ushnu* make them central to Inka ceremony. No better evidence for this exists than the presence of centrally located *ushnu* in Inka settlements throughout Tawantinsuyu. *Ushnu* are not necessarily represented by any one particular feature, but rather by a complex of features such as drains, stones, basins, or platforms.

Through most of the Inka state, *ushnu* is expressed by the central platform in or near the center of the plaza. The plaza is, in turn, usually situated near the center of the site. In several cases the platform was located on the edge of the plaza. In such cases the basin and sacrificial stone occupied the central plaza location. In still other examples, it appears that the central platform incorporated a basin or drain. There clearly was more than one way to build an *ushnu*.

The centrality of *ushnu* becomes more complicated when one considers that in Cuzco there may have been two *ushnu*, one for *hanan* and one for *hurin*. The "Account of the Shrines . . ." (Rowe 1979: 34, 35, An-5: 1) reports a stone called *ushnu* in *hurin* Haukaypata, possibly in or near Limacpampa plaza. The other early accounts, in describing Cuzco's *ushnu* stone, mention only that in the main plaza, *hanan* Haukaypata. Cuzco's *hurin ushnu* was apparently less significant and less centrally located. Most Inka settlements with *ushnu* have only one (Inkawasi in the Cañete Valley of Peru is a notable exception). The centrality, not the duality, of *ushnu,* is its notable characteristic throughout much of Tawantinsuyu.

Whereas the centrality of *ushnu* is an obvious feature of Inka architectural planning, a less-well-known aspect of *ushnu* is their architectural connection to a nearby area of high ceremonial importance. At Cuzco the *ushnu* was connected to Qori Kancha, the city's most important temple, by a drain. At provincial Inka sites the central platforms are often "connected" to a side of the plaza where there is a special sector. That connection may be expressed in a number of ways. A stairway from the platform to the plaza may point to the special sector, or a road or drain may connect the two. The sector may have a gateway aligned with the platform, and a large patio or patios inside. In the cases where the platform is located on the plaza's edge, its stairway points to the plaza's center, where, in some cases, there is evidence for the stone and basin component of *ushnu.* Thus the *ushnu* platform must not be considered an isolated architectural phenomenon, although it may often appear as such.

Summary

The ceremonies carried out at the Cuzco *ushnu* indicate its symbolic complexity. Thus many rituals—agricultural rites, initiation ceremonies, ancestor worship, and military reviews—took place at *ushnu.* These ceremonies usually involved sacrifices of liquids, animals, and even children, as well as the ashes from valued burned goods such as textiles. Outside the Cuzco region, the *ushnu* took on a more obvious public role, and perhaps more obvious political role, as it was constructed with a highly visible platform. Thus the *ushnu* was pivotal to Inka ceremonial life, as reflected by its central location in Cuzco and in settlements throughout the state.

The solid platform characterizing *ushnu* in subject territories has uncertain origins. It may have developed from the Cuzco model of a seat or bench where the sun image was placed, or where the Inka king sat. Less possibly, it was an architectural idea borrowed from non-Inka coastal architecture, or was characteristic of pre-Inka highland settlements.

In provincial Inka planning, the development of the *ushnu* platform did not do away with its stone, basin, and drain aspects. Drains or canals have been identified by some platforms, and in a few cases there is evidence of a large stone in the plaza, particularly when the platform was placed on the plaza's edge. It is not certain to what degree *ushnu* platforms incorporated basins and drains. Only a few platforms appear to have had basins or drains on their surface. In other cases, the basin is known to have rested in the plaza in front of the platform. Unfortunately, this detail is difficult to study at many Inka sites, since basins on plazas or platforms have been removed by priests or treasure seekers.

The architectural prominence of the *ushnu* in Inka provincial site planning appears to be related to its enhanced military-political role in conquered or subject territories. The platform fulfilled a political function where Inka kings and governors came together with local leaders, and where troops could be reviewed. The Inka solar religion was a ritual closely tied to the *ushnu*. This state cult was one of the few religious obligations imposed by Cuzco on all subject peoples.

Many questions about *ushnu* remain unanswered. Why, for example, are *ushnu* not present in the Cuzco area (other than in the city of Cuzco)? Were they just built differently, and therefore are not recognized? Did *ushnu* platforms incorporate the sacrificial stone, basin, and drain, or were they often separate, as at Vilcas Waman? Finally, why is there no archaeologically detectable *ushnu* in such seemingly important centers as Hatuncolla, Chucuito, and La Centinela?

In terms of Inka settlement planning, second only in importance to an *ushnu*'s centrality is its alignment with an important ceremonial area. That link—expressed architecturally by doorways, stairs, roads, or drains—ties the prominent *ushnu* platform to the site's general layout. The platform *ushnu*, while crucial for some of the most public ceremonies, was poorly equipped for more private rites. Platform *ushnu* were thus often aligned with enclosed quarters where such exclusive rituals took place.

4
Rocks and
Outcrops

The architecture of Inka settlements is frequently integrated with stones and outcrops. Whereas some were no doubt sacred, that status varied from rock to rock. To the Inka mind no two rocks were exactly alike—nor were their histories, myths, and meanings the same. The manner in which stones and outcrops were treated also varied, as did the groups responsible for performing rituals at them. Inka culture's integration of rocks and outcrops into architectural planning is unique among ancient American civilizations.

All visitors to the Cuzco area, the Inka heartland, are impressed with the important role of rock in Inka architecture. The significance of rock does not end with fine masonry (chap. 1), but rather extends to stones and outcrops, which affect the shape of buildings as well as the placement and design of settlements. Indeed, to ignore the subject of outcrops and boulders in Inka architecture is to neglect its fundamental Andean roots.[1] In Inka architecture, boulders and outcrops may form parts of terraces or freestanding walls, rest conspicuously on terraces, platforms, or plazas,[2] be placed in or between buildings, or simply be freestanding features (fig. 4.1). In some cases these large stone features may have been incorporated in constructions because it would have been too much work to remove them. In other cases the boulders or outcrops are displayed in such a way that there can be little doubt that architecture was planned around them because of their special importance.

There are hundreds of carved stones throughout Tawantinsuyu, ranging from small rocks to large outcrops. In still other cases very large outcrops, segments of hills, or mountain slopes are carved. The symbolism becomes more complex when dealing with the many boulders or outcrops unaltered by human hands, but that, as is known, carried as much importance as other, carved rocks. In some cases these unworked rocks can be identified as *waqa* (sacred places) by historical accounts. In still other cases, an architectural feature defines an important unworked stone. In short, modern Andean people and archaeologists alike may often wander in a sea of lost meaning as they walk among the boulders and outcrops of an Inka settlement. This chapter attempts to search for some of that meaning and to analyze how it affected the construction and layout of Inka settlements.

Carved or Uncarved

Simply viewing a stone does not reveal its meaning, since its carvings (or lack thereof) provide no immediate clues to its significance. Two types of carving in boulders or outcrops, however, are relatively comprehensible. The first are shelves and niches carved in stones, which probably provided surfaces or spaces for offerings or sacrificed items. Commonly sacrificed commodities were sea shells, clothing (both large and miniature), llamas, human and llama figurines, objects of gold and silver, coca leaves, and children. Sometimes the sacrificed items were burned, and the fires would have been set on stone shelves. One particularly good example of the seats or shelves is on Rodadero Hill, overlooking the walls of Saqsawaman (fig. 4.2). It was a *waqa* in Cuzco's ritual system.[3]

4.1. *The stones of Kenqo in the north of Cuzco. One (center) has a platform built around it. The other (left) is a large carved outcrop with a passageway and niches beneath it.*

4.2. Carved shelves known as the "Inka's Throne" on Rodadero Hill on the north side of Saqsawaman's plaza. The shelves may not be seats, but special places for offerings or sacrifices.

The second type is carved channels, which may be straight, curving, or in the form of single or double zigzags (figs. 4.3, 4.22). These are generally connected to small or large depressions or basins and indicate that they were used to pour special libations such as *chicha*. Similar channels are found on Inka libation vessels, *paccha* (chap. 5). Occasionally, sets of steps (not to be confused with shelves) or animals are carved on boulders. Their exact meaning is not known, although there is little doubt that much symbolism surrounded animals such as felines in Inka culture (Zuidema 1983a).

Unworked stones may have served a somewhat different purpose, since they are not carved to receive offerings or libations. Indeed, it is clear from the list of Cuzco *zeque waqa* that some stones marked a spot whose importance was not related to any history or characteristics of the stone itself. Thus in some cases it may have been incidental that a stone or outcrop marked an important place, since the stone was important only in that it marked a fixed place important in the ritual system (e.g., a water source).

There is, however, evidence that at least some uncarved stones were venerated and received offerings. Such is the case of the Guanacauri stone, one of the most important *waqa*, or sacred items, in the Inka Empire. It not only demonstrates how complex the mythology of an uncarved stone could be, but illustrates that a structure could be built around such a rock. The "Account of the Shrines . . ." (Rowe 1979: 47, Co-6: 7) relates that the Guanacauri stone was "of moderate size, without [representational] shape, and somewhat tapering." Originally resting on the top of the Guanacauri Hill at Cuzco, it formed part of many rituals, and was thought to have been originally a brother of the first Inka. The "Account" also notes that it was elaborately adorned with feathers for a solar feast, and Wayna Qhapaq took it to Ecuador whence it returned with his mummy. After the Spanish conquest, the stone remained untouched by the Europeans because it was uncarved and thus considered unimportant. Soon, however, it was hidden by the Indians, and then taken by Paullu Inka, who had just returned from Chile. Paullu Inka built a house for the Guanacauri stone next to his, but later it was seized by the Christians, who found with it miniature clothes for figurines and earspools for the initiation of young men.

This is but one of a number of examples in which an early historical source provides information on an uncarved special stone. Such accounts are of limited value unless placed within the broader context of Inka religion and related to how the Inkas used boulders and outcrops.

4.3. A carved zigzag channel terminating in a small basin on the large carved outcrop at Kenqo near Cuzco.

105

Historical Evidence for the Symbolic Content of Stones

Inka religion was fundamentally animistic, giving a spiritual content to inanimate objects. Thus the landscape, sky, regions beyond the horizon, the sea, and the underworld were filled with religious meaning. Sixteenth-century Catholic priests soon learned of this complex aspect of Andean religion and found that its eradication was very difficult. Concerned with the destruction of paganism, one of the priests' tactics was to destroy the cult objects of Andean religion.[4] They were confronted by cultures whose religion and sacred places were so ubiquitous that some priests went to considerable lengths to define those places, guiding others in the extirpation of idolatry. *Idolatry* was a common sixteenth- and seventeenth-century word used to describe the worship of anything considered sacred by Andean people. The word does not honor the extraordinary design that Andean and Inka religion had developed for sanctifying the surrounding world.

One important summary of the objects worshiped in the Andes was written by the Jesuit José de Arriaga (1968: 201–205), who listed the sun, moon, certain stars, the sea, earth, rivers and springs, hills, snow-capped mountains, ancient giants, *pacarinas* (see below), and caves. He made special mention of rocks and stones, associating them with hills and mountains, and reports that there were a thousand stories relating the transformations and metamorphoses of men into stone.

Stones also play an important role in a second list compiled by Arriaga, dealing with portable items. Such movable objects were often carved or uncarved stones, each with its own name and meaning. Not only was the stone worshiped, but so was the place where it was kept. Stone was also the major medium for *conopas*, domestic religious objects. Carved in the shape of a llama, alpaca, or other animal, these small stone figurines were often made from an apparently special stone and were passed down within families.

Some portable objects of great significance were the mummies that were regarded as the sacred progenitors of social groups. Often kept in caves or stone niches, these locations became sacred in and of themselves. Finally, Arriaga warns that a tall stone in a field could be sacred or a *waqa*. Similarly, some stones in or by rivers or canals were sacred and would be worshiped before planting and after the rains to ensure the success of the irrigation and crops. This last observation explains why some special boulders and outcrops are not found within, but distant from, a settlement.

Sometime near the end of the sixteenth century another priest, Cristóbal de Albornoz, wrote a manuscript (1967) specifically dedicated to informing how sacred places and things (*waqa*) could be discovered and destroyed. He discusses a wide range of *waqa*, from small colored stones carried by people in their bags, "like the Christians who carry figurines of saints, which they worship," to fragments of weapons or textiles, deformed children, certain fruits and animals, and so forth. Albornoz's list is more detailed than Arriaga's, but it is similar in that it stresses the importance of outcrops and stones. Like Arriaga, he notes that certain stones were found in isolated places. Thus a stone or outcrop in a pasture might be revered to ensure the fertility of the llama herds.

In referring to massive outcrops and rock mountains he laments (1967: 20): "It is impossible to take from them this superstition because taking apart these *waqa* would require such energy that all the people of Peru are not sufficient to move these stones or mountains. Thus is necessary the admonishment and preaching of the good doctrine for all."

Albornoz's discussion of *pacarina* is particularly detailed and helps explain how the Inkas and other Andean peoples were able to establish sacred or special stones outside of their native territory. He defines *pacarina* as "creators of their beings." By this he means that they were worshiped as origin symbols of different groups of people. *Pacarina* could be rivers, animals, lakes, springs, caves, and rocks or stones. No Andean *ayllu* was without its *pacarina*. Albornoz points out that the number of *pacarina* increased in Inka times, since many groups of people were moved to different places as *mitmaq*—the state-organized policy of colonization. These colonists were able to duplicate their *pacarina* and to carry them to their new homes. This phenomenon aided the Inkas' conquest policy, which ensured that *mitmaq* would have access to their traditional and familiar religious objects. *Pacarina* could be transferred from one place to another in a number of ways. If it was a stone, a fragment of the original could be moved. Conversely, a piece of cloth was used to cover the original; when the textile was transferred it would carry the *pacarina*'s powers and meaning to an appropriate stone a great distance away.

Sacred Stones in Cuzco

The Inka capital probably had more special stones than any other settlement within Tawantinsuyu. Two lists, by Albornoz and Cobo,[5] describe such stones in and near Cuzco. Although many of these stones have been removed or intentionally destroyed, their presence in Inka times is certain. The list by Albornoz (1967: 25–26) mentions over thirty *waqa*, of which more than half are stone or rocks. They range from "round stones" in the Carmenca district to a "large crag at the house of Wirakocha Inka."

107

A much more detailed list is found in "An Account of the Shrines of Ancient Cuzco," written somewhat earlier, between A.D. 1559 and 1572 (Rowe 1979: 5). This list of sacred places on lines is the description of the *zeque* system described in more detail in chapters 2, 5, and 7. Nearly a third of more than three hundred *waqa* are listed as stones or groups of stones. Thus within and near Cuzco there were many dozen sacred locations represented by rock(s). At least fourteen were *pururaucas*, or stones that, according to myth, turned into soldiers during an early Inka war against their Chanca neighbors. Other stones were used as sites for sacrifice or worship, to ensure the health of a king, to indicate the location of a miraculous event, to have dangerous powers, to be a *pacarina*, to bring victory in war, to be a mythological person, or to ensure a safe journey. Some are described as having been created by an Inka king; others are simply called "very old." One stone called Maychaguanacauri on the Antisuyu road was shaped like the Guanacauri Hill (Rowe 1979: 34, 35, AN-4: 7) near Cuzco.

Many of the stones are associated with canals, or water sources. Indeed, a stone's proximity to an important water source frequently endowed it with a special, sacred status. As discussed in chapter 5, water is crucial to understanding the meaning and organization of Cuzco's ritual system. Water also appears to be important for discerning the meaning of special stones and their relation to social structure.

In short, the two lists contain some conflicting information,[6] but do agree that stones and outcrops were important in the capital's ritual system, and thus were integrated into the architecture of the Inka capital.

Stones and Architecture in the Cuzco Area

Most of the larger settlements and some smaller complexes in the Cuzco region have one or a number of places where stone or outcrops

4.4. The carved stone known as intiwatana at Machu Picchu, Peru. Its purpose has been the subject of much speculation, including its unsubstantiated role as a "hitching post of the sun."

Rocks and Outcrops

0 50 m

4.5. *Machu Picchu. Arrows indicate the locations of some special stones and outcrops. Bingham (1930: fig. 219).*

4.6. *A large, flat outcrop surrounded by a platform on the north side of Machu Picchu, Peru. Some have suggested that it was shaped to model the horizon (not visible here) beyond it. Bingham (1930: 79).*

are integral aspects of the architecture.[7] Unless these stones are extraordinarily prominent and worked, such as the case of the *intiwatana* at Machu Picchu (fig. 4.4), little attention is paid to them. Nevertheless, their presence should be noted, and their influence on site design be studied.

Machu Picchu

The famous site of Machu Picchu is a case in point. Bingham (1913: 471) noted that each of several groups of buildings had a "religious center, consisting of more or less carved granite in position. In several cases, caves had been excavated under these rocks, and in one case the cave was beautifully lined with finely cut stonework."

Indeed, special boulders and outcrops are more apparent at Machu Picchu than at almost any other known Inka settlement. This has been noted by MacLean (1986: 72), who writes:

> Buildings in all parts of the site were planned around standing boulders. Inca stonemasons certainly possessed the skills to cut or move boulders to fit a plan; however, many of the structures incorporating such boulders seem to have been built because of and not in spite of them. In a physical sense, they were probably a stabilizing feature. In a metaphysical sense, carved or uncarved, these boulders were crucial elements in the animistic Inca religious philosophy. Therefore, they had to have been a strong consideration in the spatial organization of the site.

The presence of so many important stones at Machu Picchu (fig. 4.5) argues for a site whose religious significance may be stronger than has been suspected. The varying treatment of rocks argues that they had different roles. Some of the stones are found above or beside burial caves. Others are in patios or buildings, on low platforms or within walls. Some may have been shaped in the form of a sacred mountain near Machu Picchu. A good example of this is a flat outcrop located on the

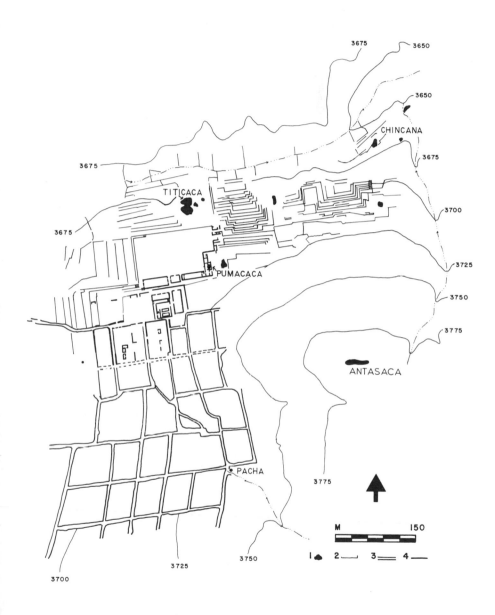

4.7. Plan of Chinchero, Peru. Buildings of fine masonry are found to the south and east of the plaza. Key: 1. important stones; 2. terraces; 3. streets; 4. Inka buildings of fine masonry. Redrawn from plans in Alcina F. (1976: 20, 22, 28, 40).

northern side of the site (fig. 4.6).[8] At least one carved outcrop may have had an astronomical or calendrical function (chap. 8). MacLean (1986: 95–96, fig. 18) maps nearly a score of special stones at Machu Picchu.

The special treatment of stones at Machu Picchu raises a number of questions. For example, was Machu Picchu's location chosen because "special" stones were there? Or did Machu Picchu's builders merely incorporate these stones into their design? All that can be said is that now that the site has been studied from many points of view, enough is known to stress the importance of its boulders and outcrops.

Chinchero

Another good example of special boulders or outcrops integrated into and near a settlement's architecture is the site Chinchero (fig. 4.7). Chinchero was once an Inka royal estate. It has always been an important potato-producing area. It may have more worked stones than any other site in the Cuzco region. There were at least four principal stones or stone clusters on the edge of the community and others associated with an important compound called Structure 11 (Alcina 1976: 99–114) on the plaza. In addition, there are a considerable number of small worked stones scattered about the site.

Chinchero has been continuously occupied since Inka times. The local people still have strong feelings about the stones. Anthropologist Edward Franquemont, who has resided at Chinchero, reports that the

4.8. *Shelves in the Titicaca stone at Chinchero, Peru.*

4.9. *A carved outcrop within the* inti-watana *sector of Pisaq, Peru. A semicircular building was constructed around it.*

worked stones are now considered dangerous, and are avoided or respected.[9] Children must not play in or near the stones.

The more important stones still have names. The largest outcrop is called Antasaca (fig. 4.7), located just east of the town on the top of the hill. Little remains of its worked surface today, but it still occupies the minds of the Chinchero people. They remember that their ancestors were forced by the Spanish to chip away all the surfaces of the stone. They feel that it was the search for gold, but more probably it was a Christian attempt to destroy a sacred place.

To the northeast is the large stone known as Chincana, with carved shelves on its top and a base with a watercourse, large vertical worked surfaces, long shelves, and a stepfret. Other small stones near the base are also worked, one with several shelves. A complex of carved boulders known as Titicaca is found below and to the north of the main plaza. It was once flanked by fine stone walls. It has a stepped tunnel entrance leading from the ground level to the top, a curving staircase, and several shelves and niches (fig. 4.8).

One important stone is located where a small hotel is now located. It is ritually linked to Ayllu Pongo, the only stone with an extant *ayllu* affiliation. Other important stones were probably located at the waterfall (*pacha*) on the south side of the community. Unfortunately, little can be seen of these because of modern construction.

Within and beside the important Inka ceremonial compound to the east of the plaza there are five stones with carved shelves. The central and largest one is known as Pumacaca. The stone is so prominent that it appears that its associated architecture is there because of, rather than in spite of, it. Alcina (1976: 105–106) presents a detailed description of its worked flat surfaces and two possible animal carvings.

Chinchero's freestanding and building-associated carved stones were and remain an important part of the settlement. As at Cuzco, the stones probably had an affiliation with a social group, although today only one maintains an association with an *ayllu*. Franquemont recalls that one massive stone in a patio was valued enough to be stolen by a character known only as Strong John (Juan Fuerte). Franquemont helped community members haul it back to its proper place. Thus some Andean people still consider that stones have their rightful place within a community's design.

Other Cuzco-Area Sites

To a lesser degree, stones enclosed within walls or surrounded by terraces are found at most Cuzco-area sites. For example, they are notable at Pisaq (fig. 4.9), Ollantaytambo (fig. 4.10), Tipón (fig. 4.11), Chacan, and Qespi Wara, to name a few. In all these cases the important stone

4.10. *A large, relatively flat upright stone with a surrounding platform is found next to important waterworks in the Incamisana sector of Ollantaytambo, Peru.*

can be identified because of one or a number of distinguishing features: they are often carved, enclosed within walls, prominently displayed on terraces, or set on platforms.

Important Stones Removed from but Part of Settlements

Some important Inka stones are part of architectural layouts that were not extensive inhabited settlements. The remarkable Sayhuite stone (fig. 4.12) on a terraced hilltop in Apurimac, Peru, is an example. Its variety of motifs making up a miniature landscape is unique in Inka stone carving. Van de Guchte's survey at Sayhuite demonstrates that the terraced hilltop is close to other archaeological remains that include steps and fountains, other carved boulders (Rumihuasi), and a large plaza (Usnu-pampa) with artificial mounds and a subterranean canal. He believes the Sayhuite stone is related to water ritual, as did Carrión (1955: 57–60) and Sherbondy (1982a: 92–93).[10] The Sayhuite stone is not as isolated from a settlement layout as was once held.

At Cuzco some of the *zeque waqa* stones lie outside the architectural limits of the capital, but are linked to Cuzco through ritual lines.

4.11. An uncarved boulder surrounded by a three-tier platform is found on a height at Tipón, Peru.

This suggests that special stones near Cuzco (and possibly other Inka sites) should be considered part of the Inka concept of a settlement. Examples of such stones at Cuzco are the Guanacauri stone (discussed earlier), the carved Kenqo outcrop (fig. 4.1), and the Tired Stone (Piedra Cansada) at Saqsawaman.

Enough is known about the Piedra Cansada (fig. 4.13) to demonstrate much of its symbolism and link to Cuzco. It is the subject of a unique structural study by Van de Guchte (1984). The Tired Stone rests just to the north of Saqsawaman. A number of sources (Cieza de León, Gutiérrez, Murúa, and Garcilaso) refer to it. Guaman Poma (1980: [159] 138–139) supplies related information about moving "tired stones." In general, the sources relate that the stone was being moved to (or from) Saqsawaman. It "tired," or could move no more, and cried blood, and thus was left near the fortress. It became part of the ritual (*zeque*) system of Cuzco and was worshiped as a general *waqa*, at which offerings were made to ensure the strength of the king (Rowe 1979: 20, Ch-4:6). The stone is related to *hanan* Cuzco and a royal *ayllu* in a territorial sense.

115

4.12. Two views of the Sayhuite stone, drawn by P. Ponce Rojas. The symbolism in its design far exceeds that of most carved Inka outcrops. Canals, terraces, human couples, buildings, felines, and other animals are combined in an animated landscape. From Carrión Cachot (1955).

*4.13. The Tired Stone north of Saqsa-
waman. Now partially destroyed, the
outcrop's complex symbolism is mentioned by a number of early histories.
Courtesy Anthony Aveni.*

Accounts vary as to where the stone came from (a nearby quarry,
Yucay, Ecuador) and where it was going (Saqsawaman, Huánuco, Ecuador), but they do appear to establish a relationship with another area.
Also, the stone's tiring and crying recall earlier critical times when, in
Andean mythology, stones took on human characteristics. In arguments
too lengthy to repeat here, Van de Guchte ties aspects of the stone into
the symbolic termination of the building of Saqsawaman and the area's
irrigation system. In short, this carved outcrop was loaded with meaning and serves as a warning that Inka stones are never understood properly if only described physically.

Accurately located by Zuidema and Aveni in 1980, the Piedra Cansada is a large limestone outcrop (and thus never could really be moved)
74.2 meters in circumference. It is located north of Saqsawaman (to the
west of the Hacienda Pucro) and is now known as the Chingana Grande.
Sculpted with geometric shapes, niches, and shelves, it has been partially destroyed. Although the Tired Stone rests outside of Cuzco's architectural limits, it is closely tied to Cuzco's mythology, ritual, and
royal *ayllu* and might properly be considered part of the urban concept
of Cuzco. Such may well be the case with other special stones in the
Cuzco area and throughout Tawantinsuyu.

Important Boulders and Outcrops throughout Tawantinsuyu

The Cuzco area has the greatest number of carved and specially displayed rocks. But the Inkas carried this important concept elsewhere,
and it shows frequently in their state architecture, often at great distances from the capital.

Examples from Argentina, Peru, and Ecuador

At the Inka fortress of Pucará de Andalgalá, for example, in Catamarca
Province, Argentina, one finds a large white stone outcrop in the center
of the patio of the highest building in the site (fig. 6.26). Somewhat to

the north, in the smaller plaza of Nevados de Aconquija in the Argentine province of Tucumán (chap. 3), one finds a large stone surrounded by a circular stone platform (figs. 4.14, 3.10). Because it is in a plaza, one could argue that this stone has *ushnu*-related properties. This is not likely, given the presence of a complete *ushnu* complex at the site's larger, nearby plaza (fig. 3.13).

An important case of apparently isolated stones possibly forming part of the Inka settlement concept is found at the administrative center of Pumpu in the department of Pasco, Peru. Beyond the periphery of the site's buildings are a considerable number of rock outcrops. The stones are found mainly in the flat *puna* to the west and south of the buildings, but similar stones may be found in the surrounding hills. At first glance these rocks appear to be insignificant, since they are removed from the "constructed" area. Upon closer scrutiny one finds that some stones are worked with small depressions and may have been used in a ritual context. More will be understood about these stones when they are accurately mapped and their relation to the design of Pumpu studied.

At the administrative center Huánuco Pampa to the north of Pumpu, there are no natural rock outcrops in the flat pampa surrounding the center. The only nearby outcrop is located within the area of storage structures, and enclosed in a rectangular building. Excavation revealed a cache of pottery and figurine fragments buried beside it (Morris 1967: 109–110).

Far in northern Tawantinsuyu, important carved stones (fig. 4.15) are found within the site of Ingapirca (Alcina 1978: 143–144; Jaramillo 1976: 127–146), just northeast of its solid oval structure by a stream. That building rests on a large outcrop (Fresco 1983; Fresco and Cobo 1978). The implications of this outcrop, part of a possible Cañari *pacarina*, are discussed in chapter 9. Northeast of Quito, one finds outcrops prominently placed within the walls of several units (nos. 3, 5, and 6)

4.14. An uncarved outcrop surrounded by a low circular platform of stones at Nevados de Aconquija, Argentina. It·is located in the smaller (northwest) of the settlement's two plazas.

within the Pambamarca fortress complex (chap. 6, "Pambamarca"). The outcrop at Unit No. 5 (Quitaloma) is particularly impressive, since it is surrounded by steep natural cliffs on one side and three artificial walls on the other.

Significant Rocks at the Titicaca Sanctuary

The great sacred rock on the Island of the Sun is discussed in chapter 3, as it forms part of an *ushnu* complex. Although rough and unworked, it was adorned with textiles and metals. Other important boulders are also found elsewhere in the sanctuary.

On the southern side of the Island of the Sun at the Inka building Pilco Kayma (Gasparini and Margolies 1980: 262–263), notable for its two-story construction (figs. 1.6, 1.7), one finds boulders integrated into the walls. One is just below a niche (fig. 4.16). Bandelier suspected that the boulders "may have been *placed there* for some purpose" and commented (1910: 195): "The boulders are so large that it would have required several men to remove them; still it is strange that people who were able to move incomparably more ponderous masses, as shown at Sillustani and Cuzco, should have left them *in situ,* building over and around them. The purpose of making a rude mass an integral part of the side of a room is not clear to me."

Given the relatively common occurrence in the Cuzco area of boulders within Inka walls made of smaller blocks, the example of the wall boulders at the Pilco Kayma does not seem extraordinary. It is quite certain that these boulders are special aspects of the building's composition, particularly since one is located under a niche where offerings could have been placed. One might even speculate that the boulders were a cause for situating the Pilco Kayma at its specific location.

One particularly significant set of carved rocks within the same sanctuary area is found on the Copacabana Peninsula, lying on the edge of

4.15. *Part of a carved outcrop associated with waterworks northeast of the oval building at Ingapirca, Ecuador.*

119

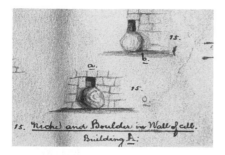

4.16. *Boulder-niche construction in the Pilco Kayma building on the Island of the Sun, Lake Titicaca, Bolivia. Courtesy Department of Anthropology, AMNH, Bandelier Collection.*

4.17. *One of a group of carved stones west of the town of Copacabana, Bolivia. It was part of the Lake Titicaca sanctuary.*

4.18. *One of several carved outcrops near Copacabana, Bolivia. In Inka times pilgrims underwent special rites before proceeding to the Island of the Sun.*

the present-day pilgrimage center and town of Copacabana (Portugal and Ibarra 1957; Portugal Z. 1977; Trimborn 1967: 19–23; Rivera Sundt 1984). Modern Copacabana covers a principal Inka settlement (Bandelier 1910: 282). The inhabitants were Inkas and *mitmaq* from various parts of Tawantinsuyu. Several carved stones rest on the western side of the town within a small area (figs. 4.17, 4.18). Some remains of Inka walls are found nearby, but there are not enough to determine the layout of buildings near the outcrops.

Ramos Gavilán (1976: 44, chap. 12) wrote that pilgrims traveling to the Islands of the Sun and Moon would undergo purification rituals on the Copacabana Peninsula before visiting the islands. It is possible that these rites took place at these stones.

One of the principal carved rocks has been called the Seat of the Sun, or Throne of the Inka, as many other carved Inka rocks with flat shelves or steps sculpted into them are known. These "seats" or "thrones" are best understood as places for offerings or as small altars. There are many such offering shelves in the complex of stones at Copacabana.[11] With the exception of Samaipata (discussed below), the Copacabana carved stones may have more shelves than any other set of carved rocks outside of the Cuzco area.

Samaipata

Farther east in Bolivia there are several other sites with Inka carved stones or outcrops (Trimborn 1967: 23–27). None are as impressive as the massive carved outcrop at Samaipata (Sabaypata) in Santa Cruz Province (fig. 4.19). It too was part of a settlement, but unfortunately the town is entangled in a forest and has not yet been mapped (Tapia 1984). Rivera (1979: 46) estimates a settlement of some thirty hectares

4.19. *View to the east over the Samaipata outcrop in Bolivia. The carved surface exceeds 10,000 square meters, the largest of all known Inka carved outcrops.*

4.20. The south side of the Samaipata outcrop. It has hundreds of niches, shelves, and steps.

in size. The Alcaya chronicle (1961: 47–50) relates that it was the seat of the region's Inka leader, who controlled the easternmost extension of the Inka state, a territory that entered into the Bolivian lowlands by the Piray and Guapay rivers (Saignes 1985: 5–31). The Alcaya historical source indicates that Samaipata was a fort,[12] but authorities disagree on this issue (chap. 6), as there is little or no evidence of fortifications, and the site itself is not found on the outer fringe of Inka-controlled territory, which is some distance farther to the east.

Samaipata may be the largest single stone outcrop ever carved under Inka direction. It is extraordinary, not only for its size, but for its location so far from Cuzco. Long the subject of interest to Bolivian and foreign scholars (D'Orbigny 1835–1847; Pucher 1945; Trimborn 1967: 130–169; Boero and Rivera 1979), the carved stone of Samaipata exceeds 10,000 square meters. Resting at about 1,950 meters above sea level, the sculpted prominence is doubtless Inka because of the great similarity of its motifs to other Inka carved stones and outcrops. The outcrop is oriented east-west, and the principal carved channels are also oriented in that direction, which raises issues related to Inka astronomy

4.21. Large and small rectangular niches are found on the north side of Samai-pata's outcrop.

(chap. 8). There are several detailed descriptions of the monument, but Trimborn's (1959: 40–70, 1967: 130–169) are the most detailed and analytical, incorporating and evaluating all previous descriptions as well as unpublished information from Nordenskiöld.

The carved monument has many steps and shelves in great abundance on its southern side (fig. 4.20), a lengthy sloped surface. On the northern side there are elaborate rectangular niches (fig. 4.21). The top of the monument is carved with numerous channels and basins, associated with libations. Three long east-west double zigzag channels forming rhomboid shapes are reminiscent of channels on Inka *paccha* (fig. 4.22) (chap. 5). On the highest part of the rock is a unique set of alternating rectangular and triangular shelves or seats forming a circle some four meters in diameter. On the eastern side of the outcrop are relief carvings of felines, a bird, and a snake (fig. 4.23). Some traces of walls are found just on the southern side of the outcrop (Trimborn 1967: 141) as well as on the eastern side. These walls are not to be confused with the yet-unstudied settlement resting in the forest a few meters to the south of the monument.

4.22. Double zigzag and straight channels run from east to west down Samaipata's top surface.

4.23. Several animals were carved on the eastern side of the top of Samaipata's outcrop. A carved puma is in the foreground.

Too little is still known about Inka stone carving to interpret the full meaning of Samaipata. It would appear, however, that it was not only part of the settlement, but that it was planned, with orderly preconceived designs and features that are interrelated in ways only faintly understood. This is not necessarily the case with all carved rocks, since many appear to be sculpted haphazardly, with niches, steps, shelves, canals, and basins jumbled together in a way that appears dictated by chance or the rock's original shape, rather than by any complex design concept.

Settlements without Important Stones

The idea that boulders or outcrops, whether sculpted or not, form part of the design of Inka settlements is not applicable to all of the larger Inka settlements. Some settlements were built where stones or rocks did not affect their general design. Such is the case on the Peruvian coast between Lima and Nasca, where large Inka settlements exist but where there is no evidence for important boulders as part of the site. This may be due in part to a general lack of large boulders at sites on the desert, or to influences from local or non-Inka cultural traditions that encouraged other aspects of a region's topography to become part of the design. Thus the relationship of a settlement to the sea,[13] nearby mountain passes or peaks, and water systems could have replaced "sacred" stones and outcrops. Also, we have no idea of the importance that portable rocks and stones may have had in such sites since none are preserved *in situ*.

South of about 18 degrees south latitude there is no good published evidence for fine Inka stone carving. The reasons for this are yet unclear (Hyslop 1984: 284), but may be related to less labor available in the southern part of the state or to the generally lower priority of such areas when compared with the more densely populated regions and larger settlements of the central and northern Andes. The lack of carved stones throughout what is now Chile and Argentina does not contradict the importance of uncarved boulders or outcrops in settlement planning. Uncarved special stones were important at settlements such as Nevados de Aconquija and Pucará de Andalgalá. The lack of carved boulders in southern Inka sites means that these settlements must be scrutinized with greater care to find the important uncarved boulders and outcrops. These rocks may sometimes be indicated by architectural features that point them out, such as surrounding walls or terraces.

Stone as a Criterion for Settlement Location

The significance of boulders and outcrops in Inka settlements raises the question of whether stones were actually powerful enough to determine a settlement's location. It would appear that important stones could at least determine the location of shrines, smaller than settlements. The Chacha Bamba site in the Urubamba region mapped by Fejos (1944: fig. 11) (fig. 4.24) is a good example of a small architectural complex centering on a carved stone.

But could a sacred rock or outcrop actually determine the location of a major human settlement? There is some evidence, albeit tentative. The Inka complex at the northern end of the Island of the Sun (chap. 3) centers around a sacred rock associated with Inka origin myths. If the rock were removed, the Lake Titicaca sanctuary's reason for existing would be lost. Is the architectural complex there because of the rock, or did building the sanctuary decree the importance of the rock?

One site in the Cuzco area, Caquia Xaquixaguana (also known as Huchuy Cuzco), had a special relationship to King Wirakocha (Cieza 1967: 131, chap. 38; Betanzos 1968: 30, chap. 10) and is generally described as being set on a great rock prominence (fig. 4.25). It is thought-provoking to consider that this great natural feature may have been central to the selection of this particular site.

MacLean raises this same question (1986: 93–96) in regard to sites in the area of Machu Picchu. She notes that several sites, including Machu Picchu, were built on particularly rocky terrain, which was incorporated into their architecture. Most of these sites have good examples of boulder sculpture. MacLean explores various practical reasons for choosing such rocky locations but leaves open the question of whether rock as a sacred commodity was a determinant of settlement location.

Outside of the Cuzco area, one might ask whether the Inka occupation of the ancient site of Pucará (Mujica and Wheeler 1981), inhabited for at least two thousand years, had something to do with the prominent rock mountain beside it. Local myths see a puma shape in the mountain, and possibly the mountain's powers were central to the symbolism of the site.

One could list many more Inka sites associated with prominent outcrops or boulders. The point is made, however, that stone and rock may be more significant than previously imagined in determining the locations of some Inka settlements.

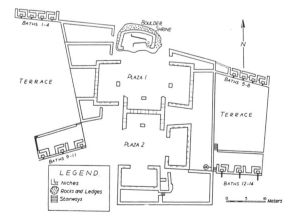

4.24. *The Chacha Bamba shrine near Machu Picchu focuses on a large carved outcrop. A complex water system with basins in the four corners enhances the ritual importance of this small architectural complex. From Fejos (1944: 38). Copyright 1944 by the Wenner-Gren Foundation for Anthropological Research, Inc., New York.*

4.25. Caquia Xaquixaguana (Huchuy Cuzco) rests on a great rock prominence overlooking the Urubamba Valley, Peru. The site is located on terraces set around a plaza in the upper-left-central part of the photograph. Courtesy Department of Library Services, AMNH, Neg. no. 334771 (photo by Shippee Johnson).

Stones and Site Design

Were important rocks consistently placed within certain recognizable sectors of Inka settlements? It seems that this may occasionally have

127

been the case, but that the varied topography of each site also influenced whether and which stones would be specially treated. Thus settlements without boulders (such as those on the Pacific coast) did not incorporate them into their design. Still other settlements have no outcrops within their architectural limits, but one might find specially treated outcrops nearby. Often, special boulders are the focal point of a set of buildings. Since the boulders were generally not moved, the placement of the buildings must have been determined in part by the boulder.

Were specific criteria consistently used to decide which boulders or outcrops would receive special attention? At sites such as Machu Picchu, Chinchero, Tipón, Pucará de Andalgalá, Ingapirca, and Pambamarca, stones resting on high prominences are specially treated. Indeed, it would seem that any Inka architect designing a settlement with a boulder or outcrop set high would incorporate it into the design.

Nevertheless, all specially defined stones are not located up high. Others appear near water sources or irrigation channels, and in important buildings, or on special agricultural terraces. They formed part of the *zeque* system of Cuzco and perhaps had a similar role in other settlements. Important boulders and outcrops are not always within the architectural limits of a site, but frequently found beside or near it.

Summary

Evidence that boulders and outcrops were integrated into Inka architectural planning and exerted some influence over it is overwhelming. Whereas some important rocks are clearly outside of settlements, those on site peripheries should probably be considered part of the settlement. The question of whether some rocks and outcrops were actually responsible for the situating of settlements beside or around them remains unanswered.

The symbolism of rocks and stone outcrops in Inka culture was so complex that one cannot simply refer to a "cult of stone" or the "sacredness of rock" and expect to explain why such stone is important. Future detailed and comparative research should delve more thoroughly into the role of these stones. Yet-undiscovered patterns in their placement, the presence or absence of carving, their associations with natural and artificial features, the types of carving, and their architectural presentation may some day clarify which stones were intended for offerings (and of what types), which were *pacarinas*, which fulfilled *zeque* functions, and which had multiple roles. Such research will be a major contribution to an understanding of Inka architecture and general site design.

5
Water

Among the many things worshiped by the Inkas, water played a role second only to that of the Sun and the Creator, Wirakocha. The thunder god, Illapa (Tunupa in Aymara), was believed to influence meteorological phenomena such as rain, lightning, thunder, and snow. This god was venerated in the Temple of the Sun in Cuzco, and is said to have had a separate house of worship in the Totocachi district of Cuzco (Cobo 1964: 160–161, Bk. 13, chap. 7), and his statue was carried to war by Inka kings.

Many Andean myths emphasize water, an element so important that it, or at least its source, was considered sacred. Fundamental to the Inka, and to some degree the Andean, world was the concept that water surrounded the world and lay beneath it. For example, the Milky Way was viewed as a great river that traversed the cosmos, and beneath the land was the sea into which all rivers and lakes ultimately drained (Urton 1978). Andean lakes thus formed part of these religious beliefs. Primary among them was Lake Titicaca, which Inka religion linked to the creation, as well as to the origin of their own people. In Andean communities, springs or other water sources were often considered founding ancestors. Sherbondy (1982a: 120–146) has written perceptively about how people's relationship to water sources was used to express concepts concerning their origins and ethnicity, and how myths relating to subterranean water passages could be used to tie people to the same lake, thus expressing "the unity of several people and nations within one kingdom or empire."

Water permeates several aspects of Andean and Inka religion.[1] It is directly tied to sacred mountains (whose worship was thought to be intimately tied to rainfall) where sanctuaries used for worship and sacrifices (Reinhard 1983) were built. Considerable evidence in pre-Hispanic Andean iconography indicates that water worship is quite ancient. There are some grounds (Demarest 1981) for thinking that the creator god Wirakocha, as its name suggests (*kocha* means lake), was closely related to water, which may have evolved originally from a concept in which a creator god controlled meteorological phenomena.

More so than in many temperate areas of the world, water in the Inka state was managed and cared for to ensure the success of agriculture and, to a lesser degree, pastures. Irrigation, possibly the most monumental heritage left by pre-Hispanic Andean peoples, is most visible on the desert Pacific coast, where dozens of valleys from northern Peru to Santiago, Chile, were converted into productive areas irrigated by these elaborate complexes of canals. Less obvious are irrigation systems in the Andean highlands, developed over a period of at least two thousand years and critical for ensuring agricultural success. Rain is plentiful in the Andes, but often erratic and occasionally sparse. Thus there are few highland Andean communities that do not maintain and esteem their canal systems. Such was the case in Cuzco, which, as noted in chapter 2, had primary agricultural territory nearby dependent on irrigation systems whose canals and water sources were regarded as *waqa,* sacred entities.

Water systems at most Inka settlements have not been studied thoroughly. This is due in part to the poor preservation at many Inka settlements of architecture and canals. Excavations rarely study channels sufficiently to reveal their complexity. In the Western world, water is sometimes displayed in fountains, but is primarily viewed as being for consumption, cleaning, and sewage. For most archaeologists, water has little symbolic value. Thus many archaeologists have not grasped why water systems around and within Inka settlements were so significant. One can be certain that the waterworks so prominently managed and displayed in Inka settlements were more than aesthetic.[2] Early historical sources usually mention water in the context of irrigation, weather, religion, or all three.

So many Andean and Inka religious beliefs concern water that it would be futile to review them all here.[3] It is, however, not difficult to understand that water played an important part in religious thought, and that water rites were a form of "technology" that was meant to prompt meteorological events, controlled water systems, determined who would use them, and in general performed roles that were critical for the very existence of Andean peoples. Thus finely constructed, sometimes elaborate waterworks are important in the planning and design of Inka settlements.

Utilitarian Water Management
The foregoing discussion about the sacred nature of water is not intended to convey the impression that all water management in Inka settlements was for religious purposes. In the few cases where areas

around Inka buildings have been excavated, channels have been found
that drain water falling from rooftops. One of the best examples is channels shown in Uhle's original maps (1923) of the buildings of Tomebamba,
Ecuador, the second Inka capital, where they are indicated on one or
both sides of the *kallanka* and other buildings. Such channels are only
partially detected in most excavations that do not clear large areas and
that usually concentrate on inside rather than outside buildings. In general, it is quite difficult to study drainage systems at unexcavated Inka
sites, since the channels near buildings have filled with earth and are no
longer visible.

Chinchero, near Cuzco, has revealed a complex drainage system (Alcina 1976: 44–46, figs. 9, 28). Here, the channels drain water from
around buildings, off the plaza, and from platforms. The drainage system is tied into Chinchero's "ceremonial" water system when it passes
by the area to the east of the plaza, where the primary ceremonial buildings are. Most of the drains at Chinchero appear to have been open, usually stone-lined channels, although some were covered. Open channels
were common throughout the Inka state. Subterranean channels were
also important, but few have been thoroughly excavated.

5.1. A bath at Ollantaytambo.

Another drainage system used in Inka settlements was the central open drains in roads. Common in Inka Cuzco, one can still see these drains in traditional Andean communities. Many of the center-road drains in Chucuito are still used. Streets with central drains, however, are not necessarily Inka. Similar drains were built in Spain in the sixteenth century (Alcina 1976: 32, 128). Thus in some Inka settlements, streets with central drains may have been installed by later Spanish residents.

The locations of Inka administrative centers do not appear to have been swampy terrain, as was the case of Cuzco, where elaborate river canalization and drains were necessary to drain the swamp in what is now the Plaza de Armas. Inka settlements were generally built in areas where elaborate and costly canalization was not necessary, or was needed only on a small scale. Sherbondy (1982a: 132–137) refers to Andean myths describing the founding of villages on top of lakes or swamps. This appears to have been useful for defining the relationship of people of separate communities via hydrological connections, often imagined subterranean ones. Whatever excess water existed under Inka centers was primarily imaginary. This is additional proof of Sherbondy's important observation (1982a: 144) that "the hydrological reality of the supply of water is different from the mythological concepts people have of it."

There is little evidence that fine Inka waterworks were used as sewage systems. Whereas it is possible that gray water was poured into the systems, the very nature of the Inka fountains, often series of connected basins, indicates that solid wastes would not have passed through them easily. There is historical evidence that libations such as *chicha*, blood, or urine may have flowed through the systems, especially since they tend to pass through areas where drinking, sacrificing, and libations were important. An early eyewitness to the ceremonies in Cuzco's main plaza (Estete 1924: 54–55) commented on the vast quantities of urine (the result of drinking much *chicha*) passing through two drains into the canalized Saphy River. In general, Inka site planning provides no evidence of water facilities used for human defecation. It is probable that such functions were performed in abandoned buildings or corrals, as is the case with rural Andean peoples today.

Baths and Fountains

Fine Inka waterworks combine a number of features such as canals, reservoirs, pools, open and closed drains, water catchments, and basins. The archaeological literature often refers to the catchments or basins as "baths." It is doubtful that most of these catchments were used for

5.2. An Inka "fountain" with a double stream falling into a basin. It is located outside the curved wall on the western side of the Sun Temple in Cuzco.

bathing, since many are quite small. Others are somewhat larger and could have been used for bathing, particularly those with steps leading into them (fig. 5.1). Since these catchments are often made of fine Cuzco masonry and placed in areas of restricted access, any bathing in them may have been more for ritual than hygienic reasons. Sometimes the word *fountain* is used if the water from the inlet or inlets falls some distance into the catchment. It is improbable that these waterworks had the same connotations of a fountain in the Western world.

There is a fine line between "utilitarian" and "ceremonial" architecture, a division denied by some persuasive logic. Nevertheless, the dichotomy is of some use to the reader. The following sections will explore how water was ceremonially handled within site planning, first in the Cuzco area and then in more distant settlements.

Fine Water Systems in Cuzco-Area Sites

Cuzco

Unfortunately, there has never been a detailed study of the water systems of Cuzco's central sector. As noted in chapter 2, two canalized rivers passed on either side of the central sector and would have been the city's principal sources of water. It is also known that the Sun

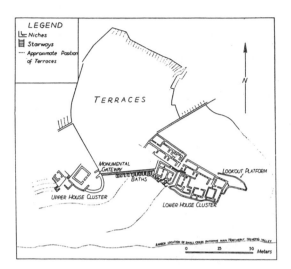

5.3. Plan of Wiñay Wayna near Machu Picchu. A series of nineteen fountains with water catchments connects the two parts of the site. From Fejos (1944: 50). Copyright 1944 by the Wenner-Gren Foundation for Anthropological Research, Inc., New York.

Temple was supplied with water from sources whose origin was forgotten early in the Spanish period (fig. 5.2). A drain also ran from the main plaza by the *ushnu* to the Sun Temple, through which libations rather than water probably passed. Certainly there were many other canals and drains in Cuzco about which we know very little.[4] One might note, however, that channels led to a compound (the Sun Temple) where the most elaborate religious activity took place. Given that Cuzco was in some ways a model for other Inka settlements, one might expect this design to be repeated elsewhere.

Cuzco-Region Sites

Margaret MacLean's analysis (1986: 65–68) of water-related constructions at sites near Machu Picchu finds all of them equipped with fountains of a generally standardized design. These have one narrow inlet about a meter wide above a rectangular basin set into the floor with a drain. They are often placed in a series on slopes such as the site of Wiñay Wayna, which has nineteen of them (fig. 5.3); Machu Picchu has sixteen. Open stone-lined channels delivered water from springs near the sites. Thus natural water sources were not required within the sites. The fountains are in the open, protected by walls on three sides, and have narrow entrances.

At Machu Picchu and Wiñay Wayna, the two largest sites in MacLean's study, the fountains are central to site design. At Wiñay Wayna they connect the two principal house clusters, whereas at Machu Picchu the fountains originate at "what was probably a very sacred point in the complex" (MacLean 1986: 92), the area called by Bingham the "Semicircular Temple," or "Torreón" (fig. 5.4). Here, waterworks unite with some of the finest buildings and more important carved boulders.

The importance of an area with an elaborate water system such as at Machu Picchu is repeated in data reported by MacLean (1986: 90) for the site of Pisaq in the Urubamba Valley. She notes how an "extraordinary channel" crosses difficult terrain to enter the *intiwatana* sector of the site and then "crosses into an open plaza and empties into a sunken basin set into the ground." From there the water drains into a series of fountains on the eastern slope. Thus Inka planners went to a considerable effort to bring water to the architecturally most impressive and elaborate part of the site.

A similar pattern can be observed at nearly all of the other larger Cuzco-area sites where the water systems have been revealed and studied. As noted previously, Chinchero's drainage system passes in front of the structure at the eastern edge of the plaza denominated by Alcina as the primary "religious" area. There, a special feeder channel, sometimes subterranean, leads directly from the central feature of that area, the carved *pumacaca* stone, into the main channel.

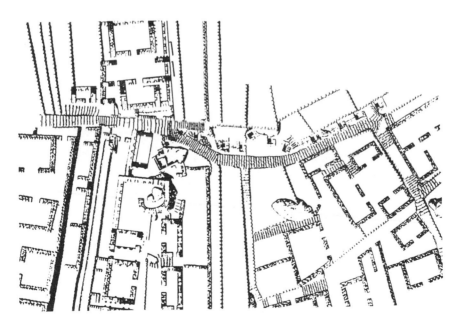

5.4. A series of sixteen fountains at Machu Picchu originates next to the Torreón and descends a slope. From Bingham (1930: 86, 88, figs. 58, 59).

Past and recent excavations at the site of Ollantaytambo (fig. 5.5) in the Urubamba Valley have revealed a complex water system in the so-called Fortaleza, or higher part of the site. Here one finds at least six fountains. An even more impressive water system is found in the lower, north-central part of the site, called Incamisana and Manyarqui, with at least twelve fountains or baths. The excavator, Gibaja (1984: 4–5), believes that the whole area was dedicated to religious activities involving water. In the Incamisana area, the canals pass on either side of a large flat rock (fig. 4.10), clearly identifiable by a surrounding platform and similar to another rock at Machu Picchu. Three of the fountains are found in a sector north of the rock (fig. 5.1), which Gibaja notes was of high religious significance. It contains a set of buildings, one constructed of masonry as fine as that used in the Sun Temple in Cuzco. In short, at Ollantaytambo elaborate waterworks were installed in the areas of finest architecture.

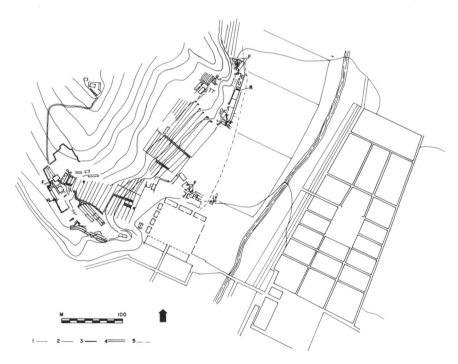

5.5. Plan of Ollantaytambo with fountains marked (F). The eastern side has a gridlike pattern. The monumental western sector has a surrounding wall and elaborate fine terracing. An upright flat rock (R) surrounded by a platform is found in the Incamisana sector. Redrawn from Gasparini and Margolies (1980: 69), with additions from Gibaja (1984).

A final example of a water system complementing an area of symbolic significance in the Cuzco area is found at the Inka settlement of Tipón (Angles Vargas 1978: 406–418), 16 kilometers southwest of Cuzco. Unfortunately, there are still no detailed published descriptions or accurate maps of the site. Tipón may have been a royal estate. The most notable aspect of Tipón is a set of twelve levels of terraces complete with elaborate channels and fountains (fig. 10.8). High above the terraces is a sector called *intiwatana*, with a large reservoir measuring about 40 by 25 meters in size. The sector contains buildings of high-quality stonework and a large outcrop set off by stone platforms (fig. 4.11). A remarkable Inka aqueduct carries water into the sector (fig. 5.6).

Water Systems throughout Tawantinsuyu
Throughout Tawantinsuyu Inka state settlements employed water-works such as fountains, baths, elaborate channels, and occasionally pools or reservoirs. They were generally not as common or as extensive as at some Cuzco-area settlements, but their similarity to those around Cuzco indicates that they were used for similar rituals.

The architectural importance of fine waterworks in the Cuzco area is undisputed. But how could water have become so sacred at sites far from the Inka homeland? Near the end of the sixteenth century, the priest Albornoz (1967: 21) wrote about this. He noted that water could be carried in a small container from a group's *pacarina* (often a water source) to a distant water source, where it would be poured with much ceremony. The new water source was thus endowed with the same importance as the old.

Water Systems at Three Administrative Centers
The administrative centers of Huánuco Pampa and Pumpu in Peru and Chilecito in Argentina are sufficiently intact to study their main waterworks in relation to site planning. Chapter 7 discusses how these settlements have a similar radial design. This may be related to their similarly arranged water systems. At Huánuco Pampa (Morris and Thompson 1985) water was taken from a small river on the southeastern side of the site to the inner part of the eastern sector denominated IIB (fig. 5.7). In describing sector IIB, Morris (1982: 163–164) writes that "no other buildings of residential dimension even approach such a high degree of architectural elaboration." With the exception of the center's *ushnu* platform, this is the only area with fine Cuzco masonry. Fine masonry is found in most of the sector's gateways, some of its buildings, and in a small "bath" (pool or tank). One canal led to the bath; the other to a much larger artificial pool nearby. They indicate that rituals connected

*5.6. The aqueduct (*lower right*) at Tipón conveys water across a depression to a sector dominated by an outcrop surrounded by a three-level platform (*center*).*

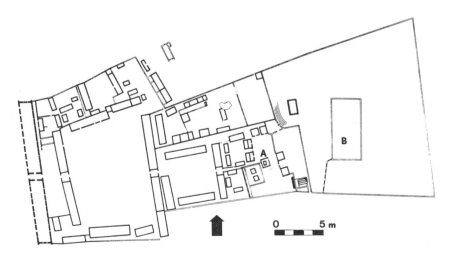

5.7. Sector IIB on the eastern side of Huánuco Pampa. A bath (A) and pool (B) are found in the innermost (western) part. The gateways leading to the waterworks are aligned with the ushnu *platform in the plaza to west. The patio enclosures were used for feasting. From Morris and Thompson (1985: 83).*

to water must have occurred within the sector. No canals apparently carried water to other parts of the site, so the exclusive use of fine waterworks in this sector adds to its importance—established by its large patios, fine masonry, and the gateways aligned with the *ushnu* platform in the plaza. The water-related architecture in sector IIB was not intended for the general use of the population. Entrance to the water facilities was through the entire series of gateways, where, it would appear, access was limited to special individuals.

Pumpu, the only other large intact Inka center in the central Andes, appears to have been designed with a layout purveying water to a ceremonial sector similar to Huánuco Pampa. At Pumpu a surface canal carries water through the large main plaza to the principal gateway on the site's eastern side (fig. 7.12). As at Huánuco Pampa, this gateway is aligned with the plaza's *ushnu* platform (fig. 3.20). Unfortunately, lack of excavation makes it impossible to discern what waterworks were present within the sector. This sector is of considerable if not primary significance, since it has the largest of all patios on the plaza (LeVine 1985: 210–221). Moreover, the only subterranean channels observed at Pumpu have been found in the eastern sector.[5] Thus the sectors fed by water at both Huánuco Pampa and Pumpu share characteristics: their location, on the eastern sides of their respective plazas; and an alignment with their respective *ushnu* platforms. Moreover, the largest patios on the plazas of both sites are found in their eastern sectors.

Another site with waterworks somewhat similar to Pumpu and Huánuco Pampa is Tambería del Inka (fig. 7.13), also known as Chilecito (Greslebin 1940), in La Rioja Province, Argentina. Located on a *barreal*, or alluvial fan, Chilecito is crossed from east to west by dry gullies (*torrenteras*), which have eaten into the alluvion. A canal led to one of them, and the gully became a stream that crossed the site from its northwest side along the north side of the rectangular plaza to the eastern side. The eastern side of Chilecito Plaza has the largest patios and buildings. The water was not directed toward a patio or enclosure, but passed beside the largest patio unit and apparently entered what appears to have been a pool, now indicated by a low depression. Chilecito's *ushnu* platform, located in the plaza, points toward the eastern side of the site. There is no visible main gateway on Chilecito's eastern side.

One might speculate that water distributed in the important eastern sectors of Pumpu, Huánuco Pampa, and Chilecito copies a Cuzco planning concept where special channels led to the Sun Temple. A major difference, however, is that the Sun Temple in Cuzco is not on the main plaza, but separated from it by some distance. In addition, Cuzco's Sun Temple lies to the southeast of the main plaza, not to the east.

Water directed to principal sectors on the eastern sides of sites might be detected with additional research at other Inka state settlements. At the sites of Shincal and Watungasta (Raffino et al. 1983–1985) in the province of Catamarca, Argentina, water also appears to have passed through the eastern sectors of their rectangular plazas. The eastern side of Watungasta is, however, poorly preserved, and Shincal has been only partially surveyed due to the heavy forest covering.

Water directed to similarly designed and oriented areas within settlements is not a generalized pattern. No known Inka military installation has similar waterworks. This may be due to the irregular topography where these sites are generally located. Nor do many settlements in the Cuzco area (with the possible exception of Chinchero), several of which were royal estates, follow this pattern. In addition, the water systems at several major Inka sites on the near south coast of Peru appear to be quite varied in their placement and design. This may reflect their locations in desert or dry terrain above irrigation channels that limited the possibilities for the delivery of water within the settlement.

Waterworks at Tomebamba

Most of the known remains of Tomebamba (fig. 5.8) are now covered by the modern city of Cuenca. Tomebamba was the second Inka capital, where Inka kings resided for considerable periods. This important settlement represented Cuzco because it often served as a capital. Perhaps because of this, there more than at any other known Inka settlement, numerous place-names from Cuzco are preserved (Arriaga 1922).

Even given the limited preservation of the settlement, there are indications that Inkas were intent on making waterworks an important part of its design. Not only is there a complex drainage system around the buildings, but there is evidence of a canal, only partially intact, within the main plaza. This canal is connected to a catchment and may have been part of a water system to supply the architecture called Puma Pungo on the southern side of the plaza (Idrovo 1984: 233–236).

To the south of Puma Pungo, beside the Tomebamba River, the Inkas built a pool, sustained by an earth dyke, which drained into a broad channel (fig. 5.9) that ran parallel to the river before draining into it (Idrovo 1984: 277–288). This large channel includes a catchment or bath built about midway along its course. The eastern side of Tomebamba has never been excavated and is now covered by modern buildings. There, Uhle (1923) believed that a Sun Temple may have been located, but his evidence was based only on a toponym. On the other hand, excavations at Tomebamba by Idrovo (1984: 127–130) reveal that the Sun Temple may be a set of structures (only partially seen by Uhle), including a semi-circular structure, on the cliffs overlooking a major drain, pool, and the

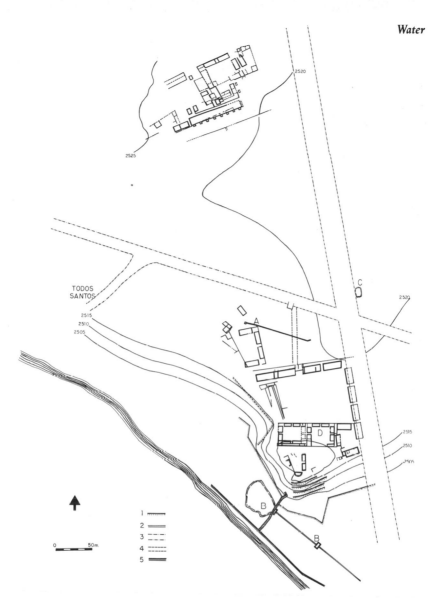

5.8. Plan of the known buildings and compounds at Tomebamba, the second Inka capital. Only a small portion of Tomebamba is depicted here, since most of the settlement is covered by the city Cuenca. A canal and water catchment are found in the plaza area (A). More elaborate waterworks (B), including a pool, canal, and bath, are found between the southern buildings and the Tomebamba River. A possible ushnu *platform (C), no longer in existence, was identified by Uhle. Recent excavations have revealed an* aqllawasi *(D) in a* kancha *in the southern zone known as Puma Pungo. The Huatana stream (not depicted) passed north of the northernmost compound. Key: 1. elaborate terraces; 2. canal; 3. modern street; 4. Inka road; 5. river barrier wall. Reconstructed primarily from plans by Uhle (1923), with some additions from a plan by Francisco Ochoa U. of the Proyecto Arqueológico Pumapungo, courtesy J. Idrovo.*

5.9. *Model of the southern sector of Tomebamba. An artificial pool drained into a canal with a large catchment or bath midway in its course. A set of four walls protects the lower terrain from the Tomebamba River.*

Tomebamba River. Thus the principal waterworks of Tomebamba may be closely associated with the main religious buildings on the southern side of the settlement.

Idrovo (1984: 117–127) has noted a similarity in the river systems of Cuzco and Tomebamba. He points out that the central sector of each city is enclosed by streams running from the northwest to the southeast. In both cases they come together after passing the main urbanized area. The northernmost stream at Tomebamba is called Huatana, a name that recalls Cuzco's Huatanay River.[6]

Could Tomebamba's location have been selected because of its river system's similarity to that at Cuzco? Do other Inka state settlements have a similar river pattern? Tomebamba's river pattern may mirror that of Cuzco, but my surveys at other Inka sites throughout the Andes have not produced convincing evidence that their locations have river patterns like those of Cuzco. Indeed, the Inka skill at building canals was such that they could often modify or supply water to varied locations selected for other reasons. Only one quite distinct case comes to mind, which may demonstrate that a natural hydrological phenomenon was instrumental in choosing a site's location. It is the large Inka fortress of Incallacta (fig. 6.18), where, on the western side, a waterfall (fig. 5.10) several stories high has been integrated into the settlement's planning. It is such an impressive feature that one cannot help wondering whether it was not a significant factor in the selection of that installation's location.

Water and the Social Structure of Settlements

Sherbondy (1982*a*) demonstrates how water sources and their canals are a critical element for understanding the design of the Inka state's *zeque* system (chap. 2). This in turn allows us to understand more about Inka social structure, since various *ayllu* and *panaqa* had access to water, and the land it irrigated in accord with their social hierarchy. The physical design of Cuzco, at least as far as its halves are concerned, appears to relate directly to different water sources. The *hanan*, or upper part, of Cuzco was situated closest to the higher and more desirable water sources. This pattern continues even today in some Andean communities, where the *hanan*, or upper half, is linked to preferential water sources. This point is critical for anyone studying settlement design, because it suggests that one tactic for determining bi- and even quadripartition of major Inka state installations may be resolved by an analysis of their nearby water systems.

The significance of this concept rests on there being little doubt that

5.10. A waterfall within the western side of the fortress Incallacta.

143

many Inka settlements, like Andean communities today, were conceived of as being in two parts, sometimes subdivided into two others. Nevertheless, few investigations at Inka settlements have attempted to understand their design using this Andean conceptual framework. These fundamental divisions probably had much to do with who occupied them and with how and when those people performed certain social obligations.

Based on the Cuzco data, one might hypothesize that the primary water source for an Inka settlement was accessible to the *hanan* division first, and the *hurin* division second. Each division would be closest to the adjoining agricultural lands utilizing the water. Such a pattern would be best detected by the distribution of water outside of the area of architecture, where the waters were used for agricultural activities. This hypothesis is simplistic at best, since some Inka centers are located in areas where irrigation activities were nonexistent or very limited. Moreover, as discussed in chapter 7, there were other factors besides water used by Inka site planners for determining a settlement's divisions.

Does the location of elaborate waterworks within a state settlement help determine its divisions? As noted in chapter 7, attempts to define those divisions at Huánuco Pampa (Morris 1980a) and at Inkawasi (Hyslop 1985) find the waterworks in the *hanan* division. In both those cases, however, the *hanan-hurin* division was defined by an analysis considering data other than the water system.

As noted earlier, in Cuzco-area sites, water is often delivered to an area of elaborate architecture, and one could speculate that the *hanan* divisions of these sites included such sectors. Before jumping to conclusions, however, we must remember that a number of the Cuzco-area sites were Inka royal estates, and it is not known if *hanan* and *hurin* divisions were always part of their design. It is more probable that such divisions were present in administrative centers and, probably, in the larger military installations, which may be more complete representations of the complexities Inkas introduced into settlement design. Moreover, historical sources tell of Inkas building "other Cuzcos" or "new Cuzcos" only in regions away from the Inka heartland (chap. 11).

One idea emerges in Latcham's analysis (1928: 193–211) of the multiple and complex meaning of the dual division (called *saya*) as regards how it was handled in regions outside Cuzco. The *hanan* division was representative of peoples directly related to Cuzco, such as Inkas themselves or loyal *mitmaq*, whereas the *hurin* division was associated with non-Inka peoples who were native or original inhabitants.[7] Research might reveal whether evidence within Inka state settlements indicates that Inka influence was stronger in *hanan* sectors and weaker in sectors considered *hurin*. None of this can be achieved, however, until a number of criteria are developed for discerning how that dual division is represented in the archaeological remains, a subject discussed in chapter 7. Water, because of its great importance in Inka economic life and religion, its clear association with Cuzco's dual division, is an important aspect of this complex puzzle.

Summary

Water systems in Inka settlements in the Cuzco area and elsewhere had the utilitarian functions of supplying water and draining rain. In addition, much energy was devoted to constructing elaborate waterworks (baths, canals, fountains), which had a symbolic role in Inka religion. Many aspects of Inka and Andean religion, and myths about the origins of Andean peoples, place water in a sacred context. Thus the fine waterworks in Inka architectural planning are closely related to ritual activities.

From the standpoint of planning and layout, the elaborate waterworks are generally found not only in elaborate agricultural terraces, but in sectors where one finds the most elaborate architecture. Patterns created by water systems, as viewed through a comparative analysis of numerous settlements, cannot yet be determined with great accuracy, since water systems are often poorly defined, even in mapped and excavated sites. An important aspect of water management in and near settlements is that it may be important for determining dual divisions (and subdivisions) within sites. Whereas understanding how these material remains express these divisions is still inconclusive, continued research of water systems should allow us to understand more closely some of the concepts used by Inka architects.

6
Military Settlements

One could argue that almost every large Inka settlement in the Andes was used for military purposes, since at some time or another each probably marshaled or housed troops and stored foodstuffs and military supplies. Nevertheless, some building complexes stand out for their clear military role. This chapter will discuss how these sites are identified and examine their contribution to an understanding of Inka architectural planning. It will also discuss reasons why and where military installations were built and make some new observations on how Inka military architecture contributes to an understanding of Inka warfare.

Some of the most notable architectural complexes created by the Inkas were military installations. They incorporate several of the planning concepts used in other settlements. Nevertheless, military sites are inevitably different. Many Inka settlements were "military" only in part, or only for a phase of their existence. It is simplistic to think that the Inkas always isolated military activities in specific sites. For example, it is probable that early in their existence some administrative centers fulfilled military requirements, particularly while they were located near expanding Inka frontiers. As the state expanded they probably assumed a less military role (Morris 1982: 160). In still other cases, military complexes became obsolete after nearby areas were conquered, and these complexes were subsequently abandoned or closed down (Hyslop 1985: 8–13). At some forts in eastern Bolivia, and even in some of the sites in the Urubamba Valley near Cuzco, military architecture is but a part of a settlement where many other activities took place. Inkas also reoccupied some military installations built by local peoples, and thus this warfare-related architecture is Inka only because they later occupied the site.

Inka Warfare
Few descriptions of Inka warfare incorporate archaeological evidence. Syntheses of historical data by Rowe (1946: 274–282), Urteaga (1919–

1920), Spurling (1982), Bram (1977), Rawls (1979: 119–156), Murra (1986), Quiroga I. (1962), and Rostworowski (1988: 95–136) mention only in passing that such installations existed. It is not unusual that syntheses of Inka militarism have barely mentioned this evidence, even though Inka forts were described by Jijón y Caamaño, Bingham, Lange, Larrabure y Unanue, and Nordenskiöld before 1920. The data in these obscure publications are so diverse that they are difficult to compare.

Thus while available syntheses omit information derived from archaeological reports, they are filled with data from early historical accounts about Inka military organization. Spurling (1982: 2) has noted that many of the first reports were by Spanish soldiers who not only were professionally interested in Inka war tactics, but were concerned with understanding them for their own survival. Thus there is plenty of information about weapons, fighting techniques, and supply systems. There are no good detailed accounts, however, of Inka fortress building or battles strictly between Andean peoples employing native strategies and weapons.

This is not the place to summarize ethnohistorical data on Inka warfare, but rather to extract some relevant points that elucidate the nature of military settlements. It is important to point out that Inka armies were composed primarily of non-Inka peoples serving their *mita*, or labor obligation. Their training was limited and their weapons (clubs, slings, lances, spear throwers, *boleadoras*, and bows) were primitive (Urteaga 1919–1920) by sixteenth-century European standards. Ethnic groups were kept together in part because they were often led by their own leaders and because different groups specialized in or were familiar with various weapons. Units were organized according to many of the same principles employed in the organization of the state itself. That is, in large campaigns, units were marshaled according to their *suyu*, and the decimal system was employed to create units of ten, fifty, one hundred, five hundred, or one thousand men. Within ethnic units the dual division, or moiety system, was maintained. Military campaigns often used three armies, a type of tripartition (Rostworowski 1988: 120, 131).

Although some ethnic leaders could and did rise to high rank in the Inka armies, the Inkas were ultimately in control of military activities. Generally, the Inka king or his half-brothers or sons were the commanders. Their military training appears to have been more substantial than that of the farmers and herders making up the bulk of the army. Young Inka males learned from experienced officers, initiation rites, and by participating in ritual battles.

A particularly important aspect of military organization was the use of both Inka and loyal non-Inka colonists (*mitmaq*), whose military duties involved manning forts or garrisons and making weapons. The link between the Inka political and military systems is evident in cases where it is known that the Inka governor, or *toricoq*, was directly in charge of the *mitmaq*. Sometimes this is expressed by the fact that leaders of the *mitmaq* were the main political authorities in a zone. There is ample evidence for the privileged position of *mitmaq* (Bram 1977: 57–59). They were given land and presents from the state and carried out surveillance on the local population. Apparently, local peoples often disliked *mitmaq* planted in their midst, considering them spies.[1]

Inka warfare techniques and technology were not purely Inka inventions. Murra (1986: 50) writes that Inka strategies must have been affected by the "centuries of *auca runa*, the age of soldiers, a time of wars" described by Guaman Poma and a few other chroniclers. Archaeological studies have now demonstrated that prior to the Inka expansion peoples throughout the Andes built fortified installations and towns. The lack of political unification in the Andes led to much intergroup warfare, since there is hardly a region in Tawantinsuyu without evidence of local military architecture.[2] Murra concludes (1986: 50) that the *Pax Incaica* regulated *auca runa* violence and redirected it to Tawantinsuyu's periphery.

Finally, there can be no doubt about the important role of religion in Inka warfare. Indeed, the two were so closely linked in Andean thought that they are difficult to separate. Rowe (1946: 280) writes:

> religion was used to justify the Inca conquest, on the pretext that the purest and highest form of religion was the Inca way of worshiping the Creator, the sky gods, and the place spirits, and that it was the Inca's duty to spread this religion throughout the world. It is difficult to state this claim without making it sound like an echo of crusading Christianity, but there is small doubt of its aboriginal character.

Thus many rituals were associated with military activities. Bram (1977: 83–85) and Spurling (1982), citing various early sources (Acosta, Cieza de León, Cobo, Guaman Poma, Molina, Polo, and Sarmiento), note that rituals and divinations guided and accompanied almost every step taken before, during, and after a military campaign. Portable sacred objects were carried to war. Rites were performed and offerings made to strengthen the Inkas' efforts as well as to diminish those of the enemy. Children and llamas were sacrificed and valuable goods ritually destroyed. Favorable auguries were necessary before important steps were taken, and the timing of important events was tied to astrological considerations.[3]

There is debate about whether the Inka expansion was driven more by economic or other motives. Conrad (1981: 18–19) has pointed out how the inheritance rules of Inka dynastic succession required each ruler to amass new properties and were therefore an important cause (but not the only one) of military expansion. Others express different points of view. Rostworowski (1988: 71) argues that the Andean reciprocity system, which required great generosity on the part of Inka kings to the *panaqa* and local lords, was a factor requiring a constant increase of state production and wealth. These growing needs are, for Rostworowski, the important factor propelling the state's expansion. Rowe (1946: 274) has noted other motives for war, such as glory and personal advancement of successful soldiers and captains. He notes that the Inka nobility was already wealthy, and that economic motives may not have been strong, adding, "Many of the conquered provinces were so poor at first they were economic liabilities rather than assets." It is indeed difficult to comment with certainty on why the Inkas built an empire. The archaeological evidence discussed below relates most directly to Inka military policies and strategies. Whereas it does not explain the cause of empire, it does add new dimensions about how Tawantinsuyu was formed, maintained, and defended.

Resettlement as a Military and Governing Strategy

Inkas established new settlements for a variety of reasons. Some were built as part of Inka resettlement policies. The true scope of these population movements is not yet known, since no attempt has been made to synthesize all of the relevant available historical and archaeological evidence. It is possible that the Inka resettlement of people equaled or exceeded that of the later Spanish viceregal administration, whose policy moved outlying populations into towns where the collection of tribute and the catechism of Indians could be controlled.

The Andean highland regions provide ample evidence for resettlement. As noted previously, the period prior to Inka domination was characterized by much warfare. A typical pre-Inka settlement was the walled hilltop town. A variant was a settlement with a nearby high, defended position to which local populations could withdraw in time of war (fig. 6.1). The Inka state histories often list, along with conquests, the local forts that were seized as well as a few that were then constructed (Rowe 1985). The danger of subject populations dwelling in their fortress towns was not lost to Inka planners, whose major objective was to neutralize local fortified settlements.

There were two forms of Inka resettlement: resettlement of people far from their home territory, and resettlement of people within their traditional area. The first is demonstrated by the *mitmaq* policy. In most regions of Tawantinsuyu there is evidence (either archaeological or historical, or both) that state colonists (*mitmaq*) were used. The reasons for instituting the *mitmaq* policy were in part military, since it was sometimes used to break up rebellious ethnic groups such as the Cañari (Ecuador) or people from the Chachapoyas area (northern Peru) and to remove people from their fortified towns.

The chronicler Sarmiento de Gamboa (1965: 244, chap. 39) indicates that the Inka king himself was responsible for important decisions such as the destruction of local (non-Inka) fortresses and the strategic movement of peoples:

> [Pachakuti Inka Yupanki] designated people to go to the subject provinces and examine them and to make clay models of them. And such was done. And the models and descriptions were placed before the Inka, who examined them and considered the plains and fortresses. He ordered the investigators to watch well what he was doing. Then he began to level the fortresses he wished, and moved those inhabitants to lower land. And he moved those of the plains to the heights and mountains, each so far from the others and so from their natural [land] that they could not return to it. . . . [The investigators] went and carried this out.

6.1. *A drawing in Guaman Poma's seventeenth-century chronicle (1936: f. 63) depicts Andean warfare before the Inkas. One group attacks another in a fortress.*

The *mitmaq* policy sent loyal peoples (from the Cuzco area or else-where) to regions of uncertain loyalty, where they manned (Inka) forts and watched over local populations.[4] But the *mitmaq* policy was also nonmilitary, or military only in that it made for good political management from an economic standpoint. Thus *mitmaq* were also removed from overpopulated zones or zones of low agricultural productivity. They were sent to underpopulated areas, or to areas from which local peoples had been removed, where extensive agricultural development was a state objective. Such was the case of the Cochabamba Valley in Bolivia (Wachtel 1980–1981).

Perhaps equally important, but less apparent in the historical sources, was the policy of resettling people within their own traditional region. It is still unclear whether resettlement of local peoples in their own region occurred throughout the Inka state. This was apparently not the case in many areas of the desert coast and northwest Argentina, where there is ample evidence that many pre-Inka settlements continued to be inhabited in Inka times.

The chronicler Cieza de León describes a resettlement policy of people in their own area. His commentary (1967: 82–83, chap. 24) relates specifically to Qollasuyu:

> In former times, before the Inkas reigned, it is well understood
> that the natives of these provinces had no towns, as is now the
> case, but only strong places with forts, which they call *pucaras*,
> whence they came forth to make war one with another; and so
> they always passed their time, living in great trouble and unrest.
> The Inkas, reigning over them, considered their manner of living
> to be bad and induced them, partly by threats and partly by favors,
> to see the wisdom of ceasing to live like savages, but rather as
> reasonable beings, establishing themselves in towns, both on the
> plains and slopes of the mountains, and settling on the land ac-
> cording to the regulations that were made.

Archaeological confirmation of the movement of people out of for-tified settlements into lower areas has been obtained in the Lupaqa area, southwest of Lake Titicaca. There, walled hilltop towns were aban-doned at the beginning of Inka times and new settlements were es-tablished on the Inka road running along the lower area near the lake (Hyslop 1976: 99–199, 1977a, 1979). The new towns included Chu-cuito, a leading Inka administrative center. Similar archaeological evidence has been described for the Jauja area in central Peru (Browman 1970: 247; Earle et al. 1980: 21, 35). Here, only one very large pre-Inka settlement continued in Inka times, but most walled sites were abandoned. A new administrative center, Hatun Xauxa, was constructed in the valley floor on the Inka road. The Inka period settlements are more accessible, and "the decrease in concern over defense indicated that, perhaps not surprisingly, the incorporation of the region into the Inca state led to a reduction of intergroup conflict, and a desire by the Inca to limit potential rebellion by settling population outside of fortified centers" (Earle et al. 1980: 40).

Thus in two areas of the Andes archaeological settlement pattern studies confirm the general statements of Sarmiento and Cieza de León that fortified settlements were abandoned while new, more accessible, and less-threatening settlements were founded. Detailed settlement pattern studies are needed elsewhere in the Andes to confirm how generalized this Inka policy was.

Identifying Military Architecture

Defensive walls surrounding an Inka settlement or some of its important buildings are frequently proof of a site's military role. As noted in chapter 1, Inka architects often enclosed important buildings and complexes of rooms within walls. An unsophisticated observer may conclude that wherever such walls occur there was a concern with defense. Such an interpretation is also supported by elaborate terracing in the Cuzco area, often found on the edge of architectural areas. These terraces augment the "defensive" nature of a settlement because of the high retaining walls. Thus an unresolved debate begun by Bingham early in the century (1911, 1930) about the supposed military role of sites in the lower Urubamba Valley area such as Ollantaytambo and Machu Picchu has continued for decades.

MacLean (1986: 83–86) discusses and compares the enclosure walls at sites in the Machu Picchu area, concluding that they served a number of purposes, none of them specifically military. In some cases a wall may simply stabilize a promontory where buildings are located. In others, they appear to separate "an encoded landscape from simple environment." In yet other cases the walls express the exclusivity of a sector, denoting privacy or access to a zone limited to specific groups of people. Finally, walls and control points such as those found at Machu Picchu are "probably most appropriately interpreted as normal protective measures for an important installation rather than as defense against a serious threat of attack." Her arguments are persuasive, but not likely to end the debate once and for all, particularly at a site like Ollantaytambo (fig. 6.2), which was actually selected and used by the Inkas as a fortress in the uprising against the Spanish. One should note the Inka preoccupation with invasion by lowland peoples on much of

6.2. A tall wall surrounds part of Ollantaytambo in the Urubamba Valley, Peru. One can debate whether such a wall was defensive or was used to delimit a special area.

the state's frontier. In the early days of the Inka state the Urubamba Valley was near a frontier.[5]

Controlled access via walls, terraces, and gates indicates major sanctuaries as well as military installations. At Raqchi (Ballesteros 1981: 10), south of Cuzco, there was a major temple to Wirakocha. The settlement is surrounded by a wall. Farther from Cuzco, one might add the walls reported by Bandelier (1910: 215–216, 282) at the sanctuary in Lake Titicaca. One wall enclosed the entrance to the Copacabana area at a neck of the peninsula; another wall and terraces isolated the all-important northern end of the Island of the Sun, where the great plaza, sacred rock, and Sun Temple were located (chap. 3). At Pachacamac, the principal Inka sanctuary on the Pacific coast, high terraces and walls delimit the Sun Temple and its associated *aqllawasi,* the Painted Building (chap. 9).

Debate about military versus the protective or symbolic role of walls will probably continue, particularly at settlements where there is little or no historical evidence for the area's political and military situation.

Such a case is demonstrated by the site Chilecito (fig. 7.13) in La Rioja Province, Argentina. Although the site was probably an administrative center, and its layout is similar to other central Andean centers, one cannot discount the possibility that its surrounding wall had a military function, particularly since Chilecito rests on an Inka border, threatened by invasion from pampas Indians. The military nature of Chilecito's surrounding wall is made more plausible by the presence of interior platforms (Greslebin 1940: 12). Such platforms are common in the surrounding walls of Inka fortresses in southern Tawantinsuyu (see below).

Thus walls surrounding sites or architectural complexes are not proof in and of themselves of direct military concerns. Additional evidence is necessary to define which sites were built primarily for defense, vigilance, or attack. This evidence comes primarily from early historical sources that, in a few cases, identify specific sites as being primarily military. No doubt, part of the archaeological puzzle defining military sites will be supplied by the analysis of a site's location within a local, defensive topography. Inka forts are often situated differently from administrative centers. They are not located directly on main Inka roads, but rather in defensive positions on hills or mountaintops. However, such a location is not necessarily a characteristic of Inka military installations. The garrison Inkawasi (described below), in the Cañete Valley (Hyslop 1985: 34–35), is situated strategically, but not on a hilltop. Its military location becomes apparent only after one considers its location within a regional perspective and understands the Inka military strategy to launch attacks against the lower Cañete Valley—Huarco.

The identification of military settlements is compounded by a curious lack of evidence of arms in the few sites that have been excavated or where extensive surface collections have been made.[6] Since almost no military sites have been excavated intensively, this may be a reflection of incomplete data. On the other hand, perhaps weapons were too valuable to be discarded in any quantity, or if they were, it was in battle and not actually within military complexes. In addition, much Inka military paraphernalia was made of perishable materials: quilted "armor," wood clubs, and braided slings.

Other evidence for military activities might include the presence of buildings frequently used for transient housing (for soldiers), such as long halls, or *kallanka*. Indeed, these are often found at Inka forts (e.g., Incallacta, Pucará de Andalgalá, Pambamarca), but some small fortifications do not have them. *Kallanka* are not necessarily diagnostic of military activities, since they are also found in *tampu* and administrative centers.

It has been noted that cemeteries are often not found in some Inka administrative centers outside of the Cuzco area (Morris 1972: 396; Hyslop 1979: 74). This has been explained by the temporary presence of the people who worked in the centers. They returned to their homes after their obligations had been fulfilled. Cemeteries at Pambamarca in Ecuador, Inkawasi in Cañete, Peru, and Cerro Chena near Santiago, Chile, provide evidence that people there may have died in warfare. Thus cemeteries in or near possible military installations may offer additional clues for determining war-related activities. Cemeteries alone are not clear indicators of military activities, since Inka artifacts are frequently found in local cemeteries throughout the Andes. In many cases, however, these Inka objects appear to have been buried with important local people as signs of prestige.

Finally, it is clear that many temporary military settlements may never be detected by archaeological tactics. The first Spaniards to view an Inka army (Xérez 1970: 69) saw cotton tents pitched over a league (approximately 5 kilometers) of terrain near the administrative center of Cajamarca in northern Peru. Thus it is apparent that permanent architecture was not always used to house a large army, particularly when it was on the move or involved in short campaigns. No such military camp-site has ever been identified by archaeologists, although this should not be entirely impossible, given the refuse that an army of thousands might leave after a short stay. The Inka use of tent camps suggests that permanent military installations were built only where there were ongoing or long-term military concerns. It also helps explain why in some parts of Tawantinsuyu there is still limited archaeological evidence for military installations.

The Distribution of Military Settlements

Why are Inka military sites concentrated in some areas and not in others? The following assessment is somewhat speculative. This is partly due to the difficulty of determining which sites are military and to the limited archaeological survey carried out in many areas, particularly on the eastern Inka frontier stretching from Bolivia to Ecuador. Moreover, there is little hope that ethnohistorical research alone can address the question, since available sources cover only certain areas and frequently do not mention forts and garrisons. Nevertheless, archaeological evidence permits at least a glimpse at military site concentrations and their significance.

In Chile, directly south of Santiago, only one, and possibly two, Inka military sites have been identified. Stehberg's careful evaluation (1976: 7–9, 33–35) of possible forts in the Santiago area and to the south suggests that there was never a great concentration of military sites in that region, although this is possibly contradicted by several Inka state histories, which emphasize the importance of military campaigns south to the Maule and Biobío rivers. The location of fortifications is intimately linked to the greater problem of the southernmost Inka frontier (Silva G. 1977–1978, 1983; Hyslop 1984: 212). It now appears that the Maipo River just south of Santiago formed the southern Inka border beyond which state institutions were not introduced. Inka incursions farther south undoubtedly took place, but the Inka affiliation of small forts there (Collipuemo and La Muralla—see below) has not been proven.

Were the walled settlements in the Atacama area of Chile constructed for military reasons? Uhle (1917: 155–157) regarded the sites of Lasana, Chuichui, and possibly Turi as such. It now appears, however, that these walled settlements were built before the Inkas (Mostny 1949; Carlos Aldunate, personal communication, 1987).

On the Argentine side of the Andes, there is no archaeological evidence for military constructions in the extreme south of Tawantinsuyu. One historical reference mentions a fort named Huentota in the province of Mendoza (Canals Frau 1946: 142–146), but it has never been found by archaeologists. It appears that the peaceful Huarpe living in the provinces of Mendoza and San Juan were only minimally affected by the Inka intrusion, and thus evidence for military activities here is notably lacking.

Farther north in Argentina, in the provinces of La Rioja, Catamarca, and Tucumán, there is some evidence for military constructions along the Inka frontier, an area where the mountains meet the dry pampas and jungle of Tucumán. In La Rioja there is the walled settlement Chilecito (chap. 7), in Catamarca the impressive fortress of Pucará de Andalgalá (see below), and in Tucumán the site of Nevados de Aconquija, which almost certainly had a military role, although it may also have been a major sanctuary (chap. 3). Given the extensive surveys carried out in these provinces in the last decades, it is not likely that many additional military sites will be located.

In the Argentine provinces of Salta and Jujuy, the identification of military sites becomes more complex, since Inkas occasionally occupied pre-Inka settlements, some of which had some defensive walls or were located on hilltops. It is questionable whether these pre-Inka fortifications were ever used in Inka times (e.g., Punta de Balasto, Fuerte Quemado, Quilmes). In other cases, the hilltops chosen for settlements may have been selected for reasons other than defense (e.g., Tilcara and Yacorite in the Humahuaca Valley, Jujuy Province).[7] The Cortaderas site (Hyslop 1984: 175–177) in Salta Province is a relatively good candidate for a military installation, since it combines a lower site with Inka architecture and artifacts with a walled hilltop with stones laid in the Inka manner. Since Cortaderas is not on an eastern Inka frontier, it may have marked an earlier southern boundary during Inka expansion.[8] In short, Salta and Jujuy provide little evidence for Inka military installations. It is possible that the Inkas relied on fortified hilltops built in pre-Inka times, but this must be confirmed.

In Bolivia there is no secure evidence for Inka fortifications in the northern high plateau or in the mountainous regions west of the eastern frontier. The southernmost known Inka fortress appears to be Condorhuasi (Schmieder 1924), lying west-northwest of Tarija. Schmieder (1926: 114–117) lists three other possible forts near Tarija, but not enough is known to determine if they are Inka. Somewhat to the north

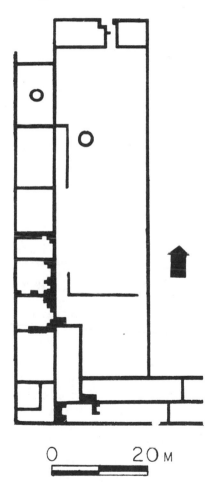

0   20 M

6.3. The main compound at Oroncota in Bolivia. Unfinished walls in the south indicate that the structure was never completed. Adapted from Walter (1959: 337).

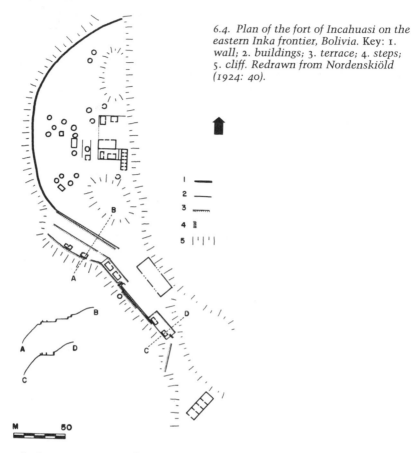

6.4. *Plan of the fort of Incahuasi on the eastern Inka frontier, Bolivia. Key: 1. wall; 2. buildings; 3. terrace; 4. steps; 5. cliff. Redrawn from Nordenskiöld (1924: 40).*

one finds Oroncota on the Pilcomayo River (Walter 1959). It is located about 70 kilometers southeast of Sucre on a high plateau about 3,300 meters above sea level.[9] The main compound at Oroncota is approximately 30 by 90 meters (fig. 6.3). Parts of it are of worked and fitted stone, which approximates fine Cuzco masonry. The compound may not have been finished. Approximately 100 kilometers east of Oroncota near the community of Lagunillas one finds the fortress of Incahuasi (fig. 6.4), mapped and described by Nordenskiöld (1924: 43–46). It is uncertain if there are other fortresses in the eastern Bolivian Andes south of 19 degrees south latitude. Given that almost no archaeological survey has taken place there in decades, great surprises may await those willing to reconnoiter that isolated zone.

Between about 17 and 18 degrees south latitude there is a considerable concentration of Inka military sites close to where the Andes meet the Amazonian lowlands. At least six sites have been located and reported by Nordenskiöld (1924), Ahlfeld (1933), and investigators from the Archaeological Museum of the university in Cochabamba (Byrne de Caballero 1979, n.d.; Sanzetenea 1975 b). They include the sites of Incallacta (see below) and Samaipata (chap. 4).[10] The Inka forts were apparently overrun by Guaraní peoples (often collectively called Chiriguanos) sometime in the 1520s (Saignes 1985: 20, 26–28; Nordenskiöld 1917).

As one proceeds northwest to the Peruvian border on the Andean slopes northeast of the Cordillera Real, there are no published archaeological data confirming any military installations. There is no doubt about Inka control over the area, which reached into the region of the upper Beni River, and forts are mentioned in some early sources (Saignes 1985: 18).

As one proceeds northwest along the eastern Inka frontier into Peru and Ecuador, evidence for Inka fortifications diminishes. It is impossible to say whether this apparent absence of sites is due in part to a lack of archaeological survey (not easy on the jungle slopes), or to social and political circumstances that may have made it less necessary to fortify the boundary.

In the area north and west of Cuzco, where considerable exploration has taken place, there is no certain evidence that the border was fortified. Some Inka settlements there may have had a military role, but are not generally so interpreted. Bingham (1911: 522) suggested that sites such as Choqquequirau and Inkahuasi[11]—located on opposing sides of the Apurimac River (Wiener 1880: 293–295)—defended the Apurimac region from encroaching Amazonian peoples, just as Ollantaytambo defended the approach up the Urubamba River. To this Bingham (1930) would add Machu Picchu, which he considered a "citadel," but which he had not discovered when he first advanced his idea. He also included Paucartambo, northwest of Cuzco, thus defining a line of possible military sites facing the Amazonian lowlands. His proposition has not been generally accepted because, as noted earlier, the walls and high terraces of some of these sites may not have been constructed for defensive purposes.

For the Apurimac River north to Ecuador there are no published archaeological descriptions of fortifications or garrisons on the eastern Inka border, which, in several areas, has not even been effectively identified (Hyslop 1988). The Ortiz inspection of 1567 (1972: 25, 34, 40, 50, 177) mentions forts in the Chupaychu region manned by *mitmaq* from Cuzco. Although the installations (not yet located by archaeologists) were situated relatively near the eastern Inka border, their role was to watch over the local Chupaychu Indians as well as to guard against intrusions.

Inka state histories and some local historical sources describe lengthy campaigns against the rebellious Chachapoyas region on the eastern Inka border (Schjellerup 1979–1980, 1984), in what is today northern Peru. *Mitmaq* were taken from the area and replaced by more loyal *mitmaq* but nothing is known about military installations. In short, given the defiant stance of the Chachapoyas region, the Inkas may have built military sites there, but they have not yet been located.

This discussion on the distribution of Inka military sites in Peru has only addressed those on the eastern frontier. Equally complex is the question of whether installations were built within the Inka territory of present-day Peru. The garrison of Inkawasi in the Cañete Valley is one of the few that have been identified.[12] Given the extensive archaeological work done in Peru, why have more Inka military installations not been identified? Many of the campaigns were rapid, not requiring the construction of forts and garrisons. Moreover, the proximity of most Peruvian territory to Cuzco, and the constant movement of armies to Ecuadorian territory (where campaigns lasting decades took place), made it possible to send troops rapidly to any rebellious area. Zones lacking military sites may never have needed them. Bram (1977: 50–53) and Rostworowski (1988: 100–105, 132), in fact, marshal historical evidence indicating that much Inka expansion was done through diplomacy—and never required warfare.

In a few cases fortified pre-Inka settlements may have been used. Since these sites generally are identified as pre-Inka, Inka components may not have been identified. Whatever the case, one suspects that there were few military sites constructed by the Inkas in Peruvian territory away from the eastern Inka border.

Two Inka "forts" in Peruvian territory may be military installations in appearance only: Paramonga (Langlois 1933) on the coast north near Pativilca, and Ungará (Harth-Terré 1933; Hyslop 1985: 41–43) in the Cañete Valley (figs. 6.5, 6.6). Both were occupied in Inka times. Paramonga, built with Inka adobe bricks, may be purely an Inka construction, although there is some debate. Ungará was constructed by local peoples and probably served to defend the Cañete Valley against Inka attack. Ungará has an *ushnu*-like square platform on its highest point, similar to Inka forts in Ecuador. One might question whether these magnificent constructions were ever used for military purposes, since they are in areas where, after their original subjugation, no military activities are known to have taken place. Paramonga, with its five tiers of high terrace walls, has only four small rooms on its summit. Its high terrace "walls" and restricted gateways might be compared to the Temple of the Sun at Pachacamac (chap. 10). Likewise, Paramonga may be primarily a religious complex. Ungará's occupation by the Inkas may have been primarily symbolic—a highly visible demonstration of Inka domination.

In Ecuador, Inka military constructions abound. They are no doubt a manifestation of the lengthy and costly military campaigns that occupied much of the time and energies of Thupa Inka and Wayna Qhapaq (Larrea 1965). High, walled fortresses, occasionally identified as such in early historical sources, are found in generally east-west tiers across the highlands, perhaps indicating successive waves of conquest (Antonio Fresco, personal communication, 1986). Several installations are located in the Azuay Mountains north of Tomebamba (modern Cuenca) but have not been studied in any detail (Reinoso 1971). Two or three lines of forts are located north of Quito (see Pambamarca, below). One line is in Pichincha; another in Imbabura; the third may be in Carchi. Sketch maps of several are published by Plaza Schuller (1976, ca. 1980) and Oberem (1968). Ongoing investigations by archaeologists of the Central Bank of Ecuador promise to clarify much about these sites.

6.5. *The so-called fort of Paramonga north of Lima, Peru. Five high terrace walls surround a summit with only four rooms. Courtesy Department of Library Services, AMNH, Neg. no. 334862 (photo by Shippee Johnson).*

In summary, if the known concentrations of military sites are any reflection of the degree of long-term Inka military activities, the above data indicate the following. First, military activities in the Santiago, Chile, area appear minimal when compared to some other areas. Second, the great concentrations in Ecuador indicate that of all parts of Tawantinsuyu, it was the most heavily militarized. This is suggested by the historical sources and is confirmed archaeologically. Third, the second-greatest concentration of forts lies in the Bolivian *oriente*, indicating great fear of invasion by Amazonian and Chaco peoples. Fourth, the eastern Inka border in Argentina was fortified by only a few installations, and on its southern extreme there may not have been any. Finally, the apparent paucity of Inka military sites in much of Tawantinsuyu may be due in part to a lack of field investigation, but perhaps is also due to factors such as proximity to roads—which could deliver armies rapidly from one quarter to the other—and to the fact that many subject peoples simply were not rebellious. It is also due to the swift nature of many conquests (Rostworowski 1988: 104–105), during which there was neither time nor need for fortress building.

6.6. *Aerial view to the south over the Ungará fortress in the Cañete Valley, Peru. This installation was seized and occupied by the Inkas. A rectangular platform is located on the summit. Courtesy Department of Library Services, AMNH, Neg. no. 334747 (photo by Shippee Johnson).*

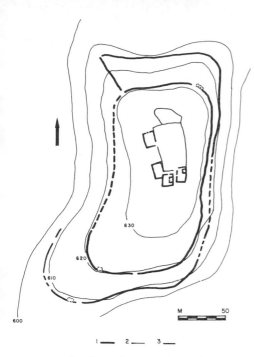

6.7. *The fort of Cerro Chena, south of Santiago, Chile. The installation appears to have been manned by* mitmaq *from north central Chile. Key: 1. surrounding wall; 2. patio wall; 3. building. Redrawn from Stehberg (1976: 37); original plan by H. Niemeyer and R. Stehberg.*

The distribution data also indicate that military installations were not automatically erected wherever the Inkas went, but depended on a number of factors such as the time necessary for conquest, the possibility of integrating a group into the state by diplomacy, and the potential threat of neighboring (yet unconquered) peoples. This last factor appears to be of primary importance, since most known Inka forts are located on or near state boundaries.

Small Forts and Outposts

Some Inka forts appear quite small, with no or few buildings placed on a hilltop surrounded by walls or steep precipices. Those in charge of the installation did not live there, but used it when danger threatened. Nordenskiöld believed that the small "forts" of Pulquina and Batanes in the *oriente* of Bolivia functioned in this manner. It is probable, likewise, that some larger Inka military installations housed few permanent residents. Their guardians would have lived on land nearby.

Plaza Schuller (1976) has mapped small military installations in the area north of Quito, Ecuador. In many cases these appear to have been simple earthworks of concentric walls and ditches located on hill- or mountaintops. Sometimes no buildings, or only a few, are present within the walls.[13] These appear to have been used by troops who lived elsewhere, possibly in larger nearby forts.

The concept of a small defensible position some distance from a main military installation has been observed at garrison Inkawasi in the

Cañete Valley, Peru (Hyslop 1985: 34–41), where two small posts are located about 6 kilometers downstream from the site. The same may be true of Collipeumo and La Muralla (Stehberg 1976: 8, 9, plate 12), sites south of the fort of Cerro Chena in the Santiago, Chile, area. The Inka affiliation of these two sites is somewhat doubtful and will require further investigation.

One particularly fine small Inka fort is Cerro Chena, located some 20 kilometers south of Santiago, Chile (fig. 6.7). It is perhaps the best studied of all Inka military sites, since it has been accurately mapped and partly excavated (Stehberg 1976). Like small military sites in Bolivia and Ecuador (mentioned earlier above), Cerro Chena has no good evidence for ceremonial or religious architecture. The fort consists of a set of concentric walls enclosing buildings surrounding a patio on the hilltop's summit. A cemetery with Inka pottery is found outside of the walls to the northwest.

The Inka pottery found in Cerro Chena is of a style that developed in the Norte Chico region well to the north of Santiago (Stehberg 1976: 5, 6, 29, 34). This Diaguita-Inka pottery is evidence that *mitmaq* from the Norte Chico were in charge of the fort. Pottery at other Inka military sites, if ever studied in detail, may also demonstrate the presence of *mitmaq* from other regions.

In summary, the small forts and outposts present little evidence for architecture relating to ceremony and ritual. Outposts appear at times linked to a nearby larger military installation. Some small forts rest above a lower settlement. The defended height was used only when necessary, a military tactic probably developed in pre-Inka times, since lower, pre-Inka settlements are occasionally found next to walled, higher ones. There are probably many other small Inka forts and outposts in the Andes, but few have been identified, since archaeologists' attentions have been drawn to larger installations with more complex architecture.[14]

Large Military Sites

Why are some fortresses and garrisons among the best examples of Inka architectural planning? In part this is explained by their location in strategic positions, which often excluded pre-existing settlements. Inkas built military complexes from the ground up with strategic characteristics that, depending on the situation, were useful for attack, surveillance, or defense. That is, they were rarely able to use and modify already-existing architectural complexes built by local populations. Also, it would seem that sites used by the army were probably built by Inkas themselves, or by *mitmaq*, since military installations were constructed in regions where a local labor supply was not available or fully dependable. Finally, the close relationship between Inka religion and warfare required that many ceremonial aspects of Inka architecture, developed in a nonmilitary context in the Cuzco heartland, be integrated even into distant army installations.

Four examples of large Inka military installations will be described and compared: Pambamarca in Pichincha, Ecuador; Inkawasi in the Cañete Valley, Peru; Incallacta in the province of Cochabamba, Bolivia; and Pucará de Andalgalá in Catamarca Province, Argentina.

Pambamarca

This Inka military establishment 32 kilometers east-northeast of Quito consists of at least fourteen walled installations, separated from one another by several hundred meters (fig. 6.8). The highest unit rests at about 4,075 meters and the lowest at about 3,400 meters.[15] The various units are considered part of the same complex because of their proximity to each other and because in some cases they are linked by trenches. The monumentality of the Pambamarca complex is notable. It extends over 6 kilometers of a mountaintop and may be the largest of Inka military complexes anywhere in Tawantinsuyu (figs. 6.9, 6.10).

The site is named after the mountain upon which it rests. Its original name may have been Quinchicaxa, a term first found in a document dated 1569 (Rowe 1985: 211) and later mentioned by Cabello Valboa, Muría, and Sarmiento. Pambamarca is just west of the old Ecuadorian

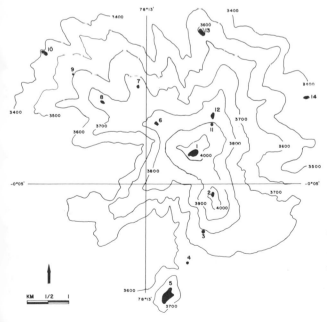

6.8. The Pambamarca fortress complex, consisting of fourteen units on a mountaintop near Quito, Ecuador. This and other military sites served the Inkas for decades against the recalcitrant ethnic groups of northern Ecuador. The numbered units are walled installations. Adapted from Plaza S. (ca. 1980: fig. 1).

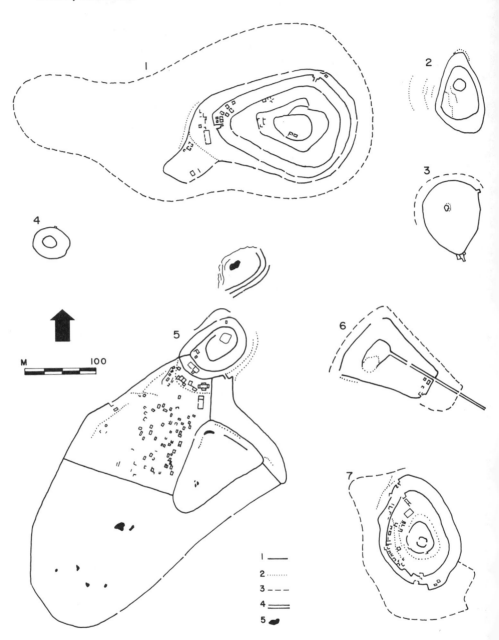

6.9. *Units 1–7 of Pambamarca. Trenches next to surrounding walls are frequently not depicted. Key:* 1. *surrounding wall;* 2. *indistinct wall or trench;* 3. *trench;* 4. *walled trench;* 5. *rock outcrop. Adapted by author from Plaza S. (ca. 1980); Unit 5 is by W. Wurster in Oberem (1968: plan 2).*

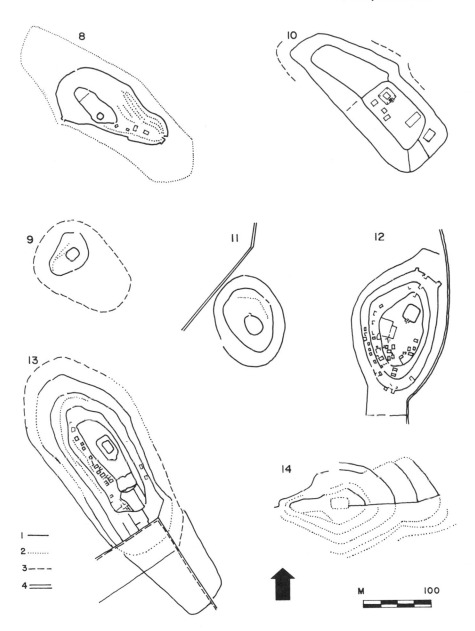

6.10. *Units 8–14 of Pambamarca. Key: 1. surrounding wall; 2. indistinct wall or trench; 3. trench; 4. walled trench. Adapted by author from Plaza S. (ca. 1980); Unit 10 is from Oberem (1968: plan 1).*

community of El Quinche, a place-name that probably identifies the location of the military complex of Quinchicaxa mentioned in the document. Early sources also relate that it was manned by *mitmaq* from different places. Cabello Balboa (1951: 320; 3d pt., chap. 16) adds that it was built by Cañari Indians as punishment for their rebellious behavior. A declaration in 1583 by a priest (Puento 1974: 22) describes the Pambamarca "fortresses" as thirteen or fourteen fortified hills with ditches built by the Inka for an eight- or nine-year war against the local population. He accurately describes some of the forts as being an "arquebus shot apart or more."

Part of the problem in identifying Pambamarca's cultural affiliation is due to its high terrain (windy, rainy grasslands) and poor preservation due to heavy rainfall and sleet, which have left limited evidence for buildings within the concentric surrounding walls. In many cases walls that once stood several meters high are only steep overgrown slopes with no visible stones. The site's cultural affiliation has been questioned by patriotic Ecuadorian scholars, who claim that military sites were built by local groups such as the Caranqui, who fought against Inka domination. There is, in fact, little doubt of the site's Inka affiliation, especially when it is compared to other Inka military sites.

The description below of Pambamarca is drawn from publications by Oberem (1968, 1980), Plaza Schuller (ca. 1980), and my reconnaissance of the site in 1986.[16]

The highest and most central part of the Pambamarca complex is dominated by a massive installation (fig. 6.9, no. 1; fig. 6.11) with five increasingly higher levels sustained by concentric walls. Frequently, deep, wide ditches are found outside of the walls. It is uncertain whether the ditches are dry moats, or whether they are simply excavations to secure earth to build up the retaining walls.[17] Nearly all of the units at Pambamarca have such ditches, which, in some cases, are visible only in aerial photographs. The walls at this and other units are made of rough stone blocks quarried nearby. There is much fill behind (on the interior of) the surrounding walls.

Many doorways are found in the concentric walls at Unit 1. Three of them are elaborately built gates. The use of many doorways, occasionally with fancy gateways (sometimes requiring a zigzag entry through successive walls) is found in several units at Pambamarca. The remains of at least two dozen buildings, all apparently rectangular, are found within the walls. Above the first wall on the north side of Unit 1 is a *kallanka* with three doorways.

Running just to the north of Unit 1 is a trench with two walls on either side. It connects Unit 1 with Units 6, 11, and probably 13.

6.11. View of the highest unit, Unit 1, of Pambamarca. Four eroded surrounding walls are visible.

The remaining units at Pambamarca are found on ridges leading down from the mountaintop. The southern units consist of four installations (fig. 6.9, nos. 2, 3, 4, and 5). Unit 2 is as high as Unit 1, but much simpler. It has three concentric walls and some artificial slopes. There is no evidence of buildings. Unit 3 is lower and still simpler, with one concentric wall. The wall surrounds a rock outcrop. Unit 4, the smallest in the complex, consists of only two concentric walls with no visible buildings. It rests directly north of an ancient road leading to the north, passing to the west of Pambamarca. Units 4 and 5 may have controlled transit.

Unit 5, known as Quitaloma, is a massive installation resting at about 3,600 meters. It is the only excavated unit and is amply described (Oberem 1968, 1980). Known locally as El Churo ("snake" in local Quechua) because of a spiral wall on its north side, Quitaloma is 280 meters wide and 450 meters long. The spiral wall encloses an earthen platform 4 meters high at its summit, where treasure hunters have dug a large hole. Two outer walls at right angles indicate that it was probably rectangular. Outside of the main walls farther to the north there is a rock outcrop surrounded by three walls on the west and steep cliffs on the east. Two concentric walls connected by three radial walls make up the greater, southern part of Quitaloma. There are several doors in the outer wall. Graves have been found on the outside of the walls. Traces of approximately eighty buildings are found in the center of the unit. Most are rectangular one-room structures, although a few have an interior dividing wall. The largest is 20.5 meters long. Small excavations have produced Inka and local pottery along with spindle whorls, sling stones, and bola stones.

Units 6, 7, 8, 9, and 10 (fig. 6.9, nos. 6 and 7; fig. 6.10, nos. 8, 9, and 10) descend a ridge leading northwest from the mountaintop. Unit 6 has two concentric walls, a half dozen small buildings, and a rock outcrop in the central, highest, part. A small high platform has been worked into the rock. Two elaborate gateways are found in the first wall. Unit 7 (known as Censo Pucará) is more complex, with four or five concentric walls, elaborate gateways, and a central platform with two entrances. More than twenty small rectangular buildings are found on the western side within the walls. The lowest concentric wall reaches a height of 13 meters on its eastern side. Unit 8 has three concentric walls or slopes and a central platform. As at most other units, the height of the concentric walls varies from 1 to 9 meters. Unit 9, similar to Unit 11, is very simple, with one or two concentric walls, a surrounding ditch, and a low central platform 20 meters across. Unit 10 is known as Achupallas and has a few rectangular structures (one appears to be a *kallanka*) and a

6.12. Unit 11 of Pambamarca. It is composed of three concentric walls with no visible buildings. A walled trench passes in front (foreground), linking it to other units.

square central platform with a stairway. It is located at an altitude of about 3,400 meters.

Units 11, 12, and 13 (fig. 6.10, nos. 11, 12, and 13) are found on the ridge descending to the north of the mountaintop. Unit 11 is composed simply of three concentric walls with no evidence of buildings. Like Unit 9, it is built on a slope and does not, as do most of the other units, take advantage of a promontory on the ridge (fig. 6.12). Unit 12 is one of the best preserved (figs. 6.13, 6.14). Most of the rectangular buildings are located within the walls on the southern and eastern side. The northern gateway requires a zigzag approach as one passes up from wall to wall. The unit is crowned with a high rectangular platform with steps. Unit 13 is larger and more complex than Unit 12, but less well preserved (fig. 6.15). Known as Campana Pucará (*campana* means bell), a rectangular platform is found at the highest central point.

Unit 14 (fig. 6.10, no. 14) is isolated some 2 kilometers to the east of Unit 1 at an altitude of 3,450 meters. Because of its lower altitude, it has been affected by farming and herding. It apparently maintains the pattern of concentric walls with a central platform.

In summary, the Pambamarca military complex is composed of large units on the top (Unit 1) and on the lower reaches of the mountain (Units 5, 7, 10, 12, and 13). Between them are found smaller units gener-

6.13. View to north of Pambamarca's Unit 12, one of the best preserved. Four walls surround numerous buildings and a central platform.

6.14. The central platform of Unit 12 of Pambamarca. It is rectangular with stone walls. A stairway leads to the top.

ally composed only of walls with few or no buildings, suggesting that troops were quartered only in the one central and several exterior units. The exterior larger units have central rectangular platforms. These platforms are similar to the *ushnu* platforms discussed in chapter 3 and suggest that ceremony and ritual were important, at least at the larger, lower units, where most of the people were housed. The larger units take advantage of promontories, whereas the smaller ones often do not. The smaller units appear to be strategic and easily defended by troops housed in the larger ones. They also link the larger, lower units with the highest central one. The larger units have buildings on intermediate levels, reached by elaborate gateways, apparently built with defense in mind. The lower walls of the larger units often have much empty space within them and have many simple doorways. Perhaps herds of llamas were kept there. Pambamarca thus appears to have been a permanent garrison from which attacks were launched, but where the threat of counterattack is also expressed by many defensive walls with protected gates.

Inkawasi
This Inka military site is discussed by the chronicler Cieza de León (1962: 205–207, chap. 73; 1967: 198–202, chap. 60) as a garrison from

which attacks were launched downriver against the Cañete (Huarco) Valley on the Pacific Coast of Peru. The war may have been King Thupa Yupanki's final conquest on the coast and lasted three or four years or campaigns. Cieza refers to the site as the "New Cuzco" and says it was abandoned after the war once a new administrative center was built in the lower valley. The ethnic composition in the section of the river valley occupied by Inkawasi is discussed by Rostworowski (1978–1980). The site has been described by Larrabure y Unanue (1904; 1941: 419–439) and Harth-Terré (1933). I (1985) have analyzed its surface artifacts and architectural planning.

Inkawasi is composed of about eight hundred "rooms" and enclosures and extends over a kilometer on gently sloping desert terrain above irrigated land in a narrow river valley (figs. 6.16, 6.17). Elaborate residential compounds are found on the eastern side of the site. South of these is a large square storage complex with more than two hundred square units or bins surrounding at least 30 larger rectangular spaces separated by low walls. Other storage units are found in the poorly preserved northeastern sector of the site and, on a more limited basis, within the struc-

6.15. View to the northeast of Pambamarca's Unit 13, Campana Pucará. A walled trench (foreground) leads into the unit, which has five surrounding walls.

tures on the southeastern side. Just to the north of the storage complex
is a zone with a trapezoidal plaza, a cemetery, and a rectangular enclosure interpreted as a compound of high ritual significance, perhaps a
Sun Temple. To the north and west of the trapezoidal plaza is a zone of
irregular architecture where there is evidence of food preparation. The
center of Inkawasi is dominated by a large trapezium plaza at least 150
meters long (north-south) set on a plateau overlooking the eastern side
of the site. A road divides it; on this road, near a large compound of unknown function south of the plaza, is an *ushnu* platform (fig. 3.21).

A rock escarpment divides the eastern part of Inkawasi from a complex zone of architecture to the southwest. That zone includes a set of
radially designed units arranged about a small plaza with a small platform in its center (fig. 7.16). It also includes a number of large compounds and patios farther west.

The evidence at Inkawasi suggests that one-third to one-half of the
rooms were used for storage. The evidence for housing is limited, and
certainly not sufficient to indicate that an army could be housed within

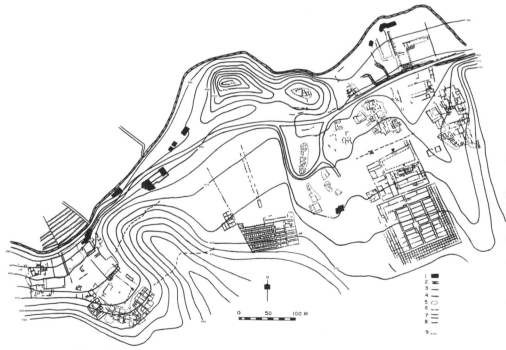

6.16. *Plan of the garrison of Inkawasi, Peru. This military installation was built by
Thupa Yupanki to carry out the difficult conquest of the Cañete (Huarco) Valley.*
Key: 1. modern building; 2. irrigation channel; 3. building wall; 4. terrace; 5. indistinct buildings; 6. road or path; 7. modern road; 8. contour line; 9. platform edge
or fallen wall. From Hyslop (1985: 137).

6.17. Aerial view of Inkawasi, Cañete Valley, Peru. The site is located in desert terrain (center to bottom) above irrigated land (top). Approximately eight hundred rooms and enclosures compose the garrison, which extends over 1 kilometer from east to west. Courtesy S.A.N.

the site. Possibly, armies camped on the side of the installation, which was used more for storage, food preparation, lodging officials, and ceremonial activities. There is little evidence for production of goods or arms at the site, suggesting that it may have been a place to which goods were primarily imported and stored.

Inkawasi's military nature is best seen when the site is examined from a regional perspective. Its strategic location upriver made it an ideal location to organize an attack on the lower valley. Walls do protect the site, but not at its architectural perimeter. One wall several hundred meters south of the main storage area closes off a dry valley. Another wall is found six kilometers downstream by an outpost known as Escalón. Escalón and another post across the river effectively control any approach to Inkawasi from the coast, where the enemy, the Huarco people, lived. The chief fortification of the local Huarco population was Ungará (fig. 6.5), occupied by the Inkas after it was seized.

There is much evidence for ceremony at Inkawasi, not only in its general design but in some of the architectural complexes. Astronomical sightlines of significance to Inkas appear to have been important in the general layout (chap. 8). Plazas with primary and secondary *ushnu*

175

(chap. 3) are integrated into the plan. The large divided plaza and two subsidiary plazas (one perfectly trapezoidal) are additional evidence for ritual activities, as is the possible "temple" compound with its accompanying cemetery next to the trapezoidal plaza.

Inkawasi appears to have been hastily built, especially when compared to Inka administrative centers in nearby coastal valleys. Inkawasi's walls are built primarily of stone mixed with clay and mud. Apparently, it was constructed rapidly with the idea that it would be occupied for only a short time. Other evidence, such as sealed doorways and limited surface debris, indicates that the site was closed after brief use.

Incallacta

In the early historical sources there is almost no information about Incallacta, department of Cochabamba, Bolivia. The site, however, is probably first mentioned in a source dating from 1569, in which it is referred to as Cuzcotuiro (Rowe 1985: 215–217). Its construction was attributed to Thupa Yupanki. A variation of this name, Cuzcotuyo, is also mentioned by Sarmiento (1965: 263, chap. 61) and Murúa (1962), who cites it as "vsco turo," a fort near Pocona taken by Chiriguano invaders and rebuilt by Wayna Qhapaq. Incallacta is situated about 20 kilometers from the town of Pocona and is the largest Inka military installation in the region (figs. 6.18, 6.19). The early histories also note that *mitmaq* and *orejones* were sent to populate and defend the area. One early report (Repartimiento de Tierras por el Inca Huayna Capac 1977: 10) relates that those *mitmaq* were Cotas and Chuis and that they were warriors. They were removed from lands near Cochabamba, which were in turn resettled by other peoples, mainly from the Andean high plateau (Wachtel 1980–1981).

Incallacta is identified as a military site because of its extensive surrounding wall and strategic location on the Inka frontier with the Amazonian lowlands. It was first mapped and described in a short article by Nordenskiöld (1915) and has been the subject of a number of popular accounts by journalists intrepid enough to get there.[18] In 1976 a detailed description of its architecture was made by González (González and Cravotto 1977) during an inspection and evaluation prepared for UNESCO. I first visited Incallacta in 1979 and returned for an additional survey in 1986.

Located at an altitude of 2,930 to 3,100 meters, most of the site is on a high river terrace between two streams. Walls surround the central part of the site and most of a steep hill to the north. Most of the building walls are constructed of double rows of stones set in mud or sand mor-

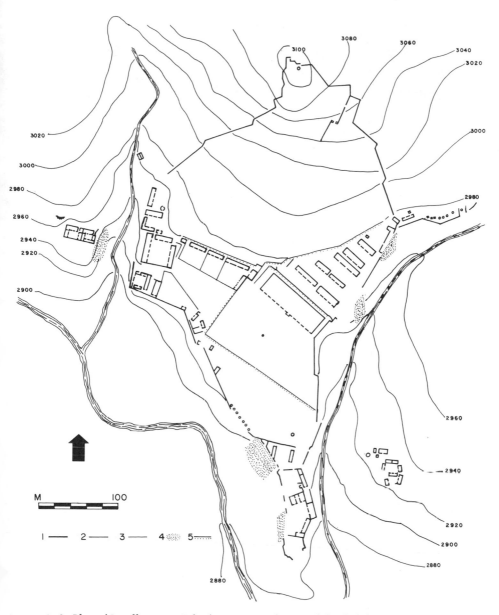

6.18. Plan of Incallacta, an Inka fortress in Bolivia. It defended the eastern Inka frontier from Chiriguano invaders, who overran it shortly before the Spanish conquest. Key: 1. building; 2. wall; 3. contour line; 4. eroded area; 5. retaining wall. Redrawn from González and Cravotto (1977: fig. 1) and original plan courtesy A. Cravotto.

6.19. View to the northeast over Incallacta, Bolivia. The large plaza (center) is divided by a terrace wall. A building with possible astronomical use, a multisided tower, was constructed on the steep cliff on the far left.

6.20. A 4–5-meter-high wall passes over the hill on the north side of Incallacta, Bolivia.

tar. Apparently, the flat wall faces were once covered with a mud plaster painted red, of which little remains.

The most notable building is a large hall (*kallanka*) on the north side of a large plaza divided by a terrace wall (figs. 1.18, 3.14). This building enclosed more than 2,000 square meters under a large gabled roof. Architectural reconstructions have been prepared by Gasparini and Margolies (1980: 207–212). It was probably used for public ceremonies and feasts, if one may draw an analogy between it and similar constructions found on the main plaza at Cuzco. A platform attached to the front (plaza side) of the building and a large flat stone in the plaza are discussed in chapter 3 as evidence for an *ushnu* complex.

The function of most of the other buildings is unknown, in part because the site has never been systematically excavated,[19] and because surface artifacts are difficult to find, given the dense, spiny vegetation covering the site. Good candidates for barracks at Incallacta are a set of seven smaller halls, or *kallanka*, behind (northeast of) the great hall. Small circular foundations in at least three parts of the site are probably correctly interpreted as the bases of *qollqa*, or storage buildings. South of the main plaza one finds a set of rectangular buildings, including one that was two stories high. Between the western side of the plaza and the stream (Quebrada Pajcha Huayco) in the western part of the site there are three *kallanka* in a row, each with an enclosed patio. Other rectangular buildings also surround patios.

A bridge must have spanned the deep gorge and waterfall of the Pajcha Huayco (fig. 5.10) to connect the main body of the site to its westernmost sector, which includes a high multisided wall (called the *torreón*), interpreted as an astronomical structure (chap. 8) and a well-

6.21. *Oblique opening in Incallacta's surrounding wall.*

built double *kancha* (fig. 1.17), which includes a gabled structure with a central wall.

The massive wall surrounding the hilltop to the north and most of the central part of the site is characterized by several features intended to increase its military effectiveness (fig. 6.20). On the hill the walls are 4 to 5 meters high and 1.5 to 2 meters thick. Their zigzag design is also found at Saqsawaman in Cuzco.[20] Small, obliquely constructed windows (*troneras*) are found in part of the wall facing the stream of Fuerte Huayco (fig. 6.21). The oblique windows would have hindered the passage of stones, darts, or arrows. On the interior part of the wall one finds an attached lower platform or wall (*banqueta*) on which troops could walk and from which they could see over the wall. In some places one finds short segments of a smaller wall on top of the main wall. The segments create open spaces, or merlons, through which one could look or discharge missiles.

Several doors are found in Incallacta's surrounding wall. Several others may no longer be detectable, particularly where the wall has fallen over the cliff.

Incallacta is the largest of a series of fortified settlements on the Inka frontier facing the lowlands of Bolivia. Its strictly military role can be questioned, since it is far more elaborate than other known fortified settlements in the region. Both González and Cravotto (1977: 39) and

6.22. *Plan of the Pucará de Andalgalá, Argentina. The main concentration of buildings is located on two hills, separated by a plaza, in the southern part of the fort. Key: A. main doorway; B. buildings in north part of the fortress. Redrawn from Lange (1892), with alterations based on author's survey.*

181

Ellefsen (1973*a*, 1973*b*) believe that it may also have been an administrative center. More recent surveys at Pocona (Céspedes 1982; Sanzetenea 1975*a*), however, indicate that it may have been the region's administrative center. Incallacta's location in a small valley suggests that its purpose was not to defend the valley, but rather the more productive Pocona region to the immediate south, through which a main Inka road passed to the east.

Pucará de Andalgalá

This elegant fortress rests on a hilltop on the south side of a plain known as the Campo del Pucará in the province of Catamarca, Argentina. The plain, rich potato-producing terrain, rests at an altitude of about 1,800 meters; the hilltop reaches 273 meters above it. The *pucará*, or fort, lies directly on the Inka frontier only a few kilometers west of the Tucumán jungle and the arid pampa beyond. The Campo del Pucará is a traditional thoroughfare for people passing from lowland Argentina into the Hualfín and Santa María areas. There are apparently no published early historical descriptions of the *pucará* and no hint of its original name. It may, however, be the fortress mentioned in a document from 1569 (Rowe 1985: 215), which records that the king Thupa Yupanki went to Tucumán (an early general term for the northern part of the Argentine northwest), built a fortress, and located (not necessarily in the fortress) many *mitmaq*.

The first description of the *pucará* (fig. 6.22) was made by Lange (1892), a topographer from the University of La Plata. He did not realize the site was Inka, and his description of the topography is far better than that of the site's architecture. He was, however, aware of some military aspects of its construction, several of which he described. In 1911 Bruch (pp. 175–187) published a more detailed description with more accurate, but less complete, architectural plans. He too did not understand that the fort was Inka, but described some pottery that clearly was. Pucará's Inka affiliation was not confirmed until González (González and Núñez R. 1958–1959: 116–119) visited the site in 1957. There have never been systematic excavations at the site.

A total of approximately 3 kilometers of wall segments enclose most of the hilltop, with prominences on its northern and southern parts. Most of the buildings and walls are found in and around the southern part. The use of unconnected walls is explained in part by the natural steepness of parts of the hilltop, which would have impeded entry. Nevertheless, other wall segments are curiously isolated, giving rise to speculation that the fortress was never finished. Another explanation is that perishable materials, such as wood and spiny brush, growing

6.23. Surrounding wall on the north side of the Pucará de Andalgalá, Argentina. It was constructed in segments (see arrows*) and has small shoot holes.*

in abundance in the zone, could have been used to construct barriers linking some of the segments (Rex González, personal communication, 1986).

The surrounding walls now stand 2 to 4 meters in height, but in some places were considerably higher. They are constructed from flat, slablike stones found in abundance on the hilltop. Apparently, no mortar was used. Sometimes a vertical segmentation is noted in the walls (fig. 6.23), suggesting that different groups may have constructed different units of the walls. Only in a few places does more than one wall impede entry to the hilltop. It appears that the concept of concentric walls was only partially employed. Some of the surrounding walls have interior platforms (fig. 6.24) and small oblique windows.

There are many 1- to 2.5-meter-wide doorways in the surrounding walls. The doors often have short, interior "entry" walls constructed at a 90-degree angle to the main wall (fig. 6.25). One doorway is clearly the principal gateway (fig. 6.22, A) with small rooms attached to the walls on either side of it. Lange suggests (1892: 7) that the zigzag form of some of the walls is intentional, used to catch attackers between two lines of fire from soldiers on the walls above. This interpretation may be disputed, since the zigzags may have been a result of the elevation contours.

6.24. View of the interior of a surrounding wall at the Pucará de Andalgalá. The platform allowed one to see over the wall, which was once somewhat higher.

The buildings in the *pucará* are rectangular structures, often with slightly irregular patios or enclosure walls. About five to seven such structures are found on the northern side of the hilltop (fig. 6.22, B), separated from the main part of the fortress about 500 meters to the south.

The southern part of the hilltop has promontories on its eastern and western sides, where most of the buildings are found (fig. 6.26). Between the two promontories there is a rectangular plaza. The plaza thus divides two main areas of constructions. As with the walls surrounding the hilltop, the buildings' walls are made of stone slabs laid with no mortar.

There is little level ground anywhere on the hilltop, and it is apparent that the plaza was constructed by using much fill, sustained by a retention wall on its southern side (figs. 6.26, A). The plaza has no evidence of structures within it, other than a circular bed of stones, disturbed by treasure hunters, about 8 meters in diameter (fig. 6.26, B). Apparently, some feature, possibly an *ushnu* stone, was once placed there. The plaza separates two main areas of buildings to its east and west. This may be an expression of Inka dual division, discussed at length in chapter 7.

The principal compound on the west is a long set of four patios, each connected to a rectangular building on its west (figs. 6.26, C, fig. 6.27).

Several other independent rectangular buildings are associated with patios. The foundations of four or five circular structures are also present.

The buildings on the eastern side of the plaza (fig. 6.28) appear to be the most significant, or at least are the most elaborately constructed. There are five compounds, each with two or more once-roofed buildings. The two easternmost ones (fig. 6.26, D_1 and D_2), not visible from the plaza, are smaller. The three fronting on the plaza (figs. 6.26, E_1, E_2, and E_3, fig. 6.28) are carefully built compounds, of which the central and highest one (E_3) has an inset doorway overlooking the plaza, the other two compounds (E_1 and E_2), and the western sector. Within E_3 there is a large white stone outcrop around which the compound has been constructed. It is noteworthy that the outcrop, evidence for ritual activity, is found in the highest building with the most elaborate door. The presence of a principal doorway on the eastern side of a plaza is similar to the layout of the administrative centers Huánuco Pampa and Pumpu in the central Andes of Peru (chaps. 3 and 7). The compounds on the eastern side of the *pucará* are variants of *kancha*.

Lange (1892: 7) notes that the number of buildings in the *pucará* is not sufficient to house an army. He speculates that those who defended the fortress lived nearby in the plain and withdrew to the fort when necessary. He also studied the question of the site's water supply, noting that it was probably drawn from the Chilca stream (fig. 6.22, C), which is now dry. The lack of any scientific investigation at the *pucará* other

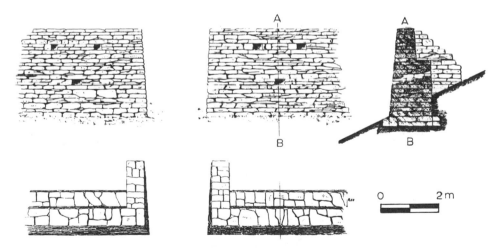

6.25. *Drawing of a wall with doorway at the Pucará de Andalgalá. The wall's exterior* (top left) *has shoot holes at different levels. The interior* (bottom left) *has a platform. The profile view* (right) *shows the entry wall of the doorway. From Lange* (1892).

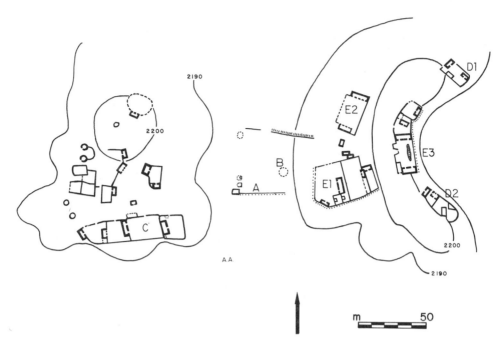

6.26. *The main buildings of the Pucará de Andalgalá, Argentina. A plaza with a retaining wall (A) on its south side separates the two groups, each on a hill. Three compounds are visible from the plaza to the east (E1, E2, E3). The highest (E3) is built around a large rock outcrop. Author's plan, with some use of Bruch (1911: 182–183).*

than surface survey and mapping makes it difficult to determine the function of any of its buildings. Thus one may entertain as a research proposition that about eight circular or more or less circular structures near the surrounding walls within the site are redoubts (Lange 1892: 8). No cemetery has been located at the *pucará*.

The Pucará de Andalgalá is unquestionably an Inka fortification on the state's eastern frontier, perhaps guarding against incursions from the neighboring marauding Lulie Indians (Lorandi 1980). Given many military aspects of the site's architecture and the limited number of roofed buildings, it does not appear to have been an administrative center. The nearest Inka administrative center is Chaquiago to the west, currently under investigation by Lorandi (1983). A line of sight connects the Pucará with the much higher site Nevados de Aconquija (chap. 3) about 60 kilometers to the north. The distance is too great to see one settlement from the other, but communication may have been possible with smoke signals or some other means.[21]

6.27. *View from compound E1 of the western side of the Pucará de Andalgalá, Argentina. A plaza (center right) separates two main groups of buildings.*

Summary

Pambamarca, Inkawasi, Incallacta, and the Pucará de Andalgalá share characteristics but are also different from each other. Together with the smaller military outposts, they elucidate our ideas about Inka warfare and help to explain concepts of military site design.

The surrounding sometimes-concentric walls that are found at Pambamarca, Incallacta, the Pucará de Andalgalá, and some smaller sites are not Inka inventions but rather features found in fortified sites of *auca runa* (pre-Inka) times. The many doorways in the surrounding walls, for example, are found in pre-Inka fortified sites. Several examples of this have been described for the Lake Titicaca area (Hyslop 1976: 110–114). Their purpose is difficult to explain, particularly since they appear to expose protected areas. Perhaps there was a way of closing the doors.[22] They could be sally ports, demonstrating the importance that Inkas attributed to the offensive in battle. At Pambamarca the inner concentric walls frequently have carefully constructed gateways through which attackers would have had difficulty advancing. The internal platform attached to walls is another pre-Inka technique observed at the sites of Pucará Juli and Tanka Tanka in the Lake Titicaca area (Hyslop 1976: 315, 320, fig. 9, 335).

The small oblique windows in surrounding walls, perhaps "shoot holes" or apertures for observation, have no certain origin. To date they are found only in some of the southern fortresses, and may be a regional architectural variant. Raffino (1983: 124) suggests that they may come from the Aymara-Atacama fort-building tradition.

Some of the variations in the installations may be ascribed to their differing strategic roles. Only Inkawasi has few surrounding walls. It may be, however, the only military site whose primary purpose was to assemble an attack on a neighboring zone. Defending Inkawasi was apparently less important than at the other sites, where attacks were a concern. Small walled fortifications with few or no buildings in them often appear in close proximity to a larger installation. Their strategic role appears to be as outposts for principal fortifications.

6.28. View from left to right of compounds E2, E3, and E1 on the eastern side of plaza at the Pucará de Andalgalá, Argentina. The plaza is in the foreground. The center compound, E3, is the highest. It is built around a rock outcrop and has a large doorway facing the plaza.

Environmental conditions may explain the differences in wall construction. At Pambamarca, the surrounding walls with much earth fill behind them are unlike those at the more southern fortifications, whose walls are freestanding. This variation may be due to the conditions in Ecuador, where one finds much more surface earth than in the south, where fortifications are built on rocky terrain. On the other hand, the different types of surrounding walls may be due to architectural traditions of the peoples used by the Inkas to construct those walls. If Cañari Indians (from south-central Ecuador) constructed Pambamarca, their traditional forms of wall construction may have been different from those of the high plateau, Argentine, or Atacama peoples, who were required to work in the construction of the southern Inka fortresses.

Occasionally, local architectural traditions are clearly responsible for the differences among fortifications. At Inkawasi the agglutinated rooms exhibit a coastal building tradition not present in highland Inka architecture.

The above-described military settlements have buildings constructed in the Inka manner. The rectangular rooms and *kallanka* are Inka hallmarks, usually alien to local architectural tradition.[23] While Inka military sites vary greatly in their general appearance, Inka architectural hallmarks appear in all of them. The absence of fine Cuzco stonework in installations outside of the Cuzco region is notable. It indicates that this outstanding Inka architectural hallmark was a feature reserved for the more accessible Inka shrines and centers.

The number and size of buildings used for housing soldiers within these sites indicates that different types of lodgings were used. At Pambamarca and Incallacta there appear to be sufficient buildings to house troops. Such is not the case at Inkawasi, the Pucará de Andalgalá, or the smaller fortifications. Apparently, soldiers lived only in the very largest installations. Otherwise, those responsible for the fortifications lived or camped nearby.

One notable characteristic at the four large sites described above is that all have ritual or ceremonial architecture. The *ushnu*-related architecture at Pambamarca, Inkawasi, Incallacta, and perhaps at the Pucará de Andalgalá indicates that this central symbolic form used in many nonmilitary sites was also found in military installations. This emphasizes the religious nature of Inka warfare, a point made with other evidence by many of the early historical sources.

The concept of the divided plaza, suggestive of the dual division in Inka society and in military organization, is clearly visible at Inkawasi, Incallacta, and the Pucará de Andalgalá. Strangely, there is no evidence yet of such at Pambamarca, although duality and more complex divisions may later be discerned in the arrangement of that complex's many units once they are studied more thoroughly.

Finally, the military sites appear to be situated in areas where Inka military operations were long term. That is, they were constructed where it was apparent that a military campaign or border vigilance might last several years or indefinitely. This clarifies why few Inka military sites are found in many parts of the state that were integrated into Tawantinsuyu through diplomacy or short military campaigns.

A study of Inka installations designed primarily for warfare reveals that their purposes were varied. They could be used for launching attacks on a neighboring area (e.g., Inkawasi). Still other sites on hilltops with defensive walls such as those of Argentina, and probably most of those in eastern Bolivia, were used to defend a frontier against invading lowland groups such as Chunchos, Chiriguanos, and Lulies. Still other sites (e.g., Pambamarca) were located amidst recalcitrant peoples and had the double function of maintaining Inka hegemony in their area as well as affording the facility for launching attacks. A primary lesson taught by these military sites is that Inka strategies of conquest, control, and defense were sophisticated and complex, requiring varied strategies and installations. This counterbalances a point of view delivered in some of the early historical sources, which describe Inka warfare as primitive.

7
Orthogonal and Radial Patterns

This chapter discusses two reoccurring patterns often found in the layout of Inka settlements. It will consider the distribution, characteristics, and meaning of both an orthogonal pattern and a radial pattern set around a center. The two are rarely found together, and each may be found in only one sector of a larger settlement. Still other Inka sites have no orthogonal or radial patterning, proof that there was no universal planning concept for Inka settlements. The lack of a general pattern throughout Tawantinsuyu suggests that Inka concepts of settlement design concepts were more varied and complex than the one used by the Spanish in the Americas who founded hundreds of towns laid out with one design principle—the grid (Stanislawski 1946).

The Spanish Grid

It is important to consider the nature of the Spanish grid so as to differentiate it from layouts used by the Inka. Inka settlements occupied by Spaniards occasionally had a grid pattern imposed over them, or an existing Inka orthogonal plan was modified to Spanish standards.

The omnipresence of the grid is relatively recent in the Americas, although it has great antiquity in the Old World. Stanislawski (1946) traces the origin of Spanish American towns back to Roman times or perhaps even to ancient India. Borah (1972: 51) compares Spanish grid towns with Roman *castra* (forts) and provincial cities:

> The *castrum* had within its walls parallel streets crossing at right angles, usually in the form of a checkerboard, two main avenues at right angles to each other running across the *castrum* from gates in the center of each wall to meet in a central square, the forum, around which were grouped the principal buildings. The Roman provincial cities when built under central direction followed the same plan; many of them not only had a gridiron arrangement of streets but one in which the forum was created

from a single, central block and the main avenues ran alongside it instead of meeting in it. The plan is the same as the standard one of Spanish-American urban centers if one accepts the substitution of a church for temples.

In general, the planned Spanish towns in the Americas have straight streets crossing at right angles. At or near the center of the town there is a principal plaza formed by dedicating one of the blocks to open space. Around the plaza lie the church and important government buildings. The settlement extends to the limits of the blocks, where the open country begins with no transitional zone. In Brazil, this pattern varied: the church was placed on higher ground away from the plaza. This particular pattern was decreed by Philip II (Stanislawski 1947: 101–104) in 1573 (*Ordenanzas de Pobladores*) but was rarely heeded in Spanish America, where it was common practice to place the church or cathedral on the main plaza.

Early Spanish grid towns could evolve into large modern cities such as Lima, laid out in 1535, or fail to develop, as was the case of the aborted Spanish settlement built in the large plaza of the Inka center of Huánuco Pampa in 1539 (Morris 1980b). The failure of the Spanish town at Huánuco Pampa resulted in the preservation of the earlier Inka settlement, one of the best examples of Inka planning in the Andes.

There is nothing "natural" about the grid concept (Stanislawski 1946: 105–106), or any other form of town design. The grid, for example, is not a particularly ideal settlement plan. Its insistence on straight lines creates problems in terrain with varied topography, and communication with the center of the town is frequently indirect. A grid design makes it difficult to place related buildings in any position other than parallel or perpendicular to each other. Grid designs, however, are easy to lay out with simple measurements and make efficient use of space. A type of orthogonal plan with some characteristics of a grid was also used in a limited way by the Inkas.

Inka Orthogonal Plans

The Inka orthogonal plan is characterized by streets that cross perpendicularly or nearly so. The streets may be exactly parallel but generally are not. They need not be separated by equal distances. The "blocks" or units formed by the streets are often rectangular or somewhat rhomboidal. The result is a patchwork of rhomboidal units, which sometimes appear similar to an irregular grid. Inka orthogonal patterns adjust to topographic variations, but are generally found on flat or sloping terrain, where major adjustments are not necessary. They do not crosscut gullies and hills, as does the Spanish grid.

One or several *kancha* often compose the units formed by the streets of an orthogonal pattern. Sometimes passageways give access to the *kancha* within a unit, but it is best not to consider these corridors or paths as streets, since they are within a unit and probably did not have the public character of a street.

The central sector of Inka Cuzco has a type of orthogonal pattern (chap. 2). In Cuzco at least four longitudinal streets were crosscut by at least five transverse streets, forming generally rectangular units. The Spanish modified this plan, although it is still apparent in parts of the old city. The dual Inka plaza was much larger than the standard Spanish plaza, and thus it was partially covered by buildings in colonial times. The plaza's location did not conform to Spanish standards, for it was not in the center of the central sector. This was soon remedied by the expanding Spanish occupation, which gave the plaza a more central location.

At least two other settlements in the Cuzco area provide examples of Inka orthogonal patterning—Ollantaytambo and Chinchero. At Ollantaytambo the pattern is found on the eastern side of the site (figs. 7.1, 5.4). Four streets are crosscut by about eight nearly parallel streets (fig. 7.2). The four streets are not exactly parallel, diverging by only about

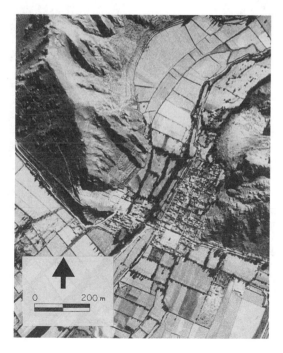

7.1. *Aerial photograph of Ollantaytambo. The orthogonal sector is on the eastern side* (center right). *Compare with the plan (fig. 5.4). Courtesy S.A.N.*

193

two degrees.[1] Two blocks in the center of the grid were left open and later were occupied by other buildings (Gasparini and Margolies 1980: 71). Another larger plaza rested south of the complex and is still used today, as are the two *kancha* found within each block or unit (Gasparini and Margolies 1980: 188–189). The western side of Ollantaytambo shows no trace of orthogonal patterning and is devoted to ceremonial and perhaps military architecture. It appears that the orthogonal area of the site was residential.[2] This was also true of much of central Cuzco, and may be characteristic of other Inka orthogonal layouts.

At Chinchero one finds another orthogonal pattern, disturbed by later construction and more irregular than at Ollantaytambo. It is found to the south of the Inka plaza and the sector of monumental Inka architecture (figs. 7.3, 4.7). The orthogonal pattern probably dates to Inka times, since Inka pottery is found within its houses and patios (Alcina 1976: 128). The layout itself consists of five or six longitudinal (generally north-south) streets crosscut by five (generally east-west) streets. The longitudinal streets bend slightly to the west in the south, probably to accommodate the curving, sloping terrain. As in Ollantaytambo, a main plaza is found on the end of the grid.

7.2. *A street in the orthogonal sector of Ollantaytambo.*

7.3. Aerial photograph of Chinchero. The orthogonal sector is south of the fine terraces and main plaza. Compare with the plan (fig. 4.7). Courtesy S.A.N.

Outside of the Cuzco area there are only a few examples of Inka orthogonal planning. Two variants are found in the Lake Titicaca area. One is Hatuncolla; the other Chucuito. Both were administrative centers for their respective areas, and both were laid out in territories incorporated early into the Inka state. Their similarities contribute to an understanding of Inka orthogonal planning. Their differences raise a number of questions.

Hatuncolla has little standing architecture dating to Inka times, but the street pattern of this settlement is probably Inka (fig. 7.4). The site is described by Julien (1979, 1983: 89−93), who refers to it as a grid. Hatuncolla is defined by two main roads, one running north-south and still called Inka Ñan (Ñan is "road" in Quechua). The second road is perpendicular to it, running east-west (Hyslop 1984: 120, 126). Two rows of long (north-south) units are placed on both sides of the east-west road. North-south paths separate the units. The two main roads meet near

7.4. *Aerial photograph of Hatuncolla in Peru. North-south and east-west roads meet near the center (A). Rectangular units separated by narrow streets are found on both sides of the east-west street. The modern plaza (B) may have been larger in Inka times. Courtesy S.A.N.*

the center of the settlement. It is difficult to tell where the Inka plaza was located. Julien (1983: 91–92) believes that the small Spanish plaza may have been part of a larger Inka one extending to the west and possibly to the north. There were apparently storage structures on the hills north and south of the settlement, but little remains of them. Some blocks of fine Inka masonry are found within the site. They may have come from an Inka building such as a Sun Temple, reported there by Cieza de León.

Chucuito lies not far to the south of Hatuncolla on the western shore of Lake Titicaca. It was once the chief town (figs. 7.5, 7.6) of the Lupaqa polity (Murra 1968). My research (Hyslop 1979, 1984: 128–130) and that by Tschopik (1946) indicate that Chucuito was founded and built in Inka times. The orthogonal pattern of Chucuito is very evident, since seven streets are crossed by at least six others. Chucuito has been permanently inhabited since its founding so the disposition of buildings within the blocks or units probably is quite different from Inka times (as at Hatuncolla). As noted by Gasparini and Margolies (1980: 77), the streets pointing toward Lake Titicaca fan out, a pattern that may accommodate the sloping, higher lands between the stream to the north and lowlands to the south. Alternatively, this pattern may be an application of the radial concept discussed below.

Chucuito appears to have had two plazas in Inka times. One was where the modern-day plaza rests, on the southwestern side of the settlement. The other lay within it, where a rectangular structure of fine Cuzco masonry, the Inka Uyu, is found. The main Inka road running along the western side of Lake Titicaca passed through Chucuito, probably on one of the two roads between the two plazas.

Between the Pacific coast and Lake Titicaca one finds an Inka center (fig. 7.7) named Torata Alta (Stanish and Pritzker 1983), perhaps the town of Cuchuna mentioned by Garcilaso de la Vega. It is situated above the present-day town of Torata in the department of Moquegua. It has at least four streets crosscut by at least five others. Stanish and Pritzker report (1983: 10): "In fact, the gridlike layout of Torata Alta is rather similar to early Spanish towns, but in mapping the many buildings we found only distinctive Inca pottery, suggesting that the site was probably a small administrative center in the elaborate Inca hierarchy."

A soccer field now occupies part of the center of the site. Given the extensive "vertical" economic relationships between the peoples of the high plateau and the Andean slopes (Murra 1972), it would not be surprising if the orthogonal pattern found on the plateau by Lake Titicaca (e.g., at Hatuncolla and Chucuito) were exported to the Moquegua area.

No other examples of Inka orthogonal planning are yet known in the Andes south of Chucuito and Torata Alta. In some cases, Spanish grid patterns may have been superimposed over the Inka ones, and archaeologists may not have thought to look for an earlier Inka one. Other *tampu* towns in the Lake Titicaca region may reveal that their grid patterns, thought to be of Spanish derivation, may have been Inka orthogonal. No examples of Inka orthogonal planning are known in the Andean highlands north of Lima. If such existed, their Inka design may have been obliterated by the construction of Spanish settlements over them.

There is an example of orthogonal patterning in the Lurin Valley near Lima. The settlement is called Nieve Nieve (fig. 7.8) or Balconcillo de Avilay and rests at an altitude of about 800 meters in the middle Lurin Valley. Alberto Bueno, an authority on Lurin archaeology, considers the site Inka (personal communication, 1986), as does Agurto (1987: 62, 63), who has mapped it.[3] Inka pottery fragments are found on its surface. Four generally north-south streets are crosscut by four others, forming an orthogonal pattern with rectangular units. Nieve Nieve is on land gently sloping southward near the edge of the Lurin River. On the south (river) side of the site one finds a plaza (probably the original Inka one), where a Spanish church was constructed.[4]

One large orthogonal center planned by the Inkas may have been Hatun Xauxa in the Mantaro Valley, Peru (Earle et al. 1980: 25–30; D'Altroy 1981: 65–89, 389–390). Unfortunately, the settlement's Inka walls are only partially intact because of modern remodeling (fig. 7.9). The mapped Inka walls are made of roughly trimmed yellowish lime-

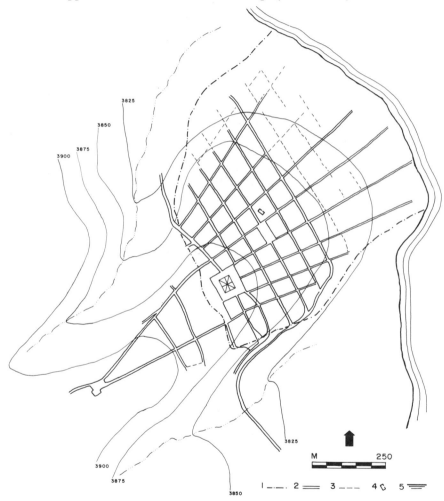

7.5. *Plan of Chucuito, an Inka center by Lake Titicaca. The streets fan out toward Lake Titicaca. Two streets come together in the southwest, where Andean ritual still takes place. Key: 1. limits of Inka pottery; 2. streets; 3. land divisions; 4. the Inka Uyu, a fine masonry building; 5. shore of Lake Titicaca. Author's plan, with assistance from Elias Mujica.*

7.6. *Aerial photograph of Chucuito. The radial street pattern opens toward Lake Titicaca. Courtesy S.A.N.*

stone and river cobbles set in mud and pebble mortar. No fine Cuzco masonry is found, but the Inka affiliation of the walls, some with rows of trapezoidal niches, is certain. One of the first Spanish visitors (Estete 1879) at Hatun Xauxa commented that it was "made like a Spanish town, very compact with its streets well laid out." Earle et al. (1980: 27) have noted that "the structures [walls] are all rectangular and apparently were laid out in the same general orientation." An area of surface pottery with no intact walls is found to the northwest of the Inka walls.

Given the partial nature of the plan, one cannot be certain that Hatun Xauxa had an orthogonal design, but the walls strongly suggest that it did. If such was the case, it would be different from other examples because it has an *ushnu* platform to one side of the buildings. That building, 28 meters square and 2.7 meters high, has an orientation somewhat different from that of the walls. A large plaza was reported at Hatun Xauxa in a letter by Hernando Pizarro (1959). If the *ushnu* platform was beside or in it as they usually are (chap. 3), the plaza at this administrative center probably would have been to one side of the orthogonal plan.

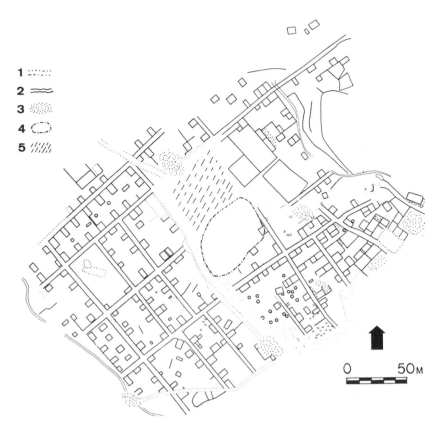

7.7. *Plan of Torata Alta in the department of Moquegua, Peru. Key: 1. modern road or path; 2. irrigation canal; 3. disturbed area or modern corral; 4. hill, 5. soccer field. Adapted from Stanish and Pritzker (1983: 9).*

7.8. *Oblique view over Nieve Nieve (Balconcillo de Avilay) in the Lurin Valley, Peru. The plaza is on the left. Four streets crosscut five others, forming rectangular units.*

In summary, Inka sites, or parts of sites, built with an orthogonal pattern share a number of characteristics. They may, for example, have a secondary plaza within the plan, but it was most common for the plaza to be on one end or side. The plazas themselves are usually not as large as are those of the Inka centers more distant from Cuzco; neither are the plans very extensive. Cuzco's and Chucuito's cover the most terrain, but at Cuzco the orthogonal plan is only the central part of the city. The "blocks" or units formed by the streets are never perfectly square, but rather rectangular or somewhat rhomboidal. The streets never crosscut topographic variations such as streambeds or hills, as do Spanish grids. All were built on flat or gently sloping terrain. Fine masonry is used in the walls of some of the "blocks" or units only at Cuzco and Ollantaytambo.

Orthogonal Plans Interpreted

Why were orthogonal plans used, and why is their apparent distribution limited to regions near Cuzco? Possibly these layouts housed permanent populations as opposed to the rotating *mitayoq* who composed the bulk of the population in most other Inka administrative centers. The presence of orthogonal plans in areas not far from Cuzco suggests that it was a planning concept used relatively early on in imperial Inka expansion. The lack of any obvious *ushnu* platforms at most of the orthogonal settlements reinforces this idea,[5] because, as noted in chapter 3, the use of large, ceremonial plazas with *ushnu* platforms apparently developed only after imperial expansion was well under way.

The meaning of Inka orthogonal patterns is not clear, since known

7.9. *Inka walls at Hatun Xauxa in the Mantaro Valley, Peru. The walls are only partially intact because the town has been occupied continuously, and altered, since Inka times. From Earle et al. (1980: 29).*

0   100   200m

201

examples are few in number and excavations have not elucidated their function. Perhaps they can be understood by counting their units. This is not easy, since they have been altered since Inka times and some blocks have been subdivided, joined, or converted to agricultural purposes. Nevertheless, it is possible to count twenty or twenty-one units at Hatuncolla, omitting the modern plaza and that next to it, considered by Julien to be the old Inka plaza. At Ollantaytambo, the grid also has twenty or twenty-one units, depending on how large the internal plaza (now built over) was. Nieve Nieve appears to have about nineteen units. Chinchero's plan may have nineteen units, although this is difficult to calculate because of alterations in the last few centuries. Chucuito has also been greatly altered since Inka times. It appears to have between thirty-eight and forty-two units, excluding the secondary plaza in the grid (proposed by Gasparini and Margolies) and omitting the units west of the modern plaza, which appear to be a Spanish enlargement, since no Inka pottery was found there. Torata Alta has about twenty-one or twenty-two units. In sum, all the orthogonal plans appear to have about twenty units, with the exception of Chucuito, which has about forty.

Unfortunately, there can be no accurate count of units in the central sector of Cuzco due to rebuilding since the Spanish conquest. Agurto's study (1980: 142–143) of central Cuzco's roads describes four principal longitudinal roads and five transverse ones. He writes that these created ten "great urban units": five in the *hanan* part and five in the *hurin* part. He also notes that some units were subdivided. My analysis of various Cuzco plans, including those produced by the UNESCO project (Agurto 1980), suggests that there were considerably more than ten units. Whether there were twenty, or nearly twenty, as with the other orthogonal settlements, cannot now be ascertained. If there were, it is possible that other orthogonal patterns built by Inkas are repeating, with variations, the number of units of Cuzco's central sector. On the other hand, even if central Cuzco's plan had fewer units, or only ten, the near multiples of about twenty and forty at the other orthogonal settlements suggest a relationship to Inka decimal organization, or the social structure of ten *panaqa* and ten *ayllu* of old Cuzco (chap. 2). This possible symbolism of the orthogonal plan is not certain. Researchers are encouraged to propose other explanations.

Radial Patterns and Centrality

Radial layouts in Inka settlements are more widespread. With the exception of radiality found in aspects of Cuzco's plan, the clear examples of Inka radial planning are generally found outside of the Cuzco area, often very far away.

As described in chapter 2, two types of radiality are found in Cuzco. The first is that of the *zeque* system, where forty or forty-one lines radiated out from a central point, the Sun Temple. The radiality of the *zeque* system did not affect the architectural plan of Cuzco. The conceptualized lines pass over the streets and blocks of Cuzco's central sector and are anchored within the system only to features such as rocks and water sources. The second type of radiality observed at Cuzco is that of streets connecting the central sector with a ring of about a dozen peripheral districts surrounding the central sector. Thus at Cuzco an orthogonal street pattern in its central sector becomes a radial pattern as the roads leave the center.

In Cuzco, the roads radiating out to the surrounding districts do not center on a single point, but rather on the area of the central sector. The lines of the *zeque* system radiate from the Sun Temple. This suggests that radiality in an Inka settlement plan involves not only the idea of a circle or arc, but that of an important central location as well. The following discussion will demonstrate how radiality can be observed as a basic planning concept in all or parts of some other Inka settlements. This will be followed by an analysis of the possible meaning of that layout.

Examples of Radiality as a Central Planning Concept

At Huánuco Pampa a radial layout was first described and interpreted by Morris (1980a).[6] The focal point of Huánuco Pampa's design (figs. 7.10, 7.11) is the large *ushnu* platform near the center of the large plaza, which measures about 520 by 360 meters. A series of streets and walls radiate out from the edges of the plaza and subdivide the city into a number of units on each of the plaza's four sides. For example, streets divide the buildings on the northern and southern sides of the plaza. These "lines" are usually open corridors or streets, but on the east they are also defined by walls defining a large, elaborate compound known as sector IIB (fig. 5.6).

Open spaces or streets are found in all four corners of the rectangular plaza and help divide the site into four main parts. Especially notable is the well-defined main Inka road, which passes into the city through the southeast and northwest corners of the plaza. Another important line, noted in chapters 3 and 5, leads from the *ushnu* platform to a series of eight gateways passing through the main compound on the east. Morris notes (1980a: 13) that it does not "go through to the outside of the site." Thus it appears to be related to the compound and did not mark a boundary, as did some other lines. Morris (1980a: 12) writes: "In my opinion this tendency of building orientation to relate to a series of lines

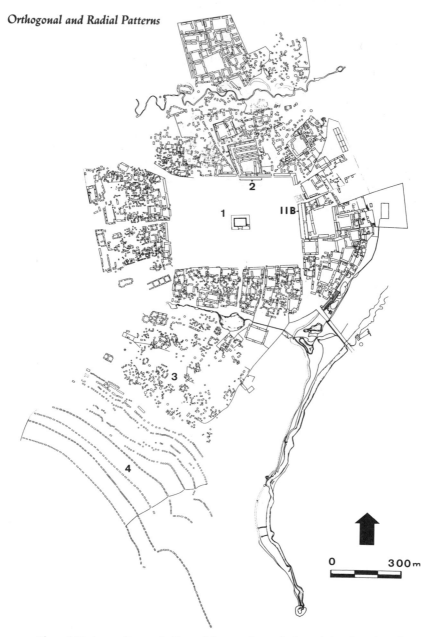

7.10. *Plan of Huánuco Pampa in Peru. A large* ushnu *platform (1) is found in the center of the plaza. Streets or walls extend outward from the plaza's four sides and corners, dividing the buildings into numerous sectors. Sector IIB, with the most elaborate architecture and fine waterworks, is found on the eastern side (fig. 5.6). An* aqllawasi *(2) is found on the north. Round houses (3), probably of* mitmaq, *are situated away from the plaza in the south.* Qollqa, *storage buildings (4), are located farther south on a hill. From Morris and Thompson (1985: 54, 55).*

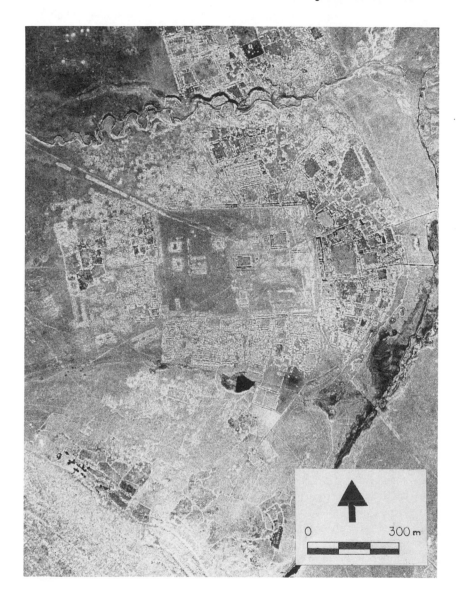

7.11. *Aerial photograph of Huánuco Pampa, Peru. Early Spanish colonial buildings are found in the rectangular Inka plaza. The main Inka road enters the northwest and southeast corners of the plaza and is highly visible. Courtesy S.A.N.*

radiating from the central plaza is a very basic principle of the city's design. It is adhered to at least in a general way even in most of the zones of irregular construction."

The administrative center of Pumpu is in the department of Pasco, Peru (fig. 10.3). Located not far south of Huánuco Pampa, Pumpu appears to have been designed with somewhat similar radial ideas. There are still no accurate published maps of Pumpu.[7] The aerial photograph of Pumpu demonstrates aspects of radiality in its design (fig. 7.12). A large *ushnu* platform is found in the large plaza, slightly to the west of its center. The plaza has buildings only on three sides. The lack of constructions on the western side and part of the northern side may indicate that the site was never completed.[8] As at Huánuco Pampa, open corridors or streets, and sometimes walls, subdivide the buildings on the sides of the plaza into radial units. This is particularly notable on the plaza's southern side, where two streets divide that side's constructions into three units. The eastern side subdivides into three or five units, depending on how one interprets poorly preserved walls and corridors. The apparently incomplete northern side has at least two sectors.

Some of the best-defined "lines" are the roads at the plaza's eastern corners. The main Inka road enters Pumpu on the plaza's southeast corner. It also enters the site on the plaza's northwest corner where there are no buildings. As at Huánuco Pampa, the road cutting diagonally across the plaza divides it into two parts. Also similar to Huánuco is a line running from the *ushnu* platform to the main gate on the plaza's eastern side (fig. 3.20) with which the platform is aligned.

A third example of radiality defining all or most of a settlement's layout is Chilecito (Tambería del Inca) in La Rioja Province in Argentina. There, about forty buildings or compounds surround a rectangular plaza with an *ushnu* platform in its center (figs. 7.13, 7.14). At Chilecito, there is a four-part division created by the rectangular plaza. The individual buildings outside of the plaza create the radial layout as they are aligned with the central *ushnu* platform. As at Huánuco and Pumpu, the *ushnu* platform is aligned with the plaza's eastern side where the site's largest patio compounds are found.

Two other examples of radiality as a central planning concept may be found at the Inka settlements of Chucuito and Maucallacta. They differ from the above examples because the buildings and streets creating a radial plan do not form a complete or nearly complete circle, but rather define less than ninety degrees of an arc.

Chucuito's orthogonal pattern (discussed above) fans out as the distance between the streets broadens nearing the shore of Lake Titicaca. One can debate whether this pattern accommodates the broadening slope on which the settlement is located, or whether it is a layout concept imposed for reasons beyond topographical consideration. One clear indication suggesting that Chucuito's radiality is an imposed concept is that two of the streets extend to the southwest and meet at a plaza where considerable ritual and ceremony is still carried out.[9] That "central point" is, however, not an *ushnu* platform. The convergence of Chucuito's streets at a point of ceremonial importance strengthens the idea that its radial layout is reminiscent of, or similar to, the more extensive radiality found at the three settlements discussed above.

7.12. *Aerial photograph of Pumpu in the department of Pasco, Peru. An* ushnu *platform (1) is found in the west center of the rhomboidal plaza. No buildings are on the plaza's western side (2). Streets or walls extend outward from the plaza's edge, dividing the buildings on the north, south, and eastern sides into several sectors. The main Inka road enters the northwest and southeast corners of the plaza. A canal (3) passes water from east to west through the plaza and arrives at the main gateway of the largest patio (4) of the east. The* ushnu *platform in the plaza is aligned with that gateway. Qollqa, storage structures, are located in the far south (5) and on a hill (6) to the east. Round house foundations (7) are found in the south, between the qollqa and the rectangular buildings just south of the plaza. A modern water channel (8) crosscuts a sector of three large patio groups in the southwest. A modern reservoir (9) is located east of the plaza's buildings and the storage structures on the hill (6). The reservoir has covered only the edge of the settlement, destroying little. Courtesy S.A.N.*

A somewhat similar example is found at the site of 7 Maucallacta (fig. 7.15) about 20 kilometers directly south of Cuzco. Maucallacta, and its accompanying large rock outcrop (Puma Orco, or Tambo Toco), is the site Paccaritampu, which plays an important role in the Inka origin myth of the Ayar brothers (Pardo 1957: 9–53; Muelle 1945). There, a large Inka settlement divided in four sectors is arranged in an arclike pattern on the in-curving slope of a mountain.[10] As at Chucuito, one could argue that the radial placement of the units simply accommodates the local topography. This is probably not the case, however, since

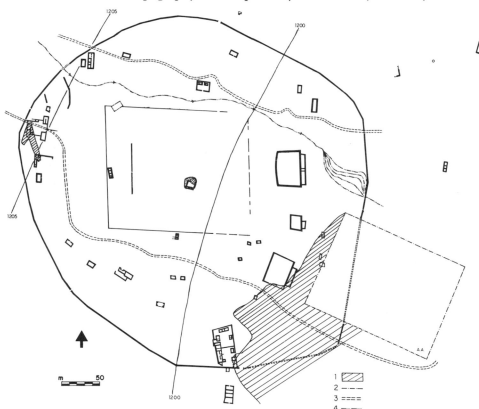

7.13. *Plan of Chilecito (Tambería del Inca) in Catamarca Province, Argentina. A nearly rectangular plaza with a central* ushnu *platform is surrounded by about forty buildings or compounds, which are pointed toward the plaza. The three largest patio compounds are found on the east. Water passed across the northern side of the plaza to the largest patio compound on the east. A wall with an internal platform, possibly defensive, surrounds the settlement. Key: 1. zone destroyed by gravel removal; 2. modern cemetery; 3. modern road; 4. water channel. Constructed from general plan in Greslebin (1940: fig. 2), unpublished drawings (Greslebin 1939), and author's survey.*

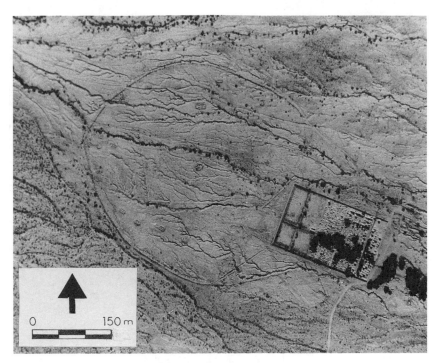

7.14. *Aerial photograph of Chilecito (Tambería del Inca). This Inka settlement is located on an alluvial fan with many gullies. Earth moving, waste dumping, modern roads, and a cemetery have destroyed some parts, but the basic design of the site is still intact. An* ushnu *platform is in the center of a rectangular plaza delineated by faint trenches. The buildings and compounds are arranged radially around the plaza facing the* ushnu *platform. Courtesy Instituto Fototopográfico Argentino, Buenos Aires, Tra. S51, Cor. 8A, Foto 522.*

the architecturally most elaborate radial unit "points" to one of the most sacred locations in all of Tawantinsuyu—the caves and carved rock outcrop related to the Inka origin myth.[11] Known now as Puma Orco, the stone outcrop is directly aligned with the site's principal corridor (found in the northern unit) and finest gateway. Although Puma Orco is located almost a kilometer from Maucallacta, it is clearly visible from all parts of the settlement. The relationship of Maucallacta (the settlement) to Puma Orco (the outcrop) demonstrates a point made in chapter 5—that an outcrop may be part of the Inka concept of a settlement, although it is located outside of the limits of its main buildings. In the case of Maucallacta, the massive outcrop is an architectural "center" of the site, although it is located quite some distance from the main inhabited zone.

7.15. Aerial photograph of Maucallacta south of Cuzco, Peru. The settlement is divided into four sectors in an arclike pattern (outlined). The main passageway and gate of the architecturally most elaborate sector (the northernmost) points to (arrow) the Puma Orco rock outcrop (circled) to the west. Courtesy S.A.N.

    Another example of radiality in Inka site planning comes from the Inka garrison of Inkawasi (chap. 6) in the Cañete Valley of Peru. It differs from the above examples in that the radial concept is used in only a part of the site. This sector is found in the southwestern part of the site (fig. 6.17) and is composed of fourteen units each of three to five rectangular rooms ascending a rocky slope around a small plaza (Hyslop 1985: 118–122) (fig. 7.16, bottom). The fourteen units are not connected, since each is separated from its neighbors by walls or corridors. Each unit is entered from the plaza. A small rectangular structure about two meters square—a secondary *ushnu*—is found in the center of the plaza. Pothunter damage has given it a U-shape. It was once filled with small black stones of a uniform size. As discussed in chapter 3, it was built to receive libations. This small platform is the "center" of the radial sector with the fourteen units arranged about it. As at several other Inka settlements, one could argue that this radial layout is merely a sensible accommodation to the surrounding mountain slope upon which the units are built. The matter is not so simple, however, since the radial

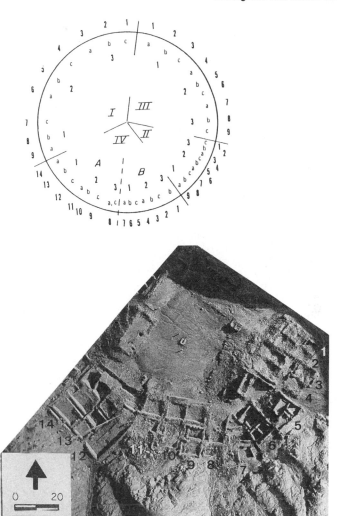

7.16. *Radial sector (below) at Inkawasi in the Cañete Valley, Peru. Fourteen units, each of three to five rectangular rooms, are arranged around a plaza with a small* ushnu-*like platform in it. Compare with the* zeque *system's Kuntisuyu sector with fourteen lines (top). This drawing (Zuidema 1982b) gives a relatively accurate view of the space occupied and the orientation of the lines of each* suyu. *The outer numbers list the lines according to the original written source (Rowe 1979). The other letters, Roman numerals, and numbers are designations formulated by Zuidema. The Roman numerals indicate the* suyu. *The small letters indicate the lines (a is Collana, b is Payan, c is Cayao). Each* suyu's *lines are grouped into units of three, expressed by the inner numbers. Those groups also have the designation Collana (1), Payan (2), and Cayao (3). Note that Kuntisuyu has two parts (A and B) defined by the division at lines 7 and 8.* Zeque *system from Zuidema and Poole (1982: 88); photo by author with Whittlesey balloon camera.*

pattern is complemented by a "center," and, as is demonstrated below, the orientation of the sector and the internal organization of its units relates to complex Inka spatial concepts.

In summary, evidence from the plans of settlements with radial layouts indicates a number of points. Throughout Tawantinsuyu such a design will have a "center," toward or upon which "lines" from a circle or arc of buildings converge. It may not be the point where they would converge with exact geometry, but there is usually little doubt about the feature or building that marks the center, since it is near the geometric center and usually isolated in a plaza or somewhat distant from the buildings.

Radial planning may involve buildings completely encircling a center, or only an arc of buildings partially surrounding a center. The most common type of center is an *ushnu* platform or a prominent rock outcrop. Whatever the nature of the center, one can be certain that it will be a point at which ceremony and ritual were important.[12]

Additional examples of radial layouts will probably be discovered far from Cuzco. Indeed, radiality has only recently been recognized in Inka settlement planning because of Morris's landmark interpretation (1980a) of the layout of Huánuco Pampa. Radial site design has not been discussed for a number of reasons. First, many Inka sites apparently have no evidence of radial planning. Second, radial layout, when it exists, is somewhat "disguised" behind other more visible planning concepts, such as rectangular or trapezium plazas and the more visible division of some settlements into several parts. In fact, the division of Inka sites and sectors of sites into two, three, and four parts is intimately related to the question of radiality. The following section will explore the meaning and greater implications of Inka radial layouts.

Prototypes for the Radial Concept

As noted in the foregoing, there are two kinds of radial planning found in Cuzco. One is in the actual layout of the capital (see chap. 2, "The Surrounding Districts" and "Roads to the Surrounding Districts"), where one finds approximately twelve districts surrounding the central sector. The streets leading out from the center form a pattern that is generally radial. Aspects of tri- and quadripartition are expressed in this layout, since the twelve districts are divided into four groups (of three districts each) attributed to the four *suyu*. As seen from the center of Cuzco, the Chinchasuyu districts lie to the northwest; the Antisuyu districts to the northeast; the Qollasuyu districts to the southeast; the Kuntisuyu districts to the southwest. The four main roads leading out from the main plaza of Cuzco lead directly into, and pass through, the four *suyu* areas formed by each set of three districts. They do not separate the *suyu* areas from each other.

One might expect that the arrangement of the twelve districts would also allow one to define the bipartition present in the plan of central Cuzco. In this case the Chinchasuyu and Antisuyu districts would define the upper, or *hanan*, half, and Kuntisuyu and Qollasuyu would define the lower, or *hurin*, half. Such is not the case, since the dual division of Cuzco is usually defined by the road to Antisuyu, which leaves the main plaza and proceeds to the northeast along Triunfo and Hatun Rumiyoc streets. The line dividing the upper and lower parts of Cuzco thus does not coincide with the divisions between the *suyu* areas formed by the surrounding districts. If one extends the division line between upper and lower Cuzco (as seen in the central sector), it cuts through the Antisuyu districts to the northeast and the Kuntisuyu districts to the southwest. This has been demonstrated by Chávez Ballón (1970), who published a map (fig. 7.17) in which the four *suyu* form an X over the city. The central sector's dual division passes through the X and crosses it (✗).

When viewing the physical plan of Cuzco, one sees concepts related to tri- and quadripartition only by viewing the organization of the surrounding districts. Dual division in the plan was expressed in the central sector. The central sector of Cuzco was inhabited mainly by Inkas, whereas the surrounding districts were inhabited by non-Inkas or Inkas-by-privilege. Thus one might say that in Cuzco's layout bipartition is particularly Inka, whereas tri- and quadripartition require the participation of other peoples.

The second kind of radial planning found at Cuzco is the large pattern formed by the *zeque* system. This set of forty or forty-one lines extending out from the Sun Temple does not appear to have influenced the architectural plan of the capital in any direct way (chap. 2, "The *Zeque* System"), but is a most useful tool available for studying how the Inkas organized space and its relation to social divisions. The primary analysis of this is by Zuidema (1964), who interpreted the *zeque* organization primarily in terms of kinship. The lines of the system are divided into four *suyu* (I is Chinchasuyu; II is Qollasuyu; III is Antisuyu; IV is Kuntisuyu).[13] Nine lines each are found in I, II, and III; fourteen lines are in IV. Within each of the four parts the lines are subdivided into groups of three. Thus tripartition emerges as a fundamental aspect of each of the four parts. Each group of three lines is assigned the designation Collana, Payan, and Cayao. The significance of these terms is complex and multifaceted. For this study, one can associate Collana with Inka, Payan with Inka and non-Inka, and Cayao with non-Inka. Similarly, Collana groups were related to Inka kings; Payan groups to *panaqa*; Cayao groups to *ayllu*. Tripartition also emerges within each group of three *zeque* lines, since each line carries a Collana, Payan, or Cayao designation. Bipartition is also present in the *zeque*'s organization, since one may pair Chinchasuyu (I) with Antisuyu (III) and Qollasuyu (II) with Kuntisuyu (IV) to form two halves.

Zuidema views the *zeque* organization from more than one standpoint. Of particular interest to this study are his "Second Representation" and "First Representation."[14] In the Second Representation, the most comprehensive, the *suyu* are clearly represented. The *suyu* I (Chinchasuyu) and III (Antisuyu) form the upper, or *hanan*, half. The *suyu* II (Qollasuyu) and IV (Kuntisuyu) form the lower half. In each *suyu* the names Collana, Payan, and Collao refer to the three groups of three *zeque* lines (fig. 7.16, top). Zuidema's First Representation views the *zeque* system by eliminating the Cayao (non-Inka) groups of lines (I3, II3, III3, and IV3). The *hanan* half thus has four groups of three lines and the *hurin* half has four groups.

The Second Representation is an imperial view, since it includes non-

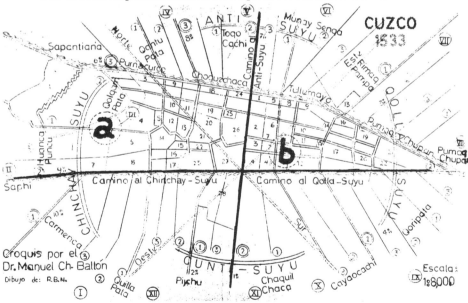

7.17. *A somewhat schematic plan depicting fundamental divisions in Inka Cuzco* (*Chávez Ballón 1970*). *The four main Inka roads* (solid dark lines) *come together in the Haukaypata Plaza.* Hanan *Cuzco* (a) *is separated from* hurin *Cuzco* (b) *by the road to Antisuyu. The districts surrounding central Cuzco are divided into four groups: Chinchasuyu* (Chinchay Suyu)*, Antisuyu* (Anti Suyu)*, Qollasuyu* (Qolla Suyu)*, and Kuntisuyu* (Cunti suyu)*. The divisions between the four groups form an* X *(broken lines). The dual division of central Cuzco, when extended, cuts through the Antisuyu and Kuntisuyu groups of districts. From Chávez Ballón* (1970)*.

Inkas and emphasizes the four *suyu.* The First Representation is more Inka, since it excludes non-Inkas and emphasizes the dual division as opposed to the four *suyu.* In another sense, one could relate the Second Representation to the entire design of Cuzco whereas the First Representation would relate primarily to Cuzco's central sector (which excluded non-Inkas).

Thus both the plan of Cuzco and the *zeque* system have a number of characteristics in common. Both have a radial design and a fundamental dual division. This bipartition can be seen dividing both Inka or subject populations. Both have a form of quadripartition relating to the *suyu,* or four quarters of the empire. Both use tripartition. In Cuzco's plan there are three districts for each *suyu.* In the *zeque* system the lines of each *suyu* can be viewed in groups of three. In the *zeque* system tripartition is more complex, since it is also used to order and rank individual lines in sequence. That aspect of tripartition cannot be seen in the physical plan of Cuzco.

The similarities between the *zeque* system and the plan of Cuzco allow one to use either one as a general model for the examination of radiality and its related forms of partitioning in other Inka settlements. The *zeque* system, possibly because it creates spatial patterns without much architectural elaboration (that "architectural" elaboration would be only the system's *waqa),* is more intricate, allowing one to see detailed aspects of spatial structure, such as the lines and their groupings within *suyu.* One important difference between the plan of Cuzco and the *zeque* system is that the dual division of the central sector of Cuzco does not coincide spatially with any dual division based on the surrounding districts, but rather crosscuts two of the *suyu.* This does not occur in the *zeque* system, where duality is achieved by pairing two of the *suyu.*

Huánuco Pampa's Design Interpreted
Morris (1980a) uses many of the principles outlined by Zuidema to interpret the plan of Huánuco Pampa. He begins with several statements of caution, noting that "structural principles are expressed with shifting relationships and perspectives." He also notes that the organization of the site may not be the result of actual *zeque* lines, since there is no archaeological indication of the forty-plus lines at Huánuco Pampa. Moreover, Morris emphasizes that kin and marriage classes related to Cuzco's *zeque* system may not be represented in the correspondences he identifies. The relationships he detects are present in the more abstract levels at which *zeque* lines were arranged. By this he means primarily the evidence for bi-, tri-, and quadripartition within a radial design.

Morris sees Zuidema's Second Representation at Huánuco Pampa by attributing a *suyu* designation to the buildings on each of the four sides of the rectangular plaza.[15] The buildings of each side are divided into three sectors by corridors and/or walls, just as the grouping of *zeque* forms a tripartition in each of the *zeque* system's *suyu*. The bipartition of the city follows the main Inka road cutting across the plaza in a southeast-northwest direction and is clearly one way of seeing the city divided into two parts. Thus the northern and eastern sides become *hanan* and the southern and western parts become *hurin* (fig. 7.18, A). The enumeration of the subzones within the four *suyu* is done according to the *zeque* model. Morris points out that a confirmation of this model's applicability to Huánuco Pampa's design is found in the way the two halves replicate each other. This similarity of I to II and III to IV is found in the city's architecture as well as in the *zeque* system. Another confirmation is that the most formalized architecture is found in *suyu* I and III, the upper, or *hanan*, part of the site.

Morris also sees the planning of Huánuco Pampa from a different perspective—that of Zuidema's First Representation. This other interpretation was prompted by the architectural indications of an east-west axis formed by a street on the west, the *ushnu* platform, and a set of gateways on the east. Dividing the site along that axis creates two symmetrical halves (fig. 7.18, B). In this case the northern half would be *hanan* and the southern half would be *hurin*. As with Zuidema's First Representation, it is possible to define four main divisions in each half. These are formed by using the widest streets in the city. Morris notes that this set of divisions, while plausible, splits the compound on the east with the gateways, which seem to be a unified activity area.

Morris's application of the First Representation to Huánuco Pampa is somewhat more daring than the first. There is, however, evidence from the actual plan of Inka Cuzco which reinforces his view of two perspectives functioning at Huánuco Pampa. If one superimposes Morris's first perspective on the second, one finds a crossed X, somewhat similar to that detected in Cuzco's plan by Chávez Ballón. The perspective emphasizing the *suyu* forms the X. The perspective emphasizing only an *hanan-hurin* division crosses the X forming a ✕.[16]

There is additional evidence for the accuracy of Morris's correspondences. As noted in chapter 5, water is significant in determining the upper and lower divisions, with primacy given to the upper, or *hanan*, division. At Huánuco Pampa the elaborate waterworks (a "bath" and artificial pool) are located just to the north of the east-west line dividing the site's most elaborate compound on the east (fig. 5.6). The waterworks are part of Morris's *hanan* halves when seen from both of his perspectives. In addition, the orientation of the *suyu* and the dual halves is

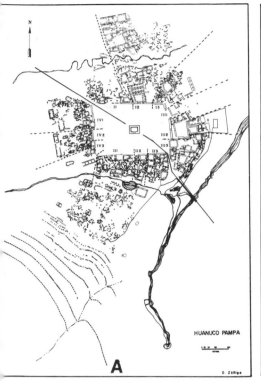 

7.18. *Two perspectives of the organization of Huánuco Pampa's plan. The first (A) views the center in four parts (suyu), represented by the sectors on each side of the rectangular plaza. Each part is subdivided into three sectors by streets or walls. The division between* hanan *and* hurin *is defined by the Inka road passing through the northwestern and southeastern corners of the plaza. This corresponds to Zuidema's Second Representation of the* zeque *system. The second perspective (B) creates the* hanan-hurin *division along an east-west line. This corresponds to Zuidema's First Representation of the* zeque *system in which Cayao (non-Inka) groups of lines are eliminated, resulting in four main divisions in each half. From Morris (1980a).*

generally that found in Cuzco's physical plan and in the *zeque* system at Cuzco. At Huánuco Pampa the *hanan* half occupies the north, or north to east (depending on the perspective). In Cuzco one finds the surrounding districts of Chinchasuyu and Antisuyu and *zeque* lines of the same *suyu* occupying the northern area of the city. The *hanan* part of central Cuzco is the northern half of the sector.

In summary, Morris's analysis of the structure of space and architecture at Huánuco Pampa by utilizing concepts developed from the *zeque* system is convincing not just because radiality can be detected in the city's plan, but the system's bi-, tri-, and quadripartition are quite evident in the city plan. Morris's analysis is sufficiently convincing to sug-

217

gest that radiality, wherever it is found in an Inka settlement, may allow further analysis with the various types of spatial patterning observed in the *zeque* system.

Bi-, Tri-, and Quadripartitioning in Other Radial Plans

The radial sector at Inkawasi (described in the foregoing) appears to be an architectural representation of at least one part of the spatial organization of the *zeque* system (Hyslop 1985: 52–56). Its fourteen units may be an architectural representation of the *zeque* system's Kuntisuyu quadrant (fig. 7.16, top). There are a number of parallels. First, the Cuzco system's Kuntisuyu fans out from southeast to southwest, as does the sector at Inkawasi. The system's Kuntisuyu is composed of fourteen lines while Inkawasi's radial sector has fourteen units. The system's lines are arranged in groups of three, and this is generally true of the units of Inkawasi's radial units.[17] Kuntisuyu's lines are divided by Zuidema into two segments (A and B) between lines seven and eight. At Inkawasi the radial sector has a division defined in the middle of its arc by the only pie-shaped unit. The other units are rectangular. It is improbable that the individual rooms of each unit represent the *waqa* of a *zeque* line. Whereas twelve of the lines of Kuntisuyu have between three and five *waqa*, which could correspond to the three to five rooms of each unit, two of Kuntisuyu's lines (one and eight) have fifteen *waqa*.[18]

Inkawasi's radial sector allows for some insight not visible in the data and analysis from Huánuco Pampa. The possibility that actual lines (not detectable at Huánuco Pampa) are represented by architectural units at Inkawasi heightens the prospect that radial design is actually representing part of the *zeque* system and not just principles derived from it. No other sector at Inkawasi is characterized by a radial design. It is unclear why only Kuntisuyu should be presented radially. The possible meaning of Kuntisuyu's unusual organization has been discussed by Zuidema in several publications (1977a: 242–244, 1982a: 209–211, 218–221, 1982b: 90–93). One reoccurring point is its relationship to foreign or non-Inka people.

Two other settlements with a more complete radial design somewhat similar to that of Huánuco Pampa are Pumpu and Chilecito. A thorough analysis of Pumpu's layout must wait the publication of accurate maps. It is probable that much of Morris's analysis at Huánuco Pampa may hold true for Pumpu. This will be difficult to show, since Pumpu may never have been completed, and one large set of formally arranged buildings and patios (on the southwest) is not closely associated with the plaza.

Chilecito is quite similar to Huánuco Pampa except that its radiality is expressed by individual buildings and compounds, not by streets defining entire subdivisions of buildings. It would appear that the four *suyu* are represented by the buildings constructed on the four sides of the rectangular plaza (fig. 7.13). As at Huánuco Pampa, bipartition could be achieved by a line cutting diagonally northwest-southeast through the plaza, or by an east-west line running through the *ushnu* platform in the center of the plaza. There are not enough buildings at Chilecito to detect or reject a tripartition scheme within the *suyu* on all sides. The eastern side (a possible Antisuyu, because of its location on the east), however, has three compounds with large patios that may well represent tripartition. Chilecito had about forty buildings or compounds in it. It is probably premature to suggest that each represents a *zeque* line (of which there were forty or forty-one), but the idea should not yet be discarded.

Chucuito is especially provoking. It is a special example of an Inka settlement design combining an orthogonal pattern with clear aspects of radiality. The nine radial streets (or the nine rows of blocks formed by the streets) may represent the nine lines typical of a *zeque* quadrant. If such is the case, the blocks do not represent *zeque waqa*, since there are far fewer blocks (about forty) than *waqa* in any of the system's quadrants. Since the fan opens to the east-northeast, it may be a representation of the Antisuyu quadrant. In Cuzco's *zeque* system, Antisuyu occupies the northeast. If Chucuito is a representation of Antisuyu, it is worth noting that at several large Inka settlements (Huánuco Pampa, Pumpu, Chilecito, and Inkawasi) the eastern or northeastern sector can be defined as Antisuyu and these sectors have the compounds with the largest patios and most elaborate architecture.

Maucallacta occupies an arc fanning out to the east-southeast. The lack of a detailed plan precludes an elaborate analysis of its design, and the aerial photograph published here (fig. 7.15) does not permit a close examination of the sectors' internal divisions. The northern sector, with the finest Cuzco-style masonry and associated plaza, is clearly divided into three parts by two corridors with fine masonry gates. When viewed from the "center"—the Puma Orco outcrop—this sector is located directly to the west. South of it one finds another sector with some fine Inka masonry. It is divided into three parts by north-south lines (one a terrace wall, one a street). South of it lies the largest sector. It has no fine masonry, but does have three parts divided by streets— a lower part and two upper ones. The southernmost sector is very small (less than a dozen buildings) and partially destroyed by modern constructions.

Maucallacta's elaborate design, when well mapped, may stimulate much discussion about Inka radial planning. One could propose that

Maucallacta has the four *suyu* represented by four sectors. Instead of being in a circle, as at several other Inka settlements, they are laid on an arc. One might associate the two sectors of fine masonry with Chinchasuyu and Antisuyu (traditionally *hanan*) and those without it with Qollasuyu and Kuntisuyu (traditionally *hurin*). The idea that the sectors represent *suyu* is supported by their participation in a radial design and by their tripartite layouts. Maucallacta has a plaza, divided into two parts by a terrace wall, suggesting an *hanan-hurin* division. The two sectors with fine masonry might be associated with the western, or uppermost, side of the plaza (to which they are closest), whereas those without the fine masonry would be associated with the lower, eastern side (to which they are closest).

If the above analysis holds, curious variations occur in the Maucallacta radial design that are not known (or have not been detected) elsewhere. The more or less standard orientations of the *suyu* are ignored or, most probably, reversed. Such is entirely possible, given the strong influence of dialectical reasoning in Andean thought (Isbell 1982).

In summary, radial design as interpreted by *zeque* spatial patterning and partitioning is quite varied, since at times it appears that only one *suyu* is represented, whereas at other times much of the system's general pattern is described in architecture. Whether the actual system or only its spatial patterns is being portrayed is less certain. Since in one or two cases the lines may be portrayed architecturally, it may be that relatively complete *zeque* spatial organization is lurking behind some Inka radial layouts. There can be little doubt that settlements arranged into two, three, and four parts employed groupings used by the *zeque* system. The growing evidence for the influence of *zeque* organization in Inka site design allows one to comprehend more fully the comments by Polo de Ondegardo (1916b: 114), an early and accurate informant of Inka affairs, who wrote that the towns and villages of the empire were "divided by their *zeques* and lines." He added (1917: 52) that he had recorded more than one hundred places with the system. He did not make it clear, or perhaps was unaware, that *zeque* concepts and spatial patterning may have been a key to the layout of some of those "towns and villages."

Understanding the role of *zeque* spatial organization in Inka settlements holds some promise for a preliminary understanding of the activities that may have been carried out in such sites. It may also permit scholars to determine when various sectors were used, since the *zeque* system's parts have a highly structured calendrical aspect (Zuidema 1977a, 1981a, 1982a, 1982b). The application of the system's principles may also aid in determining what kind and rank of people were associated with specific architectural units, since one of the system's preoccupations, at least at Cuzco, was to define which social groups would carry out ritual and other tasks.[19]

Summary

Two patterns used in Inka settlement layouts are orthogonal and radial designs. The orthogonal designs differ from the later Spanish ones by often having the plazas at one end or on the side. A few known Inka orthogonal plans appear to have a smaller, secondary plaza within the grid. Spanish grids most often have the main plaza in the grid's center. In the orthogonal plan, the units or blocks formed by the streets are rectangular or slightly rhomboidal and of varying size. The Inka orthogonal plans may be modeled after the central sector of Cuzco, but the correspondence is not clear due to the inability to know the exact design of central Cuzco, remodeled since the Spanish conquest. It may be significant that Inka orthogonal plans appear to have block or unit counts in multiples of ten, a possible symbolic representation of decimal organization or of the original ten *panaqa* and ten *ayllu* of Inka Cuzco. Orthogonal layouts are found within the Cuzco area and regions relatively near the capital. This suggests that they were used early in the state's expansion, and that the concept was not exported to the extremes of the empire.

Radial patterns, as with grids, are found in the layout of entire sites, or just parts of them. Although there are examples in the Cuzco area, the radial pattern appears most commonly used in Inka settlements in conquered or assimilated areas of the state. Radiality is observed in the plan of Cuzco outside of the central sector. It is also the primary pattern formed by the *zeque* system at Cuzco. Either or both of these could be the model for other radial layouts, but the *zeque* system is a more complete demonstration of how Inkas integrated ideas of bi-, tri-, and quadripartition in the organization of a complete radial pattern. In general, bipartition in a radial design refers to dual division and expresses the moiety concept. Dual parts are composed of quadrants, or *suyu*, of which Chinchasuyu and Antisuyu form the upper, *hanan*, half, and Qollasuyu and Kuntisuyu form the lower, or *hurin*, half. The quadrants, among other things, express the four-part division of the Inka Empire. The *suyu*, or quadrants, are commonly divided into three parts. This tripartition relates the Inka concepts of Collana, Payan, and Collao, which refer to the higher, middle, and lower status of Inka, Inka and non-Inka, and non-Inka groups.

When a radial design is found in Inka settlements it may portray an entire circle or just a quadrant. When an entire radial plan is represented, the four quadrants, or *suyu*, are generally found on each of four sides of a rectangular or rhomboidal plaza. The upper-lower, or moiety, division can be detected by dividing the four quadrants into two groups, as in the *zeque* system. The upper, or *hanan*, part usually has the more elaborate architecture and is commonly, but not always, associated with an arc in the northwestern to southeastern side of the site. The lower, or *hurin*, half is less elaborate architecturally and commonly found in the arc occupying the southeastern to northwestern part of the site. There is another perspective by which the *hanan-hurin* division can be observed, but this has been demonstrated only at Huánuco Pampa and Cuzco. The quadrants, or *suyu*, are most commonly divided into three architectural groups, just as the lines in most *suyu* in the *zeque* system are grouped into three units. This tripartition appears to be an expression of the Collana, Payan, and Collao concepts and may be expressed in decreasingly elaborate architecture.

It is still uncertain to what degree the Inkas are actually portraying *zeque* systems in radial layouts, or just the principles and spatial relationships found in the system. The Kuntisuyu sector at Inkawasi is evidence that a part of the actual system may be portrayed, since architectural units, possibly representing lines, are generally oriented and grouped, as in the *zeque* system.

The use of the *zeque* model in the layout of an architectural plan allows for the expression of some of the most fundamental Inka concepts concerning the organization of society, the state, and even the world. It permitted some settlements to be total or partial representations of the known Inka world. They were thus replicating Cuzco, whose plan incorporated a world view by the use of the fundamental bi-, tri-, and quadripartitioning. No one has said it better than Morris (1980a: 30), who sees such a plan as an Inka attempt "to build a new order in the foreign world it 'administered.'"

8
Orientation and Alignment: Astronomical Concerns

Did astronomical concerns influence the design of some Inka settlements, buildings, and other architectural features? This complex topic is still in its infancy, since detailed astronomical measurements have only been carried out in a few places. Moreover, only in the past decade has some sense been made of the astronomical evidence found in and around Cuzco and in the early historical sources.

Many details of Inka religion and calendrics and their relation to astronomy are beyond the scope of this chapter. Thus it is useful to mention the relevant literature. Recent advances are based on work by Zuidema (1977a, 1982b) on the Inka calendar. This research is based on calendrical data in ethnohistorical accounts and on the organization of some aspects of Cuzco's *zeque* system, some of whose *waqa*, or sacred shrines, served as observation points or sighting landmarks for astronomical observations. This evidence for Inka astronomy, backed up by field survey, has been presented by Zuidema (1981a, 1981b, 1981c, 1982a) and his collaborator Aveni (1981a, 1981b).

Other researchers (Dearborn and White 1982; Dearborn, Schreiber, and White 1987) have investigated the astronomical aspects of Machu Picchu. In addition, I carried out an archaeoastronomical study at Inkawasi (Hyslop 1985). The information on Inka astronomy has been supplemented by ethnographic work on Quechua cosmology by Urton (1978, 1981) and by alignment data from numerous Andean coastal sites (Urton and Aveni 1983), some of which are Inka. Outside of Peru, only limited archaeoastronomical work has been done, namely at Ingapirca in Ecuador (Ziolkowski and Sadowski 1984), Copacabana in Bolivia (Rivera Sundt 1984), and Incallacta in Bolivia (Sanzetenea 1973).[1]

In 1986 and 1987 I visited a number of Inka settlements outside of Peru. No detailed archaeoastronomical study was carried out at any settlement, but possible astronomical implications do emerge from a comparative study of the plans and individual monuments. Since most Inka archaeoastronomical research has been carried out in the Cuzco region, one goal of this chapter is to present and evaluate data from elsewhere in Tawantinsuyu. First, however, it is useful to consider briefly the nature of Inka astronomy at Cuzco.

Inka Astronomy

The main Inka deities were the sun, the moon, some stars or star groups, and meteorological phenomena, such as thunder and rainbows. Also of cosmological concern were some "dark cloud" constellations and the Milky Way. Inka astronomy was based in great part on horizon observations of celestial phenomena (Zuidema 1981b; Aveni 1981a). Important days in the annual cycle were defined by the rising and setting of important celestial bodies, particularly the sun, at certain points on the horizon.

At Cuzco, these events on the horizon were viewed from observation points in and near the city. From them, specific points on the horizon were marked by towers or pillars (chap. 2, "Astronomical Towers"). Other observations may have been made through windows and by shadows cast by specifically designated pillars or windows (Dearborn and Schreiber 1986: 16).

Some of the important observations at Cuzco were made from points outside of the city limits. Zuidema (1981a) and Aveni (1981a) present evidence for observations made on the June solstice (Inti Raymi) and December solstice (Capac Raymi), major Inka feasts. The day of the zenith passage was determined to fix an antizenith date important in the agricultural calendar.[2]

A number of Inka settlements (discussed below) outside of the Cuzco area are oriented generally east-west, possibly indicating a concern with the equinox. Within the tropics the sun rises and sets on an east-west line on the equinoxes. An Inka concern with the equinoxes is, however, poorly documented. No research in the Cuzco region has found physical evidence for such observations, and the sole historical account of such interests comes from the often unreliable Garcilaso de la Vega,[3] who described a shadow-casting technique that might have determined the equinox, but basically describes a means of observing the zenith when at midday "the sun bathed all sides of the column and cast no shadow at all."

Finally, the Inkas appear to have had a special interest in the southern circum-polar region from about 146 to 155 degrees. There, important constellations arose, and the Milky Way, the river, or *mayo*, to Andean people, was centered (Urton 1978, 1981; Zuidema 1982a: 209–211, 218–221).

Astronomical Influence on Cuzco's Design

Did astronomical observations influence Cuzco's physical plan? The Inkas made several observations from points outside the city's architectural limits. Columns or towers on hills were necessary for these observations. As noted in chapter 2, these columns or pillars were found on hills surrounding the city and might properly be considered part of it. At least two important compounds in central Cuzco may have had an astronomical alignment. Zuidema (1982a) presents evidence that the Qori Kancha was aligned either with the Pleiades rise azimuth, or the nearly similar sunrise around May 25, which, according to an early historical source (Molina 1943: 25), signaled the lunar "month" that included the December solstice.[4] Zuidema (1981a: 326) also notes that the central gutter and axis of the round tower (Muyujmarca) at Saqsawaman and the rectangular complex surrounding it are "all very close to the ZSR (zenith sun rise at 103 degrees 30 minutes) and AZSS (anti zenith sun set) direction." The location of the *ushnu* stone in the plaza of Cuzco may have been selected because of an interest in defining an antizenith date (Aveni 1981a: 309–316).[5]

It appears that the orthogonal pattern of central Cuzco, the basic plan of the city's center, was probably not defined by astronomical alignments. The matter, however, might be investigated in greater detail. The longitudinal streets (Ahuacpinta and Arequipa) are oriented at 158 degrees, 6 minutes and 151 degrees, 57 minutes. Two main transverse streets (Hatun Rumiyoc and Cabracancha Maruri) are oriented between 62 and 63 degrees.[6] One might speculate that the longitudinal streets were seen as pointing to the important circum-polar region and the transverse streets to the areas of the June solstice sunrise, the May 25 sunrise, or the Pleiades rise azimuth, all within a restricted arc where the sun moves on the northeastern horizon. The solar solstice azimuths occur at about 24 degrees north and south of an east-west line at Cuzco and within the tropics. Exact correspondences with these astronomical azimuths depend on horizon heights, which vary along a street and from street to street.

An alternative astronomical interpretation of central Cuzco's layout is that it was laid out along orientations formed first by the Qori Kancha and its associated Intipampa Plaza. As Cuzco's primary religious building, its orientation may have been established prior to the street pattern, which followed that of the temple. As noted above, there is some consensus that the Qori Kancha is astronomically aligned. It is still speculative to view an astronomical pattern in Cuzco's layout.

In summary, Cuzco presents evidence that at least two compounds

(Qori Kancha and Muyujmarka) may have been oriented to or aligned with astronomical azimuths important to the Inkas. Other observations were made at Cuzco, particularly the solstices, that influenced the city's physical plan only in that their observation required the construction of towers or columns on hills about the capital. The evidence of an active and complex Inka concern with astronomy at Cuzco encourages investigators to search for the influence of astronomical concerns in the design of other settlements.

Physical Evidence for Astronomical Towers beyond Cuzco

During my surveys of several dozen Inka state settlements since 1979, horizons around the sites were scanned with binoculars for evidence of towers or columns such as those at Cuzco. It was hoped that some might have remained, particularly since some of these sites were little disturbed by Spaniards intent on destroying religious-calendrical-astronomical devices, as in Cuzco, where the towers were dismantled early in the colonial period. Dearborn and Schreiber (1986: 35) report none near Machu Picchu,[7] an area apparently never reached by the Spanish. My search for towers or columns at Inka settlements outside of the Cuzco area has produced little evidence.[8] Two towers or columns, however, each quite different, deserve description.

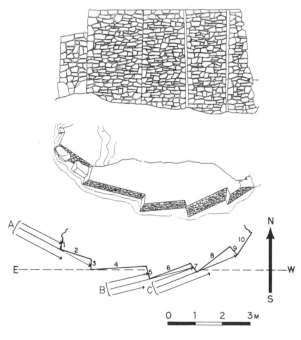

8.1. *Diagrams of the astronomical tower at Incallacta in Bolivia.* Top: *a horizontal view of the broad faces;* middle: *an oblique view of the tower's faces;* bottom: *a vertical view of the ten faces. Arrows indicate which faces the sun's rays illuminate during the June solstice sunset (A), the sunset on the day of zenith passage (B), and the December solstice sunset (C). Middle and top drawings courtesy R. Sanzetenea and D. Pereira.*

8.2. The tower on the cliff face at Incallacta as seen from below.

A tower with possible astronomical use is found at the Inka fort In-callacta in Bolivia. A curved structure with ten zigzag vertical faces is found on a cliff on the westernmost part of the site (figs. 6.18, 6.19). Its orientation is generally east-west (figs. 8.1, 8.2). Located on a precipitous slope, its type of construction rules out its being part of a residential building or the surrounding "defensive" wall. The structure is approximately 6.8 meters long and 4.5 meters high, built with the flat sides of stones forming the wall faces. Nothing quite like it has been recorded at any other Inka state settlement.

This tower was first interpreted as an astronomical device by Ramón Sanzetenea, an archaeologist at the Archaeological Museum in Cochabamba, Bolivia. Sanzetenea (1973) considers that the structure uses the western sunset to illuminate different faces depending on the time of year. I took the angles of faces 2, 4, 6, and 8 with a Brunton's compass and corrected for magnetic deviation.[9]

The available measurements are not sufficient to determine with certainty how the tower might have functioned. It is apparent, however, that only face 1 would have been illuminated completely during the June solstice sunset. During the following six months the sun would set farther to the south, illuminating successive faces. On an equinox Sanzetenea observed face 5 illuminated, as the measurements suggest. It would seem that face 9 should be illuminated only during the December solstice, but the measurements indicate that it is not, or only

8.3. The Horca del Inka, a lintel placed between two crags on a hilltop south of Copacabana by Lake Titicaca in Bolivia. It may have served as part of an Inka astronomical device.

partially. In fig. 8.1 (bottom), arrows indicate the solstice and zenith sunsets (for 17 degrees south latitude, corrected for horizon elevation), events that might have been marked (with no certainty) by the tower.

If the tower of Incallacta is an astronomical device, its faces indicate that it served to mark several times of the year. It may be similar to a "wall" described by the seventeenth-century priest Montesinos (1882: 71, chap. 12): "An honest and talkative *criollo* showed me four very old walls on a hill, and assured me that this structure served as a timepiece for the ancient Indians."

The tower of Incallacta occupies a prominent place in the site's design. It is visible from most of the site because of its position high on a cliff to the west. Additional research on the tower may clarify whether it marked important days in the Cuzco calendar. Another option is that it marked days in the Incallacta agricultural calendar. Such days would have been different from those at Cuzco, since Incallacta is located at nearly 17 degrees south latitude.

A different sort of possible astronomical device, involving a natural crag or column, has been described by Rivera Sundt (1984). It is located on Mount Kesanani just south of the town of Copacabana, Bolivia, once an Inka settlement (figs. 8.3, 8.4). A hole in a natural crag casts the light of the June solstice on an artificial lintel set between two crags.[10] On June 21, 1978, the June solstice, at approximately 8:00 A.M. (somewhat after the sunrise), Rivera S. and several others observed the sunlight passing through the hole and projecting on the rectangular lintel stone. This lintel between the two crags is known as La Horca del Inka (The Gallows of the Inka). There is no evidence that it was ever used for hangings. Trimborn (1959: 6–8) suggests that it might have had an astronomical use but makes no observations on the solstice or other types of measurements. He notes that it was once known as "intiwatana."

Rivera also writes that a stone projection 39.63 meters to the east casts a shadow on the lintel on September 21, marking the equinox. It is unclear whether Rivera witnessed this event, but the layout of the *horca* and the stone projection indicate that it might function in such a way.

Is the crag with the hole an astronomical "pillar"? The hole through which the light passes appears artificial. No confirming study with a transit has yet been made.[11] The location of the crag with the hole and the associated *horca* near what was once an important Inka settlement suggests that it is an Inka construction. The crag with the hole functions by light casting, a technique described by Sarmiento for some columns with holes near Cuzco (see description below). If the *horca* and associated crag is an observational device used to mark the solstice, it did not influence the planning of the Inka settlement below it. It was, however, a part of the settlement and could be seen from it.

Windows, Light, and Shadow Casting at Machu Picchu

One of the unique buildings at Machu Picchu is the Torreón (figs. 8.5, 8.6). Located above a burial chamber, the Torreón is built of fine Cuzco masonry and surrounds a large shaped rock. The Torreón rests beside

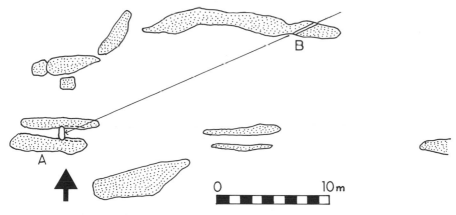

8.4. *Diagram of the Horca del Inka with two crags supporting a lintel (A) and the nearby crag with a hole (B), which casts light (arrow) on the lintel during the morning of the June solstice. Shaded areas are stone crags or prominences. Redrawn from Rivera S. (1984: 106).*

the uppermost fountain of a set of sixteen fountains. Studies by Dearborn and White (1982, 1983) propose that it served as an astronomical observatory. The primary evidence for this is the orientation of a cut edge on a raised portion of shaped rock found within the Torreón. It points out a window in the Torreón at an azimuth of 60 degrees, 95 minutes, nearly identical to that of the June solstice sunrise in the fifteenth century. The window itself points toward the Pleiades rise azimuth at 65 degrees. Postulating that stone projections outside the window held a string or some other device in the window,[12] Dearborn and White performed an experiment indicating that such a device could have been used to predict the actual day of the solstice. A string or some other apparatus in the window is necessary, since "an observer located at the rear of the stone could sight along the edge only to see the wall below the window" (Dearborn and Schreiber 1986: 23).

Whether the Inkas used some device to cast the crucial shadow on the rock's edge is speculative but important because of its implications. Limited evidence on Inka light and shadow casting comes from Garcilaso (see note 3, this chapter), who described it in conjunction with a stone pillar. Another description is by Sarmiento (1965: 236, chap. 30), who describes stone columns in Cuzco with holes around which paving stones with lines were placed. "Leveled lines corresponding to movements of the sun entering from the holes of the columns" were made in the paving stones. Sarmiento adds that this apparatus served as a timepiece for determining planting and harvesting dates. Sarmiento's description indicates that cuts in rocks could be used for solar observations. He mentions "holes" through which sunlight passed, but not windows. Guaman Poma (1936: 235), however, described morning observations of the sun through a window that established important days in the agricultural calendar.

A fine masonry structure (fig. 4.9) in the Intiwatana sector of Pisaq near Cuzco also surrounds a shaped rock with a cut edge oriented at

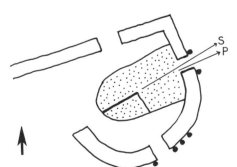

8.5. *Schematic of the Torreón at Machu Picchu. The central rock (dotted area) has a cut edge with a June solstice sunrise (S) orientation. The window is aligned with the Pleiades rise in the fifteenth century (P). Black dots represent stone pegs on the exterior of the building. If a shadow-casting device was hung on the pegs, the cut edge could be aligned with the June solstice sunrise. Redrawn from Dearborn and Schreiber (1986: 24).*

8.6. The Torreón at Machu Picchu surrounds a central rock with a debated astronomical role.

about 63 degrees—varying from 60 to 66 degrees (Dearborn and White 1983: S46–S48). At Pisaq's Intiwatana, the June solstice sunrise azimuth is at 64 degrees. Unfortunately, the building's walls are not high enough to indicate whether they blocked light or had windows. A crucial alignment device is missing. The cut edge on the central rock at Pisaq is somewhat similar to that on the rock in Machu Picchu's Torreón, and it is offered as supporting evidence that such cut edges were not random.

The implications of Machu Picchu's Torreón reach beyond the possible function of that building. Dearborn and Schreiber (1986: 17) and Dearborn (1986: 120) use it to claim that Inkas were capable of very precise alignments, and they judge the validity of other archaeoastronomical studies accordingly. The high precision of Inka astronomical observations, however, remains as debatable as the postulated apparatus in the Torreón's window.

Other difficult-to-evaluate astronomical aspects of the Torreón at Machu Picchu are explored by Dearborn and White. A window facing southeast may have been used to observe the southern circum-polar region, where several important Andean constellations appear. When sunlight passed through the Torreón's two windows, a period of five or six days before and after the zenith passage was defined. A window at the entrance to a cave (Intimachay) at Machu Picchu may have been designed to admit the light of the December solstice sunrise (Dearborn, Schreiber, and White 1987).

Archaeoastronomical research at Machu Picchu (and Pisaq) is useful for a number of reasons. It suggests, but does not prove, how observations may have been made through light or shadow casting. Physical evidence for this technique has not been researched in Cuzco, where most investigations deal with observations made from observation points to horizon towers marking important solar azimuths. The Machu Picchu research also proposes how cuts on some rocks may have served for astronomical observations. This may be helpful for understanding some of the meaning of carved rocks and boulders (chap. 4). The evidence (supported in part by a hypothetical string) for a June solstice alignment suggests that it was observed somewhat differently than at Cuzco (where a June solstice sunset observation by horizon towers has been described by Zuidema and Aveni). At present there are no data concerning whether astronomical alignments influenced the layout of Machu Picchu.

Astronomical Alignments at Inkawasi

Was the general design of Inka settlements influenced by Inka astronomical interests? This proposition has been studied in detail only at Inkawasi (figs. 6.16, 6.17), the Inka garrison in the Cañete Valley of Peru (Hyslop 1985: 46–77, 129–137). Inkawasi's military aspects are discussed in chapter 6. Fig. 8.7 is a simplified map of Inkawasi presenting the orientations of major compounds and architectural axes of the site. The orientations are to true north as established by solar and stellar observations.

The orientation data from Inkawasi suggest that several compound or site axes were aligned with horizon azimuths important to Inkas. This argument is subject to debate for a number of factors discussed below. Details concerning the measurements are found in Hyslop (1985). The alignments may be summarized as follows: (1) to the zenith sunset azimuth—the large compound south of transit station D is aligned with a zenith sunset. The northern wall of the compound (equivalent to the southern side of the main plaza) misses the zenith sunset azimuth by about half a degree; (2) to the June solstice sunrise and Pleiades (or May 25 solar) azimuths—the trapezoidal plaza creates an arc of less than seven degrees on the northeastern horizon, within which these azimuths may be observed. The point from which this alignment was

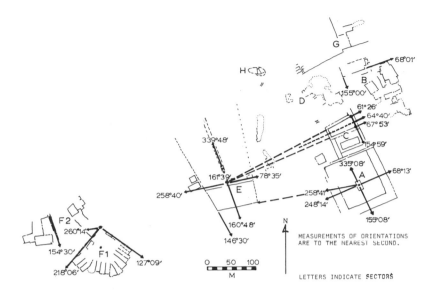

8.7. *A simplified map of Inkawasi with the orientations of major compounds and buildings. Several do not correspond to azimuths of interest to the Inkas. A trapezoidal plaza (at* A *and* B*) defines an arc on the northeastern horizon that included the azimuths of the June solstice sunrise, the Pleiades rise, and the May 25 sunrise. A corridor oriented at 155 degrees points to the region of the quasi-circum-polar constellations and the Milky Way. The compound south of point* D *is aligned with the zenith sunset. The compound defines the southern side of the main plaza, which has an* ushnu *platform in it (*E*). From Hyslop (1985: 58).*

laid out may be debated and affects (because of different horizon elevations) where, within the arc, the proposed azimuths occur; (3) to the circum-polar region on the southeastern horizon—the main corridor passing southeast through transit station C points to this area. The circum-polar area is not a specific sight-line defined by research in the Cuzco area, but is an arc on the horizon of interest in Inka and contemporary Quechua cosmology. The main corridor is aligned with the lowest point on the southern horizon, which forms a bowl-like depression within which the quasi-circum-polar constellations rose.

At Inkawasi, no architectural alignments were observed that correspond to other solstice sunrises or sunsets, some of which were important in Cuzco. Likewise, no other alignments appear to have been directed to Andean star group azimuths. No east-west alignments were detected that might indicate an Inka interest in representing the equinox.

Dearborn (1986) has evaluated the above proposed alignments, raising questions concerning their precision.[13] As noted earlier, what constitutes a precise alignment is still in question. Whether or not Inkas

233

made extremely precise measurements does not rule out their constructing "aligned" buildings or compounds without great precision, particularly if the architecture was not intended to serve for observation (Hyslop 1985: 70). Site axes or compounds aligned with Inka horizon azimuths may have been intended to symbolize ideas or the time associated with the azimuth and did not serve as observatories.

One means of determining whether "imprecise" architectural alignments were intentional is to compare a number of Inka settlements. General patterns with astronomical origins may be detectable among a range of sites. In the context of an individual settlement such a pattern may be less convincing. The following section discusses such a possibility.

The Shape and Orientation of Inka Plazas

Since planned Inka settlements are often arranged around a central plaza, the shape of the plazas frequently defines or repeats major architectural alignments of buildings and compounds found near them. Given the lack of detailed archaeoastronomical studies at most Inka settlements, one may search for clues relating to the use of astronomical alignments in architectural layout by comparing the plazas' shape as represented in existing and corrected site plans.

Inka site plans, or their plazas, cannot be compared without establishing true north, since the magnetic north (used on most plans) varies from 0 to 5 degrees, depending on the site's location and when a plan was made. The plans consulted for this study have been oriented to true north.[14]

Inka plazas are found in varying shapes and sizes. Some authorities refer to Inka plazas as trapezoidal, a plane figure two of whose sides are parallel. In Tawantinsuyu there is secure physical evidence for only one trapezoidal plaza, a secondary plaza at the Inka garrison Inkawasi.[15] Quite a number of Inka plazas are generally rectangular.[16] A limited number of Inka plazas have the form of a trapezium, a plane figure with four sides, no two of which are parallel. Finally, some Inka plazas have an irregular shape. These categories of plaza shape are discussed below.

Rectangular Plazas

Four-sided rectangular plazas are oriented with their sides within a few degrees of a north-south or east-west axis. There is no evidence that Inka concepts of direction included the Western concepts of direction. The basis and meaning of this plaza orientation will be discussed below.

The best-known and largest of the Inka rectangular plazas is found at Huánuco Pampa (figs. 7.10, 7.11). The central axis running through the plaza, parallel to the northern and southern sides, is about 88 degrees. Although no plan is yet published, the rectangular plaza at La Centinela (Chincha Valley, Peru) is within two degrees of an east-west line. The generally rectangular plazas at Tarma Tambo (LeVine 1985: 336) and Tunsucancha (Morris 1966) are oriented to within three degrees of an east-west line.[17] The large Inka settlement of Lima La Vieja in Peru's Pisco Valley is now in ruins. Recent mapping (Carmichael 1984) and an early aerial photograph (fig. 8.8) indicate an east-west rectangular plaza. At Hatuncolla in the department of Puno, Peru, the size of the plaza is uncertain, but it probably fits within the cross of the north-south and east-west main roads which form the basis of the site's orthogonal pattern (fig. 7.4). In southern Tawantinsuyu several settlements had generally rectangular east-west plazas, particularly in Argentina. At the Pucará de Andalgalá (fig. 6.22) in Catamarca Province the southern border of the plaza is oriented at 92 degrees. The plaza of Watungasta

8.8. Aerial view of Lima La Vieja, an Inka center in the Pisco Valley, Peru. In the center of the rectangular plaza is a platform with a cross on it. It is unknown if an ushnu *platform once rested there. Most of the settlement has been destroyed in the last decades. Courtesy Department of Library Services, AMNH, Neg. no. 334700 (photo by Shippee Johnson).*

in Tinogasta is within less than two degrees of a true east-west line (Raffino et al. 1983–1985: 443–449). Shincal's plaza (fig. 3.22) in Catamarca has a southern edge oriented at 94 degrees, as does the plaza at Chilecito (fig. 7.13) in La Rioja.

The evidence for rectangular east-west plazas comes mainly from outside the Cuzco area.[18] The large plaza at Saqsawaman (fig. 2.11) in Cuzco is somewhat irregular due to the zigzag wall on its south side and the slightly curved Rodadero Hill on the north. Its long sides are oriented generally along an east-west axis. It might be classified as a variant of the rectangular east-west plazas, but there can be no certainty.

The considerable number of generally east-west rectangular plazas suggests that their orientation may not be accidental. In most cases the plaza's east-west length is longer than the north-south width. One must consider, however, that the orientation of these plazas is a random occurrence, since a number of rectangular Inka plazas are not oriented east-west.

Known rectangular plazas with other orientations include that at Pachacamac (Lurin Valley, Peru), whose central dividing road is at about 55 degrees (figs. 9.9, 9.10, 9.12). The main plaza at Catarpe (Atacama, Chile) is at 63 degrees (fig. 8.9); the plaza at Viña del Cerro (Copiapó, Chile) at 53 degrees (fig. 10.2); the plaza at Turi (Atacama, Chile) at 53 degrees (fig. 9.5). In all cases, the northeast to southwest length of the plaza is greater than the northwest to southeast width.[19] Whether this represents a group of plazas oriented to between 53 and 64 degrees for a specific reason, or is a random occurrence, is uncertain.[20] Only one rectangular plaza has been found whose long side is oriented well off east-west, but at considerably less than 53 degrees. That is the plaza at Chinchero (fig. 4.7) oriented at approximately 76 degrees.[21]

The non-east-west rectangular plazas do not appear to be oriented to known or suspected Inka astronomical azimuths. At Pachacamac, the plaza appears to fit within the alignment of two main perpendicular streets built before the Inkas. Similarly, at Turi, the plaza is oriented with the central (pre-Inka) street. It appears that pre-Inka architectural axes were used for some plazas constructed by Inkas, particularly where a pre-existing site was remodeled.

Trapezium Plazas

A limited number of Inka plazas are trapeziums. The dual plaza in Cuzco (Haukaypata and Kusipata) appears to have been two joined trapeziums (fig. 2.3). At Tomebamba, the second Inka capital in Ecuador, most buildings defining the plaza are now covered by the modern city of Cuenca. The mapping by Uhle (fig. 5.7) of some buildings on three sides

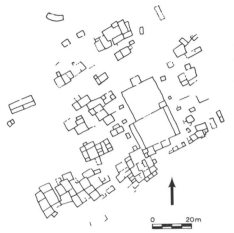

8.9. *The eastern sector of Catarpe near San Pedro de Atacama, Chile. The two large enclosed rectangles may be interpreted as a divided or dual Inka plaza. Redrawn from map by Thomas F. Lynch.*

0   20m

of the plaza indicates that it was a trapezium. Its longest axis appears to have been from east-northeast to west-southwest. Unfortunately, the destruction and remodeling at Tomebamba and Cuzco make it impossible to determine their plazas' exact orientations.[22]

Three other important Inka state settlements have trapezium plazas sufficiently intact to compare (fig. 8.10): Pumpu (Pasco, Peru), Tambo Colorado (Pisco Valley, Peru), and Inkawasi (Cañete Valley, Peru). As noted above, the southern side of the main plaza at Inkawasi (figs. 6.16, 6.17) is aligned within half a degree of the zenith sunset. A zenith alignment with about a half degree error is found on the northern side of the plaza at Tambo Colorado (Urton and Aveni 1983: 226, 227, 229) (fig. 8.11). At Pumpu (fig. 7.12) the line from the *ushnu* platform to the main gate on the east is about two degrees off a zenith sunrise azimuth.[23] Although not measured in the field, the north side of Pumpu's plaza (fig. 8.10, C) may point to the zenith sunrise. None of Pumpu's plaza sides are precisely aligned with solstice azimuths or other azimuths of possible interest to Inkas.

There is some evidence that Inka plazas in the form of a trapezium may have been influenced by a zenith alignment. Confirming measurements should be taken at Pumpu. In all cases, nevertheless, one could argue that the trapezium shape is a distortion of the more common rectangular form due to nearby river or stream embankments. The long sides of the trapezium plazas (with the exception of Inkawasi) are oriented generally east-west or from west-northwest to east-southeast. This may be a variation of the rectangular plazas' east-west orientation. It is notable that very few rectangular or trapezium plazas have their long sides oriented well away from east-west.

Irregularly Shaped Plazas

Inka plazas are sometimes irregularly shaped, with five sides or curving sides, apparently influenced by topography. Examples include the terraced plaza at Machu Picchu with natural prominences on two sides, and the large divided plaza at Incallacta (figs. 4.5, 6.18), where steep natural slopes determine the form of two of its sides. Similarly, the five-sided plaza at Nevados de Aconquija and the plaza with a curved side at Potrero de Payogasta (Salta, Argentina) are defined in part by the topography. The slightly curving four sides of the plaza on the Island of the Sun in Lake Titicaca appear to conform to the ridge, rock face, and slope between which it is located. At Raqchi (Cuzco, Peru) the plaza's shape is defined by hill slopes on two sides.

Whether topography influenced some other Inka plazas is uncertain. Due to remodeling, the shape of the plaza at Vilcas Waman (Ayacucho, Peru) cannot be reconstructed with accuracy. Reconstruction drawings by Gasparini, Harth-Terré, and Cosmopolis (in González C. et al. 1981) depict it differently, and only one rendering might have been rectangular. The *ushnu* platform at Vilcas Waman defines one side of the plaza. It is oriented within 2 degrees of an east-west line. The plaza at Ingapirca (Cañar, Ecuador) is so small it might best be defined as a patio, but its shape is irregular (fig. 9.15).

The irregular Inka plazas indicate that at a number of settlements, astronomical alignments or concepts were not important in defining the

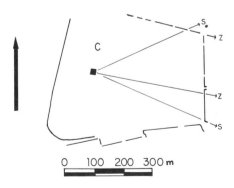

8.10. Three intact Inka trapezium plazas. Both Tambo Colorado (A) and Inkawasi (B) have a side aligned with the sunset on the day of zenith passage (Z). Pumpu's (C) northern side may point to a zenith sunrise (Z). A sightline from the ushnu platform to the zenith sunrise azimuth (Z) misses the alignment of the platform with a main gate slightly to the north by about 2 degrees. Sightlines to the solstice sunrise azimuths (S) as viewed from the platform are also indicated in the Pumpu plaza diagram. They are not precisely aligned with the plaza corners. Based on author's measurements.

8.11. The trapezium plaza at Tambo Colorado in the Pisco Valley, Peru. An ushnu *platform is on the plaza's side (center right). The view is to the south-southeast. The bed of the Pisco River is beyond the site.*

plaza's shape. Topography and perhaps other unknown factors often appear to have influenced the plaza's shape. This is particularly true at Inka royal estates near Cuzco and some military installations elsewhere, many of which are built on irregular terrain.

Analysis

No astronomical alignment pattern was found defining plazas at all Inka settlements throughout Tawantinsuyu. The considerable number of rectangular plazas with a generally east-west alignment suggests that, given certain conditions, they represent an Inka ideal of plaza shape and orientation. Such plazas are usually found in Inka settlements built from the ground up on flat or gently sloping terrain.

When Inkas remodeled a pre-Inka settlement, installing a plaza, it was often rectangular, but its orientation may have been dictated by principal streets or compounds within the older settlement.

When Inka state settlements are built on irregular terrain, particularly in the case of some royal estates near Cuzco and military installations elsewhere, the plaza shape often has no clear four-sided shape.

The most common Inka plaza has four sides. Whether a rectangle or the less-common trapezium, the long sides are, with very few exceptions, oriented much closer to east-west than to north-south. Since these settlements are found over many degrees of latitude, it is improbable that the azimuths of star groups (variable according to latitude) were used to determine the plazas' orientations. The east-west orientation suggests an interest in the equinox, but at Cuzco there is almost no historical evidence (except Garcilaso), and poor physical evidence, that such an observation was important in Inka astronomy.

Another possibility is that the observation of the solstices was a basis for the rectangular east-west plaza concept. The June and December solstice sunrise and sunset azimuths form a rectangle with a long east-west axis at any latitude. Similarly, the quadripartition of the sky by the movement of the Milky Way (forming a cross over the sky) may have inspired a plaza's design. When the rectangular plazas' corners are viewed from a central *ushnu* platform or from the geometric center of the plazas, the corners are not aligned with precision to solstice azimuths; thus the plazas might have been laid out with a solstice-defined rectangle in mind, but with no interest in accurate alignments to solstice azimuths.

The four-sided plaza has meaning well beyond astronomical considerations. As discussed in chapter 7, the four sides of a plaza usually divide a settlement into four parts. Those quarters are fundamental to Inka social structure and cosmology (chap. 7 and below). It is probable that the four-sided plaza symbolizes this important concept. The lack of well-defined four-sided plazas at several Inka royal estates may reflect topographical influences, but also a disinterest in defining quadripartition in their layout. Most four-sided plazas are found at administrative settlements outside of the Cuzco area.

Astronomical Alignments of Other Buildings and Compounds

Are Inka buildings or architectural features aligned with astronomical azimuths at sites other than Cuzco, Machu Picchu, and Inkawasi? Lack of study at other sites makes this impossible to answer. Investigations by Ziolkowski and Sadowski (1984) at Ingapirca (Cañar, Ecuador) suggest that alignments may have been important in the layout of the great oval building (a zenith alignment), the rooms on top of it (to equinoxes and the zenith), and the Pilaloma sector's main corridor (a June solstice sunrise) (fig. 9.15). The orientations of these buildings were taken from topographic site plans whose geographic north varied. Moreover, no horizon elevations were available for the analysis. Given the margin of error that may exist, the authors point out that their results should be considered hypothetical.

I measured the orientations of the square or rectangular *ushnu* platforms throughout Tawantinsuyu, since astronomical observations may have been made from them, and because they are generally centrally located. Some are oriented within a few degrees of east-west (Huánuco Pampa, Vilcas Waman, Shincal); many others are not. The orientations of the platforms appear to conform to the plazas' sides within which or on which they were located. There is no precise pattern for the orientation of *ushnu* platforms.

Given the evidence from Machu Picchu, Inkawasi, Cuzco, and a few other settlements, it does appear that at least some Inka buildings or architectural features were aligned with important astronomical azimuths. Such alignments, however, do not appear to have been common.

Nonastronomical Alignments

Astronomical alignments are only one type of alignment found in Inka settlements. Alignments may be made between architectural features and buildings. For example, *ushnu* platforms are often aligned with gateways or *ushnu* stones (chap. 3). Chapter 9 discusses how some compounds or buildings may be aligned with sacred mountain peaks and passes. In some cases, those peaks and passes may be associated with astronomical azimuths, but more archaeological and ethnographic research is needed to clarify the implications and certainty of such alignments. The investigator must consider that Inka architectural alignments cannot be interpreted without considering the surrounding geography and relationships of buildings and features within sites.

The Orientation of Duality and Quadripartition

A reoccurring theme in this book (chaps. 5 and 7) is tactics for detecting and interpreting how Inka state settlements may have been organized into two and four parts, types of partitioning fundamental to Inka spatial organization. Does the orientation of proposed halves and quarters of sites allow one to propose which moiety (*hanan* or *hurin*) or *suyu* (Chinchasuyu, Antisuyu, Kuntisuyu, and Qollasuyu) they represent? The orientation of halves or quarters of sites may be a useful indicator in some cases. Cuzco's physical plan and the design of the *zeque* system places Chinchasuyu in the northwest, Antisuyu in the northeast, Qollasuyu in the southeast, and Kuntisuyu in the southwest. The *hanan* half is in the north; *hurin* is in the south. Morris (1980a) proposes dual and four-part divisions at Huánuco Pampa, which have orientations generally similar to those at Cuzco. He bases his partitioning of the site on its architectural layout (without directly considering orientations). My partitioning of Inkawasi (Hyslop 1985: 46–77) uses the Cuzco orientations as only one of a number of guides for determining its major divisions. At In-kawasi, the proposed orientations of the site's halves and four parts are similar to those in Cuzco. One could argue here that the use of Cuzco models (be it the physical plan of the city or the design of the *zeque* system) results in a circular logic. In the two cases above, however, independent architectural data are also used to identify the dual division and *suyu*. Whether the orientations of Cuzco's halves and four parts were applied at other state settlements should remain a topic for investigation.

Today and in Inka times, Andean people handle spatial patterns with considerable flexibility. A rigid application of the Cuzco orientations to define halves and quarters at many state settlements would be simplistic. The propensity for Andean thought to work with mirror images and inverse dualism suggests that some sites might have their orientations reversed or transformed in different ways. Moreover, irregular terrain clearly affects the layout of some settlements and may often override the influence of orientation in the placement of main site divisions. Topography also affects water resources and the road pattern, both important in Inka settlement design. Since roads and corridors are often used to define site divisions, their entry and exit points may define sectors with orientations dissimilar to Cuzco's halves and quarters. Finally, chapter 5 notes that primary access to water may be crucial for determining the *hanan* and *hurin* dual division of settlements. This geographical factor may alter site organization over whatever desire there was to orient sectors like those at Cuzco.

In short, the orientation of the divisions of Cuzco is one factor that should be considered while analyzing the design of other settlements. Other influences and transformations, however, may prevail over the importance of the Cuzco orientations.

Summary

Given the diverse, contested, and incomplete nature of research on Inka orientations and alignments, one might ask if their influence on Inka settlement design can yet be evaluated. Many aspects are yet uncertain, but investigations have now established some facts and hypotheses that could not have been expressed a decade ago. One objective of this chapter is to display and evaluate data from beyond the Cuzco area. This information cannot be used to evaluate Inka astronomy, but in some ways supplements the Cuzco findings. Sufficient research has now accrued so that ignoring Inka astronomy's potential influence on site design would be hazardous.

There is good evidence from Cuzco and less reliable data from Copacabana and Incallacta that pillars or towers used for astronomical observations were part of Inka settlements. These structures were visible from the settlements, but did not affect their layout. At Machu Picchu, proposed observatories did not significantly affect site layout. At Inkawasi, some aspects of the layout appear affected by the alignment of walls with astronomical azimuths. In all of the above cases, the investigators propose independently that the physical evidence indicates a concern with the June solstice.

Different types of physical evidence from Inkawasi, Machu Picchu, Tambo Colorado, and possibly Pumpu, Incallacta, and Ingapirca indicate that some structures were built to detect the zenith passage or reflect a zenith alignment. Physical evidence for equinox observation or alignment has been proposed but remains unconfirmed for Ingapirca's oval building, the tower at Incallacta, and the Horca del Inka complex at Copacabana. Inka plazas oriented generally east-west may also indicate a concern with the equinox, but this is not certain, given the lack of historical and physical data for such an observation at Cuzco.

Proposed astronomical layout alignments and observational devices are best considered two categories of evidence for Inka astronomy. Observational devices, designed to mark a specific date, might be more precise than aligned architecture, which did not serve for observation, but where concepts associated with the time marked by the azimuth are expressed via the alignment. It is still uncertain what accuracy was acceptable to Inka astronomers and site planners when and if alignments were expressed in architecture.

A number of Inka plazas throughout Tawantinsuyu, particularly outside of the Cuzco area, are generally rectangular, often with long east-west sides. A few trapezium plazas may be variants of this. Other Inka plazas were shaped in part by the settlements' natural geography and sometimes have more than four sides or have curving sides. The model for the generally rectangular east-west plazas, found over a wide range of latitudes, might have been the solstice azimuths, which form a rectangle with east-west sides longer than north-south sides. The corners of the east-west plazas are not precisely aligned with the solstice azimuths from suspected observation points such as plaza centers or *ushnu* platforms. Thus the solstice-defined rectangular concept may have been used to design those plazas with little concern for accurate alignments of the corners from some central point. This proposal, however, must be viewed as speculative. The four-sided plazas, whether rectangles or the less-frequent trapeziums, often divide a settlement into four parts, which may symbolize the quadripartition so important in Inka social structure and cosmology.

9
Mixed Inka-Local Settlements

Readers familiar with Andean archaeology will note that quite a number of Inka settlements have not been mentioned, or are cited only in passing, in the previous pages. In some cases the omission is intentional, since these are often sites built before the Inka domination of an area, but later used for the business of Tawantinsuyu. These settlements convey limited information about Inka planning, since only a part or parts were constructed in Inka times. Most areas of these sites often continued to be used in Inka times. Thus the authorities from Cuzco sometimes contented themselves with settlements whose layout was dictated by many factors quite foreign to principles originating in their home area.

This chapter will examine some settlements where Inka buildings, and possibly Inka planning, are only a part of a larger architectural layout.

Residences of Local Lords and Elites
Inka architecture is found in some settlements that are not really Inka, but more closely related to local cultural groups that formed part of the Inka state. Since both Inka and local pottery and architecture are found in these sites, it would be easiest to classify them as some sort of Inka-local mixture. A deeper understanding of the matter is achieved if one attempts to isolate settlements of where Inka architecture is a state venture and not a local copy or imitation. Settlements where local, non-Inka lords and elites lived are good examples where Inka building forms are found but were probably not the result of Inka state planning. The following four cases help elucidate this.

Ichu
Ichu is located about 80 kilometers due east of the administrative center of Huánuco Pampa. Thompson's study (1967; Morris and Thompson 1985: 138–142) of Ichu was aided by a historical source from 1549 that

identified it as the home of the local Chupaychu chief. The Chupaychu ethnic group was controlled by the Inka state through the administrative center, Huánuco Pampa. At Ichu, Thompson found two long rectangular buildings subdivided into two or three rooms.[1] Built with fieldstones, they were more carefully constructed than local Chupaychu houses and more closely resembled an Inka plan than a Chupaychu one. Polychrome Inka pottery was found in one of the buildings, but was never found in other village sites in the region. Both of the buildings had niches and there was evidence for a well-used kitchen in one small side building. Morris and Thompson (1985: 142) concluded that these structures housed the Chupaychu chief and some of his relatives:

> Since it was Inca policy to rule through the local leadership, these Inca traits [of pottery and architecture] and the obvious importance of the buildings would be reflections of the status of the occupants in the Inca political system. The separate, heavily used, kitchen is also indicative of high status, because under the Andean systems of reciprocity it was the obligation of the leaders to provide abundant food and drink to those who served under them.

La Paya

Another residence of a local chief during the Inka period is found at the site of La Paya (Puerta de Paya) in Salta Province, Argentina. La Paya was first studied by Ambrosetti between 1904 and 1907 (1907–1908). Ambrosetti excavated many tombs in this settlement built in pre-Inka times but inhabited through the Inka into the early Spanish periods. The local architecture at La Paya is composed of several hundred irregularly shaped or more or less circular buildings. There is one notable exception, known as the Casa Morada (Dark Red House) because of its reddish sandstone blocks. This is rectangular and 3 meters wide (fig. 9.1). It has two patios and, to its west, four storage units built with Inka architectural traits. Shortly before Ambrosetti's excavations, a group of pothunters digging inside the Casa Morada found a burial with a gold treasure, which Ambrosetti (1902) was able to recover in part.

In 1981 the Casa Morada was re-excavated by González and Díaz. González notes (1981: 18–20) that the rectangular house form is Inka and not typical of the local architecture. The Inka and Santa María artifacts accompanying the burial are indicative of an important local individual. Considerable Inka pottery was found in the house. González concludes that the architecture and artifacts indicate that the Casa Morada was the house of the local chief in Inka times.[2] González (1983b) argues convincingly that La Paya is the prehistoric town of Chicoana,

9.1. *A rectangular foundation of dark red stones is all that remains of the Casa Morada, the home of a local lord in La Paya during Inka times. The rectangular shape was not typical of houses of the local Calchaquí population.*

known from historical sources to have been important in Inka times. Diego Almagro, on an expedition to the southern realms of Tawantinsuyu, was the first European to enter it in 1535. He obtained a large quantity of maize stored there, no doubt because Chicoana controlled the surrounding area along the Calchaqui River.

Hatunmarca and Marca

In the upper Mantaro region of central Peru, near the Inka administrative center of Hatun Xauxa, one finds numerous examples of house compounds or patio groups of elite members of the local Wanka people.[3] The buildings are constructed of rough limestones set in mud and pebble mortar. Before Inka rule the patio groups were composed of round buildings. After the Inka conquest, these patio groups occasionally incorporated one or two rectangular buildings. Two sites with an essentially Wanka occupation, Hatunmarca and Marca, demonstrate this point (D'Altroy 1981: 122–143; Earle et al. 1987: 44–73). Both were probably about the same size in Inka times.

Hatunmarca is a large settlement originally built in the centuries before Inka rule and occupied through the Inka period into Spanish colonial times. It is located about 8 kilometers northwest of Hatun Xauxa. A couple of thousand buildings at Hatunmarca are circular and several dozen are rectangular. In Inka times the settlement became smaller, but elite patio groups were built or remodeled incorporating rectangular buildings (fig. 9.2) along with circular ones.

The settlement of Marca is smaller, with more than four hundred buildings, almost all of which are circular. It is located only 5.5 kilometers north of Hatun Xauxa and was built and occupied in Inka times. The few rectangular structures at the site are found in elite patio groups.

Several features found in some of the rectangular buildings indicate that they are the result of Inka influence. Interior niches (some trapezoidal), interior tenons, gabled roofs, and multiple rooms were never used in Wanka architecture but were common in Inka. Although most of the pottery at both sites is local Wanka, Inka pottery is concentrated near and in the elite patio groups with rectangular buildings. The higher incidence of Inka pottery and architectural features at Marca is explained by its lack of a pre-Inka population. D'Altroy (1981: 139–143) feels that these data indicate that Wanka elites had a greater interaction with the Inka state than did the commoners. Indeed, in most parts of Tawantinsuyu the Inka commonly ruled through local lords and elite members of society, as stressed in several of the early historical sources.

Rectangular houses are not inherently better than round ones. The adoption of the rectangular form by Wanka elite symbolizes their new relationship to the Inka state. The rectangular buildings probably increased the prestige of their inhabitants, who demonstrated their link to the state by the shape of their household. In the upper Mantaro region this phenomenon has been more effectively demonstrated archaeologically than in many other parts of Tawantinsuyu.

Lupaqa Houses and Chulpas

In the Lupaqa region on the southwestern side of Lake Titicaca, Inka architectural features played an important role in "housing" elite members, both dead and alive, of the local Aymara-speaking society. In the centuries prior to Inka domination of the area, houses were circular (Hyslop 1976: 99–137, 1977a). At the Lupaqa village site Lundayani (Hyslop 1976: 377–380) near the town of Juli in the department of Puno, Peru, Inka rectangular buildings were used along with the local round form during the Inka period. Since Lundayani was occupied briefly into the Spanish colonial period and has the remains of a church, it is possible that some of its rectangular buildings are Spanish. Most are not, however, since Inka pottery and local Inka-period Chucuito pottery are found in several rectangular structures.[4] Lundayani has not been studied carefully enough to determine if rectangular buildings were used only by its elites.[5] It is clear, however, that only important members of Lupaqa society were buried in buildings strongly influenced by Inka architectural traits (Hyslop 1977b).

Important members of high plateau society were traditionally buried in aboveground (generally round) structures called *chulpas*. Prior to the Inkas, most of these structures were igloo-shaped, built with rough fieldstones. After the Inka domination of the high plateau near Lake Titicaca, the burial structures frequently became square or rectangular, although round ones continued to be built. Fine Cuzco-style masonry was often used in these structures (fig. 9.3) and expressed the prestige of their deceased occupants. Thus in the Inka period, members of the local Lupaqa society began to use the typical Inka rectangular plan in houses and a square or rectangular plan in their burial structures. That this was a prerogative of the elite is best demonstrated by the *chulpas*, which were used only for the burial of important individuals.

In summary, many non-Inka lords and elite members of society were familiar with Inka architectural ideas, since they were required to travel to Cuzco, where they would have seen Inka state architecture. More-

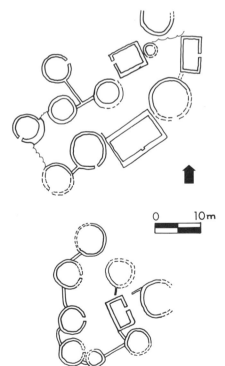

0   10m

9.2. *Elite members of the Wanka people began building rectangular houses after Inka domination. Two patio groups at Hatunmarca demonstrate the use of the rectangular form. Before Inka domination Wanka residences were circular. Redrawn from Earle et al. (1987: 52, 56).*

9.3. Six burial towers of the Lupaqa elite near the town Acora on the southwest side of Lake Titicaca. Four are square; two are round. The fine Cuzco-style masonry and square plan were borrowed from the Inka for these buildings, which housed the remains of important members of high plateau society.

over, many of their subjects participated in the construction of Inka public works and administrative centers and thus learned basic Inka architectural concepts. The use of Inka architectural forms by important local people is not necessarily a pattern in all of Tawantinsuyu. Much additional research will be required to determine the range of residences occupied by the non-Inka Andean lords. In all of the above examples, the use of Inka architectural traits appears primarily symbolic, a means by which local non-Inka elites expressed their relationship to the dominant state. Where such buildings are found, they generally are not part of a planned Inka settlement, but are rather a town or village that grew randomly or was arranged according to non-Inka, local principles. Since these sites appear to have Inka buildings and often contain some Inka pottery, it is easy for the archaeologist to mistake them for state settlements.

Areas with No Inka Architectural Planning

The distribution of Inka architecture discussion in chapter 1 noted that no good examples of Inka architecture are found in several areas of Tawantinsuyu. In some cases this is due to a lack of archaeological survey.

In at least one large region, the Chimú area of the north coast of Peru (Rowe 1948; Kosok 1965; Schaedel 1951, 1966), the lack of Inka architecture is related to local political and cultural circumstances. The Chimú region extended over about 1,000 kilometers along the Pacific coast from Túmbez in the north to just north of Lima. The Chimú state was the largest political unit ever conquered by the Inkas. Its capital, Chan Chan (Moseley 1975; Moseley and Day 1982; Moseley and Mackey 1974), was the biggest "city" in the Andes at the time of the Inka conquests.

Rowe (1948: 45) notes that the Chimú king was kept in "honored exile" in Cuzco, but that the Chimú state was dismembered by making the old dynastic lords of the individual valleys directly responsible to Inka rulers. Thus the Chimú king did not receive, as did some other lords, a powerful position within the Inka state. The intentional destruction of the upper level of the state apparatus may explain why the Inka occupation at Chan Chan is so minimal. A survey of sites on the main Inka road covering 200 kilometers north of Chan Chan (Hyslop 1984: 37–55) found no evidence of Inka architecture. Many of the roadside settlements, however, have Inka-related pottery. Thus they must have been used in Inka times (Helsley 1980; Keatinge and Conrad 1983). It appears that this absence of Inka architecture on the north coast is due to the strong local building tradition. The north coast had the most elaborate "urbanization" of any part of the Andes. The Inkas apparently decided to occupy existing buildings and settlements. If new ones were built, local architects, engineers, and workmen were available for the task (Hyslop n.d.a).

One good example of a complex (without Inka architecture) built and used in Inka times is the site Chiquitoy Viejo (Conrad 1977) on the southern edge of the Chicama Valley. Its general layout, U-shaped rooms, ramps, and burial platform are all architectural characteristics of the north coast. Chiquitoy Viejo has been interpreted as an Inka administrative center, and no doubt it served some role in Inka administration. One might doubt, however, that it was the seat of an Inka governor. The important person residing at Chiquitoy Viejo may well have been a local lord.[6] Evidence for this is the low percentage of Inka-related pottery found in the excavations (8.6 percent), and the north coast mortuary platform, where it is improbable that an Inka governor was buried.

The lack of Inka architecture on the north coast may have more far-ranging implications. The Inkas' planned political degradation of the area may have been expressed by the lack of planned Inka settlements. In addition, there is archaeological and historical evidence that in Inka times much of the north coast may have been governed from the highlands to the east, or settlements well upriver from the flat, irrigated coastal plain (Hyslop 1984: 53; Dillehay 1977). If such was the case, perhaps there were no major Inka administrative centers on the north coast. This role was fulfilled by settlements to the east.

Does lack of Inka architecture on the north coast suggest that other areas of Tawantinsuyu had no Inka architecture for similar or different reasons? At present there is no answer to this question, since the areas where no Inka architecture has yet been identified are poorly surveyed, or the Inka constructions may have been destroyed.

Inka Buildings within Local Towns and Cities

Throughout Tawantinsuyu one finds settlements where most of the architecture is of a local, non-Inka type, but where in one or more parts of a site there are clear examples of Inka architecture. In many cases, it is uncertain whether some of these settlements were founded in Inka times or before. Nevertheless, both historical and archaeological data often suggest that these settlements are not simple *tampu*, but rather Inka governmental centers or major sanctuaries. They are different from towns where local lords lived in that the Inka component is more com-

9.4. *The square* kancha *at La Puerta in the Copiapó Valley. It has eight rectangular rooms and three square storage units. A tree stands in the central patio. Only foundations remain of the rooms and surrounding wall.*

251

plex. That is, forms of Inka architecture such as *kancha,* plazas, storehouses, and *kallanka* are found in them, indicating that Inka architecture fulfilled a role beyond that of housing local important people. Moreover, analyses of these sites' size, location within a region, and relationship to contemporary settlements often indicate that Inka administrative activities took place at them.

The sites described and discussed below have been selected because more information exists about them than about some others.

La Puerta

La Puerta lies at an altitude of about 1,000 meters on the Copiapó River in Chile and is composed of about 200 houses and 150 identifiable tomb mounds. The houses are subcircular stone foundations or depressions. Niemeyer (1986: 174–176, 239), the leading authority on prehistoric Copiapó, has mapped and analyzed the site. He concludes that La Puerta was the principal Inka administrative center for the valley. This evaluation is based primarily on the site's size, its critical location, and a large Inka *kancha* with rooms and storage units (Hyslop 1984: 284) built near the center of the settlement (figs. 1.17E, 9.4).

The *kancha* measures approximately 27 by 30.5 meters, with four rooms each on the north and south. Each has a door facing an internal patio. Three rectangular storage units are found on the western side of the patio. Analysis of the excavated materials is still under way, but Niemeyer notes that there is evidence that the rooms were residential. It has not been ascertained whether some of the surrounding local architecture was built before Inka domination.

0   50M

9.5. Plan of Turi, a local settlement in the Atacama Desert with a few Inka additions. The square plaza with the kallanka on its southwest side is the major Inka modification. From Mostny (1949: 167).

9.6. Aerial view toward the west over Turi. The Inka plaza and kallanka *are in the right center. A hole made by pothunters in the plaza may have destroyed remains of an* ushnu. *Courtesy Carlos Aldunate.*

Turi

Turi is located about 50 kilometers northeast of the city of Calama in Chile's Atacama Desert and was first described by Mostny (1949: 165–176). This walled settlement was probably built prior to the Inka invasion, but then occupied by the Inkas to administer the area. The wall encloses a subrectangular area of buildings and streets measuring about 240 by 160 meters (figs. 9.5, 9.6).[7] Some structures, probably corrals, are found outside the enclosing wall. An Inka road passes along the northeastern side of the site.

The Inka buildings consist of a *kallanka* on the southwest side of a square plaza and several other rectangular buildings on the eastern side of the plaza, where a door leads to the plaza from the Inka road. The *kallanka* has stone foundations; the upper parts of the walls are built with rectangular adobe bricks. It is 26 meters long, 9 meters wide, has a gabled roof and three doors facing the plaza. The rectangular plaza measures 40 by 46 meters. Local buildings were pushed aside to create the plaza (Carlos Aldunate, personal communication, 1986). The plaza's orientation is similar to plazas at Catarpe, Viña del Cerro, Potrero de Payogasta, and Paria, discussed in chapter 8. A hole left by pothunters in the plaza suggests that some important feature was once located there— possibly a stone or small platform that could have been part of an *ushnu* complex.

Fuerte Quemado

On the Argentine side of the Andes there is a considerable array of sites with both Inka and local architecture (Raffino 1983). The difficult problem of distinguishing the specific activities and role of each site has only begun (González 1983a), since there are often little or no excavation data and few historical records. One settlement currently under investigation is Fuerte Quemado in the Santa María (Yocavil) Valley, Catamarca Province. Preliminary excavations and mapping by Kriscautzky (1983, 1986, 1987) reveal a site nearly 4 kilometers square with semi-subterranean houses and patios typical of the local, Santa María culture. On the western side are a set of at least six Inka patios with rectangular buildings (fig. 9.7). Because of its numerous Inka constructions and because there is no other convincing candidate nearby, the settlement may have been a local Inka administrative center.

9.7. *A rectangular Inka building in the Inka sector at Fuerte Quemado in the Santa María Valley.*

Along the Santa María River there are other large settlements with typical Santa María architecture, but with little evidence of Inka presence. One site in particular, Tolombón, may have been the seat of a powerful local chief in pre-Inka and Inka times (González 1982: 327–335).[8] Thus in the Santa María Valley, Fuerte Quemado is unique in having a major local settlement and a substantial Inka occupation. As one might expect, Kriscautzky (1983: 6) found that Inka pottery predominated in the sector with Inka architecture. He also found evidence for many different activities, including a foundry. In short, Fuerte Quemado appears to be an Inka administrative center built into a large, older local town.[9] Since the Inka sector is on one side of the site, however, no houses of the local architecture were destroyed to make space for the Inka buildings.

Pachacamac

Pachacamac was one of the greatest ancient cities in the Andes (fig. 9.8) and is located in the Lurin Valley just south of Lima, Peru (Uhle 1903). The occupation at Pachacamac began at least two thousand years ago and continued up until the Spanish conquest (Bueno 1982). During Wari times (A.D. 700–1000) Pachacamac participated in a pottery and tapestry art style that spread over a considerable part of the coast. The city began its major period of growth after Wari influence diminished. When the Inkas conquered the central coast, they showed great respect for Pachacamac, in part because of its oracle, which Inka kings consulted on several occasions, although they were not often pleased with its pronouncements. As Tello (1940) noted, Pachacamac is two or three times larger than any map indicates. Surface pottery found well to the north and northwest of the existing architecture suggests a large inhabited area, most probably constructed of perishable cane and mat structures.

Many of the buildings now visible at Pachacamac were built in the centuries after Wari. During this time two perpendicular streets were laid out: one north-south and the other east-west (fig. 9.9). The streets' division of the site into four parts may demonstrate that Andean concepts of bi- and quadripartition were applied in site planning before Inka times. The primary type of compound at Pachacamac consisted of an enclosure with storage units, patios, and stepped "pyramidal" structures with ramps (Paredes and Franco 1987), three of which have been excavated. There are at least fifteen "ramped pyramids" at Pachacamac. These appear to have been associated with various social groups that came to Pachacamac for religious-political purposes (Jiménez B. and Bueno 1970: 16–17). One of the first Spanish eyewitnesses (Estete 1879) to see Pachacamac noted that much of the city seemed to be in ruins. It

9.8. Aerial view of Pachacamac. This ancient city was much larger than the standing architecture indicates. Buildings were once located in the desert beyond the adobe buildings. Courtesy Department of Library Services, AMNH, Neg. no. 334837 (photo by Shippee Johnson).

is possible that in Inka times, the goods once destined for the storage units of the ramped pyramid compounds were diverted to the Inka Sun Temple. Thus with Inka sovereignty over the city some of the older compounds fell into disuse.

Pachacamac became a leading administrative and religious center under the Inkas. Lanning (1967: 170) writes that "the city seems to have shrunk after the Inca conquest to little more than a ceremonial center, but it was a very important ceremonial center."[10] Much excavation and restoration in Pachacamac in the last decades gives a somewhat different view, since it is now clear that the Inkas remodeled and constructed several new buildings and compounds around the old city (Bueno 1982: 43–51; Jiménez and Bueno 1970: 16–25). Pachacamac's economic role requires that one not consider it just the seat of an oracle. Several early historical sources note that goods for the Inka state were collected from a large part of the coast at Pachacamac.

The areas constructed by the Inkas in Pachacamac are known as

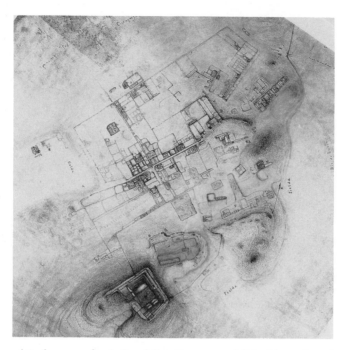

9.9. Map of Pachacamac by A. Bandelier. He never published it, perhaps because a plan by Uhle (1903) was more detailed. Note the two central streets (north-south and east-west), which divide the center of the settlement into four parts. Courtesy Department of Anthropology, AMNH, Bandelier Collection.

the Sun Temple, Mamacuna, the Pilgrims' Plaza, the Tauri Chumbi group, and the Painted Building (fig. 9.10). There are other smaller Inka buildings on the southeastern side and cemeteries with Inka artifacts. The names given to the various Inka compounds are often capricious. Whereas the Sun Temple (fig. 3.16) is accurately identified, the Mamacuna is an uncertain *aqllawasi*. Tello (1940), who found fine Inka masonry in corridors leading to it, thought it was a Temple of the Moon (fig. 9.11). The main plaza is clearly the site's principal plaza, but whether it was used by "pilgrims" is merely conjecture. The Tauri Chumbi complex was named after the Inka governor in Pachacamac at the time of the Spanish conquest. One cannot be certain he lived here, although it is a large elite Inka residential complex. Tello, Jiménez Borja, and Bueno agree that the "Painted Building" was a type of *aqllawasi* related to the Sun Temple.[11] It is unfortunate that many of the archaeological investigations carried out at Pachacamac in the last half century have never been fully published.

9.10. *Aerial photograph of Pachacamac. Several Inka architectural complexes were constructed in and around the older, pre-Inka buildings. The Inka constructions are* 1. *the Sun Temple;* 2. *the Mamacuna;* 3. *the Pilgrims' Plaza;* 4. *the Tauri Chumbi;* 5. *the Painted Building. Courtesy S.A.N.*

Considering the difficulty of understanding the activities carried out in the Inka compounds and buildings at Pachacamac, it is still possible to see aspects of Inka remodeling and even planning. The remodeling is particularly clear in the Pilgrims' Plaza (fig. 9.12). Tello excavated in the plaza and noted (1940):

> In the location considered the "camp of the pilgrims," we have found remains of small structures, superimposed rectangular chambers separated by partitions of refuse and sand. They reveal continual mixing of the earth and successive constructions. Deep excavations have permitted an understanding of the structural details in this area, which on its surface appears as a flat, leveled, clean, rectangular plain some 200 meters long by 50 meters wide, with low stone roads and remains of longitudinal columns set in rows.

Tello's observations confirm archaeological observations made at some other settlements such as Turi. That is, the Inkas' occupation of older "cities" sometimes resulted in the destruction or leveling of existing structures to construct their buildings and plazas.

A number of Inka architectural traits are found in the plaza, along with a sense of planning typical of Inka sites. First, the plaza is rectangular. A road divides the plaza through its center. The road is marked by columns of rectangular adobe bricks (fig. 9.13) and may have been covered by a perishable roof. On the south side of the plaza is a mound of Inka-style adobe bricks with a stairway leading down into the plaza. That building is probably an *ushnu* platform (fig. 3.16). The rectangular plaza divided into two parts is a hallmark of Inka planning, as is its association with a platform.

The plaza is not centrally located as one would expect at a settlement completely planned by Inkas, but rather slightly to the west of the site's architectural center. Whereas the Inkas leveled and filled in earlier structures to construct the plaza, they apparently were unwilling to disturb the earlier central area of the site with its ramped pyramid complexes and two perpendicular streets. Indeed, most of the Inka buildings at Pachacamac are constructed on what was empty terrain, or where abandoned buildings of a much earlier period rested. It is not known whether the ramped-pyramid complexes were left intact out of respect, or simply because they were too large to destroy easily. This raises

9.11. The heavily reconstructed architectural complex known as the Mamacuna. It has some fine Inka masonry, rare on the Pacific coast, in an entry corridor.

an important question about Inka planning. To what degree were pre-existing settlement plans taken into account by Tawantinsuyu and to what extent did they influence the location of Inka additions?

Other aspects of Inka planning at Pachacamac are more difficult to define and perhaps somewhat speculative. It may be significant that a main Inka compound (Tauri Chumbi) is found on the eastern side of the site (fig. 9.14). It might be the architectural equivalent of the elaborate structures and patios found on the eastern side of Inka centers such as Huánuco Pampa, Pumpu, Inkawasi, and Chilecito (chap. 7). It is noteworthy that the design of the Sun Temple at Pachacamac has little in common with that of the Sun Temple in Cuzco. Bueno (1982: 47) has noted its many traits typical of coastal architecture, particularly the use of a large, solid, stepped mass, and compares it to the Inka complex Paramonga (fig. 6.5).

In conclusion, Pachacamac is probably the most monumental example of Inka planning that coordinated and adjusted its design to a pre-

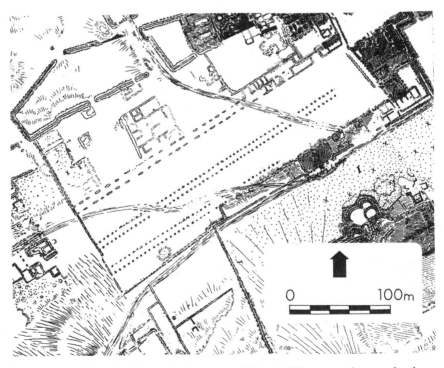

9.12. Map of the Inka plaza at Pachacamac. Older buildings were destroyed to lay out the rectangular area. A structure of Inka adobe bricks, an ushnu *platform, rests on the plaza's southeast side* (dark hatching). *From Uhle (1903).*

9.13. A road marked by two rows of the foundations of square columns of Inka adobe bricks divides the plaza of Pachacamac into two parts.

existing layout. Why certain areas were destroyed and others left undisturbed is still uncertain, although it appears that complexes still in use at the time of the Inka conquest were generally left intact. Equally perplexing is what aspects of the pre-Inka settlement influenced the locations of Inka buildings. Inka planners did not always pay heed to an earlier layout, a point demonstrated below.

Ingapirca

Few Inka settlements have caused as much speculation as Ingapirca in the province of Cañar, Ecuador. Data from the excavations (Alcina 1978) by the Spanish Scientific Mission (1974–1975) and the Castillo Commission of Ingapirca (Fresco 1979, 1983, 1984) offer interpretations of many aspects of the site, which, nevertheless, remains only partially excavated. Ingapirca is best known for the large oval structure of fine Cuzco masonry (fig. 1.5), interpreted as everything from a fort to a castle.[12] The recent investigations have produced particularly interesting data regarding the site's relationship to the earlier Cañari occupation.

A considerable area of Inka buildings south of the excavated sector

9.14. The Tauri Chumbi compound, possibly the residence of an Inka governor.

(fig. 9.15) remains unstudied. Thus the observations here about how Inkas integrated their architecture into a pre-existing settlement are valid only for the excavated area. Pre-Inka walls have been found under Inka constructions in the southern part of the plaza, under and to the north of the storage area, and within and near the "Gran Kancha" (fig. 9.16). They consist of single rows of river stones. Some stone-surfaced oval platforms, probably house floors, are also present (Fresco 1983: 209–210, 1984: 96–100). The architecture, radio carbon dates, and associated pottery (Cashaloma) indicate an earlier Cañari occupation. At least in the excavated zones, the Inka constructions at Ingapirca leveled or covered the Cañari architecture. This might be seen as one of many Inka attempts to demolish the Cañari, since it was a recalcitrant ethnic group punished by the Inkas.

Several other aspects of the Inka occupation at Ingapirca indicate that the earlier Cañari occupation may have strongly influenced the site's location and design. Fresco's study (1979: 11–13) of the early historical information for the area indicates that Ingapirca was called Hatun Cañar in Inka times and that it was the principal Cañari settlement of the zone. The location of Inka Ingapirca appears to have been selected because of the pre-existing Cañari settlement. Fresco interprets Ingapirca as a second-category Inka administrative center with a very strong religious component. He argues that the sacred aspects of the site have their basis primarily in the Cañari beliefs.

Fresco and Cobo (1978: 155–161) note that the rock prominence upon which the oval platform (*castillo*) was built may have been the *pacarina* (sacred origin place) of the Cañari nation. Fresco (1983: 209, 1984: 100) also suggests that the oval shape (unique in Inka architecture) of the *castillo* may have been derived from the oval Cañari house form. In addition, an elaborate Cañari burial group (Fresco and Cobo 1978) was found in the center of the Pilaloma *kancha* of Ingapirca. The principal person of this burial is interpreted as a *waqa*, symbolic of Cañari origins. On top of the burial was a circle of stones and a large upright stone (*wanka*). Thus the Pilaloma sector and the great oval building may be Inka buildings constructed in relationship to Cañari religious ideas. The Inka occupation at Ingapirca may demonstrate a point made by the priest Albornoz in the late sixteenth century (1967: 17), that throughout Tawantinsuyu the Inkas sought out local sacred places and maintained them with rites. He adds that some of the foreign *waqa* were "ennobled" with special rituals and offerings. At Ingapirca Inka architecture apparently ennobled the Cañari *waqa*.

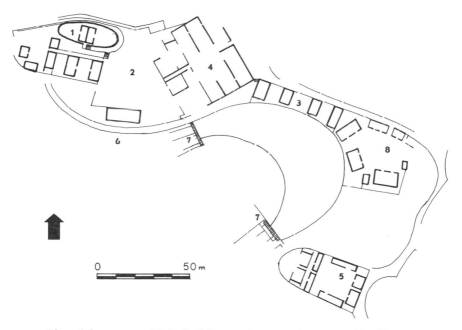

9.15. Plan of the excavated Inka buildings at Ingapirca. Key: 1. *oval building;* 2. *plaza;* 3. *storage units;* 4. *La Condamine;* 5. *Pilaloma;* 6. *agricultural terracing;* 7. *waterworks;* 8. *big* kancha. *Redrawn from Fresco (1983: 196).*

If Fresco and Cobo are correct in their interpretation, Ingapirca provides one of the best examples of how Inka architectural planning could be linked to local religious beliefs. Inkas apparently destroyed the local community, but preserved and embellished what to the Inkas was most important—the religious location. This also explains why such monumental Inka architecture was located relatively close to Tomebamba, the second Inka capital, only 40 kilometers to the south (Hyslop 1984: 19–36; Idrovo 1984). Ingapirca's proximity to Tomebamba precludes its being considered a major administrative center. Thus religious and symbolic interpretation is central to understanding the location and architecture of Inka Ingapirca.

Tomebamba

Tomebamba, the second Inka capital (now Cuenca, Ecuador) (chap. 5), was destroyed on one or two occasions by rival Inka armies during the Inka civil war (Rostworowski 1988: 148–178), which raged for several years before the arrival of Pizarro in 1532. Excavations directed by Jaime

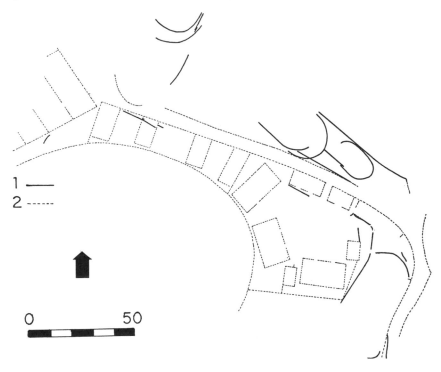

1 ——
2 ------

0   50

9.16. Cañari buildings under Inka Ingapirca. Key: 1. Cañari walls; 2. Inka walls. Adapted from Fresco (1983: 210).

9.17. *Fragments of fine masonry blocks destroyed in the Inka destruction of the second Inka capital, Tomebamba, in Ecuador. Rival Inka armies destroyed the city during the Inka civil wars shortly before the Spanish invasion in* A.D. *1532.*

Idrovo have found thousands of fragments hacked from blocks of fine Cuzco masonry used in Tomebamba's walls (fig. 9.17). Ash covering the floors of some buildings indicates that Tomebamba was burned. This discovery suggests that, given special circumstances, the Inka could be "destroyers of cities." The destruction of the fine masonry blocks suggests an aggressiveness that the Inkas did not generally exercise toward the architecture of non-Inka groups. Elsewhere, local settlements were remodeled, added on to, or forced into abandonment, but there is little evidence for their systematic destruction.

The dismembering of Tomebamba had its basis in the rivalry between two imperial contenders, their *panaqa,* and the Cañari in whose home territory Tomebamba rested. Those special factors apparently led to a destructiveness beyond that which was typical of Inkas.

Other Mixed Inka-Local Settlements

Many other sites in the Andes demonstrate that the Inkas frequently integrated their constructions into local ones built before or during Inka rule. Unfortunately, research at such sites is only beginning or not sufficiently advanced to explore this integration in depth. Several examples deserve to be mentioned, which will someday reveal more about the mix of Inka and local planning.

The near-south coast of Peru provides numerous examples of Inka local mixtures (Menzel 1959, 1971). The Tambo de Mala in the Mala Valley has Inka buildings, once of great elegance with double-jamb doors, located on a prominence beside a large settlement that developed in the centuries prior to the Inkas. The same may be said of Cerro Azul (Marcus, Matos, and Rostworowski 1983–1985; Marcus 1987) in the

9.18. Aerial photograph of La Centinela in the Chincha Valley. It was once the seat of a powerful coastal lord. Inka buildings and a plaza are located in the foreground before a high pre-Inka solid structure. Courtesy Department of Library Services, AMNH, Neg. no. 334733 (photo by Shippee Johnson).

Cañete Valley, where once-spectacular Inka buildings (systematically destroyed over the centuries) are located just to the north of a very large pre-Inka site.

In the Chincha Valley, La Centinela (Menzel and Rowe 1966) has elaborate Inka constructions and a rectangular east-west plaza (Hyslop 1984: 113) closely integrated into a set of pyramidal structures built earlier (fig. 9.18). Rostworowski's (1988: 100–104) analysis of a historical source from 1558 (Castro and Ortega 1974) points out how successive Inka generals or kings constructed new buildings in Chincha, among them a compound called *hatuncancha*, probably an administrative complex. This demonstrates that the Inka additions to a local settlement were not necessarily planned and built at one time. The growing number of Inka buildings and public works in Chincha also reflects the increasing control of Cuzco over a valley that probably found that its obligations to the Inka state grew beyond that originally expected.

Ongoing research there directed by Craig Morris can expect to define new aspects of the planning used by the two quite different cultures.

Inka aspects of settlements on Peru's south coast share a number of features, creating an architectural subarea. Whereas adobe brick walls, trapezoidal niches and apertures, and plastered and occasionally painted wall surfaces are typical of the Cuzco area,[13] other characteristics are adapted from the local architectural tradition. The use of rooms sharing walls, for example, is a local trait found in many primarily Inka compounds. This characteristic gives Inka coastal settlements a more compact appearance. Occasionally, important Inka buildings are built on artificial raised platforms and have rectangular or square doors and niches, other coastal traits. Friezes, a local tradition, are also found in Inka buildings. Since rainfall is scarce on the coast, roofs were generally not gabled or inclined (as was often the case in Cuzco and other parts of the highlands) but flat. At Tambo Colorado in Pisco, Inkawasi in Cañete, and some other primarily Inka settlements one finds many walls constructed with a mud-clay and stone mixture typical of local pre-Inka architecture. The Inka incorporation of local architectural features is generally explained by their use of coastal construction labor familiar with traditional building techniques from local traditions, and often adaptations to desert environmental conditions. Flat roofs and agglutinated rooms, for example, are sensible architectural features in an area where there is very little rain.

In the highlands, the Inkas built or remodeled many large settlements that existed well before their arrival. Such appears to have been the case of the administrative center at Cajamarca (Ravines 1976), where the modern town now covers the old city.

Inka remodeling of a very ancient highland "city" is found at Pucará in the department of Puno, Peru. This settlement was continuously occupied for more than fifteen hundred years before the Inkas, who reconstructed one of the upper terraces at Pucará with their tall trapezoidal niches. One ancient stairway was rebuilt (fig. 9.19) with some fine Cuzco-style masonry blocks (Mujica and Wheeler 1981: 82–95). Mujica points out that Inka pottery is found throughout the large site and under the modern town beside it. The lack of much identifiable Inka architecture at Pucará may be due to the Spanish colonial occupation and to the Inka tendency in the high plateau to construct buildings with earth walls. Once in disuse, these eroded with the heavy rains. Several early historical sources note that Pucará was important in Inka times. The only archaeological proof of that is the broad distribution of Inka pottery and some architectural modifications in the terrace walls.[14]

Summary

Inka architecture in a settlement outside of the Cuzco area does not necessarily imply that the site was a state installation. Local lords and the elite sometimes adopted Inka architectural ideas, particularly the rectangular house, for use in their own towns. To date, no archaeologists or historians have located the residence of a local lord at an Inka center characterized only by Inka architecture. It appears that local lords generally lived in their traditional communities away from such centers.[15] There may, however, be important exceptions, particularly at settlements with a mix of Inka and local architecture. Fuerte Quemado, Chucuito, La Centinela, and Pachacamac may well have been centers of Inka administration as well as places where local lords lived, although archaeological or historical proof is still lacking.

Inka architects did not always build their settlements from the ground up. They were often willing to use and modify pre-existing architectural complexes. Such modifications occasionally required the leveling of some pre-existing buildings, but usually the principal buildings were left intact. Thus at Pachacamac and Fuerte Quemado major pre-Inka constructions were not disturbed. In order not to destroy a local settlement, Inka buildings were constructed on the side or perimeter of pre-existing ones. When local architecture was destroyed, the Inkas apparently leveled some of the abandoned or less-important buildings (Pachacamac, Turi, possibly Puerta). In non-Inka settlements occupied by Inkas, the sectors with older or local architecture often continued in use. This is demonstrated by the broad distribution, not just in the Inka sectors, of Inka pottery at several of these sites. Inkas rarely destroyed an important local community, although some were forced into abandonment (chap. 6).

9.19. A stairway with some fine Inka masonry blocks built into a much older terrace wall at Pucará.

Mixed settlements range from the relatively simple to the extremely complex. At several sites, it is often difficult to determine the extent of Inka planning, since only a few Inka buildings or compounds are found. Moreover, whatever planning may have existed in the parts defined by local architecture is so poorly understood that little is still known about how Inka architects may have situated and integrated their buildings to non-Inka ones. In the case of the more complex settlements such as Pachacamac, where several Inka areas can be defined, some elements of Inka planning can be observed.

The Inkas' use of towns and cities of subject peoples for their own purposes is common throughout Tawantinsuyu. The manner in which they occupied and altered these settlements varies from place to place, and no doubt had to do with factors such as settlement's role in the local political and religious system, its proximity to an Inka road, the trustworthiness of the local population, and the amount of local labor available for construction projects.

All the settlements discussed other than residences of local lords are located on main Inka roads. There is little evidence that large pre-Inka settlements became Inka centers if they could not be located on such Inka roads. Since the course of those roads (Hyslop 1984: 245–253) was often dictated by topography, local political circumstances, and political strategy involving areas separated by great distances, it was often only by chance that an important local settlement was located on an Inka road. There is no good evidence that the Inkas made major additions at local settlements not located on main roads. When buildings with Inka architectural traits are found in sites off the roads, they may have been built by local lords and elites.

Where local populations were untrustworthy, the Inkas often forced important local settlements to be abandoned (chap. 6). Here, one is more apt to find Inka centers built from the ground up. In most cases mixed local-Inka settlements were located in areas for which there is little or no history of an Inka fear of rebellion after the area's assimilation into the state by peaceful or military means. At Ingapirca, located in "dangerous" Cañari territory, the Inka takeover of the site appears to have been inspired by religious considerations rather than by reuse of the local settlement, much or all of which was leveled.

10
Environmental
Influences

This chapter will explore how environmental factors influenced the location of the larger Inka settlements and how, in turn, the construction of those settlements modified the natural environment.

Settlement Location

One cannot really say that "Inkas always built in high locations" or that "Inkas always built where there was a spectacular view." Such simplifications, although common in some texts, ignore the multitude of factors that determined site location and disregard contradictory data from many other settlements.[1] The idea that Inkas tended to construct on a height with a view has been presented by writers familiar with Inka settlements in the Cuzco area, primarily in the Urubamba Valley, where such was often the case.

An examination of settlements throughout Tawantinsuyu requires one to consider a myriad of factors, many non-environmental. If one can generalize at all, suffice it to mention that many related influences, environment included, were part of any Inka decision concerning a settlement's design and placement.

In chapters 4 and 5 it was suggested that aspects of "sacred geography" such as rock outcrops or water sources may have determined the locations of some settlements. This cannot yet be proven, but is quite probable, given the great Inka concern with such natural features. Other features that may also have influenced settlement placement are sightlines pointing to ritually important mountain peaks and passes. This has been suggested for Machu Picchu (Reinhard, personal communication, 1986) and is no doubt an idea present in the minds of scholars who have spent much time studying Inka settlements. This concept was expressed early on by Bandelier (1910: 275), who was convinced that Pilco Kayma and Iñak Uyu (fig. 10.1), large buildings at the Lake Titicaca sanctuary, were placed on the eastern side of their respective islands so as to be oriented directly toward the high peaks to the northeast (Mount Llampu) of the Cordillera Real. Determining whether geographical features beyond settlements may influence settlement location and design is one of the thorniest questions concerning where and how Inka sites were planned.

In other cases, the proximity of an Inka settlement to natural resources clearly shows why a specific location was chosen. An example is the Inka metallurgical site of Viña del Cerro (Niemeyer 1986: 176–186) in the Copiapó Valley of Chile (fig. 10.2). Several buildings and twenty-six smelters are placed on a prominence where the winds, necessary for the smelters, are particularly strong and constant throughout the year and through most of the daylight hours. It is relatively certain that the copper ore processed at Viña del Cerro came from several mines found in the vicinity. Thus nearby mines and strong winds determined the site's location. It is easier to relate the location of a specialized production center to specific natural resources than administrative centers, whose locations depended on environmental, cultural, and political concerns.

Locations of Administrative Centers

Typical Topography

When settlements were primarily administrative centers, factors affecting their placement differed considerably from those that determined the locations of sanctuaries, specialized production centers, *tampu,*

10.1. View over the second story of Pilco Kayma across Lake Titicaca to the snowcapped Cordillera Real. The building points toward the highest peak, Mount Llampu. This and other Inka buildings or compounds may have been aligned with sacred passes or peaks.

271

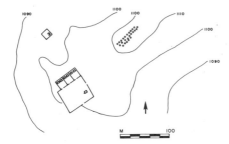

10.2. *Plan of the metal smelting site of Viña del Cerro in the Copiapó Valley, Chile. It is set on a prominence in the valley to take advantage of constant daytime winds necessary for the proper function of the smelters (circles). The plaza has a small* ushnu *platform with steps. Redrawn from Niemeyer (1986: 240).*

local population centers, or military installations. This is complicated by some settlements' combining of several roles. Pachacamac, for example, on Peru's central coast, was both an administrative center and a major sanctuary. Chilecito in Argentina is a fortified administrative center. Inka administration was important at Fuerte Quemado in Argentina and La Centinela in Peru, although both were also local population centers. It is therefore somewhat deceptive to speak of a "primary role" for large Inka settlements, since activities carried out at them were multiple. Nevertheless, some large settlements were mainly administrative (chap. 11), whereas others (such as sanctuaries and fortresses) were used for quite different purposes.

10.3. *View to the west over Pumpu, a large administrative center on the high plateau of central Peru near Lake Junin.*

272

In cases where essentially administrative activities can be established for large settlements, certain environmental considerations essential to their locations can be isolated. Indeed, if any topographical factor characterizes classic Inka administrative centers, it is their location on flat or gently sloping terrain.[2] Examples of Inka sites built from the ground up and located in such terrain include Quito and Tomebamba (Cuenca) in Ecuador; Huánuco Pampa, Pumpu (fig. 10.3), Hatun Xauxa, Vilcas Waman, Hatuncolla, and Chucuito in Peru; Paria in Bolivia; and Potrero de Payogasta, Chilecito, and Shincal in Argentina. As noted in chapter 9, some Inka administrative centers were installed in pre-existing local settlements, most of which are also located on generally flat or mildly sloping terrain. Examples are Cajamarca and Huamachuco in Peru, Fuerte Quemado in Argentina, and La Puerta and Catarpe in Chile. It appears that local hilltop settlements were rarely, if ever, converted into Inka administrative centers, probably because, as noted in chapter 6, it was Inka military policy to relocate the inhabitants of such towns.

In the irrigated coastal desert valleys of Peru, Inka buildings are occasionally found on slight prominences. This appears to follow the local custom of constructing important buildings on slight elevations, and not building on valuable agricultural lands. Thus in the Lurin, Mala, Cañete, and Chincha valleys, Inka buildings of main settlements are set

on prominences next to older settlements, rather than on the nearby flat irrigated terrain. In these cases, there is no indication that the Inka buildings' elevated positions were chosen for defensive reasons, but rather to utilize undisturbed terrain, and possibly for other reasons, such as a view of the sea (chap. 5).

Most Inka administrative centers were probably placed on generally flat or slightly sloping terrain because it was easier to build on land without topographical obstacles. There was another reason. Level locations in the Andes are often found on valley edges or bottoms, where the local population tended to concentrate and to work their fields. Other generally level sites in high plateau regions were often surrounded by rich pasturelands with considerable population. There is reason to believe that in Inka times different climatic conditions prevailed at high altitudes, permitting agriculture in regions above 3,800 meters in the Peruvian Andes and the high plateau of Bolivia (Cardich 1980). Whenever possible it was important to place administrative centers within a manageable range of the local populations, which supplied the labor necessary for the functions of the center.

Nevertheless, access to nearby labor did not always determine the location of administrative centers, as demonstrated by the role of the Inka road system in establishing such centers' locations.

Roads and Administrative Locations

Inka administrative centers were connected to each other and the capital, Cuzco, by the road system (Strube E. 1963) (fig. 10.4). Major centers were located on principal roads, and the course of the roads may often have preceded decisions concerning the placement of administrative centers. Many environmental and political factors dictated where Inka roads could and would be placed, and thus the regional topography was evaluated before the road system was laid out, particularly in areas where no earlier roads existed. In a previous study, I discussed a number of environmental factors governing the placement of roads (Hyslop 1984: 245–253). In brief, roads rarely ran across great arid stretches, over particularly rugged natural obstacles, or where rain and snow caused heavy erosion or drainage problems. There are notable exceptions, but these are usually found where there simply was no alternative. In general, Inka roads passed through the Andes using the flatter valley edges and bottoms and the level plateau. At times mountain crests were the driest, least precipitous route. When deserts were traversed the shortest routes between water sources and local population centers were designed. Occasionally, a major route might have avoided deep gorges and high natural barriers only by making major detours,

10.4. *The Inka road system. The map depicts approximately 23,000 kilometers (14,300 miles) of roads located by archaeological survey or historical research. The system is actually much larger, but additional investigation will be necessary to define the missing routes. Adapted from Hyslop (1984: endpapers).*

which was unacceptable, given the need for the roads to link the state quickly and economically. In such cases, gorges and passes were traversed, but usually the topographically least demanding route was selected. Given the ruggedness of much Andean terrain, even a "least demanding route" might often carry the road through abysses or over spectacular passes. Sometimes no roads, or roads with major detours, were constructed where environmental obstacles were insurmountable.[3] In short, the layout of the Inka road system was an interplay between the need of the state to join its territories efficiently, and environmental features that required that some natural barriers be avoided. The placement of administrative centers, inevitably on roads, was thus influenced by distant and local factors, often environmental, which governed the layout of the road system.

Environmental constraints on the Inka road system were juxtaposed against the political needs of the state, which preferred a relatively straight route for the transport of goods, people, and rapid communication. Every detour lengthened the distance between Cuzco and Quito, or between Cuzco and Santiago. Thus it appears that principal arteries occasionally avoided major population zones, although it may have been politically astute for a major route to have passed through them. A particularly good example of this is found in the central Andes where the main north-south Inka road is located in the high, flat *puna* region to the west of the more populated valleys on the eastern Andean slopes. There the north-south artery was constructed along a route with the least obstacles, and the main administrative centers such as Huánuco Pampa and Pumpu were placed on the road rather than in the areas where most of the subject populations lived. Of course, smaller subsidiary roads connected the centers to the populated valleys. Here it appears that a topographically easy route and a political need for a direct north-south artery were critical in the layout of the road, which in turn specified a general location for the centers. In this case, distant political and environmental factors determined that administrative centers not be placed near or within areas of dense subject populations.

Even given this special case, one can generalize that Inka roads were directed to subject peoples whose labor formed the backbone and source of wealth and power of the state. Sometimes this required that local populations be resettled (chapter 6). This was common policy in certain parts of the state, particularly where populations were evicted from defensive hilltop settlements. The decision where local populations would be resettled was no doubt closely linked to road politics.

In summary, the locations of Inka administrative centers required an understanding of the often-distant influences of environmental factors

10.5. Overlooking Machu Picchu, Peru. The irregular terrain was terraced to accommodate buildings. The central plaza was also leveled by using terraces. Inka architects generally terraced sloping land where buildings were to be erected.

and state politics that governed the locations of Inka roads. This was counterbalanced by a desire, if possible, to place the centers near local populations. If road engineering considerations made this impossible, populations might be moved closer to the roads, or linked to the centers by secondary routes.

Spacing between Centers

It has been suggested that the Inka state placed its administrative centers at relatively specific intervals (Agurto 1987: 37). Cobo (1964: 129, Bk. 12, chap. 32) wrote that the major provincial centers were separated by 20 to 30 leagues (approximately 100 to 150 kilometers).[4] The idea that major administrative centers are regularly spaced is not supported by other historical sources, even those written by individuals who traveled great lengths of the Inka roads in the early Spanish colonial period. The notion of a determined distance between the centers may come from the experience of those who traveled the Quito to Cuzco road, where several centers appear to be situated at intervals of several days' walk. Regular spacing of administrative centers may also be a false extrapolation from the generally regular spacing between *tampu*, roadside lodgings, which are found at a day's walk or less on roads throughout Tawantinsuyu.[5] The irregular spacing between centers is more notable in the southern part of the Inka state than in the central Andes.

Larger administrative centers were placed on main roads and, if possible, in or near concentrations of local ethnic groups. It also appears that generally flat or sloping terrain with access to water was also an important consideration in the selection of the site. Two examples demonstrate the diverse factors that led neighboring centers to lie, in one case, very close together and, in another case, very far apart.

The first example is that of the administrative centers Hatuncolla and Chucuito by Lake Titicaca. They are separated by about 35 kilometers. Each was responsible for the administration of a large population, and both controlled a "nuclear" territory at least 90 kilometers in length from north to south. Both are towns founded in Inka times on the main Inka road. The deeper explanation for their proximity probably has to do with each center's being near the ancestral communities (Sillustani and Cutimbo) of their local dynastic leaders. Thus Chucuito and

10.6. *The main plaza at Nevados de Aconquija, Argentina, has a three-level retaining wall on its eastern side, indicating that the plaza was leveled with much earth fill.*

Hatuncolla are relatively close to each other (about two days' walk) because they were located close to important pre-Inka communities.

The second example includes two centers in Chile, Catarpe (near San Pedro de Atacama) and La Puerta (in the Copiapó Valley), separated by more than 400 kilometers of the Atacama Desert. There is little possibility that any Inka sites larger than *tampu* lie on this road, since it passes through one of the most barren and unpopulated areas of the Andes (Hyslop 1984: 150–167; Iribarren and Bergholz 1971). In this case the distance between the centers was very great because of the lack of subject peoples living between them.

In summary, it was not Inka policy to place centers at specific intervals on the main roads. When centers appear regularly spaced, factors other than an intentional design were the cause.

Remodeling the Landscape for Buildings and Plazas

Notable examples exist where Inka architects required that considerable earth be moved to shape the terrain for their needs. This landscape architecture has not frequently been discussed, since previous studies have been more interested in the buildings themselves than in the land

10.7. Aerial view of the western side of Ollantaytambo. Fine agricultural terraces line slopes within the site. Courtesy S.A.N.

279

on which they were placed. Also, it is sometimes difficult to tell if the terrain of a settlement has been altered substantially. Only in some cases do archaeological information or other data clarify the issue. In some settlements, more energy may have gone into altering the landscape for the buildings than into the construction of the buildings themselves.

The chief Inka method of modifying the landscape for the construction of settlements is by terracing. Terraces are most common in the Cuzco area, particularly in settlements in the Urubamba Valley (fig. 10.5), and are often located in rugged terrain. Many of the buildings in Cuzco were set on terraces (chap. 2). The use of terraces to level sloping terrain for buildings has great antiquity in the Andes, and is not an Inka invention. The relationship between terraces used for buildings and agricultural terraces is uncertain. It is even unknown which may have developed first. Donkin (1979: 131) writes that "perhaps refinements in agricultural terracing owe something to the use of the platform or 'terrace' in architecture."

Evidence from some settlements shows that earth fill was used to level the surfaces of Inka plazas. Excavations in the plaza at Huánuco

10.8. Fine agricultural terraces at Tipón near Cuzco, Peru. They mold the landscape's natural curves into geometric patterns.

10.9. Aerial view of part of Pisaq in the Urubamba Valley, Peru. The Pisaqa and Intiwatana architectural complexes are visible on the ridge (center and center right). Courtesy Department of Library Services, AMNH, Neg. no. 334763 (photo by Shippee Johnson).

Pampa (C. Morris, personal communication, 1987) revealed that part of the plaza's eastern side was leveled by earth fill. At the southern frontier settlements of Nevados de Aconquija and Pucará de Andalgalá, retaining walls show that the main plazas of both sites were leveled partially with earth fill. A three-tiered wall (fig. 10.6) sustains the plaza of Nevados de Aconquija. A simpler retaining wall about 4 meters high supports part of the southern side of the plaza at Pucará de Andalgalá. Sometimes an Inka plaza would not be leveled into one plain, but rather divided by a terrace wall into a two-level plaza, such as at Incallacta in Bolivia, Maucallacta near Cuzco, or Inkahuasi on the edge of the *puna* in the upper drainage of the Pisco River. Plazas divided by a terrace wall not only allowed a large flat space to be constructed with less effort, but divided it into two parts, a division expressed in many other Inka plazas by a road or other distinguishing feature. Machu Picchu is a relatively special case where several terraces are used to level the main plaza. Elsewhere in Machu Picchu, earth fill was used to level a very irregular terrain (Valencia Z. 1977: 3).

AGOSTO
CHACRAIAPVI
quilla

tiempo se la bransa — haylli nmi ynca —

²⁵⁰ *10.10. A drawing from Guaman Poma's seventeenth-century chronicle (1936: f. 250) depicting an Inka king and others "breaking open" the earth with an Andean footplow. This activity ritually linked the Inka king to the beginning of the annual agricultural cycle.*

Elaborate Agricultural Terracing

Cuzco Region Terraces:
Types, Locations, Use, and Symbolism

It appears that sites with much landscape architecture are a phenomenon observed primarily in the Cuzco area and in some settlements within a few days' walk of the capital. Agricultural terraces are the principal form of landscape architecture. Agricultural terraces (Donkin 1979) are, in great part, a complex, broad, and important subject somewhat removed from this discussion. They have been used for millennia in the Andes, but in many places terraces were not part of the settlement concept. On the other hand, agricultural terracing within Cuzco and nearby settlements formed an integral part of their planning.

Niles (1982: 173) has noted that terracing was indeed part of the Inka settlement concept. Other studies of Inka architecture mention terracing only in passing, probably because terraces are usually associated with agriculture and are not seen as a significant part of what some authorities consider architecture.

In her study of agricultural works near Cuzco, Niles (1982) distinguished different types of terracing on the basis of their construction. The first and most common are "production" terraces, built of rough field-stones and with relatively low walls. Such terraces tend to follow the natural contours of slopes and are not necessarily closely associated with nearby settlements. The second type is known as "high-prestige" terracing, such as is found at the sites Tipón, Yucay, Ollantaytambo (fig. 10.7), Pisaq (fig. 11.4), and Chinchero. These terraces are more limited in extension, but are integrated into the human settlement. They are typified by high walls defining strips of fields. The walls are made of finely cut stones and may slant toward the slope. They often have peg stone or inset stairways and complex water systems, sometimes with "fountains" or "baths." These special terraces conform less to the natural contours, molding the slopes into straight lines, zigzags, and curves. In the Cuzco area, high-prestige terraces and their variant are far less common than are production terraces.

A third variety of terracing falls between the production terraces and high-prestige terraces, with the size and quality of its masonry between that of the two other types. This terracing molds the landscape or open areas into new forms, but not as dramatically nor with as fine stonework as high-prestige terracing.

Several points distinguish why elaborate terracings might be both part of a settlement and "high-prestige." First, they are near to the remains of important buildings. The terraces may be found on one side of the buildings, or within and around them. At Tipón, a wall surrounding the buildings also encloses the fine terraces (fig. 10.8). The terraces not only are elegantly constructed, but also are associated with some of the finest building complexes in the Cuzco area, often those of Inka royal

10.11. *Fine agricultural terraces to the north of the Inka plaza* (center right) *at Chinchero near Cuzco, Peru. A large carved boulder complex called Titicaca is found within the terraces* (foreground). *Courtesy Chinchero Archive/E. Franquemont.*

estates (Rowe 1967: 69; Rostworowski 1970: 253, 258; MacLean 1986: 129). These settlements, many of which are considered the finest examples of Inka architecture in the Cuzco area, were built or improved by Inka kings as country residences. They were probably more than just royal estates, since their complexity and varied layouts suggest that activities other than the occasional lodging of a king took place at them. Ollantaytambo, Chinchero, Yucay, Caquia Xaquixaguana (Huchuy Cuzco), Pisaq, Calca, Huayllabamba, and even possibly Machu Picchu and Tipón functioned, at least during the reign of one king, as such estates. Nearly all have high-prestige terraces. The terraces, at least when viewed from a distance, are the most imposing architectural feature of the sites (fig. 10.9). Thus there is a close association between the presence of royal estates and the settlements where such terraces are often found.[6]

The connection to royal estates is not sufficient to explain why elaborate agricultural terraces became part of these settlements. The introduction of such terracing into settlement design is influenced by aspects of Inka religion, which involved complex rites based on the grow-

10.12. The elaborate Inka terracing at Huaytará, upper Pisco Valley, Peru, is among the most extensive outside the Cuzco area.

ing cycle of various crops, maize being particularly important (Murra 1960). Some of the rituals were performed by the Inka king and other nobles (fig. 10.10). Numerous early historical sources note that special lands were set aside for the Inka and the state religion.[7] Thus one must consider the high-prestige terraces as highly symbolic, places where maize and other crops could be grown, where agricultural rituals could be carried out close to areas of royal residence.[8]

One point arguing for the symbolic nature of high-prestige terraces is that the energies invested in their construction went far beyond that necessary to terrace slopes by simpler means.[9] That is, the use of fine masonry instead of rough fieldstones, or the reworking of slope contours into geometric layouts, would not have been necessary to build equally effective production terraces. Chinchero, a royal estate near Cuzco, provides an example of this.

At Chinchero (fig. 10.11) the elegant terraces border on two sides of the main plaza (Alcina 1976: 131–140), near some of the finest buildings (figs. 4.7, 7.3). Important worked boulders are set within the terraces (fig. 4.8). Until recently, some of the terraces belonged to the Catholic church, which, in early Spanish colonial times, often took over the lands designated for the royal Inkas or the state religion. Alcina (1976: 140) points out that the limited terrain made available by the fine terraces at Chinchero was somewhat irrelevant if they were intended only for production. He notes that lying beside Chinchero there is an extensive, well-irrigated plain used for agriculture. Even given their ritual role, the yields from the elaborate terraces within royal estates were probably part of the economic base of Cuzco's *panaqa*, a subject raised in chapter 11.

Fine Terracing throughout Tawantinsuyu

Beyond the region of Cuzco are found examples of agricultural terracing similar in elegance but not often in dimensions to those in the Inka heartland. We shall examine below some examples of fine Inka terraces within settlements well away from Cuzco.

Small low terraces have been noted by Morris (personal communication, 1987) below an irrigation canal on the southeastern side of Huánuco Pampa. Their presence within the site leads Morris to postulate an essentially ritual role for them. As with Inka royal estates, large highland administrative settlements and sanctuaries also have fine terracing, unless their flat terrain rules out terrace construction. All of the following examples of high-prestige terracing are found at important Inka settlements that have some pronounced slopes near the main buildings.

10.13. Drawing by A. Bandelier of fine Inka terraces located on the Island of the Sun near the island sanctuary's main plaza and sacred rock. Courtesy Department of Anthropology, AMNH, Bandelier Collection.

One of the best but yet unstudied fine Cuzco-style sites of agricultural terracing outside of the Inka heartland is found at Huaytará (Hyslop 1984: 106–108) in the upper reaches of the Pisco Valley drainage system.[10] Located on the main Inka road leading from Hatun Xauxa to the coast, these terraces at 2,600 meters rival those in the Cuzco area (fig. 10.12). The main Inka structure at Huaytará (fig. 1.9) is one of the finest Inka buildings found anywhere outside of the Cuzco area (Gasparini and Margolies 1980: 255–259).

Particularly fine examples of Inka terracing outside of the Cuzco area are found at the sanctuary of the Islands of the Sun (Titicaca) and the Moon (Coati) in Lake Titicaca. Like many sites in the Cuzco area, they are closely associated with the most important architectural complexes. On the Island of the Sun, the terraces form part of the barrier, defined elsewhere by a wall, that isolates the northern tip of the island where the great "Sacred Rock" and main plaza are found (chap. 3). Bandelier (1910: 226–227) noted that they were the most "regular" system of terraces on the island, and mapped them (fig. 10.13).

Other fine terraces at the Lake Titicaca sanctuary are found on the Island of the Moon (Coati) by the building known as Iñak Uyu (Bandelier 1910: 275, 261). Iñak Uyu (fig. 10.14) is built on the first and highest of four terraces descending in a northeast direction to the lakeshore. It is, in Bandelier's words, the "largest and most handsome edifice on either island," and at one time most of its rooms were two stories high (fig. 10.15). An early historical source (Ramos Gavilán 1976: 62, chap. 18, 90, chap. 28) indicates that it was a Moon Temple with female attendants. The terrace immediately below it is supported by a wall of the finest Cuzco-style masonry about 2.5 meters high. No other walls or terraces at the lake sanctuary are made of fine Cuzco masonry. The elegance of the terrace wall suggests that it was at least as important as the great building above it.[11] Bandelier notes that many of its stones were removed to build churches in the town Juli on the southwestern side of the lake.

No elegant Inka terracing in settlements has yet been found south of Lake Titicaca. The reasons for this are uncertain, but may have to do with the limited development or lack of agricultural terracing, even in earlier periods, in parts of the Inka state now occupied by Argentina and Chile (Field 1966: 12, 259, 480). Local labor knowledgeable in fine terrace building may not have been available.[12]

Far in the north of Tawantinsuyu another set of fine terraces, probably high-prestige agricultural constructions, is found on the southern side of Tomebamba (Cuenca) (Idrovo 1984: 266–270) in Ecuador where the plain on which the settlement rests descends to the river (figs. 10.16, 5.8). These terraces have been only partially revealed by recent excavations, and their extent is still uncertain. Similar terraces are noted south of the plaza at Ingapirca (Fresco 1983: 200–201). They too are only partially excavated, but some walls are up to 3 meters high.

In summary, most large Inka settlements maintained sacred lands, often elaborate terraces, which were dedicated to the use of the Inka, *panaqa*, or the state religion. Where fine terraces are absent, it is probable that nearby fields performed the same role. Fields used for ceremonial purposes are less detectable archaeologically, since it has not been determined what differentiates a "sacred" field from one that was not, unless elaborate terracing was used. In the case of administrative centers located on very flat terrain, such terraces could have been constructed. Fine terraces do not appear to be associated with Inka military sites, which are often built on hilltops and by steep slopes.[13] This may indicate that agricultural ritual or production was not particularly important at military installations.

As in the Cuzco area, fine Inka terracing in other parts of Tawantinsuyu is associated only with the most important Inka architectural

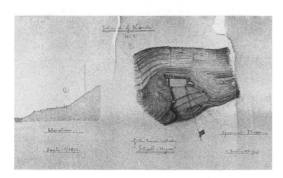

10.14. Drawing by A. Bandelier of special terraces lying between the Iñak Uyu and the shore of Lake Titicaca on the Island of the Moon (Coati). The first (highest) terrace below the Iñak Uyu has a wall built of the finest Cuzco-style masonry. Courtesy Department of Anthropology, AMNH, Bandelier Collection.

complexes, generally sites thought to have been major sanctuaries or administrative centers. During my survey of Inka roads and their associated smaller sites such as *tampu* (Hyslop 1984), no such terraces were observed. That survey, however, did not encompass the Cuzco area, where elaborate terraces may not always be intimately associated with architectural complexes.

Summary

This chapter examines two ways in which environment influenced the planning of Inka settlements: how and why locations were selected, and how these locations were then modified by the construction of the settlement.

Environmental factors instrumental in the selection of locations range from Inka religious concepts to ideas guided by engineering concerns and architecture. Although not yet well demonstrated, "sacred geography," the presence of sacred rock outcrops, water, and nearby mountain peaks and passes may have played a role in selecting the location of some settlements. Most administrative centers outside of the Cuzco area were built on flat or slightly sloping terrain. Generally, level

10.15. *Drawing by A. Bandelier of the Iñak Uyu building, the largest in the Lake Titicaca sanctuary. It was probably a Moon Temple with female attendants. Courtesy Department of Anthropology, AMNH, Bandelier Collection.*

10.16. Recently excavated terraces with fine masonry walls on the southern side of Tomebamba (Cuenca) in Ecuador.

terrain was but one factor contributing to the selection of a center's location. Other important factors included the site's proximity to local sources of labor, the possibility of using a pre-existing town or village, and the need to be on an important road. The routes of main roads were often influenced by distant environmental and political considerations.

There was no fixed Inka policy of separating administrative centers by a determined distance, although in the central Andes the distances between centers is somewhat regular.

Once a major Inka settlement's location was selected, the remodeling of the landscape was often necessary, particularly where the terrain was irregular, as at many sites in the Cuzco area and at some Inka military installations. The principal type of landscape engineering involved the construction of terraces to create level ground for buildings, plazas, and agricultural activities. There are exceptions, but in general, Inka site planners did not place buildings directly on slopes. Sloping terrain would first be leveled with earth or fill and sustained by a retaining wall, a technique similar to that used in agricultural terraces. Large, level plazas were also created by retaining walls sustaining earth fill.

289

Important Inka settlements both in and away from the Cuzco area were also distinguished by fine agricultural terracing. Examples include Inka royal estates near Cuzco, important sanctuaries, and distant administrative centers, but not necessarily military installations. Built with large expenditures of labor that modified the landscape into geometric patterns with fine masonry walls, these terraces were royal, religious, or state lands where ritually important crops such as maize were grown and where agricultural rites were performed.

The Inka propensity to remodel the terrain of some of their settlements far exceeds that of earlier Andean civilizations.

11
Final Considerations

This chapter considers questions relating to planned Inka settlements and queries touched upon in prior chapters that require additional comment or summary.

Research Objectives

More than a thousand articles and books have been written on Inka archaeology and ethnohistory, but very few scholars, including those studying the Inka, have attempted to read most of this literature. Investigation of Inka settlements will progress more rapidly when scholars begin to consider data other than their own and to expand their understanding of Tawantinsuyu.

No large Inka fortress or garrison has been excavated systematically. Beyond a survey of surface remains, Cuzco, the Inka capital, has never been the object of comprehensive archaeological investigations. The royal Inka estates of the Cuzco region await ethnohistorical and archaeological analysis and comparison. Many sixteenth- and seventeenth-century historical sources, both archival and published, require ethnohistorians to work them into insightful interpretations of Inka affairs. Large regions of the Andes (northern Ecuador, northern Peru, and southern Bolivia) have undergone very limited archaeological survey. In short, very little is known about large regions of the Inka domain, including the Inka heartland, Cuzco.

Housing the Population of the Empire

No one really knows how many people lived in the Inka Empire in its final years. Its population could have exceeded 14 million.[1] It is doubtful that exact estimates will ever be made due to the lack of surviving census data from Inka times. Whatever Tawantinsuyu's population, however, two points are noteworthy. First, only a very small percentage of the population included Inkas originating from the Cuzco area. Second, planned settlements throughout Tawantinsuyu could have housed only an extremely small part of the state's population.

To date there is secure evidence for only one large city within the Inka state, Cuzco, whose population probably exceeded 100,000 people. Even some of the largest planned settlements, such as Huánuco Pampa and Pumpu in Peru's central Andes, could have housed only a few thousand people at any given time.

Some historical sources, however, appear to contradict this point. Cieza de León, for example, mentions that many thousands served at centers such as Huánuco Pampa and Hatun Xauxa. These figures should be interpreted in Andean terms, as the number of people who provided the rotating labor service (*mita*) to the state. These individuals would come to the centers and work at or near them for a limited amount of time, generally only a few weeks. An administrative center could thus be filled with thousands of people throughout a year, although only a fraction were working in it at any one time. Thus planned Inka settlements were never very large. The biggest in the central Andes may have housed several thousand at a time; state settlements in the south Andes could have housed only hundreds of people. In some areas of the Inka state, particularly Qollasuyu, planned settlements rarely exceed several dozen buildings.

The majority of Tawantinsuyu's subjects resided in their traditional communities. Some of these were villages; others were houses dispersed over the countryside in such a fashion that it would be difficult to call them villages. In the centuries just before Inka domination, Andean populations began concentrating into villages, probably for defensive reasons, since warfare was endemic, at least in the highland areas. Reliable data are lacking because there are few detailed settlement pattern studies, but it appears that the tendency for Andean peoples to live in rural areas reasserted itself in Inka times. Defended agglutinated villages were no longer necessary during the *Pax Incaica*, and the state encouraged or forced their abandonment, at least in some areas (chap. 6). Cobo (1983: 194, Bk. 2, chap. 24) describes this Inka policy and the type of settlements that resulted:

> When the Inca subjugated a province, he obliged the inhabitants to leave their former dwellings and come down from the high and rugged places where they lived to other more appropriate places that were designated for them, and there they were to settle and live as a community under the authority of superiors who were put in charge of them. It is true that, although we give the name "towns" to these settlements or groups of huts into which the vassals of the Incas were organized, the name "town" is appropriate only by comparison with the groups of dwellings where they lived before; in fact, ordinarily these places were so small and

poorly designed (except for the provincial capitals, which were usually larger and better constructed) that they did not even resemble our most humble villages.

Cobo's description of dispersed populations is a general observation, most valid for the central and south-central Andean highlands, which he knew best. Some large towns, however, did function in Inka times. Marca near Hatun Xauxa may have had a population of over four thousand individuals (Earle et al. 1987: 58). Some of the conglomerate villages in the Argentine northwest could have had resident populations in excess of several thousand people. Archaeologists have recorded smaller villages of dozens of concentrated houses in other places (Lavallée and Julien 1983; Morris and Thompson 1985: 119–162). In many parts of the Andes it simply has not been determined where most of the people lived in Inka times. On the desert coast of Peru, many large pre-Inka settlements continued to be occupied during Inka rule, but there are still no secure estimates of how many people lived in settlements as opposed to in houses dispersed throughout and on the edges of irrigated valleys.

11.1. The settlement Tilcara in the Humahuaca Valley of Argentina was occupied in Inka times but has none of the type of planning that characterizes Inka state settlements. It does have a complex array of streets and buildings.

Some early historical reports refer to the non-Inka Andean towns as unplanned and randomly developed. When compared with Inka state settlements, it indeed appears as if little general planning was used (fig. 11.1). Agurto C. (1987: 57) refers to this type of village or town as "informal urbanism," characterized by poorly defined sectors, irregular lots of space, and uneven paths of variable width. He notes that some villages appear to have a central plaza with larger buildings. A detailed study of whatever planning exists within such settlements is in its infancy and beyond the scope of this study, but it is worth noting that such settlements were not as random or spontaneous as a cursory examination of their layout might suggest. Many villages were probably organized using the concept of a dual division. Paths or spaces, however tortuous, separated social units. Evidence for this is found in present-day indigenous settlements in the Andes, some of which have layouts somewhat similar to towns and villages in Inka times. Anthropological studies of these contemporary villages reveal that there is much structure and organization behind their apparent disorder. They do not, however, demonstrate the high degree of planning imposed by the Inka state.

The Role of Administrative Centers

Given that most people at Inka administrative settlements were temporary workers or officials, who were its permanent residents? Early historical sources reveal that Inka governors were common, but archaeological studies of state settlements have yet to define with certainty the residences of governors. Related to this is Rostworowski's surprising observation (1988: 118) that she has found no documents mentioning the presence of Inka administrators living amongst the ethnic groups. It is possible that Inka governors who actually resided outside of the Cuzco area were rare. They may have traveled, visiting areas when problems arose, as some historical evidence suggests (Rostworowski 1988: 110).

Whatever evidence there is for fancy residential compounds, sometimes called palaces, in Inka centers is not proof for resident governors. Until this situation is clarified, one might speculate that such buildings were used by important officials who were passing by, be they technical or religious specialists, loyal local lords, Inka governors, leaders of Cuzqueñan *mitmaq*, or Inka kings. This interpretation suggests that the fancy residential sectors of administrative centers had a function directly tied to bureaucracy.

A somewhat different opinion is expressed by Morris (1982: 162, 163), whose research at Huánuco Pampa was unable to "pinpoint a concentrated bureaucratic and administrative core." He notes that, "except

11.2. Large Inka storage jars, sometimes used for chicha *(a fermented beverage, usually of maize), provide evidence for feasting at Inka centers.*

for purely record-keeping matters, administration *per se* was probably not strongly differentiated as a separate activity. It was rather part and parcel of the ceremonial and hospitality functions." In discussing the nature of Huánuco Pampa's most elaborate residential enclave, sector IIB (fig. 5.6), Morris (1982: 162, 163) writes that if it was reserved for the Inka king, it must have usually been unoccupied. It may have symbolized his presence and would have played down the importance of any other high-level authority at the center. Indeed, the center may not have had a concentration of administrative authority, a possibly decentralizing element.

What, then, was the role of an elaborate residential enclave in an Inka center? Morris argues that its purpose was essentially one of state hospitality. Sector IIB at Huánuco Pampa produced "a whole complex of culinary pottery, food remains, and literally tons of large jars [*arybolloi*] [fig. 11.2] thought to be primarily associated with *chicha*" (Morris 1982: 165, 166). He notes that Andean political power and economic rights were closely associated with state hospitality and drinking, and that such ceremonies, although nominally religious, "were a way of establishing and maintaining a relationship between leaders and the led." Morris concludes (1982: 166):

If our preliminary interpretations are correct, the elaborate space provided along with the thousands of jars of beer represents one of the principal investments made by the Inka state at Huánuco Pampa. In terms of state-local relationships, this may even have been the key function, and many of the other spaces and activities in the center served to support it. An elaborate setting had been constructed for the ceremonies that forged a relationship between the Inka and those whose service was important to him.

For Morris, the Inka administrative center is an extension of Cuzco, which maintained its links to local lords and subjects through ceremony, hospitality, and the distribution of sumptuary goods such as textiles. Its central role used reciprocity and Andean ceremony to legitimize and create the larger units necessary to form a large state. Inka administrative centers were not the bureaucratic capitals we associate with Western political states, but they did create the necessary links between the center of power, Cuzco, and its subjects.

11.3. Excavated foundation of an aqllawasi *at Tomebamba in Ecuador. Archaeologists have found many spinning artifacts and female burials with gold objects in this compound.*

Related to this is Morris's interpretation of the storage facilities found in and near Inka centers. He believes (1986: 63) that they had a small role in the economy of the local towns and villages other than, perhaps, some supply to local leaders. The foodstuffs stored at Inka centers provided for the needs of state hospitality necessary for its building projects and feasting.

Several Inka centers outside of the Cuzco area have produced evidence for specialized production. *Aqllawasi,* residences of "chosen women" who brewed *chicha* and made textiles for the state, were noted in many places by the first Europeans to travel through the Andes (Alberti 1985). Of all long-term residents of centers, these appear to have been particularly important (fig. 11.3). They produced the important food and beverages which fueled the *mita* labor system. They also produced the fine textiles so important in Inka ritual and in reciprocal exchange relationships (Morris 1974, 1979, 1982).

Morris's view of the Inka administrative center as a place for feasting, drinking, and much political-religious ceremony makes it appear that solidarity rituals and hospitality typical of less-complex societies were employed in the formation of a large state. It complements, but does not necessarily contradict, the conception of the Inka state as a highly organized entity capable of organizing much state production, massive storage systems, and great building projects such as the road and *tampu* system.

Morris's formulations about the nature of the Inka administrative center are based primarily on ethnohistorical data and archaeological evidence from one settlement, Huánuco Pampa. How generalized were these patterns? Or were they restricted to the better-known Inka administrative settlements of the central Andes? My study of state planning suggests that these patterns have considerable universality.

The role of state storage is a case in point. Throughout Tawantinsuyu administrative centers frequently have identifiable storage areas. They are sufficiently extensive in only a few cases to suggest that they supplied foodstuffs to populations not attending the center. In the case of Cochabamba, Bolivia, a storage complex of more than two thousand buildings, the foodstuffs were destined for state military activities elsewhere (Wachtel 1980–1981). The storage complexes at and near Hatun Xauxa in Peru include more than two thousand buildings (Earle and D'Altroy 1982). Most are located at or near the administrative center and appear to have been used by it. A few other small storage complexes are most closely associated with local towns and villages. They may have been used to support state activities in those villages, or may have been cared for by their inhabitants (T. N. D'Altroy, personal communication, 1988). This pattern is somewhat different from that found at Huánuco Pampa, where storage was heavily concentrated at the center. To date, there is no pattern of extensive Inka storage in local towns and villages throughout Tawantinsuyu. The goods stored at Inka settlements appear to have supported activities at them. Their role was not to provide commodities to the local economy. The comparative data from Tawantinsuyu, therefore, indicate that Inka administrative centers' storehouses did not interfere in local economic relations.

A comparative study of major Inka settlements also indicates that they may not have bureaucratic zones of any size. Although excavations will be necessary to confirm this point, the potential bureaucratic enclaves within Inka state settlements are not large and are frequently difficult to identify by examining the site plans and the way buildings were constructed. They are generally built around or beside large patios.[2] It is not unusual to suggest that large states could be managed with a minimum of bureaucracy. Finley (1987 : 15) points out that Greece and Republican Rome were both relatively free of the administrators and *paperasserie* that characterized later empires.

Underlying Morris's interpretations is the idea that Inka ceremonial activities and state administration are categories that may not be separated easily. This investigation of Inka settlement planning provides confirming evidence. The previous chapters have described numerous ceremonial and symbolic aspects of Inka settlements often lying at great distances from Cuzco. Plans incorporating rocks, ceremonial water systems, radiality, two-, three-, and four-part divisions, elaborate terraces, and so forth all express Inka concepts about the nature of society and the universe. They indicate the physical expressions of Inka ritual and symbolism far beyond that which would be necessary to accomplish strictly administrative tasks.

Much of the symbolism found in the design of Inka administrative centers may have been educational, demonstrating the Inka world view to subjects and local lords. When visiting the centers, subjects would enjoy Inka hospitality, supply labor for state operations, and learn about the Inka way of thinking from the surrounding buildings and associated features. The result was a vast subject population that, although it did not live in the centers, was indoctrinated on visits to them.

The Royal Estates

Some kinds of Inka settlements found near Cuzco, for example, the royal estates (chap. 10) of Inka kings and *panaqa,* may never have been replicated away from the Inka heartland, although components of their design were certainly important elsewhere. The plans of the royal es-

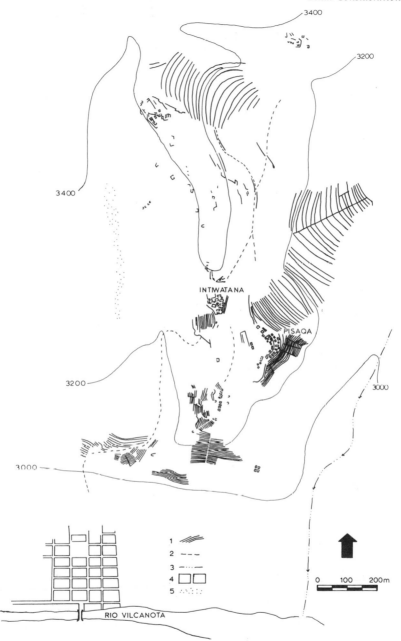

11.4. Plan of Pisaq in the Urubamba River Valley near Cuzco. It was an Inka royal estate and is dispersed over a considerable area. There are several sectors of build-ings and several zones of elaborate terracing (dark lines). Key: 1. terraces; 2. road; 3. stream; 4. modern town; 5. cliff burials. Redrawn from Angles Vargas (1970).

299

tates may serve only indirectly as models for the more numerous state installations throughout Tawantinsuyu.

When one compares the plans of royal estates (several have not been mapped) such as Yucay, Ollantaytambo (fig. 5.4), Pisaq (fig. 11.4), and Chinchero (fig. 4.7), their designs are quite different from state settlements beyond the Cuzco area. In general, the estates are characterized by layouts with extensive and fine agricultural terraces, elaborate waterworks, important carved and uncarved rock outcrops, and numerous buildings constructed of various types of fine masonry. They do not have large plazas or *ushnu* platforms and they generally are not arranged around four-sided plazas.

Much human energy was invested in their elegant terrace and wall construction and landscape engineering, more so than at most other Inka settlements beyond the Cuzco region. Their expensive construction sets these royal preserves apart from most state settlements. The diversity of the estates' plans, often constructed all or partially on irregular terrain, suggests that integration with the environment was a prime factor guiding their design. Given the importance Inkas associated with the sacred, animate landscape, these settlements more than others throughout the state appear to be places where Inka architects created a synthesis between environment and settlement, not only by accommodation to natural features, but also by modifying the landscape.

The royal estates were the personal property of Inka kings and their *panaqa*. Special, perhaps unique, design concepts may have been used in their planning. There is yet no evidence that they were considered "other" or "new" Cuzcos, as was the case of some of the larger settlements farther from Cuzco.[3] There is yet no concrete evidence that they were designed to express spatial and temporal concepts to subject peoples, or that they served as hospitality centers for subjects. Indeed, royal estates appear built for Inkas, although it is known in some cases that some foreign *mitmaq* helped construct and maintain them. A basic concept, yet to be explored, is that the design of royal estates did not require the kinds of symbolism and distribution of space important in dealing with foreign subjects.

Further ethnohistorical and archaeological research is necessary to define the role of those estates within the Inka system. Until then it will be difficult to understand many aspects of their design. It is necessary to repeat, as do several chroniclers, that they were used for the recreation and relaxation of Inka kings. Was that their sole purpose? Their role as a source of wealth directly accessible to the *panaqa* must be considered. That wealth would not have come primarily from the produce of their elaborate fine terraces, whose use may have been primarily ritual, but from the extensive agricultural areas around the settlements. It may also have come from production areas such as *aqllawasi* within the settlements, which created the sumptuary goods used in the reciprocal gift giving between Inkas and local lords. Rostworowski (1988) has demonstrated the great influence that the *panaqa* played in Inka politics, particularly as concerned disputes over royal succession. Might the royal estates have been the *panaqa*'s most reliable and lucrative economic base?

It is provoking to think that these elegant settlements and their surrounding lands may have produced the wealth used by the elite Inka groups that not only created an empire, but, because of their infighting (including a civil war for royal succession), also gave rise to some of the conditions for the successful European invasion of the Andes.

A Sanctuary Pattern

Early historical sources indicate that a few state settlements were almost entirely devoted to religious activities. Often called sanctuaries, they were dedicated nearly exclusively to ceremonial activities that extended well beyond the support of administrative, economic, or military activities.

One of the best examples of an Inka sanctuary is the religious complex found in Lake Titicaca on the Copacabana Peninsula and the nearby Islands of the Sun (Titicaca) and the Moon (Coati) in Bolivia. First described and interpreted by Ramos Gavilán in the seventeenth century (1976) and more recently by Bandelier (1910), the Titicaca sanctuary (chap. 3) is characterized by several Inka buildings and other constructions spread out over a considerable area. Today there are no remains of a major Inka settlement, although a settlement of some sort probably rests under modern Copacabana. Understanding how the sanctuary functioned explains much about its dispersed nature. This may help identify other sanctuaries and allows for the elucidation of yet another type of Inka settlement planning.

Pilgrims to the Titicaca sanctuary first went through the Copacabana Peninsula, passing through a wall with guarded gates. In Copacabana ethnic Inkas lived surrounded by *mitmaq* from forty ethnicities. Here, the visitor would undergo rituals, probably at a place where there are numerous carved outcrops (figs. 4.17, 4.18). The visitor would then cross by boat to the southern end of the Island of the Sun to a reception point and continue on the Inka road to the northern part of the island (fig. 11.5). Along the way the pilgrim would encounter fine Inka buildings such as the two-story Pilco Kayma (figs. 1.6, 1.7), a waterworks or bath, and arrive at a set of buildings which could house the traveler (Kasapata).

11.5. Aerial photograph of Lake Titicaca with the Island of the Sun (left), the northern tip of the Copacabana Peninsula (right), and the Island of the Moon (beyond the peninsula). Pilgrims walked from one end of the Island of the Sun to the other as part of a sacred route. The main plaza and large sacred rock are on the north (far left) end of the island.

At that point the pilgrim was a short distance from the most sacred part of the island, where the main ceremonial plaza and its great sacred rock were located (chap. 3). Upon reaching the point where one first glimpsed the rock and plaza, one passed barefoot through three gateways, after additional ritual. The pilgrim then passed a Sun Temple and arrived at the plaza and rock. One could also make a side trip to the nearby Island of the Moon, where there was a Moon Temple maintained by female attendants.

A pilgrim visiting the Lake Titicaca sanctuary thus spent several days proceeding along a route marked by sacred places where different types of ritual were carried out. The dispersed pattern of buildings thus appears to be the result of important constructions placed along a sacred route. The origin of this pattern is not certain, but its similarity to *zeque* lines with their sequences of sacred points, or *waqa*, should be noted. Travel along sacred routes was frequently marked by stopping points or stations where ritual was carried out. Zuidema (1982c: 439–443) describes a 100-kilometer Inka pilgrimage route with twenty-one stations from Guanacauri at Cuzco southeast to Vilcanota. He argues that it may have extended to the Lake Titicaca region, a distance of 300 kilometers. He refers to this particular route as a long-distance *zeque* because of its straightness, at least on the approach.[4]

Are other Inka sanctuaries typified by a pilgrimage route with sacred points along the way? Several high-altitude sanctuaries in the southern part of the Inka state have been studied sufficiently to suggest that there, too, visitors to the mountain sanctuaries passed along routes that had sacred points on them (Beorchia 1987: 67–71, 106–123, 124–130, 148–152, 237–242) (fig. 11.6). The stages of entry to a sacred place could also be very localized. Hernando Pizarro's letter (1959) in 1533 describes two stages of entry to the Sun Temple at Pachacamac where fasting was required before each advance.

The idea that sanctuaries or sacred places are approached via stations where ritual was carried out has implications for Inka planning. It suggests that the occasional isolated Inka building or other construction (e.g., waterworks or architecturally modified stone outcrops) may form part of a dispersed set of stations on a route, and not be an independent phenomenon. The small sites on the Inka Trail leading to Machu Picchu, each with its waterworks and carved rocks, are evidence that Machu Picchu was a major sanctuary (fig. 11.7).

Other Cuzcos

Some early historical sources mention "other" or "new" Cuzcos. At the beginning of the seventeenth century Guaman Poma wrote that there were other Cuzcos in Quito, Tomebamba, Huánuco Pampa, Hatuncolla, and Charcas (Bolivia) (1980: 185 [187]). As with several of his lists, it was probably not complete. What did he mean by "other" Cuzcos? Some insight is recorded by Cieza de León (1959: 342), who wrote that the Inka garrison Inkawasi (Cañete, Peru) was known as the New Cuzco. He wrote that its streets, hills, and plazas were given the same names as those of Cuzco. It is clear that names from Cuzco were used within and around some Inka settlements. Arriaga's study (1922) records numerous Cuzco toponyms at Tomebamba (Cuenca, Ecuador). The main plaza on the Island of the Sun in Lake Titicaca was called Haukaypata, the same as half of Cuzco's plaza. The similarity of major Inka settlements with Cuzco, however, is only superficially elucidated by noting that place names from Cuzco were transferred to settlements far from the capital.

At Cuzco one finds planning concepts employed in many other settlements. The orthogonal plan of Cuzco's central sector was used in some places. The radial concept found in Cuzco's surrounding districts and in its *zeque* system is used in all or parts of some settlements near and far from Cuzco. Other elements of planning at Cuzco found distributed widely throughout the state include the use of central *ushnu* complexes, *kallanka* on or near plaza edges, waterworks and drains in or near areas of considerable ceremonial importance, and site axes defined by the use of roads and astronomically based models. At settlements in and near Cuzco and throughout Tawantinsuyu important boulders and stone outcrops formed important aspects of site planning. Terraces were used to level space for buildings and plazas and for the cultivation of ritual crops. These aspects of planning only demonstrate physical similarities between Cuzco and numerous far-flung settlements. It is, however, the meaning of these design components that makes for the profound similarities with Cuzco. Their meaning expresses much about how Inkas viewed their own social structure, the

11.6. *Mount Mercedario in the province of San Juan, Argentina. The mountain may have the highest sanctuary in the Inka Empire. A route leading to it has several stations where ritual materials were buried. Courtesy A. Beorchia.*

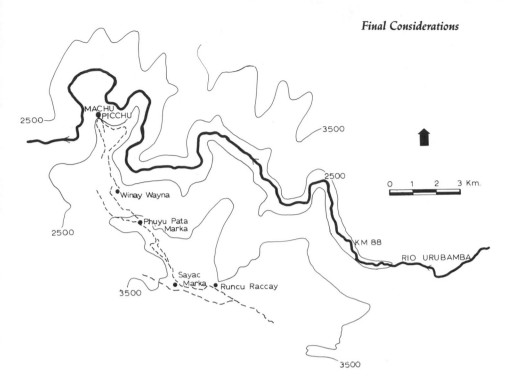

11.7. The road to Machu Picchu (the Inka Trail) has a number of small sites on it that may be ritual stopping points along the route. Adapted from Fejos (1944: fig. 2) and MacLean (1986: fig. 1).

organization of their state, and their relationship to the environment and the cosmos.

Inka settlements are thus not precise physical replications of Cuzco, but represented what Rostworowski (1979–1980: 190) has called its "mythical space." That is, Inka social, religious, and political concepts developed in Cuzco are spread to diverse parts of the state via the design and specific features of the larger state settlements. This was done in part by the flexible use of spatial divisions. The use, for example, of four-sided plazas may be taken as a form of quadripartition that expresses the *suyu* spatial concept symbolizing the four quarters of the empire. The use of astronomical concepts to align plazas and some compounds relays ideas about the Inka calendar and the organization of time. The alignment of buildings with mountain peaks and passes and the integration of rock outcrops express the deep Inka concern with the animate, sacred landscape. Where settlements can be divided into two parts, often by roads or an architectural alignment through the main plaza, it is probable that they represented the moiety or dual division fundamental to Inka social structure. Elaborate agricultural terraces integrated into some site designs were used for the agricultural ritual so prevalent in Inka religion. Central *ushnu* complexes allowed for a set of political, military, and religious rituals (child sacrifice, solar worship, and so forth) that were pivotal to Inka life and, according to Inkas, basic for achieving the integration of their subjects into the state.

Administrative settlements were extensions of Cuzco in more than a ceremonial way. As noted above, Morris sees these settlements not as semi-independent administrative capitals, but as direct links between the capital and subjects where ceremony, feasting, and hospitality solidified the bonds between the rulers and the ruled, creating the conditions by which it was possible to extract the rotational *mita* labor that was the basis for the state's wealth. It is probable that the larger Inka forts and garrisons may have functioned as hospitality centers somewhat similar to administrative centers. Whatever feasting and hospitality occurred at them was, however, probably intended for soldiers, who often came from great distances. Military installations may also be viewed as "other" or "new" Cuzcos, since they, too, have many of the same symbolic elements found in and near Cuzco.

Variations in Inka Settlements

No two Inka state settlements are identical. There were no universal principles followed in selecting a location and planning the layout of major Inka settlements. Rather, a complex set of concepts was used, based on the major activities to be carried out in the settlement, its topography, the distance and amount of local labor, and local cultural influences. Even given considerable variations in site planning, state settlements from Argentina to Ecuador indicate that their planners were aware of numerous Inka architectural forms and building styles. The ubiquity of the *kancha, kallanka,* terracing techniques, and elaborate water systems suggests that Inkas themselves, not just loyal subjects, planned and directed the construction of state installations.

What makes the design of Inka settlements vary from place to place? A considerable number of crosscutting and varied influences are apparent. Certainly, the principal activities of a settlement were important. Inka forts, surrounded by walls often located in irregular terrain, required a type of planning different from that of administrative centers. At military installations, some spatial patterns seen in administrative centers may have been sacrificed or transformed due to the irregular terrain. Sanctuaries may have included dispersed constructions and features along a specified route. Administrative centers were built on generally flat terrain and their designs express spatial concepts least transformed by topography. Estates near Cuzco were so extravagant that their occupants (kings and *panaqa*) could only have been royal.

The population density and the political status of the surrounding area also affected the design of settlements. A pacific local population indicated that pre-existing towns and centers might be used and re-modeled by the Inkas. The density of an area's population influenced the size of state administrative settlements, since its construction depended on local and *mitmaq* labor. Thus Inka centers in the central Andes, where populations were dense, are much larger than those in the southern Andes, where there were fewer people and population was more dispersed. The Inkas' political degradation of the Chimú region on Peru's north coast, and the Chimús' great existing infrastructure of roads and settlements, resulted in very little Inka influence on architecture or site planning.

The use of local or *mitmaq* labor and local building techniques created variations in Inka settlement design. On the near-south coast of Peru, Inka settlements retain the compact design of local sites, with joined, not independent, rooms. Wall construction throughout Tawantinsuyu's state installations is often characteristic of local building traditions.

Dozens of state settlements throughout Tawantinsuyu demonstrate that Inka architecture and site design cannot be fully understood by just analyzing settlements in the Cuzco area. Indeed, several types of Inka settlement planning are best seen outside of the Cuzco area. For example, sites with large rectangular or trapezium plazas, usually with *ushnu* complexes, are best defined in areas distant from Cuzco. Military influences on site design are best studied at settlements on Inka borders far from Cuzco. Finally, some of the best-known Inka sanctuaries are not in the Cuzco area.

Settlements within the Context of Empire

This book discusses how Inkas organized state settlements for military, economic, and political purposes, generally within a ritualized context. Inka settlements were but one means used by the Inka state to expand and maintain its control. They alone do not clarify the state's strengths and weaknesses. It is unnecessarily judgmental to claim that Inka settlements contributed to the management of an empire in a way that was good or bad, fragile or strong, intelligent or dull.

The Inkas knew far better than we do what was needed to create and manage their realm. Nevertheless, given both the Inkas' monumental expansion and their rapid demise in the face of the European invasion, scholars waver between noting Inka weaknesses and noting their strengths. Some point out their great power and organization, which united the largest region ever governed by a state in pre-Columbian America. They note the grand array of insightful tactics by which territories were assimilated or conquered and then governed.[5] On the other hand, others, concentrating on many disruptive elements within the state from ethnic disobedience to *panaqa* rivalry, deny that Tawantin-suyu should be called an empire, claiming that it never developed cohesion.[6]

Was Tawantinsuyu an empire? What is an empire if not the agglomeration of many ethnic groups over a great and varied environment, with rulers who govern those who govern? Tawantinsuyu, like most older and some more recent empires, occasionally confronted severe ethnic resistance and probably suffered from overexpansion. As with many other empires, there were disruptive quarrels among the ruling elite. The Inkas nevertheless achieved an empire in the common definition of the word.[7]

What does the study of Inka settlements contribute to the imperial debate? The distribution of state-planned settlements from Santiago, Chile, to the Colombian-Ecuadorian border, a distance of over 5,000 kilometers, along with other large state construction enterprises such as the road system, demonstrates that the Inkas organized for the continuation of their enterprise. The Inka Empire was not a political enterprise joined together with little or no infrastructure. That physical network of roads, *tampu,* and larger settlements is physical evidence that an imperial design was not only planned but executed. Solidarity rituals in the administrative centers may have been an occasionally weak link between rulers and governed, but Inka armies, supported by massive stored supplies and an efficient transport system, were never far away and were occasionally called upon to enforce obedience. Tawantinsuyu, moreover, employed many strategies that went beyond reciprocity and military threats to teach, regulate, and enforce cohesion.

The weaknesses that brought the Inka Empire crashing down in the 1530s are as much a part of the definition of empire as are its notable strengths. Many other empires were not long-lived, many grew too quickly, and most saw great internal discord among the governed as well as among the rulers. Fragility and lack of cohesion, as well as power and organization, are part of the essence of empire. Uneasy lay the crowned heads of Old World emperors. Great dangers also accompanied the Inkas who wore the imperial fringe.

Accepting the imperial status of Tawantinsuyu allows scholars to compare it to other large, hierarchically organized, multiethnic states. To insist that it was unique among world political structures denies the use of comparison, a necessary methodology employed by scholars wishing to define general cultural and historical patterns.

This book describes and interprets the design of Inka settlements. It does not enter into cross-cultural deliberations about the nature of the preindustrial city, urbanism's relation to cultural evolution, or the symbolism of urban structures. It should, however, serve others who make such inquiries.

Major Inka settlements might be compared with fine Andean textiles, which served practical ends, but had much symbolism woven into them. As in weaving, the planning and layout of Inka settlements must have been a major intellectual, religious, and possibly aesthetic endeavor. It is clear that before designing a settlement, Inka architects had to be aware of a multitude of religious, political, economic, and ethnic factors before they could weave these influences into a coherent architectural layout. But are the designs of Inka settlements works of art, as are fine Andean textiles? I leave this question, about which the chroniclers say nothing, for the reader to ponder.

Notes

1. Introduction

1. Due to the perishable nature of Inka roofing materials, it is difficult to reconstruct roofing techniques with accuracy. Studies by Agurto (1987: 177–251) and Lee (1988) explore the topic. Other useful sources on Inka roofing include Bouchard (1983: 45–55), and especially Gasparini and Margolies (1980).

2. Strangely, no circular *qollqa* have ever been positively identified in the Cuzco region.

3. Rostworowski (1972: 39) presents evidence for the sacred nature of red coloring.

4. An intact ramp leading up to an unfinished burial tower is present at the Lake Titicaca habitation and burial site Cutimbo (Hyslop 1977b: 165, fig. 21). It is more than 18 meters in length and composed of fieldstones.

5. Protzen (1980, 1983) has performed experiments demonstrating how the Inkas fitted stone blocks. His investigations of quarries and stone extraction techniques provide especially valuable information not available in early historical accounts. Outwater (1978) also discusses quarrying in his work on the construction of Ollantaytambo in the Urubamba Valley, near Cuzco.

6. Agurto (1987: 135) notes that stonemasons in Cuzco were able to duplicate easily and accurately Inka and colonial stonework during the restoration of monuments damaged in the earthquake of 1950.

7. The walls of Tanka Tanka may be compared with a wall in Cuzco, that of Quiscapata Street (Agurto 1980: 105, photo on facing page). Agurto C. feels this may be one of the oldest visible walls in Cuzco (personal communication, 1986).

8. The debate centers on whether the early Inka kings have historical validity or are inventions that express the social organization of Cuzco.

9. An exception is the evaluation of Rowe's scheme found in Wedin (1963). Wedin warns against the use of exact dates for the reigns of the late Inkas, but produces no alternative chronology.

10. Rostworowski (1988) analyzes these sources, citing many reasons why Inka histories carry divergent information. She points out that conflicting accounts are not due simply to the inaccuracies of oral traditions (the Inkas were illiterate until the arrival of Europeans), or to early European writers, who misunderstood Andean culture, but to the political views of diverse Inka groups and other Andean people who supplied the information recorded after A.D. 1532.

11. Vincent Lee (1985) has published the best preliminary plans of the neo-Inka settlements Rosas Pata and Espíritu Pampa (Vilcabamba). His ongoing work in that region will supply more detailed maps.

12. Rostworowski's description (1988: 71–87) of Inka buildings and public works is ordered according to the succession of kings who built them.

13. The method has pitfalls, since one must weigh the accuracy of varied early historical sources, and evaluate to what extent buildings were remodeled or added after a site's original construction. Another difficulty, particularly evident in Inka sites outside the Cuzco area, is discerning which characteristics are introduced into Inka architecture by local, non-Inka traditions. For example, the corbeled vault of the Titicaca region becomes Inka, but only in that region where it originated.

14. The Inkas had length measurements, which were used in the design of settlements and the layout of buildings and terraces. Rostworowski (1981) discusses the evidence in the early historical sources and dictionaries. Agurto C. (1987: 255–280) examines the physical evidence from measured buildings in the Cuzco area. Farrington (1984) finds patterns of measurement in terrace dimensions. There appears to have been a common length measure of about 1.6 meters or 3.2 meters. Agurto argues that Inka measurements were based on human dimensions, but that they were subdivided into a base ten (decimal) system. The Inkas used the decimal system for some types of accounting, but Rostworowski and Farrington do not mention use of the decimal system in length measurements. The origin of Inka length measurements in human proportions is noted by Rostworowski and by Valencia E. (*n.d.*).

2. Cuzco

1. Agurto (1980: 96) writes: "The destruction of archaeological remains is continual and permanent, and a large number of walls listed in the survey of 1934 have disappeared as well as an appreciable number of those that figure in the Registry of 1950."

2. Interpreting Garcilaso's descriptions of Cuzco is enough to leave the most patient scholar in a quandary. His characterization, found in many sections of his famous chronicle, is by far the most detailed of any person who lived in Cuzco before 1560. He writes much that cannot be backed up by other written accounts, however. When it is possible to test his veracity, he fails on some occasions to be accurate. On many other points he passes such tests with flying colors and appears to have a clearer conception of the data than the shorter accounts that confirm him. Rostworowski (1988: 56–58) demonstrates how some of his intentional distortions of historical events are due to allegiance to his *panaqa*.

3. See illustrations and a discussion of such drawings in Gasparini and Margolies (1980: 63–66).

4. The early historical accounts of the Inkas have numerous references to state-organized ventures that required carrying heavy loads, such as stones, over very great distances. This commentary about the sand of Cuzco's plaza coming from the sea, 450 kilometers away, is particularly interesting, since it appears to be true, verified by a particularly astute informant, Polo.

5. The *sunturwasi,* or *cubo,* of Garcilaso was not described by other chroniclers. He notes that he saw it, but that it was destroyed in his childhood (the 1540s). Since Garcilaso provides us with the sole description, one might doubt its existence, or confuse it with the round buildings of Qasana. Tom Zuidema has supplied me with evidence supporting Garcilaso. In the *Actas de los libros de Cabildos del Cuzco—Año 1549* (1959: 188, 197–198, 207–208) one finds an order from 1549 to Hernando Pizarro's caretaker, Diego Velázquez, to reconstruct a building (*cubo*), recently destroyed by Pedro de Cuevas, at Hernando Pizarro's house, which was in Amarukancha. Hernando Pizarro took over Amarukancha when he was governor after its original Spanish owner, Hernando de Soto, left for Spain in 1535. It is thus possible to confirm that there was a *cubo* associated with Amarukancha and that it was destroyed before 1549.

6. The name of one building may have been Ochullo (*Libro Primero* 1965: 33). The first Spanish town hall (*cabildo*) and foundry were located in a *galpón* on the terrace on the northeast side of the plaza (*Libro Primero* 1965: 33). That large hall may have been called Cuyusmanco. Zuidema (1968: 47–49) notes that both Pachacuti Yamqui (1879: 295) and the dictionary of González Holguín (1952: 58) associate it with the *cabildo.* Zuidema also found a seventeenth-century source referring to the district behind the cathedral as Cuismanco.

7. Pedro Pizarro (1978: 88) attributes it to "Yngas antiguos." Garcilaso (1963II: 261, Bk. 7, chap. 10) says that it was Wayna Qhapaq's. Sarmiento de Gamboa (1965: 265, chap. 63) says that it was built by Waskar. Finally, the Anonymous Jesuit (1879: 149) claims that it was a temple with a serpent idol.

8. The curved wall on the southwest side of Qori Kancha is considered by some to be indicative of a Sun Temple. Three other identified Sun Temples (at Pachacamac, Vilcas Waman, and the Island of the Sun) have no curved wall.

9. Colcampata is a notable exception. Excavations there by Valencia (1984) have found Qotakalli pottery, indicating a human presence there before the expansion of Tawantinsuyu.

10. Garcilaso described three towers (1963II: 287, Bk. 7, chap. 29), but a third remains unconfirmed by Valcárcel's excavations (1934: 7–9). Two are clearly defined, one round with a cistern in the center (Muyujmarka) and a rectangular one (Sallajmarca).

11. Excavations in recent years have exposed considerable areas of walls, terraces, and enclosures. Still unpublished, the results of these endeavors should amplify the knowledge about this site. The *anfiteatro* described by Valcárcel has, with additional excavation, become a magnificent round enclosure.

12. See Lee (1987) for some interesting ideas (some unconfirmed) on technical aspects of the construction of Saqsawaman.

13. Duality at many levels of authority is maintained by Zuidema (1964, 1983*b*), Duviols (1979), and Rostworowski (1983: 130–179).

14. The point was not lost on even the earliest Spaniards to enter Cuzco, soldiers whose accounts are descriptive but rarely have much analytical depth. One account from 1535 (Estete 1924: 48) records that "four roads from four very large kingdoms or provinces came together in a cross in Cuzco. [The provinces] were subject to them [the Inkas] and were named Chinchasuyu, Qollasuyu, Antisuyu, and Kuntisuyu."

15. The number of *panaqa* may have been greater, depending on the historical source. See Sherbondy (1982*a:* 18–21) for a useful review of the *panaqa-ayllu* similarities and differences. Both had a putative male genitor, but the *panaqa* were possibly never really kinship groups, although kinship terms were used to define them. The *panaqa* were units of Inka people with specific political and calendrical tasks. They were ranked, and it is possible that they could be joined voluntarily (Zuidema 1983*b*). Rostworowski (1988: 35–41) also reviews the evidence on *panaqa*. She views them as true kinship groups, possibly matrilineal.

16. The *zeque* system has been studied by others such as Chávez Ballón (see Morrison 1978) and Vescelius (see Sullivan 1974), neither of whom published their important knowledge dealing with the thorny subject of the locations of many of the system's *waqa*, many of which can only be identified or located approximately. Even today there is no comprehensive published source defining the locations, however approximate, of most of the known *waqa*. It is difficult for the larger community of scholars to evaluate published research relating to the system without such a study.

17. San Andrés de Machaca is a native community in Bolivia where the custom still prevails of assigning pie-shaped lands surrounding the town to the community's *ayllu*.

18. Sherbondy (1986: 53–55) believes that her findings contribute to the debate about whether the *panaqa* and their "founder" kings have any historical reality. She writes that the distribution of waters, lands, and Inka groups is the result of a total reorganization of Cuzco, which created or changed the *panaqa* into a Cuzco institution. The distribution of the irrigation districts, with their intricate symmetry and parallels (as seen in the *zeque* system), could have taken place only at one time, probably during the rule of Pachakuti or Thupa Yupanki. She argues, as does Zuidema, that the genealogical lists really define ranking among the *panaqa*, and that the language of descent is really the language of hierarchy.

19. Sherbondy also suggests (1982*a:* 93–95), but does not demonstrate conclusively, that the *zeque* divisions were used for labor organization, particularly for the important task of canal cleaning. In addition, she notes (1982*a:* 86) that many calendrical aspects of the *zeque* system are based on factors specific to Cuzco, such as the functioning of the Chacan canals and the maize crop. Thus the dates for irrigating, planting, cultivating, and harvesting would have to be adjusted in other areas, where local agricultural calendars must have been used in coordination with the Inka state's.

3. The Center

1. Some of the preliminary data and ideas appear in Zuidema (1978: 157–162). Rowe (1979: 74–75) also presents some of the historical evidence for *ushnu*.

2. In all fairness, the report (1943: 30, 36) also described the *utcu* (*ushnu*) of Cuzco as a basin where *chicha* was sacrificed and noted that it had a drain to the Sun Temple. Attributed to Cristóbal de Molina, el "Almagrista," the text is probably by Bartolomé de Segovia.

3. One early report by Bartolomé de Segovia from 1553 (1943: 22) mentions "a high, square platform with a very high stairway" supporting *ushnu* pillars. Archaeologists have never observed an *ushnu* stone on top of an *ushnu* platform.

4. "*Intiwatana*," or "hitching posts of the Sun," appear to be important stones whose name is of recent origin. The term used by the Inkas for these monuments is unknown.

5. González Carré et al. (1981: 51) believe that the sacrificial stone reported by Cieza de León in the middle of the plaza may be a large rectangular stone now on one side of the plaza. It may have been moved when the Inka plaza was remodeled and covered with cement walks.

6. An *ushnu* platform is found closer to Cuzco, at Curabamba (department of Apurimac, Peru). A sketch map of the site and brief description were made by Wiener (1880: 278–280). The platform is a stepped structure located on the eastern side of the plaza. Lechtman (1976: 27–32) investigated the dubious metallurgical activity at Curabamba and published a photograph of the plaza and platform.

7. Zuidema (1980: 351) compares the *ushnu* platform of Vilcas Waman with the Cuyusmanco of Cuzco. As mentioned, evidence for the Cuyusmanco, and its association with *ushnu*, is limited.

8. The leading source on the Inkas in the Copacabana area was written by the priest Alonso Ramos Gavilán, who lived in Copacabana beginning in 1618. His *Historia de Nuestra Señora de Copacabana* (1976) was published in 1621. The other detailed source is Bernabé Cobo, who at the same time was living nearby in Juli on the southwestern side of Lake Titicaca. Cobo's account, completed in 1653, closely parallels that of Ramos and suggests that he had access to Ramos's work. Cobo (1964: 189–194, chap. 18) does include some new details, but omits many others covered by Ramos.

9. One could argue that it is the first detailed study of Inka archaeological remains. It is remarkable in that it remains one of the best studies despite innumerable problems. Bandelier wrote (1910: xv): "Climate, nature and man conspire to impede, annoy and obstruct." Surprisingly, Bandelier's work has rarely been consulted by scholars, many of whom assume that more recent or contemporary works are the only ones "scientifically" valid.

10. A similar observation was made by the visitor E. G. Squier (1877: 336, 337) in the last century: "But this rock today—alas for the gods dethroned!—is nothing more than a frayed and weather worn mass of red sandstone."

11. There is a remote chance that the round stone basin by the Inka baths in Copacabana may have been brought there from the plaza by the sacred rock. Local memory claims that it is an Inka artifact, but recalls nothing of its history.

12. Paulotti (1958–1959: 127, 129) describes these stones as forming a double circle. Argentine colleagues and I visited the site in 1986 and found the stones to form a rectangle. A hole is in the center of the rectangle. This is the place where the rough stone was seen and photographed by Paulotti.

13. Incorrectly drawn in Gasparini and Margolies (1980: 208, 212), who portray the platform between the sixth and seventh doorway instead of in front of the seventh. The distinction may be important, since its location in front of the

doorway means it could be seen, and entered, from the plaza as well as from the *kallanka* behind it. Zuidema (1980: 350) was the first to point out the possible significance of this platform.

14. Shea (1966) excavated two small structures on the southeastern side of the first platform at Huánuco Pampa. Their relationship to the *ushnu* complex remains uncertain. They do demonstrate that a centrally located *ushnu* platform was not necessarily just a platform. Morris and Thompson (1985: 59, 60) report a subterranean canal between the platform and the ceremonial area to the east with its series of gateways, fine Inka masonry, and large patios. Not only a canal, but a major architectural axis formed by elaborate gateways linked the *ushnu* platform to the eastern side of the plaza. At Pumpu the "drain" connecting the platform with the eastern gateway may be the open channel passing just north of the platform to the eastern doorway (fig. 7.12).

15. In both his field seasons at Tambería del Inca, Greslebin used the southeast corner of the platform as the point for measurements to other structures in the site. His published plan (1940) shows lines radiating from the platform, much like a *zeque* system. In fact, Greslebin had no knowledge of the *zeque* system, nor was he aware the site was Inka, even given its name.

4. Rocks and Outcrops

1. Gasparini and Margolies (1980: 267) express a different view, writing: "The deeply rooted cult of the rock, whether the rock was natural or modified in multiple ways by the stone carver, represents an area of investigation apart from architecture."

2. The use of special stones in plazas, an important aspect of the *ushnu* concept, is dealt with in chapter 3.

3. This *waqa,* called Sabacurina, listed in "An Account of the Shrines . . ." (Rowe 1979: 22, 23, Ch-5: 6), was used for "solemn sacrifices" and "worship" of Saqsawaman. The "Account" also relates that Inkas sat there. This is a rare case where early information notes that the shelves were seats. There is a tendency to consider all such shelves as "thrones" or "seats" of the Inka. It is probable that most were for offerings or sacrifices.

4. Means (1928: 301) reports that the Viceroy Don Francisco de Borja y Aragón, a zealous extirpator of idolatry, wrote the Spanish king in 1619, saying that since 1615 no fewer than 10,422 "idols" had been seized or destroyed. The viceroy might have been less pleased with these achievements had he known that there were a very large number of "idols" still intact. The reason for this is that sacred parts of the landscape and objects not only were omnipresent in the Andes, but could be reproduced or multiplied.

5. The "Account of the Shrines of Ancient Cuzco" was found in Cobo's seventeenth-century work, but not actually authored by him. See Rowe (1979).

6. Rowe makes a careful comparison (1979: 72–79) of the two lists, noting that each has independent information about *waqa* in and near Cuzco and that Albornoz's list may be a summary of a more lengthy original.

7. Useful sources with photographs of carved stones in the Cuzco area are Hemming and Ranney (1982: 165–177), Ubbelohde-Doering (1966: plates 257–267), and Angles Vargas (1978: unnumbered plates).

8. The photograph is reproduced from Bingham (1930: fig. 56). It does not show the peak beyond, which the rock appears to imitate. A photograph in Hemming and Ranney (1982: 52) portrays both the stone and the horizon beyond. The rock forms one side of an architectural unit that has been excavated (Valencia Z. 1977).

9. I thank Edward Franquemont, who kindly supplied the data cited here on Chinchero's important rocks and outcrops.

10. Sherbondy compares the Sayhuite rock with those of Lanlankuyoq and Laqo of Cuzco. Now in territory frequented by Sendero Luminoso (Shining Path) revolutionaries, the stone is difficult if not dangerous to visit. A life-size model may be viewed in the Parque de las Leyendas in Lima. It is occasionally attached to the park's water system, which allows the rivers and canals on the stone to flow with water. I thank Maarten Van de Guchte for this yet-unpublished information on Sayhuite.

11. There are still others at Qopa Qati, three kilometers south of Copacabana (Portugal Z. 1977: 300), carved into three separate outcrops.

12. So does a newer source discussed and published by Rowe (1985: 215, 226).

13. Santacruz Pachacuti (1879: 273) refers to the construction of "observation points on the seashore at Pachacamac and Chincha."

5. Water

1. The clear importance of water in historical accounts and archaeological remains was called the "water cult" by Carrión Cachot (1955), and the term persists in much present-day literature. There is, however, no evidence for a "cult" in the modern accepted usage of the term. Indeed, water ritual blended with and complemented many other aspects of Inka religion and might be best viewed as one component of a complex of religious beliefs rather than as a separate entity. The fact that this chapter concentrates on water in architectural planning should not detract from water's integration with other beliefs.

2. MacLean (1986: 66, 68, 90) suggests that the manipulation of water in Machu Picchu–area sites may have been related to "the pleasure derived from the sight and sound of water purling down through channels and splashing into basins." There is, however, little historical evidence that Inkas created waterworks in settlements for aesthetic reasons. She is quite aware (1986: 90) that water management "often transcended purely utilitarian function and was important in ritual."

3. Carrión Cachot (1955: chap. 3) reprints and comments on a number of these. The greater part of this lengthy work reviews the evidence for *paccha*, devices for pouring libations that are a long Andean tradition. One might question whether all these devices are in any sense clear evidence for a water cult, since, according to several myths, they were often used with *chicha* and employed in rites quite removed from water-related themes.

4. One study is by Ardiles (1986), who describes subterranean channels in the Inka fields known as Saucero. Today the zone is known as San Judas Grande in the district of Huanchac. Saucero had sacred lands where at least two annual agricultural rituals were carried out. Maize was planted here in land that was dedicated to the Sun and Mama Huaco. Fifteen segments of channels were lo-

cated, some at depths of 2 meters. They are stone lined and stone capped, often parallel and equidistant. This complex drainage system recuperated wet terrain for agricultural-religious purposes and secured water for irrigation.

Ongoing and as yet unpublished excavations in Saqsawaman (Suchuna sector) have found elaborate waterworks, including a reservoir.

5. The mapping of Pumpu is an ongoing project of Ramiro Matos M., who directs a team from San Marcos University, Lima. Matos detected the subterranean channels in the eastern sector when the waters of the modern reservoir on the side of the site were lowered, revealing channels in the embankment.

6. Tomebamba has many toponyms in common with those of Cuzco (Arriaga 1922). Using names from Cuzco for places and natural features in and around Tomebamba was one certain way in which the second capital took on characteristics of Cuzco (see chap. 11, "Other Cuzcos").

7. This is a conception that would seem to oppose the well-known division into *hanan* and *hurin* of non-Inka people throughout much of the state. There is no necessary conflict, however, since the dual division within an Inka settlement may have followed criteria somewhat different from the way local populations were organized. It would appear that the dual division of many non-Inka people was present before the expansion of Inka rule, but that it was more rigidly applied and often altered by Inka administration.

6. Military Settlements

1. Another important point of Inka military organization has been elaborated by Murra, who has presented the evidence for the evolution of the military apparatus from an entity of many ethnic groups performing their service as *mita*, to a more professional corps of troops that no longer returned to their homes, and some of whom were permanently removed from their territory and resettled near Cuzco. Freed from traditional *mita* obligations to their own lords, "most of their time was now to be devoted to royal and army matters" (Murra 1986: 56).

2. One example of a region's militarization is found in survey work carried out by Elias Mujica and me in the region to the southwest of Lake Titicaca (Hyslop 1976, 1977a). There, many settlements were located on hilltops and surrounded by concentric walls. This pattern appears to have been repeated throughout much of the Andes from Chile and Argentina to Ecuador, although there are few investigations documenting it with detailed settlement pattern studies (but see Le Blanc 1981). Unfortunately, the period of several hundred years between the demise of the Wari and Tiwanaku cultures and Inka expansion has been of little interest to archaeologists working in the Andean highlands. They have preferred to study the more "glamorous" larger states and empires.

3. Kubler, in his study of the colonial Quechua, notes how the ritualized nature of Inka warfare was one of its greatest weaknesses in battles with the Spanish. He describes the Inka siege of Cuzco (1946: 383): "Manco's great mass attacks were launched periodically at the full moon, when his men were at the mercy of the cavalry counter attack. At all times his troops were massed so densely that their pikes were of no avail against the horses. Then, at new moon, when the horses would have been at disadvantage in the dark night, the Indians

ceased attacking to perform sacrifices to the lunar deity, thus forfeiting the advantage of sustained pressure upon the enemy. This 20-day rhythm of battle was known to the Spaniards, and they exploited it accordingly."

4. A good example of extensive use of *mitmaq* on the Pacific coast is the Cañete Valley, where local populations were apparently decimated in war with the Inkas, and groups from several different areas replaced them (Rostworowski 1978–1980).

5. Other evidence for military installations in the Urubamba Valley includes Pumamarca near Ollantaytambo (Gasparini and Margolies 1980: 289, 293, 294), which may have been built before the Inka expansion into more distant regions (Niles 1980). Kendall (1985: 293–308, 407) reports the hilltop "fort" of Huillca Raccay in the Cusichaca area. Ceramic evidence indicates that it was built prior to the imperial expansion. Thus some fortifications in the Urubamba Valley may not have been built to defend the Inka state. Additional research on this matter is necessary to clarify the military situation in the Late Intermediate Period in the Urubamba Valley.

6. At Quitaloma (see section on Pambamarca) Oberem (1968: 339, 342) did find *bolas* and sling stones.

7. Raffino (1983: 257–260) presents a map of Inka fortresses in the southern Andes. He includes these sites and some others for which there is even less evidence of Inka military concerns (the Inka affiliation of Angostaco is not at all certain; Osma has no clear Inka military architecture). I have reviewed the literature and visited most of the sites indicated by Raffino to be Inka military installations. Many of these sites should be discounted as military until better evidence is available, since few of them have clearly defined Inka military architecture. Similarly, Raffino includes three fortresses south of Cerro Chena in Chile whose Inka affiliation is still doubtful.

8. Pío Pablo Díaz and I made a return visit to Cortaderas in 1986. It revealed it to be somewhat larger than depicted on the published map (Hyslop 1984: 176). Several dozen rectangular foundations in rows, generally interpreted as storage units, are located south of the central part of the site.

9. The site is identified by Cobo and in a document from 1559 (Rowe 1985: 216, 226) as a fort. See a published photograph in Ibarra and Querejazu (1986: 330), who call Oroncota a temple (1986: 337), but comment perhaps more accurately that it is the biggest and most important Inka site in Potosí. The only adequate published source on Oroncota is by Walter (1959), who describes only the main building. A photograph of a double-jamb doorway in the site has been published by Paddock (1984: 63), who apparently did not realize he was in Oroncota and describes the complex as "a mesa-top fort." Indeed, the fort rests on an extremely high mesa. Some stonework approximates fine Cuzco masonry (Walter 1959: figs. 1, 4). In 1986 I had the good fortune to speak with Dr. F. Ortiz Sanz, former Bolivian ambassador to the United Nations, whose family once owned Oroncota. His recollections of the fort confirm observations published by Walter about its difficult access and spectacular view of the Pilcomayo Valley.

10. Trimborn (1967: 163–169) discusses the military aspects of Samaipata, noting that not all authorities agree on its military role.

11. Bingham appears to have been in error with many of his ideas about Machu Picchu, so scholars are loath to accept him on interpretive matters. His strong insistence on Machu Picchu's military nature should be balanced by the thoughtful refutation by MacLean, cited earlier in this chapter.

Readers may be perplexed at the number of Inka settlements named Inkawasi (Incahuasi, Inkahuasi). The name means "house of the Inka" in Quechua and is a general toponym applied to sites and regions in early colonial times after the original names were lost, but when local people recalled that Inkas had been there. There are hundreds of places now called Inkawasi, Incahuasi, or Inkahuasi throughout the domain of Tawantinsuyu.

12. Pardo (1957: 417–454) reports two fortresses, Molloccahua, about 100 kilometers south of Cuzco, and Huaccrapucara, about 60 kilometers south of Cuzco. The descriptions are not sufficiently detailed to determine if these are truly military sites.

13. Once thought generally to be pre-Inka, recent investigations now suggest that they are Inka (Antonio Fresco, personal communication, 1986), a point later partially noted by Plaza Schuller (ca. 1980: 40, 47).

14. See chapter 9, note 14.

15. It is possible that two additional units resting 3 to 5 kilometers to the northeast of the complex were part of it. These installations are not included in the discussion, since their distance from the main complex suggests that they may not have been part of it. They are lower, affected by farming, and in very poor condition. If indeed they form part of the complex, one might note that they are as large as Unit 5, Quitaloma.

16. Oberem surveyed and mapped two of the lowest units, Achupallas and Quitaloma, and made small excavations at Quitaloma. Plaza Schuller surveyed the remaining units but did not excavate. He was the first to note that the units make up a unified military system and tentatively suggested that it was built under Inka orders.

17. The latter appears to be the case when one observes that the broader, deeper ditches are found in front of some of the larger walls. On the other hand, the exterior ditch surrounding this highest fortification is often quite distant from the lowest walls. It is nearly 1.5 kilometers in length. Perhaps the ditches served as both a dry moat and a source of earth.

18. A thorough review of the popular literature about the site is found in González and Cravotto (1977: 7–8).

19. Nordenskiöld did excavate "some pits" but tells little about his finds other than that there was only a thin, superficial cultural layer (1915: 174–176, 181). Some of the pottery he found is clearly Inka. He looked for but found no graves, speculating that they might be found in caves in a nearby precipitous mountain slope.

20. Nordenskiöld (1942) believed that zigzag walls were an Inka invention that may have influenced the military architecture of Europe. He notes that building walls *en tenaille*, i.e., so that a storming party could always be fired at from two sides, was unknown in Europe until after the invention of gunpowder. Europeans fighting in the Andes may have carried the idea back to the Old World.

21. Nevados de Aconquija may also be a border fortification, but is not discussed here, given the absence there of surrounding walls and its extraordinarily high location. If Nevados de Aconquija performed a military role, hints of this are its several *kallanka* and its location on an Inka boundary. It is distinguished by much architecture relating to Inka ceremonial concerns.

22. The fortified pre-Inka settlement Llaquepa near Desaguadero, Puno, Peru, has three concentric walls with numerous doorways. I observed two such doorways with a large pile of stones perched precariously above each (Hyslop 1976: 300). Apparently, the stones could have been released to close the doors. No similar closing mechanism has yet been reported from any Inka fortress.

23. Rectangular buildings in prehistoric sites (not only fortresses) in Ecuador, eastern Bolivia, Chile, and Argentina are generally considered an indicator of Inka building. Pre-Inka local cultures rarely used a rigidly rectangular form (the Atacama area may be an exception) in these areas of Tawantinsuyu.

7. *Orthogonal and Radial Patterns*

1. Gasparini and Margolies (1980: 68, 70) interpret this slight broadening of the longitudinal streets as an attempt to create a trapezoidal shape. The broadening is, however, very slight and allows for the sector to occupy fully the generally sloping terrain between the mountain slope on the east and a river on the west. Some examples of radial planning might be considered trapezoidal if one did not consider their true complexity.

2. Luis G. Lumbreras has suggested (personal communication, 1988) that the orthogonal sector of Ollantaytambo might be conceived as one single unit or "building," although no wall surrounds it. In this case the streets should be considered passageways within a unit that might have been dedicated to a specific activity. The common loom attachments on walls in the sector suggest that it was inhabited by *aqlla*, chosen women.

3. Others may argue that the settlement is an early Spanish *reducción*, a possibility that cannot be ruled out until there is a better understanding of the planning used in such settlements. *Reducciones* were towns of Indians created by the early Spanish colonial administration to facilitate the collection of tribute and the propagation of Catholicism (Gade and Escobar 1982).

4. Another possible Inka orthogonal plan is found at the site Malanche 3 in the dry Malanche streambed about 25 kilometers west of the site Pachacamac. The orthogon of Malanche 3 is composed of three streets crosscut by at least three others (Elías Mujica, personal communication, 1987). It is placed on sloping terrain, with the plaza at the lower side of the slope. Inka pottery is found at the site, but its occupation continued into Spanish times, a point demonstrated by the remains of a church constructed north of the plaza. Perhaps the construction of Malanche 3 was never completed, since there are considerable open spaces within the units formed by the streets. As at Nieve Nieve, the possibility exists that the settlement is an early Spanish *reducción*.

5. At the Malanche site there is a very small adobe platform in the plaza. If it represents an *ushnu*, it is probably the smallest in Tawantinsuyu. At the Nieve site one finds an oval platform about 1.5 meters in height on the edge of the

plaza. Since there are no proven oval *ushnu* platforms elsewhere in Tawantinsuyu, it is probably not an *ushnu* platform.

6. Written in 1980 and submitted for publication in 1981, this important contribution to Inka architectural planning remains unavailable because of publication delays. The author has graciously permitted me to cite segments of "Architecture and the Structure of Space at Huánuco Pampa" here.

7. This task is being completed by Ramiro Matos and students from San Marcos University. Matos has kindly supplied me with copies of the detailed mapping of the buildings around the plaza. These have been used to define the units (described here) into which the plaza's buildings are arranged. They are a far better tool for this analysis than the best aerial photographs. A map of Pumpu based on an aerial photograph is found in LeVine (1985).

8. It has been suggested that the large three-unit complex in the southwestern part of the site should be interpreted as the buildings that are "structurally" those west of the plaza. If so, there is no clear indication of why this complex was not built directly on the western side of the plaza. There is relatively secure evidence that Pumpu was never completed. Good proof are rows of small mounds for *qollqa* where the silos were never constructed. At Huánuco Pampa, the western side of the plaza may have been the last constructed (Morris, personal communication, 1988). If Pumpu was built in a similar sequence, a western side may have been planned but not completed.

9. That plaza does not mark the geometric center of the point where the radial streets might meet, but is slightly to the south. This appears to adjust to topography, since the streets thus avoid a steep embankment.

10. Bauer will publish the first accurate plan of the site. See description and partial plan by Kendall (1985: 377–382, 403).

11. Descriptions and photographs of Puma Orco (Tambo Toco) are found in Pardo (1957) and Muelle (1945) and in Hemming and Ranney (1982: 60–63, 173, 175). This massive stone protrusion is one of the largest carved outcrops in the Cuzco area. It includes three stone caves, shelves, steps, channels for liquids, and carved felines.

12. There are some other examples of Inka radial planning at all or parts of settlements, which have not been thoroughly studied. The sector called Pisaqa at Pisaq has more than twenty rectangular structures arranged in an arc (Angles Vargas 1970: 53–58, 1978: 180–181). The "center" of this radial sector appears to be stone outcrops, not indicated on any published map, or two large adobe structures on the slope to the west. One could argue that the site of Shincal in Catamarca Province, Argentina (fig. 3.23), has elements of radiality somewhat similar to Chilecito, but not as pronounced. At Shincal one finds a large *ushnu* platform near the center of a large, square plaza. The surrounding buildings are aligned with the plaza's sides, or placed somewhat obliquely so as to face the plaza. The buildings and compounds, while not necessarily pointing to the *ushnu*, are arranged about and face the plaza.

13. The notational system devised by Zuidema will be used here. The Roman numerals indicate the *suyu*. Arabic numbers indicate the individual *zeque* lines. Small letters indicate if the line is Collana (a), Payan (b), or Cayao (c). See fig. 2.15.

14. Wachtel's useful summary (1973) of Zuidema's work classifies Zuidema's Second Representation as the "first" structure because it is the most comprehensive and fundamental.

15. The quadripartition of Huánuco Pampa was first advanced in a paper presented by Morris in 1976 (1980b).

16. The crossed ✳ is a highly formalized way of observing the way the dual division may crosscut two of the four parts. Presented here as a tool to instruct the reader, there is no direct evidence that Inkas used a crossed ✳ as a visual pattern.

17. See Hyslop (1985: 55) for a more thorough discussion of the groupings of units and their correspondence to the groupings of lines in the *zeque* system's Kuntisuyu.

18. The number of *waqa* for each line of Kuntisuyu is as follows:

Line	No. of *Waqa*
1	15
2	4
3	4
4	5
5	5
6	5
7	5
8	15
9	3
10	4
11	4
12	3
13	4
14	4

Twelve of Kuntisuyu's lines have between three and five *waqa*, similar to the number of rooms in each unit. However, two lines (one and eight) have fifteen *waqa*. Thus in two units the number of rooms could not correspond to the number of *waqa*.

Exact room counts are difficult to make in several of the radial units at Inkawasi because of rock and mud slides. Apparently no unit had more than five rooms.

19. Morris (1980a) is the only one who has tentatively attempted to compare archaeologically detectable activity patterns against what might be expected at locations where the *zeque* system provides some hint as to possible activity.

8. Orientation and Alignment: Astronomical Concerns

1. Ibarra Grasso has attempted to summarize the data on Inka astronomy (1982), drawing evidence from his own sources, Zuidema, Urton, and Wachtel. The presentation is a confused, questionable contribution. Mention is made of this book because of its wide distribution in South American bookstores.

2. Dearborn and Schreiber (1986: 19–36) feel that additional evidence is necessary to prove just how some of these observations were made. The complex and unique data indicating that the Inkas reversed a zenith observation to establish a day important in the agricultural calendar will not be evaluated here due to ongoing work revising the astronomical argument (Aveni *n.d.*).

3. The text from Garcilaso de la Vega (1987: 117, Bk. 2, chap. XXII) follows: "To ascertain the time of the equinoxes they had splendidly carved stone columns erected in the squares or courtyards before the temples of the Sun. When the priests felt that the equinox was approaching, they took careful daily observations of the shadows cast by the columns. The columns stood in the middle of great rings filling the whole extent of the squares or spaces. Across the middle of a ring a line was drawn from east to west by a cord, the two ends being established by long experience. They could follow the approach of the equinox by the shadow the column cast on this line, and when the shadow fell exactly along the line from sunrise and at midday the sun bathed all sides of the column and cast no shadow at all, they knew that the day was the equinox."

Aveni (*n.d.*) notes that many of Garcilaso's descriptions of Inka sundials, shadow casting, and so forth come more from his Renaissance mentality than from any detailed knowledge of Inka astronomy.

4. Dearborn and Schreiber (1986: 18–19) find the Qori Kancha's alignment "quite precise" if aligned with the sun around May 25. A greater discrepancy (1.4 degrees) is found with the Pleiades alignment. They note that the difference with the Pleiades rise azimuth might not be significant if the compound was not used as a true observing instrument, but was "merely oriented to a star group."

5. Dearborn and Schreiber (1986: 33) find that alignment has an uncertainty "too large to unambiguously associate it with an anti-zenith passage observation." They note Zuidema's supporting structural evidence (1981*a*), which is "difficult to evaluate quantitatively but must be considered." That type of logic, not easily handled by physical science, is central to the investigation of Inka astronomy and the calendar. Without its unique insights, it is doubtful that Zuidema and Aveni would have developed the leads that allowed them to lay the basis for Inka astronomy. Aveni (*n.d.*) has responded to Dearborn and Schreiber's comments, noting technical flaws in their analysis and methodological problems with their positivist approach.

Dearborn's rigorous search for the exact physical evidence leads him to question some alignments for which the physical evidence is only partial, or where an alignment is not a nearly exact correspondence with a horizon azimuth. His approach is a useful examination of published research, but his rejection of some alignments may find him discarding valuable leads. This is particularly the case with buildings or compounds that may have been oriented or aligned for symbolic reasons, but that were not observing instruments. In such cases the Inkas may have been willing to accept alignment variations beyond those acceptable to Dearborn.

6. The exact measurements for Hatun Rumiyoc from two different points on the wall are 62 degrees, 11 minutes and 61 degrees, 57 minutes. Cabracancha

Maruri measured 61 degrees, 24 minutes. I thank Anthony Aveni (personal correspondence, June 10 and 22, 1983) for supplying these data.

7. They did find a natural rock prominence (with a hole in it) on a ridge, which could not be demonstrated to have an astronomical use.

8. At Fuerte Quemado in Catamarca, Argentina, towers were once placed on the nearby hill of Ventanita (also called Intiwatana). A nineteenth-century painting by Maetfessel portrays these structures, but no evidence for them remains today (Kriscautzky 1986). Ziolkowski and Sadowski (1984: 111–112) report a mound on Cerro Cubilán to the east of Ingapirca, Cañar, Ecuador. It is aligned with the eastern axis of the eastern room on top of the oval structure and may have been used to determine the day of zenith passage. They report that excavations will be necessary to determine if it is a natural or artificial formation.

9. The orientations of these faces are probably accurate to within a degree or two. No broad face is perfectly flat or completely vertical, each slightly sloping from its base into the slope of the cliff (north). The magnetic deviation was determined by solar observations used to establish the orientations of other walls within the fort. That deviation of about 4 degrees, 30 minutes agrees with that indicated by the Bolivian Military Geographic Institute's topographic map "Punata" (Hoja SE 20-5). Measuring the angles of the faces with a transit would require building a scaffold on the cliff.

The orientations of the broad faces and their respective western horizon elevations are *face 2*—285 degrees, 30 minutes (elevation 8 degrees); *face 4*—265 degrees, 30 minutes (elevation 14 degrees); *face 6*—247 degrees, 30 minutes (elevation 16 degrees); *face 8*—230 degrees, 30 minutes (elevation 14 degrees); *face 10*—212 degrees, 30 minutes (elevation 15 degrees). At Incallacta, the June solstice sunrise azimuth with an 8-degree horizon is at 297 degrees, 41 minutes (A). The zenith sunset azimuth with a 14-degree horizon is at 256 degrees, 36 minutes (B). The December solstice sunset azimuth with a 14-degree horizon is at 249 degrees, 42 minutes (C).

10. The lintel rests on a shelf carved in each crag. The shelf is sufficiently long (indicated by the dashed lines in fig. 8.4A) for there to have been several more lintels. If such was the case, several lintels could have formed a platform.

11. My examination of the site on June 4, 1986, found Rivera's diagram properly scaled and accurately oriented. A Brunton's compass was used to check the angles, which were then corrected for magnetic declination.

12. As noted in chapter 1, projections or knobs on stones in fine masonry blocks are thought to have been used for moving or fitting the stones, not for hanging devices from them. The Torreón has similar projections on stones not beside windows.

13. I have responded to several of these points and questioned aspects of Dearborn's methodology (Hyslop *n.d.b*).

14. At many sites I visited in 1986, a solar observation was made to establish true north. In some cases, current magnetic declinations supplied by geographical institutes were used to orient plans. In other cases, declination information on topographic maps was used to make the correction. The latter is the least accurate means and was avoided when possible.

15. It is possible that the Intipampa Plaza on the northwest side of the Sun Temple in Cuzco was a true trapezoid. The Santo Domingo Church has destroyed the foundation that defined one of the long sides.

16. The slightly imperfect rectangular plazas are occasionally described here as "generally rectangular." Their corners may vary from 90 degrees by up to 6 degrees.

17. I did not check the orientation data from Tarma Tambo and Tunsucancha in the field. They rely on the accuracy of the site plans' north arrows (which I corrected for magnetic declination). The plan of Tarma Tambo may be quite inaccurate, as it appears to have been drawn from an aerial photograph and may have a casually placed north arrow.

18. There are no good published plans of the plazas at Pisaq, Limatambo, Tipón, Maucallacta, and Huchuy Cuzco in the Cuzco area. Aerial photographs indicate that Huchuy Cuzco's plaza may be east-west and rectangular. The same may be the case at Maucallacta.

19. Such may not be the case at Catarpe if one considers the two large adjacent enclosures a form of dual plaza. Lynch (personal communication, 1988) reports a "well built doorway" in the wall shared by the two "plazas."

20. To this group one might add two possible plazas at Chucuito. The exact placement of these plazas is uncertain because of remodeling.

21. Divergent north arrows in the published architectural plans of Chinchero (Alcina 1976) indicate that its plaza may have had an orientation of about 91 degrees. Most of the plans suggest an orientation of about 76 degrees.

22. For the record, possible measurements of three sides of Tomebamba's plaza are (1) *south side*—82 degrees, 30 minutes. This was determined by my Brunton's compass measurement of the re-excavated Mullucancha's north side. This measurement was used to orient Uhle's plan of the Palacio de Huaina Capac. From that map the fence on the north of the *cuarteles*, the apparent south side of the plaza, was measured; (2) *west side*—346 degrees. This sector has been re-excavated. The measurement is by Brunton's compass; (3) *north side*—68 degrees. A measurement taken from the magnetic north arrow on Uhle's plan of the Templo del Díos Viracocha. No part of the north side of the plaza is visible today. The compass measurements were corrected for a magnetic declination of 3 degrees. The north side misses a June solstice alignment within 2 degrees (3-degree horizon). It misses the Pleiades rise azimuth in the sixteenth century by less than a degree. Several factors could alter this possible alignment: the accuracy of Uhle's plan (much of which cannot be checked by an examination of the re-excavated foundations); the accuracy of Uhle's north arrow; and the lack of additional buildings to define the plaza sides more completely.

23. At Pumpu's latitude it is at 101 degrees, 6 minutes (horizon elevation of 2 degrees). The *ushnu* platform is truly aligned with the main gate on the eastern side of the site at 98 degrees, 56 minutes.

9. Mixed Inka-Local Settlements

1. A third long rectangular building in the site is the ruin of a colonial-period church.

2. In another publication González (1982: 327) writes that the Casa Morada is most probably the residence of the local lord and less likely that of an Inka leader.

3. The Upper Mantaro Archaeological Research Project studying the Wanka settlements has differentiated the elite from commoner patio groups on the basis of building and patio size. The patio groups with several buildings, frequently more centrally located, often have the larger buildings and are considered elite. The preliminary report of excavations (Earle et al. 1987) in both commoner and elite groups confirms the validity of this distinction. The term "Wanka" is used here inclusively for the Xauxa and Wanka peoples.

4. A more thoroughly researched high plateau village occupied in Inka times is Cchaucha del Kjula Marca, south of Lake Titicaca. It is composed mainly of round houses (Rydén's no. 2) with one large rectangular one (Rydén 1947: 256–264, table 2). Inka pottery predominated in the large rectangular house, which was also occupied into Spanish times. Its excavator, Rydén (1947: 320–325) believed that it was a settlement of Inka *mitmaq.* In light of the evidence from sites studied in this section, one might consider it a local settlement where the largest house was that of an important Aymara person who adopted the rectangular house shape.

5. Not all important members of high plateau society used rectangular houses, since there is ample evidence from early historical sources and archaeological research (Rydén 1947: 184–225, 300–302) that some important Aymara lived in large circular houses both during Inka times and early in the Spanish period.

6. Conrad's important research (1977: 15) does not address the question of who might have been buried in the mortuary platform at Chiquitoy Viejo, although such a question is related to determining what type of administration took place there. His evidence for a succession of two "officials" can be used to advance the idea that it was the seat of local hereditary rulers in Inka times. If such was the case, Chiquitoy Viejo might better have been included in the discussion of the previous section, which deals with the residences of local lords and elites in Inka times. It would vary from those examples in that the important occupants of Chiquitoy Viejo did not care or wish to imitate Inka architectural forms. Netherly and Dillehay (1986: 89) suggest that Chiquitoy Viejo is the seat of one of two local lords. Their indirect evidence comes from an analysis of historical documents and the hydrological system.

7. Many of the "local" house units in Turi are generally rectangular. This does not indicate Inka influence, since that form was used in the area prior to the rise of Tawantinsuyu. The Atacama-area rectangular houses are one of few examples in southern Tawantinsuyu where a local people did not use circular houses. In general, rectangular buildings in much of the southern Inka state indicate Inka influence. The architecture of Turi is particularly complex when compared with other "cities" of the Atacama region. Ongoing investigations directed by Carlos Aldunate will clarify much about the different activities and organization of the site. Mostny (1949: 166) has defined four wall types, the most common being rough stones laid without mortar. The site also has nu-

merous rectangular storage units and circular aboveground burial structures (*chulpas*).

8. Rex González (personal communication, 1986) has also noted the same for the monumental site of Quilmes (Ambrosetti 1897), a few kilometers to the north of Fuerte Quemado. Quilmes has typical Santa María architecture, but one rectangular structure to the side of the site might prove to be the house of the local chief in Inka times. Otherwise, no Inka architecture has been identified in Quilmes. Research at Tolombón is very limited (Aparicio 1948). It appears to have no Inka architecture.

9. The question of Inka administrative districts in the northwest of Argentina is closely related to determining which Inka settlements are administrative centers, which are the towns of local chiefs, which are *tampu,* and which are sites with specialized activities (metalworking, fortifications, and so forth). González (1982, 1983*b*) has written the most thorough examination of Inka "provinces." These two lengthy and detailed articles contain a wealth of helpful observations, including some debatable conclusions. They are fundamental for scholars wishing to understand the political structure of the Inka state in the Argentine northwest. One article (1982) was published in Lima with one missing manuscript page. That page would have been placed before the last paragraph on page 333.

10. Uhle (1903) may have originated the impression that it was small, since he considered only the compounds known as Mamacuna and the Sun Temple to be Inka.

11. Tello's interpretation (1940) of the religious structures at Pachacamac is unique. He felt that the two principal temples were the Sun Temple and the older Pachacamac temple to its southeast. Each had a "twin." Pachacamac's twin was the old pyramidal structure lying between the Sun Temple and Mamacuna, which he called Urpay Wachac. According to myth, Urpay Wachac was the wife of Pachacamac. The twin of the Sun Temple was the compound known as Mamacuna, which Uhle considered the Temple of the Moon. In Inka mythology, the moon was the wife of the sun. Using evidence from Middendorf and from a plan made in 1793 by Joseph Juan, he notes that Uhle erroneously classified the Painted Building as the Temple of Pachacamac. Tello considered the Painted Building the true *aqllawasi* of the Sun Temple.

12. Gasparini and Margolies (1980: 289, 296–299) note that this platform is oval, not elliptical, and could have been designed by a pattern formed by three circles lined up along the same axis. Ziolkowski and Sadowski (1984: 104–105) point out that three aligned circles cannot be used to form an accurate plan of the building. Gasparini and Margolies used an older simplified and somewhat idealized plan.

13. Fine Cuzco masonry even appears used in limited fashion in a number of sites on the south coast. It has been found at Huaycan and Pachacamac in the Lurin Valley, Cerro Azul in the Cañete Valley, and Paredones in the Nasca area. Historical reports indicate that it was used extensively at Cerro Azul, but little remains today (Bueno 1982).

14. See Rowe (1942) for data on late Colla fortified hilltops near Pucará and a

site, Sicllani, with a ten-room *kancha.* Rowe suggests that Sicllani may have been an Inka garrison or barracks built after the Colla revolt.

15. Chucuito by Lake Titicaca may be an important exception. There is good evidence that the Lupaqa lords were forced out of their fortified community, Cutimbo, and resettled in Chucuito, which was laid out in Inka times. The Lupaqa lords Cari and Cusi were living in Chucuito in 1567 when interviewed by the Spanish inspector Diez de San Miguel (1964).

10. Environmental Influences

1. Some Inka religious sites, principally in regions south of Cuzco, are found at very high altitudes indeed. These remarkable high-altitude sanctuaries are the subject of a growing literature. Schobinger et al. (1966), Beorchia (1987), and Reinhard (1983) provide an introduction to the topic. These sites are dealt with only briefly in this volume (chap. 11), since they were not populated settlements, but rather sanctuaries visited from time to time where offerings were made and rituals performed.

2. This is quite different from many of the Inka military installations, which are often placed on, or incorporate within their plan, a hilltop or other easily defended position. Inka military sites are discussed in chapter 6.

3. Good examples of the Inka roads' evasion of major environmental obstacles was their skirting of some deserts (Sechura, Atacama). A more direct coastal route would have placed the road along the Pacific coast, but the lack of water and population centers required that the road swerve inland.

4. One of the more elegant general descriptions of Inka roads is by Cobo (1964: 126–131, Bk. 12, chaps. 31, 32). More recent research on the road system (Hyslop 1984) indicates that many of Cobo's generalizations are valid for the roads he traveled, mainly the principal north-south highland and coastal routes in present-day Peru. There is much greater variation in the nature and types of Inka roads than Cobo reports. Several of the other early descriptions of Inka roads have the same characteristic. Their authors consider their personal experience or observations to be valid for all Tawantinsuyu. The tendency to generalize about the Inka state on the basis of limited data, often from one region or zone, has masked much regional variability, making a complicated situation seem much simpler than it was.

5. My survey of roads throughout Tawantinsuyu (Hyslop 1984: 294–303) found a generally regular placement of *tampu* on Inka roads. Many factors, however, intervened to cause variations within the limits of the daily walk that supposedly separated them. Thus the Inka state did not use a rigidly defined distance to determine the spacing even between *tampu.*

6. Fine agricultural terraces are also found at sites not known to have royal affiliations. Examples are those at Choquequirau of Challachaca, with special circular systems (Niles 1982: 165) greater in diameter at the bottom than at the top, and Moray (Donkin 1979: 117, 118), where the inverse is found, namely, circular systems forming depressions. Earls and Silverblatt (1981) explore the cosmological meaning of Moray. The terraces at Zurite bordering on the Anta Plain west of Cuzco belonged to Tumipampa *panaqa* (Wayna Qhapaq) (Rostworowski 1988: 266).

7. Rostworowski (1988: 238–251) discusses the possession of land in Tawantinsuyu, defining several categories of land that served the interest of the state or the king personally. She views as excessively simple the idea conveyed by some chronicles that all land in Tawantinsuyu was divided into three categories—those of the Inka, the Sun (state religion), and the *ayllu* or people.

8. Another line of thinking also sees terraces as visually symbolic. Nickel (1982) has proposed that the stepped terrace patterns of horizontal and vertical lines are closely related to Andean dialectical thinking, expressed in stepped patterns in many other media (stone, pottery, textiles, and so forth). She believes that the opposition of horizontal, vertical, and diagonals has its counterparts in cosmology, language, and iconography. The oppositions so common in Andean thinking are thus imprinted on the landscape by terraces, which also provide practical and symbolic agricultural benefits.

9. Niles (1982: 169–171) presents data indicating that high-prestige terraces are often watered by special sources, including reservoirs.

10. Another example of fine Inka terracing is at Pomacocha near Vilcas Waman (Luis G. Lumbreras, personal communication, 1988). The area has been controlled by Peru's revolutionary movement, the Shining Path, for the last several years, so there are few prospects that this Inka settlement will be investigated in the near future.

11. Two reports (Cobo 1964: 189–194, Bk. 13, chap. 17; Ramos Gavilán 1976: 23, chap. 5) contain a unique description of a failed Inka attempt to plant coca, a tropical plant, in excavated depressions near the beach on the Island of the Sun. It was thought that the trenches would protect the plant and keep it warm. The experiment was unsuccessful not only because of the climate, but because the trench walls collapsed, burying the coca and many of the people who were in charge of it. One generally assumes that maize was the principal plant cultivated on Inka elaborate terraces. Maize is still cultivated by local populations in protected areas near Lake Titicaca's shore.

12. Some Inka settlements are found in regions outside or on the edge of the southern limit of all forms of traditional terracing as defined by Field (1966: 480). The Pucará de Andalgalá in Catamarca, Argentina, is an example. Although it has a terracelike retention wall sustaining its plaza, its buildings are constructed on slopes that are not terraced, an unusual characteristic in Inka state settlements (figs. 6.27, 6.28).

13. The garrison Inkawasi in the Cañete Valley of Peru has extensive terracing on the riverbanks by the site. The terraces appear to have been constructed in Inka times and are uncharacteristic of "coastal" terraces found in the lower reaches of that and nearby valleys. Because of their fieldstone construction, they do not qualify as "high-prestige" terraces, nor are they integrated into the settlement plan.

11. Final Considerations

1. Estimates of the population of Peru in 1520 by Cook (1981: 111) range from 4 to 14 million just for Peru. Cook uses several approaches, which yield different results. His tentative estimate for Peru in 1520 is 9 million. Much of Tawantinsuyu is excluded from this calculation. His estimates do not include

the densely populated Ecuadorian highlands and valleys of the Argentine northwest. They also exclude the less densely occupied regions of Chile and southern Bolivia.

2. Examples of such enclaves are the compounds found at Tambo Colorado (north of the plaza), Chilecito, Pumpu, Inkawasi, and Pucará de Andalgalá (east of their respective plazas).

3. The royal estate Caquia Xaquixaguana has become known as Huchuy Cuzco, or New Cuzco. There is no evidence that it was considered a "new" or "other" Cuzco in Inka times, however.

4. Zuidema (1982c) makes a detailed argument for the straightness of pilgrimage routes in Inka times. These include the *zeques* surrounding Cuzco. Zuidema notes that the imperial pilgrimages of the *capac hucha* involved traversing straight directions, avoiding the Inka highway, over great distances (Molina 1943: 75–76). The *capac hucha* involved sending an immaculate child to Cuzco or another ritual center, where he or she would be sacrificed. Sometimes the child was returned, often to his or her place of origin, for sacrifice. Zuidema (1978) also cites Bastien, noting that modern Andean peoples traveling to a shrine do so in as direct a way as possible. The return, however, is done in a nonritual way.

5. These include population resettlement to near and distant areas, the use of Quechua as a lingua franca, the development of new productive areas, the acceptance of local religions along with Inka beliefs, the use of local lords as regional governors, the resolution of boundary and other quarrels between polities, the education of sons of local lords in Cuzco, and the residence (some would say, hostaging) of local gods and lords in Cuzco.

6. The leading proponent of this view is Rostworowski (1988: 15, 16), who believes the word *empire* carries too many Old World connotations. Noting that the Andean world, isolated from other continents, is unique, she prefers the word *Tawantinsuyu* for the Inka state. This critique of her position on the word *empire* is not intended to detract from the importance of her *Historia del Tawantinsuyu* (1988), one of the more important if somewhat controversial books to emerge in the Andean literature in some years.

7. Definitions of empire do not vary much. The *Oxford English Dictionary* (vol. 3, 1969: 128) defines it as "an extensive territory (esp. an aggregate of many separate states) under the sway of an emperor or supreme ruler; also, an aggregate of subject territories ruled over by a sovereign state." The *Encyclopedia Americana* (vol. 10, 1984: 312) defines empire as "a form of political organization in which a central authority exercises sovereignty over a vast and diverse territory and often over a multitude of nationalities."

Glossary

Inka language (Quechua) words used frequently in the text are defined below. Definitions are adapted primarily from Murra (1978: 24–26) and "Glosario-índice del Quechua" (Guaman Poma 1980: 1075–1108). Some words have several, varied meanings; only that used in the context of the book is noted here.

Apacheta: a shrine; a stone pile placed as an offering beside a road at high points.
Aqlla: a woman chosen for state and religious service.
Aqllawasi: the building or compound where *aqlla* lived, wove, and brewed.
Ayllu: subdivision of a social unit, based on genealogy, lineage, or kinship.
Chicha: a fermented beverage, generally of maize; originally a Caribbean word.
Chulpa: a burial; an aboveground burial structure.
Hanan: one half (literally, the upper half) of the Inka dual or moiety social structure; one of two parts of an Inka settlement.
Hurin: one half (literally, the lower half) of the Inka dual or moiety social structure; one of two parts of an Inka settlement.
Kallanka: a long hall, often with a gabled roof.
Kancha: an enclosure; several rooms placed around a patio, generally within a rectangular perimeter wall.
Mamacona (pl.): similar to *aqlla.*
Mita: literally, one's turn; the temporal prestation of labor to one's ethnic group or to the state.
Mitayoq: A corvée laborer; one who supplies *mita* service.
Mitmaq: a settler from some other place; an Inka state colonist.
Pacarina: a sacred place—generally a feature of the landscape—of a group's origin.
Paccha: device for pouring libations.
Panaqa: Inka royal *ayllu,* alleged lineage group of royal Inkas.
Pucará: fortress.
Puna: high regions of the central and south Andes, often grasslands.
Qollqa: storehouse; silo.
Suyu: a share or province; one of four parts of the Inka state.
Tawantinsuyu: the Inka Empire; land of the four (*tawa*) parts or provinces (*suyu*).
Tampu: an Inka state lodging on the road system.
Toricoq: an Inka governor or inspector.

Ushnu: a centrally located ritual complex consisting of a drain with a stone, basin, and platform within Inka settlements.

Waqa: a shrine; a place or object for ritual.

Wasi: a house; a building or buildings.

Zeque: a ceremonial line or path; a radial system of forty-one lines in Cuzco that integrated Inka kinship, cosmology, and calendrics.

Bibliography

Acosta, Joseph de
   1985   *Historia Natural y Moral de las Indias*, [1590] 2d ed. Biblioteca Americana, Fondo de Cultura Económica, Mexico City.
Acta
   1948   "El Acta Perdida de la Fundación del Cuzco," [1534] (notes by Raúl Porras Barrenechea). *Revista Histórica*, Vol. 17, pp. 74–95, Lima.
"Actas de los libros de Cabildos del Cuzco—Año 1549."
   1959   Año 10, No. 10, Universidad Nacional del Cuzco.
Agurto Calvo, Santiago
   1980   *Cuzco—Traza urbana de la ciudad Inca*. Proyecto Per 39, UNESCO, Instituto Nacional de Cultura del Perú. Cuzco: Imprenta Offset Color S.R.L.
   1987   *Estudios acerca de la construcción, arquitectura, y planeamiento incas*. Lima: Cámara Peruana de la Construcción.
Ahlfeld, Friedrich
   1933   "Die Inkaische Festung Cuticutuni in der bolivianischen Ostkordillere." *Zeitschrift für Ethnologie*, Vol. 64, pp. 260–262, Berlin.
Alberti Manzanares, Pilar
   1985   "La influencia económica y política de las acllacuna en el incanato." *Revista de Indias*, Vol. 45, No. 176, pp. 557–585, Madrid.
Albornoz, Cristóbal de
   1967   "La instrucción para descubrir todas las guacas del Pirú y sus camayos y haziendas," [end of sixteenth century], ed. Pierre Duviols. *Journal de la Société des Américanistes*, Vol. 55, No. 1, Paris.
Alcaya, Diego Felipe de
   1961   Relación Cierta que el padre Diego Felipe de Alcaya, cura de Mataca, envió a su Excelencia el Señor Marqués de Montes Claros, Visorrey de estos reynos, sacada de la que el Capitán Martín Sánchez de Alcayaga, su padre, dejó hecha, como primer descubridor y conquistador de la Gobernación de Santa Cruz de la Sierra, [ca. 1610] *Cronistas Cruceños del Alto Perú Virreinal*, ed. Hernando Sanabria Fernández, pp. 37–86, Publicaciones de la Universidad Gabriel René Moreno, Santa Cruz de la Sierra, Bolivia.

Alcina Franch, José
  1976 *Arqueología de Chinchero.* 2 vols.: 1. *La Arquitectura,* 2. *Cerámica y Otros Materiales.* Misión Científica Española en Hispanoamérica, Junta para la Protección de Monumentos y Bienes Culturales en el Exterior, Dirección General de Relaciones Culturales, Ministerio de Asuntos Exteriores, Madrid.
  1978 "Ingapirca: arquitectura y áreas de asentamiento." *Revista Española de Antropología Americana,* pp. 127–146. Facultad de Geografía e Historia, Universidad Complutense, Madrid.
Almeida Reyes, Eduardo
  1984 Investigaciones arqueológicas en el Pucará de Rumicucho, El Pucará de Rumicucho. *Miscelánea Antropológica Ecuatoriana,* Serie Monográfica 1, pp. 9–27, Museo del Banco Central del Ecuador, Quito.
Ambrosetti, Juan B.
  1897 "La antigua ciudad de Quilmes." *Boletín del Instituto Geográfico Argentino,* Vol. 18, pp. 33–70, Buenos Aires.
  1902 "El sepulcro de La Paya últimamente descubierto en los valles Calchaquies, Provincia de Salta." *Anales del Museo Nacional,* Vol. 8, pp. 119–148, Buenos Aires.
  1907–1908 Exploraciones arqueológicas en la ciudad prehistórica de "La Paya" (Valle Calchaquí, Provincia de Salta). *Revista de la Universidad de Buenos Aires,* 8 (Sección Antropología, 3), 2 vols. Facultad de Filosofía y Letras. Buenos Aires: M. Biedma é hijo.
Angles Vargas, Victor
  1970 *P'isaq—Metrópoli Inka.* Lima: Industrial Gráfica.
  1978 *Historia del Cuzco,* I. Lima: Industrial Gráfica.
Anonymous Jesuit
  1879 De las costumbres antiguas de los naturales del Pirú. *Tres Relaciones de Antigüedades Peruanas,* [1594] pp. 137–227. Ministerio de Fomento. Madrid: Imprenta y Fundición de M. Tello.
Aparicio, Francisco de
  1940 "Ranchillos—Tambo del Inca en el Camino a Chile." *Anales del Instituto de Etnografía Americana,* Vol. 1, pp. 245–253, Universidad Nacional de Cuyo, Mendoza.
  1948 "Las Ruinas de Tolombón." *Actes du XXVIII Congrès International des Américanistes,* pp. 569–580, Paris.
Ardiles N., Percy E.
  1986 "Sistema de drenaje subterráneo prehispánico." *Allpanchis,* Año 18, No. 27, pp. 75–97, Instituto de Pastoral Andina, Cuzco.
Arriaga, Jesús
  1922 *Apuntes de Arqueología Cañar.* Cuenca: Imprenta del Clero.
Arriaga, José de
  1968 Extirpación de la idolatría del Pirú. *Biblioteca de Autores Españoles,* [1621] Vol. 209, pp. 191–277. Madrid: Atlas.

Aveni, Anthony F.
1981a "Horizon Astronomy in Incaic Cuzco." *Archaeoastronomy in the Americas,* ed. Ray Williamson, pp. 305–318. Santa Barbara: Ballena Press.
1981b "Comment." *Latin American Research Review,* Vol. 13, No. 3, pp. 163–166.
n.d. Response to Dearborn and Schreiber. *Archaeoastronomy,* in press.

Azevedo, Paulo de
1982 *Cusco—ciudad histórica: continuidad y cambio.* Proyecto Regional de Patrimonio Cultural PNUD/UNESCO. Lima: Ediciones PEISA.

Ballesteros Gaibrois, Manuel
1981 "Racchi (Perú), un enigma arqueológico." *Investigación y Ciencia* (Spanish edition of *Scientific American*), No. 54, pp. 7–16.

Bandelier, Adolph F.
1910 *The Islands of Titicaca and Coati.* Hispanic Society of America, New York (reprint by Kraus, 1969).

Barreda Murillo, Luis
1982 "Asentamiento humano de los Qotakalli de Cuzco." *Arqueología de Cuzco,* ed. Italo Oberti Rodríguez, pp. 13–22. Cuzco: Ediciones Instituto Nacional de Cultura.

Bennett, Wendell C.
1934 Excavations at Tiahuanaco. *Anthropological Papers of the American Museum of Natural History.* Vol. 34, Pt. 3, New York.
1936 Excavations in Bolivia. *Anthropological Papers of the American Museum of Natural History,* Vol. 35, Pt. 4, New York.

Beorchia Nigris, Antonio
1987 *El enigma de los santuarios indígenas de alta montaña.* Centro de Investigaciones Arqueológicas de Alta Montaña, San Juan (*Revista del C.I.A.D.A.M.,* Año 1985, Vol. 5, San Juan, Argentina).

Berberian, Eduardo E.; Juana Martín de Zurita; and J. D. Gambetta
1977–1978 "Investigaciones arqueológicas en el yacimiento incaico de Tocota (Prov. de San Juan, Rep. Argentina)." *Anales de Arqueología y Etnología,* Vols. 32–33, pp. 173–210, Universidad Nacional de Cuyo, Mendoza.

Bertonio, Ludovicio
1956 *Vocabulario de la lengua aymara,* [1612] facsimile edition, La Paz, Bolivia.

Betanzos, Juan de
1968 Suma y Naración de los Incas, [1551] *Biblioteca de Autores Españoles,* Vol. 209, pp. 1–56. Madrid: Atlas.

Bingham, Hiram
1911 "The Ruins of Choqqequirau." Reprinted from *American Anthropologist* (N.S.), Vol. 12, No. 4, pp. 505–525, 1910.

1913   "In the Wonderland of Peru—The Work Accomplished by the Peruvian Expedition of 1912, under the Auspices of Yale University and the National Geographic Society." *National Geographic Magazine,* Vol. 24, No. 4, pp. 387–573, National Geographic Society, Washington, D.C.

1930   *Machu Picchu—A Citadel of the Incas.* New Haven: National Geographic Society and Yale University Press (reprint by Hacker Art Books, 1979).

Boero Rojo, Hugo, and Oswaldo Rivera Sundt

1979   *El Fuerte Preincaico de Samaipata.* La Paz–Cochabamba: Editorial Los Amigos del Libro.

Borah, Woodrow

1972   European Cultural Influence in the Formation of the First Plan for Urban Centers That Has Lasted to Our Time." *Urbanización y proceso social en América* (originally a symposium at the 39th International Congress of Americanists, Lima, 1970), pp. 35–54. Instituto de Estudios Peruanos, Lima.

Bouchard, Jean François

1976a   "L'architecture inca: une signification sociale." *La Recherche,* No. 69, pp. 679–683, Paris.

1976b   "Patrones de agrupamiento arquitectónico del Horizonte Tardío." *Revista del Museo Nacional,* Vol. 42, pp. 97–111, Lima.

1976c   "Charpentes Andines Inca et Modernes: observations et reflexiones." *Bulletin de l'Institut Français d'Etudes Andines,* Vol. 3–4, pp. 105–117.

1983   *Contribution a l'Etude de L'Architecture Inca.* Paris: Fondation de la Maison des Sciences de l'Homme.

Bram, Joseph

1977   *Análisis del Militarismo Incaico,* trans. D. Tauro H., Universidad Nacional Mayor de San Marcos, Lima (Doctoral dissertation, Department of Anthropology, Columbia University, New York, 1941).

Browman, David Ludvig

1970   "Early Peruvian Peasants: The Culture History of a Central Highlands Valley." Doctoral dissertation, Anthropology Department, Harvard University, Cambridge, Mass.

Bruch, Carlos

1911   Exploraciones arqueológicas en las provincias de Tucumán y Catamarca. *Biblioteca Centenaria de la Universidad Nacional de La Plata,* Vol. 5, La Plata.

Bueno Mendoza, Alberto

1981   "Orígenes del Tawantinsuyu: Un Planteamiento." *Boletín de Lima,* No. 11–12, offprint, pp. 1–20.

1982   "El Antiguo Valle de Pachacamac: Espacio, Tiempo y Cultura." *Boletín de Lima,* No. 24, pp. 3–52.

Byrne de Caballero, Geraldine

1978   "Incarracay: Un centro administrativo incaico." *Arte y Arqueología,* Vol. 5–6, pp. 309–316, La Paz.

1979   "Los monumentos incaicos en Cochabamba, tesoros del patrimonio nacional." *Los Tiempos*, Jan. 14, Cochabamba.

n.d.   "Nuevas investigaciones arqueológicas en la provincia de Ayopaya, departamento de Cochabamba." *Los Tiempos*, probably 1975, Cochabamba.

Cabello Valboa, Miguel

1951   *Miscelánea Antártica*, [1586] Instituto de Etnología, Facultad de Letras, Universidad Nacional Mayor de San Marcos, Lima.

Canals Frau, Salvador

1946   "Etnología de los Huarpes—Una síntesis." *Anales del Instituto de Etnografía Americana*, Vol. 8, pp. 9–147, Universidad Nacional de Cuyo, Mendoza.

Cardich, Agusto

1980   "El fenómeno de las fluctuaciones de los límites superiores del cultivo en los Andes: su importancia." *Relaciones de la Sociedad Argentina de Antropología*, N.S., Vol. 14, No. 1, pp. 7–31, Buenos Aires.

Carmichael, Patrick

1984   "Reconocimiento de Lima La Vieja, Valle de Pisco." *Patrimonio Monumental*, Epoca II, Año VII, No. 1, pp. 6–7, Centro de Investigación y Restauración de Bienes Monumentales, Lima.

Carrara, María T.; A. M. Lorandi; S. Renard; and M. Tarragó

1960   "Punta de Balasto." Investigaciones Arqueológicas en el Valle de Santa María, ed. Eduardo M. Cigliano et al. *Publicación del Instituto de Antropología*, No. 4, pp. 13–41, Facultad de Filosofía y Letras, Universidad Nacional del Litoral, Rosario.

Carrión Cachot, Rebeca

1955   "El culto al agua en el antiguo Perú." *Revista del Museo Nacional de Antropología y Arqueología*, Vol. 2, No. 2, pp. 50–140.

Castro, Cristóbal de, and Diego de Ortega Morejón

1974   "Relación y Declaración del Modo que este Valle de Chincha y sus Comarcanos se governavan antes que oviesc Ingas y despues q(ue) los vuo hasta q(ue) los Cristianos entraron en esta Tierra," intro Juan Carlos Crespo, [1558] *Historia y Cultura*, No. 8, pp. 91–104, Lima.

Céspedes Paz, Ricardo

1982   "La Arqueología del Area de Pocona." *Cuadernos de Investigación*, Serie Arqueología, No. 1, pp. 89–99, Instituto de Investigaciones Antropológicas (Museo Arqueológico), Universidad Mayor de San Simon, Cochabamba.

Chávez Ballón, Manuel

1970   "Cuzco, Capital del Imperio." *Wayka*, No. 3, pp. 1–14, Universidad Nacional del Cuzco.

1971   "Cuzco y Machu-Pijchu." *Wayka*, Nos. 4–5, pp. 1–4, Universidad Nacional del Cuzco.

Cieza de León, Pedro de

1962   *La Crónica del Perú* (Part 1), [1553]. Madrid: Espasa Calpe.

1967   *El Señorío de los Incas* (second part of *La Crónica del Perú*), [1553]. Instituto de Estudios Peruanos, Lima.

1976   *The Incas*, [1553] trans. Harriet de Onís, ed. Victor W. von Hagen. Norman: University of Oklahoma Press.

1984   *Descubrimiento y conquista del Perú*. Madrid: Zero-Jamkana.

Cobo, Bernabé

1964   Historia del Nuevo Mundo, [1653] *Biblioteca de Autores Españoles*, Vols. 91–92. Madrid: Atlas.

1983   *History of the Inca Empire*, [1653] trans. Roland Hamilton. Austin: University of Texas Press.

Collapiña, Supno, et al.

1974   *Relación de los Quipucamayos*, [1542]. Lima: Biblioteca Universitaria.

Conklin, William

1986   "Inka Architecture" (review of *Inca Architecture* and *Monuments of the Incas*). *Archaeoastronomy*, Vol. 9, Nos. 1–4, pp. 128–133. Center for Archaeoastronomy, College Park, Md.

Conrad, Geoffrey W.

1977   "Chiquitoy Viejo: An Inca Administrative Center in the Chicama Valley, Peru." *Journal of Field Archaeology*, Vol. 4, pp. 1–18, Boston.

1981   "Cultural Materialism, Split Inheritance, and the Expansion of Ancient Peruvian Empires." *American Antiquity*, Vol. 46, No. 1, pp. 3–26.

Cook, Noble David

1981   *Demographic Collapse, Indian Peru, 1520–1620*. Cambridge: Cambridge University Press.

D'Altroy, Terence Norman

1981   "Empire Growth and Consolidation. The Xauxa Region of Peru under the Incas." Doctoral dissertation, Department of Anthropology, University of California, Los Angeles.

Dearborn, David S. P.

1986   Review of *Inkawasi: The New Cuzco. Archaeoastronomy*, Vol. 9, Nos. 1–4, pp. 114–122, Center for Archaeoastronomy, College Park, Md.

Dearborn, David S. P., and Katharina J. Schreiber

1986   "Here Comes the Sun: The Cuzco–Machu Picchu Connection." *Archaeoastronomy*, Vol. 9, Nos. 1–4, pp. 15–37, Center for Archaeoastronomy, College Park, Md.

Dearborn, David S. P.; Katharina J. Schreiber; and Raymond E. White

1987   "Intimachay, a December Solstice Observatory." *American Antiquity*, Vol. 52, pp. 346–352.

Dearborn, David S. P., and Raymond E. White

1982   "Archaeoastronomy at Machu Picchu." *Ethnoastronomy and Archaeoastronomy in the American Tropics*, ed. Anthony F. Aveni and Gary Urton, pp. 249–259. *Annals of the New York Academy of Sciences*, Vol. 385, New York.

1983   "The 'Torreón' of Machu Picchu as an Observatory." *Archaeoastronomy*, No. 5, pp. S37–S49.

Demarest, Arthur A.

1981   *Viracocha—The Nature and Antiquity of the Andean High God*.

Peabody Museum Monographs, No. 6, Harvard University, Cambridge, Mass.

Diccionario de Autoridades

1963   Edición Facsímil, [1726, 1723, 1737] 3 vols. Madrid: Gredos.

Diez de San Miguel, Garci

1964   "Visita hecha a la provincia de Chucuito por Garci Diez de San Miguel en el Año 1567," [1567]. *Documentos Regionales para la Etnología y Etnohistoria Andina*, Vol. 1, pp. 1–299, Casa de la Cultura, Lima.

Difieri, H.

1948   "Las ruinas de Potrero de Payogasta." *Actes du XXVIII Congrès International des Américanistes*, pp. 599–604, Paris.

Dillehay, Tom D.

1977   "Tawantinsuyu Integration of the Chillon Valley, Peru: A Case of Inca Geo-Political Mastery." *Journal of Field Archaeology*, Vol. 4, pp. 397–405, Boston.

Discurso

1906   "Discurso de la sucesión y gobierno de los Yngas," [ca. 1580]. *Juicio de Límites entre el Perú y Bolivia*, Vol. 8, *Chunchos*, ed. Víctor M. Maurtua, pp. 149–165. Madrid: Imprente de los Hijos de M. G. Hernández.

Domingo de Santo Tomás

1951   *Lexicon o vocabulario de la lengua general del Perú*, [1552] facsimile edition. Instituto de Historia, Universidad Nacional Mayor de San Marcos, Lima.

Donkin, R. A.

1979   *Agricultural Terracing in the Aboriginal New World*. *Viking Fund Publications in Anthropology*, 56, Wenner-Gren Foundation for Anthropological Research, University of Arizona Press, Tucson.

D'Orbigny, Alcide

1835–1847   *Voyage dans l'Amérique méridionale*. Paris.

Duviols, Pierre

1979   "La dinastía de los Incas: ¿Monarquía o diarquía?" *Journal de la Société des Américanistes*, Vol. 66, pp. 67–83, Paris.

Earle, Timothy, and T. N. D'Altroy

1982   "Storage Facilities and State Finance in the Upper Mantaro." *Contexts for Prehistoric Exchange*, ed. Jonathan E. Ericson and T. Earle, pp. 265–290. New York: Academic Press.

Earle, Timothy K.; T. N. D'Altroy; C. Hastorf; C. Scott; C. Costin; G. Russell; and E. Sandefur

1987   *Archaeological Field Research in the Upper Mantaro, Peru, 1982–1983: Investigations of Inka Expansion and Exchange*, Monograph 28, Institute of Archaeology, University of California, Los Angeles.

Earle, Timothy K.; T. N. D'Altroy; C. J. LeBlanc; C. A. Hastorf; T. Y. LeVine

1980   "Changing Settlement Patterns in the Upper Mantaro Valley, Peru." *Journal of New World Archaeology*, Vol. 4, No. 1, Institute of Archaeology, University of California, Los Angeles.

Earls, John, and Irene Silverblatt
   1981   "Sobre la instrumentación de la cosmología inca en el sitio arqueo-
          lógico de Moray." *La tecnología en el mundo andino,* Vol. 1, ed.
          Heather Lechtman and Ana María Soldi, pp. 433–473, Instituto de In-
          vestigaciones Antropológicas, serie antropológica, No. 36, Univer-
          sidad Nacional Autónoma de México, Mexico City.
Ellefsen, Bernardo
   1973*a*   "La división en mitades de la ciudad incaica." *Bulletin de l'Institut
          Français d'Etudes Andines,* Vol. 2, No. 4, pp. 23–28, Lima.
   1973*b*   "El patrón urbano incaico según el Prof. Zuidema y su relación con
          Incallacta." *Bulletin de l'Institut Français d'Etudes Andines,* Vol. 2,
          No. 4, pp. 29–34, Lima.
Estete, Miguel de
   1879   Relación del viaje que hizo el señor capitán Hernando Pizarro por
          mandado del Señor Gobernador, su hermano, desde el pueblo de Ca-
          xamarca á Panama, y, de allí a Juaca, [1533] *Biblioteca de Autores Es-
          pañoles,* Vol. 26, pp. 338–343. Madrid: Librería y Casa Editorial
          Hernando.
   1924   Noticia del Perú [1535]. *Colección de Libros y Documentos Refe-
          rentes a la Historia del Perú,* second series, Vol. 8, pp. 3–56, ed.
          Horacio H. Urteaga and Carlos Romero, notes Carlos M. Larrea.
          Lima: Sanmartí (authorship questioned).
Farrington, Ian S.
   1983   "Prehistoric Intensive Agriculture: Preliminary Notes on River Cana-
          lization in the Sacred Valley of the Incas." *Drained Field Agriculture in
          Central and South America,* ed. J. P. Darch, pp. 221–235. Proceedings
          of the 44th International Congress of Americanists, Manchester, BAR
          International Series 189, Oxford.
   1984   "Medidas de Tierra en el Valle de Yucay, Cusco." *Gaceta Arqueo-
          lógica Andina,* No. 11, pp. 10–11, Instituto Andino de Estudios Ar-
          queológicos, Lima.
Fejos, Paul
   1944   Archaeological Explorations in the Cordillera Vilcabamba. *Viking
          Fund Publications in Anthropology,* No. 3, New York.
Field, Chris
   1966   "A Reconnaissance of Southern Andean Agricultural Terracing."
          Doctoral dissertation, Department of Geography, University of Cali-
          fornia, Los Angeles.
Finley, Moses I.
   1987   *Ancient History, Evidence and Models.* New York: Penguin Books.
Fresco, Antonio
   1979   "Arqueología de la Sierra Sur del Ecuador: Ingapirca." Doctoral dis-
          sertation, Departamento de Antropología y Etnología de Américas,
          Universidad Complutense, Madrid.
   1983   "Arquitectura de Ingapirca (Cañar-Ecuador)." Miscelánea Antropo-
          lógica Ecuatoriana, *Boletín de los Museos del Banco Central del Ecua-
          dor,* Año 3, No. 3, pp. 195–212, Cuenca-Guayaquil-Quito.

1984   "Excavaciones en Ingapirca (Ecuador): 1978–1982." *Revista Española de Antropología Americana*, Vol. 14, pp. 85–101, Universidad Complutense, Madrid.

Fresco, Antonio, and Wania Cobo

1978   "Consideraciones etnohistóricas acerca de una tumba de poso y cámara de Ingapirca (Ecuador)." *Revista española de antropología americana*, pp. 147–161, Facultad de Geografía e Historia, Universidad Complutense de Madrid, Madrid.

Gade, Daniel W., and Mario Escobar

1982   "Village Settlement and the Colonial Legacy in Southern Peru." *Geographical Review*, Vol. 72, No. 4, pp. 430–449.

Garcilaso de la Vega, Inca

1963II   Comentarios Reales de los Incas (Primera Parte), [1604]. *Biblioteca de Autores Españoles*, Vol. 133. Madrid: Atlas.

1963III Comentarios Reales de los Incas (Segunda Parte), [1604]. *Biblioteca de Autores Españoles*, Vol. 134. Madrid: Atlas.

1987   *Royal Commentaries of the Incas and General History of Peru*, [1604] Part 1, trans. Harold V. Livermore. Austin: University of Texas Press.

Gasparini, Graziano, and Luise Margolies

1977   *Arquitectura Inka.* Centro de Investigaciones Históricas y Estéticas, Facultad de Arquitectura y Urbanismo, Universidad Central de Venezuela, Caracas.

1980   *Inca Architecture*, trans. Patricia J. Lyon. Bloomington: Indiana University Press (originally in Spanish, 1977).

Gibaja Oviedo, Arminda

1982   "La ocupación neo Inca del valle del Urubamba." *Arqueología de Cuzco*, ed. Italo Oberti Rodríguez, pp. 81–96. Cuzco: Ediciones Instituto Nacional de Cultura.

1983   "Arqueología de Choquepujyo." *Arqueología Andina*, ed. Arminda Gibaja O., pp. 29–44. Cuzco: Ediciones Instituto Nacional de Cultura.

1984   "Excavaciones en Ollantaytambo, Cusco." *Gaceta Arqueológica Andina*, Año 3, No. 9, pp. 4–5, Instituto Andino de Estudios Arqueológicos, Lima.

González, Alberto Rex

1966   "Las ruinas del Shincal." *Primer Congreso de Historia de Catamarca—Ciencias Auxiliares de la Historia*, Vol. 3, pp. 15–28, Junta de Estudios Históricos, Catamarca.

1981   "La Ciudad de Chicoana—Su importancia histórica y arqueológica." *Síntomas*, No. 3, pp. 15–21, Buenos Aires.

1982   "Las 'provincias' inca del antiguo Tucumán." *Revista del Museo Nacional*, Vol. 46, pp. 317–380, Lima.

1983a   "Inca Settlement Patterns in a Marginal Province of the Empire: Sociocultural Implications." *Prehistoric Settlement Patterns: Essays in Honor of Gordon R. Willey*, ed. Evon Z. Vogt and Richard M. Leventhal, pp. 337–360. Cambridge: Harvard University Press.

1983b "La provincia y la población incaica de Chicoana." *Presencia Hispánica en la Arqueología Argentina*, Vol. 2, ed. Eldo S. Morresi and Ramón Gutiérrez, pp. 633–674. Museo Regional de Antropología "Juan A. Martinet," Facultad de Humanidades, Universidad Nacional del Nordeste, Resistencia, Chaco, Argentina.

González, Alberto Rex, and Antonio Cravotto

1977 *Estudio arqueológico e inventario de las ruinas de Inkallajta*, UNESCO Informe Técnico PP/1975–76/3.411.6, Paris.

González, Alberto Rex, and V. Núñez Regueiro

1958–1959 "Apuntes preliminares sobre la arqueología de Campo de Pucará y alrededores (Dpto. de Andagalá, Pcia. de Catamarca)." *Anales de Arqueología y Etnología*, Vol. 14–15, pp. 115–162, Universidad Nacional de Cuyo, Mendoza, Argentina.

González Carré, Enrique; J. Cosmópolis A.; and J. Lévano P.

1981 *La ciudad inca de Vilcashuamán.* Universidad Nacional de San Cristóbal de Huamanga, Ayacucho.

González Corrales, José A.

1971 "Lítica Inca en la zona del Cuzco." Doctoral dissertation, Universidad de San Antonio Abad del Cuzco.

1984 "Arquitectura y cerámica Killke del Cusco." *Revista del Museo e Instituto de Arqueologia*, No. 25, pp. 37–46, Universidad Nacional de San Antonio Abad, Cuzco.

González Holguín, Diego

1952 *Vocabulario de la Lengua General de Todo el Perú llamada Qquichua o del Inca*, [1608] Edición del Instituto de Historia, Universidad Nacional Mayor de San Marcos, Lima.

Gordon, Robert B.

1985 "Laboratory Evidence of the Use of Metal Tools at Machu Picchu (Peru) and Environs." *Journal of Archaeological Science*, Vol. 12, pp. 311–327.

Greslebin, Héctor

1939 "Revelamiento y descripción de la Tambería del Inca de Chilecito, provincia de La Rioja, República Argentina." Unpublished report to the Comisión Nacional de Cultura, Buenos Aires. Made available by Alberto Rex González.

1940 "Arqueología de la Tambería del Inca (Chilecito, La Rioja, República Argentina), un ensayo de urbanismo prehispánico que auspicia la Sociedad Central de Arquitectos," pp. 3–27, Buenos Aires.

Guaman Poma de Ayala, Felipe

1936 *Nueva corónica y buen gobierno*, [1614] facsimile edition. *Travaux et mémoires de l'Institut d'Ethnologie* 23, ed. Alfred Métraux, Paris.

1980 *El Primer Nueva Corónica y Buen Gobierno*, [1614] ed. John V. Murra and Rolena Adorno, trans. Jorge I. Urioste, 3 vols. Mexico City: Siglo Veintiuno.

Gutiérrez de Santa Clara, Pedro

1963 *Quinquenarios o Historia de las Guerras Civiles del Perú, Biblioteca de Autores Españoles*, [ca. 1555] Vols. 165–167. Madrid: Atlas (references here drawn from Vol. 166).

Harth-Terré, Emilio

1933   "Incahuasi—Ruinas incaicas del Valle de Lunahuaná." *Revista del Museo Nacional*, Vol. 2, No. 1, pp. 101–125, Lima.

1938–1939   Mapa de Tambo Colorado, in Urteaga 1938–1939, p. 91.

1962–1963   "Técnica y Arte de la Cantería Incaica." *Revista Universitaria*, Nos. 122–125, pp. 152–168, Cuzco.

1964   "El Pueblo de Huánuco Viejo." *Arquitecto Peruano*, No. 320–321, pp. 1–22, Lima.

Helsley, Anne M.

1980   "Excavations at Cerro Tambo Real—Lambayeque, Peru." B.A. thesis, Department of Anthropology, Princeton University, Princeton, New Jersey.

Hemming, John, and Edward Ranney

1982   *Monuments of the Incas*. Boston: Little, Brown and Company.

Hyslop, John

1976   "An Archaeological Investigation of the Lupaca Kingdom and Its Origins." Doctoral dissertation, Department of Anthropology, Columbia University, New York.

1977a   "Hilltop Cities in Peru." *Archaeology*, Vol. 30, No. 4, pp. 218–225, New York.

1977b   "Chulpas of the Lupaca Zone of the Peruvian High Plateau." *Journal of Field Archaeology*, Vol. 4, pp. 149–170, Boston.

1979   "El área Lupaca bajo el dominio Incaico—Un Reconocimiento Arqueológico." *Histórica*, Vol. 3, No. 1, pp. 53–79, Departamento de Humanidades, Pontificia Universidad Católica del Perú, Lima.

1984   *The Inka Road System*. New York and San Francisco: Academic Press.

1985   *Inkawasi—The New Cuzco*. International Series 234, *British Archaeological Reports*, Oxford, England.

1988   "Las fronteras estatales extremas del Tawantinsuyu." *La Frontera del Estado Inca*, ed. Tom Dillehay and Patricia Netherly, pp. 35–57. International Series 442, *British Archaeological Reports*, Oxford, England.

n.d.a   "Factors Influencing the Transmission and Distribution of Inka Cultural Materials throughout Tawantinsuyu." Paper presented at Dumbarton Oaks Symposium "Latin American Horizons," October 11–12, 1986, Washington, D.C., in press.

n.d.b   Response to Dearborn, *Archaeoastronomy*, in press.

Ibarra Grasso, Dick Edgar

1982   *Ciencia astronómica y sociología incaica*. La Paz–Cochabamba: Editorial Los Amigos del Libro.

Ibarra Grasso, Dick, and Roy Querejazu Lewis

1986   *30,000 años de prehistoria en Bolivia*. La Paz–Cochabamba: Editorial Los Amigos del Libro.

Bibliography

Idrovo Urigüen, Jaime
  1984   "Prospection archeologique de la vallée de Cuenca—Ecuador (Secteur Sud; ou l'emplacement de la ville Inca de Tomebamba)." Doctoral dissertation, 2 vols., Université de Paris I, Panteon Sorbonne, Paris.
Iribarren Charlin, Jorge, and Hans Bergholz
  1971   "El camino del Inca en un sector del Norte Chico." Actas del VI Congreso de Arqueología Chilena, ed. Hans Niemeyer F., pp. 229–265, Santiago. (Published separately in 1972 with additional photographs by the Compañía de Cobre Salvador, Depto. de Comunicaciones, Potrerillos, Chile.)
Isbell, Billie Jean
  1982   "Culture Confronts Nature in the Dialectical World of the Tropics." Ethnoarchaeology and Archaeoastronomy in the American Tropics, ed. Gary Urton and Anthony Aveni, Annals of the New York Academy of Science, Vol. 358, pp. 353–363.
Jaramillo P., Mario
  1976   Estudio histórico sobre Ingapirca. Universidad Cátolica del Ecuador, Quito.
Jijón y Caamaño, Jacinto
  1934   "Los Orígenes del Cuzco." Tercera Parte, Anales de la Universidad Central de Quito, Vol. 53, No. 289, pp. 91–129, Quito.
Jiménez Borja, Arturo, and Alberto Bueno Mendoza
  1970   "Breves notas acerca de Pachacamac." Arqueología y Sociedad, No. 4, pp. 13–25, Museo de Arqueología y Etnología, Universidad Nacional Mayor de San Marcos, Lima.
Joyce, T. A.
  1923   "Pacha." Inca—Revista Trimestral de Estudios Antropológicos, Vol. 1, No. 4, pp. 761–778, Museo de Arqueología, Universidad Nacional Mayor de San Marcos, Lima.
Julien, Catherine J.
  1979   "Investigaciones recientes en la capital de los Qolla, Hatunqolla, Puno." Arqueología peruana, ed. R. Matos M., pp. 199–213, Seminario, Investigaciones Arqueológicas en el Perú 1976, Universidad Nacional Mayor de San Marcos, Lima.
  1983   Hatunqolla: A View of Inca Rule from the Lake Titicaca Region. University of California Publications in Anthropology, Vol. 15, Berkeley and Los Angeles: University of California Press.
Kalafatovich, Carlos
  1970   "Geología del grupo arqueológico de la fortaleza de Saccsayhuaman y sus vecindades." Revista Saqsaywaman, No. 1, pp. 61–68, Cuzco.
Keatinge, Richard W., and Geoffrey Conrad
  1983   "Imperialist Expansion in Peruvian Prehistory: Chimu Administration of a Conquered Territory." Journal of Field Archaeology, Vol. 10, pp. 255–283, Boston.
Kendall, Ann
  1974   "Architecture and Planning at the Inca Sites in the Cusichaca Area." Baessler Archiv, n. F., Vol. 22, pp. 73–137, Berlin.

1976   "Descripción e Inventario de las Formas Arquitectónicas Inca." *Revista del Museo Nacional*, Vol. 42, pp. 13–96, Lima.

1985   *Aspects of Inca Architecture—Description, Function, and Chronology*, 2 vols., International Series 242, *British Archaeological Reports*, Oxford, England.

Kosok, Paul
1965   *Life, Land, and Water in Ancient Peru*. New York: Long Island University Press.

Kriscautzky, Néstor
1983   "Excavación en Fuerte Quemado, Provincia de Catamarca." *Aportes*, No. 19, pp. 1–18, Dirección General de Extensión Universitaria, Universidad Nacional de Catamarca, Argentina.

1986   "Análisis de los restos de fauna y flora recuperados en las excavaciones arqueológicas del Sector I—yacimiento Cerro de la Ventanita—Fuerte Quemado, Santa María, Catamarca." *Primeras Jornadas de Ciencia y Tecnología*, pp. 1–16, Secretaría de Ciencia y Tecnología, Universidad Nacional de Catamarca.

1987   "Interpretación de las excavaciones arqueológicas realizadas en el yacimiento incaico de Cerro de la Ventanita 'Intihuatana,' Fuerte Quemado, Valle de Santa María, provincia de Catamarca." Paper submitted to the Second Jornadas de Ciencia y Tecnología, Catamarca.

Kubler, George
1946   "The Quechua in the Colonial World." *The Andean Civilizations*, pp. 331–410, *Handbook of South American Indians*, gen. ed. Julian H. Steward, Vol. 2, *Bulletin* 143, Bureau of American Ethnology, Smithsonian Institution, Washington, D.C.

1952   Cuzco: reconstrucción de la Ciudad y restauración de sus monumentos, Informe de la misión enviada por la UNESCO en 1951, Museos y Monumentos, III, UNESCO, Paris.

La Barra, Felipe de
1962   "Comprobaciones del Arte Militar Incaico y Características Principales." *Actas y Trabajos del II Congreso Nacional de Historia del Perú*, Vol. 2, pp. 347–357. Lima: Centro de Estudios Histórico-Militares del Perú.

Ladrón de Guevara A., Oscar
1967   "La Restauración del Ccoricancha y Templo de Santo Domingo." *Revista del Museo e Instituto Arqueológico*, No. 21, pp. 29–95, Universidad Nacional de San Antonio Abad del Cuzco.

Lange, Gunardo
1892   "Las ruinas de la fortaleza del Pucará." *Anales del Museo de La Plata*, Arqueología III, Universidad Nacional de La Plata, La Plata.

Langlois, Louis
1933   "Las Ruinas de Paramonga." *Revista del Museo Nacional*, Vol. 7, pp. 23–52, 281–307, Lima.

Lanning, Edward P.
1967   *Peru before the Incas*. Englewood Cliffs, N.J.: Prentice Hall.

Larrabure y Unanue, Emilio
1904   *Incahuasi, ruinas de un edificio peruano del siglo XV.* Lima: El Lucero.
1941   *Historia y Arqueología—Valle de Cañete.* Manuscritos y Publicaciones, Vol. 2. Lima: Imprenta Americana.
Larrea, Carlos Manuel
1965   La Cultura Incásica del Ecuador—Notas Históricas y Cronológicas, *Publicación* 25, Plan Piloto del Ecuador, Instituto Panamericano de Geografía e Historia, Mexico City.
Las Casas, Bartolomé de
1958   Apologética Historia, [ca. 1550] III, *Biblioteca de autores españoles,* Vol. 105. Madrid: Atlas.
Latcham, Ricardo E.
1928   *Los Incas—sus orígenes y sus ayllus.* Santiago: Balcells y Co.
Lavallée, Daniele, and Michele Julien
1983   *Asto: curacazgo prehispánico de los Andes Centrales.* Lima: Instituto de Estudios Peruanos.
LeBlanc, Catherine
1981   "Late Prehispanic Huanca Settlement Patterns in the Yanamarca Valley, Peru." Doctoral dissertation, Department of Anthropology, University of California, Los Angeles.
Lechtman, Heather
1976   "A Metallurgical Site Survey in the Peruvian Andes." *Journal of Field Archaeology,* Vol. 3, pp. 1–42, Boston.
Lee, Vincent R.
1985   *Sixpac Manco: Travels among the Incas.* Privately published, P.O. Box 107, Wilson, Wyoming.
1987   "The Building of Sacsayhuaman." Privately published, P.O. Box 107, Wilson, Wyoming.
1988   "The Lost Half of Inca Architecture." Privately published, P.O. Box 107, Wilson, Wyoming.
Lehmann-Nitsche, Robert
1928   Arqueología Peruana: Coricancha, el Templo del Sol en el Cuzco y las imágenes de su altar mayor. *Revista del Museo de La Plata,* Vol. 31, pp. 1–260.
LeVine, Terry Y.
1985   "Inka Administration in the Central Highlands: A Comparative Study." Doctoral dissertation, Department of Anthropology, University of California, Los Angeles.
Libro Primero
1965   *Libro Primero de cabildos de la Ciudad del Cuzco,* [1534], ed. Raúl Rivera Serna. Universidad Nacional Mayor de San Marcos, Lima.
Lorandi, Ana María
1980   "La frontera oriental del Tawantinsuyu: el Umasuyu y el Tucumán. Una hipóthesis de trabajo." *Relaciones de la Sociedad Argentina de Antropología,* N.S., Vol. 14, No. 1, Buenos Aires.

1983 "Olleros del Inka en Catamarca, Argentina." *Gazeta Arqueológica Andina*, No. 8, pp. 6–7, Lima.

Lumbreras, Luis Guillermo
1974 *The Peoples and Cultures of Ancient Peru*, trans. Betty J. Meggers. Washington, D.C.: Smithsonian Institution Press. (Originally *De las artes, los pueblos y las culturas del Antiguo Perú*, 1969, Lima.)

Lynch, Thomas
1978 "Tambo incaico Catarpe—este." *Estudios Atacameños*, No. 5, pp. 142–147, Museo Arqueológico, Universidad del Norte, San Pedro de Atacama, Chile.

McEwan, Gordon
1984 "Investigaciones en la cuenca del Lucre, Cusco." *Gaceta Arqueológica Andina*, Año III, No. 9, pp. 12–15, Instituto Andino de Estudios Arqueológicos, Lima.

MacLean, Margaret Greenup
1986 "Sacred Land, Sacred Water: Inca Landscape Planning in the Cuzco Area." Doctoral dissertation, Department of Anthropology, University of California, Berkeley.

Maidana, O., et al.
1974 "Osma, un yacimiento indicador para el Valle de Lerma." Ediciones Culturales del Depto. de Información Parlamentaria, Bibliográfica y de Prensa de la Legislatura de la Provincia de Salta.

Mansfeld, Franz
1948 "La ciudad legendaria del Ancoquija." *Revista Geográfica Americana*, Vol. 30, pp. 53–59, Buenos Aires.

Marcus, Joyce
1987 Late Intermediate Occupation at Cerro Azul, Perú. University of Michigan Museum of Anthropology, Technical Report 20, Ann Arbor.

Marcus, Joyce; Ramiro Matos M.; and María Rostworowski de Diez Canseco
1983–1985 "Arquitectura inca de Cerro Azul, valle de Cañete." *Revista del Museo Nacional*, Vol. 47, pp. 125–138, Lima.

Mariscotti de Gorlitz, Ana María
1978 Pachamama Santa Tierra: contribución al estudio de la religión autóctona en los Andes centro-meridionales. *Indiana; Beiträge zur Völker- und Sprachenkunde, Archäologie und Antropologie der indianischen Amerika*, Beiheft 8.8.

Matienzo, Juan de
1967 Gobierno del Perú, [1567] *Travaux de l'Institut Français d'Etudes Andines*, 11, Paris-Lima.

Means, Philip A.
1928 "Biblioteca Andina—Part One." *Transactions of the Connecticut Academy of Arts and Sciences*, Vol. 29, pp. 271–525, New Haven.

Mena, Cristóbal de (ascribed to; also called Anónimo sevillano de 1534)
1967 La conquista del Perú, [1534] *Las relaciones primitivas de la conquista del Perú*, ed. Raúl Porras Barrenechea, pp. 79–101, Instituto Raúl Porras Barrenechea, Universidad Nacional Mayor de San Marcos, Lima.

Menzel, Dorothy
  1959 "The Inca Occupation of the South Coast of Peru." *Southwestern Journal of Anthropology*, Vol. 15, No. 2, pp. 125–142, Albuquerque.
  1971 "Estudios Arqueológicos en los Valles de Ica, Pisco, Chincha y Cañete." *Arqueología y Sociedad*, No. 6, Museo de Arqueología y Etnología de la Universidad Nacional Mayor de San Marcos, Lima.
Menzel, Dorothy, and John H. Rowe
  1966 "The Role of Chincha in Late Pre-Spanish Peru." *Ñawpa Pacha*, No. 4, pp. 63–76, Berkeley.
Molina, Cristóbal de (el Almagrista). See Segovia, Bartolomé de, 1943.
Molina, Cristóbal de (el Cuzqueño)
  1943 Relación de las Fabulas y Ritos de los Incas, [1575] *Los Pequeños Grandes Libros de Historia Americana*, Serie I, Vol. 4, pp. 5–84 (second document). Lima: Librería e Imprenta D. Miranda.
Montesinos, Fernando
  1882 *Memorias antiguas historiales y políticas del Perú, Colección de Libros españoles raros o curiosos*, [ca. 1644] Vol. 16. Madrid: Miguel Ginesta.
Moorehead, Elizabeth L.
  1978 "Highland Inca Architecture in Adobe." *Ñawpa Pacha*, Vol. 16, pp. 65–94, Berkeley.
Morris, Craig
  1966 "El Tampu Real de Tunsucancha." *Cuadernos de Investigación*, No. 1, Antropología, pp. 95–107. Huánuco: Universidad Nacional Hermilio Valdizán.
  1967 "Storage in Tawantinsuyu." Doctoral dissertation, Anthropology Department, University of Chicago.
  1972 "State Settlements in Tawantinsuyu: A Strategy of Compulsory Urbanism." *Contemporary Archaeology*, ed. Mark Leone, pp. 393–401. Carbondale: Southern Illinois University.
  1974 "Reconstructing Patterns of Non-Agricultural Production in the Inca Economy: Archaeology and Documents in Institutional Analysis." *The Reconstruction of Complex Societies: An Archaeological Symposium*, ed. Charlotte Moore, pp. 49–60, American Schools of Oriental Research.
  1978–1980 "Huánuco Pampa: nuevas evidencias sobre el urbanismo inca." *Revista del Museo Nacional*, Vol. 44, pp. 139–152, Lima.
  1979 "Maize Beer in the Economics, Politics, and Religion of the Inca Empire." *Fermented Food Beverages in Nutrition*, ed. Clifford F. Gastineau, W. J. Darby, and T. B. Turner, pp. 21–34. New York: Academic Press.
  1980a "Architecture and the Structure of Space at Huánuco Pampa." To be published in *Cuadernos del Instituto Nacional de Antropología*, Buenos Aires.
  1980b "The Spanish Occupation of an Inca Administrative City." *Actes du XCIIᵉ Congrès International des Américanistes*, Vol. 9-B, pp. 209–219, Paris.

1981   "Tecnología y Organización Inca del Almacenamiento de Víveres en la Sierra." *La Tecnología en el Mundo Andino,* ed. Heather Lechtman and Ana María Soldi, Vol. 1, pp. 327–375. Mexico City: Universidad Nacional Autónoma de México.

1982   "The Infrastructure of Inka Control in the Peruvian Central Highlands." *The Inca and Aztec States, 1400–1800,* ed. G. A. Collier, R. I. Rosaldo, and J. D. Wirth, pp. 153–171. New York and London: Academic Press.

1986   "Storage, Supply, and Redistribution in the Economy of the Inka State." *Anthropological History of Andean Polities,* ed. J. V. Murra, N. Wachtel, and J. Revel, pp. 59–68. Cambridge and London: Cambridge University Press.

Morris, Craig, and Donald E. Thompson

1974   "Huánuco Viejo: An Inca Administrative Center." *The Rise and Fall of Civilizations,* ed. C. C. Lamberg-Karlovsky and Jeremy A. Sabloff, pp. 191–208. Menlo Park: Cummings Publishing Co. (Originally in *American Antiquity,* Vol. 35, No. 3, pp. 334–362, 1970.)

1985   *Huánuco Pampa—An Inca City and Its Hinterland.* London: Thames and Hudson.

Morrison, Tony

1978   *Pathways to the Gods.* New York: Harper and Row.

Moseley, Michael E.

1975   "Chan Chan: Andean Alternative of the Preindustrial City." *Science,* Vol. 187, pp. 219–225, Washington, D.C.

1985   "The Exploration and Explanation of Early Monumental Architecture in the Andes." *Early Ceremonial Architecture in the Andes,* ed. Christopher B. Donnan, pp. 29–57, Dumbarton Oaks, Washington, D.C.

Moseley, Michael E., and Kent C. Day, eds.

1982   *Chan Chan: Andean Desert City.* School of American Research Advanced Seminar Series. Albuquerque: University of New Mexico Press.

Moseley, Michael E., and Carol J. Mackey

1974   *Twenty Four Architectural Plans of Chan Chan, Peru—Structure and Form at the Capital of Chimor.* Peabody Museum of Archaeology and Ethnology, Harvard University. Cambridge, Mass.: Peabody Museum Press.

Mostny, Grete

1949   "Ciudades Atacameñas—Norte de Chile." *Boletín del Museo Nacional de Historia Natural,* Vol. 24, pp. 125–204, Santiago de Chile.

Muelle, Jorge C.

1945   "Pacarectambo." *Revista del Museo Nacional,* Vol. 14, pp. 153–179, Lima.

Mujica, Elias, and Jane Wheeler

1981   "Producción y Recursos Ganaderos Prehispánicos en la Cuenca del Titicaca, Perú—Trabajo de Campo 1979–1980." Informe final presentado al Instituto Nacional de Cultura, Lima.

Murra, John V.

1960 "Rite and Crop in the Inca State." *Culture in History, Essays in Honor of Paul Radin,* ed. Stanley Diamond, pp. 393–407. New York: Columbia University Press.

1968 "An Aymara Kingdom in 1567." *Ethnohistory,* Vol. 15, pp. 115–151, Bloomington, Indiana. (Also in Murra 1975.)

1972 "El Control Vertical de un Máximo de Pisos ecológicos en la economía de las sociedades andinas." *Visita de la Provincia de León de Huánuco,* Vol. 2, pp. 429–476. Universidad Nacional Hermilio Valdizán; Huánuco, Perú. (Also in Murra 1975.)

1975 *Formaciones económicas y políticas del mundo andino.* Instituto de Estudios Peruanos, Lima.

1978 *La Organización Económica del Estado Inca,* trans. Daniel R. Wagner. Mexico City: Siglo Veintiuno (doctoral dissertation 1955; publication in English, 1980).

1986 "The Expansion of the Inka State: Armies, War, and Rebellions." *Anthropological History of Andean Polities,* ed. J. V. Murra, N. Wachtel, and J. Revel, pp. 49–58. Cambridge and London: Cambridge University Press, and Paris: Editions de la Maison des Sciences de l'Homme (originally in French in *Annales [ESC],* Vol. 33, Nos. 5–6, Paris, 1978).

1980 *The Economic Organization of the Inca State.* Greenwich, Conn.: JAI Press (doctoral dissertation 1955, Department of Anthropology, University of Chicago).

Murúa, Martin de

1962 *Historia General de Perú, Origen y Descendencia de los Incas* [1590–1600]. Colección Joyas Bibliográficas, Biblioteca Americana Vetus, Madrid.

Netherly, Patricia, and Tom Dillehay

1986 "Duality in Public Architecture in the Upper Zaña Valley, Northern Peru." *Perspectives on Andean Prehistory and Protohistory,* ed. Daniel H. Sandweiss and D. Peter Kvietok, pp. 85–114, Latin American Studies Program, Cornell University, Ithaca, New York.

Nickel, Cheryl

1982 "The Semiotics of Andean Terracing." *Art Journal,* Vol. 42, No. 3, pp. 200–203, College Art Association, New York.

Niemeyer F., Hans

1986 "La ocupación inkaica de la cuenca alta del Río Copiapó." *Volumen Homenaje—45° Congreso internacional de americanistas,* Simposio—El Imperio Inka, *Comechingonía—Revista de Antropología e Historia,* Año 4, Número Especial, pp. 165–294, Córdoba, Argentina.

Niemeyer F., Hans; Miguel Cervellino G.; and Eduardo Muñoz

1984 "Viña de Cerro: Metalurgía Inka en Copiapó, Chile." *Gaceta Arqueológica Andina,* No. 9, pp. 6–7, Instituto Andino de Estudios Arqueológicos, Lima.

Niemeyer F., Hans; V. Schiappacase F.; and I. Solimano R.
1971 "Patrones de poblamento en la Quebrada de Camarones (Prov. Tarapacá)." *Actas del VI Congreso de Arqueología Chilena,* pp. 115–137, Santiago de Chile.

Niles, Susan
1980 "Pumamarca: A Late Intermediate Period Site near Ollantaytambo." *Ñawpa Pacha,* No. 18, pp. 47–62, Berkeley.
1982 "Style and Function in Inca Agricultural Works near Cuzco." *Ñawpa Pacha,* Vol. 20, pp. 163–182, Berkeley.
1984 "Architectural Form and Social Function in Inca Towns near Cuzco." *Current Archaeological Projects in the Central Andes—Some Approaches and Results,* ed. Ann Kendall, pp. 205–219, Proceedings of the 44th International Congress of Americanists, Manchester, BAR International Series 210, Oxford.

Nordenskiöld, Erland von
1915 "Incallacta, eine befestigte und von Inca Tupac Yupanqui angelegte Stadt." *Ymer,* Heft 2, pp. 169–185, Stockholm.
1917 "The Guarani Invasion of the Inca Empire in the Sixteenth Century: An Historical Indian Migration." *Geographical Review,* Vol. 9, pp. 103–121, American Geographical Society, New York.
1924 *Forschungen und Abenteuer in Südamerica.* Stuttgart: Strecker und Schröder.
1942 "Fortifications in Ancient Peru and Europe." *Ethnos,* Vol. 7, pp. 1–9, Lund.

Noticia del Perú. See Estete, Miguel de, 1924.

Oberem, Udo
1968 "Die Bergfestung Quitoloma im Nördlichen Hochland Ecuadors." *Baessler Archiv,* n.F., Vol. 16, pp. 331–354, Berlin.
1980 "Festungsanlagen im Andengebiet." *Allgemeine und Vergleichende Archäologie—Beiträge,* Vol. 2, pp. 487–503, Deutsches Archäologisches Institut, Bonn.

Oberti R., Italo
1983 "Cuzco arqueológico y etnohistórico. Una introducción bibliográfica." *Revista Andina,* Vol. 1, No. 2, pp. 443–474, Centro Bartolomé de Las Casas, Cuzco.

Ortiz de Zúñiga, Iñigo
1967, 1972 Visita de la Provincia de León de Huánuco en 1562, [1562] *Documentos para la Historia y Etnología de Huánuco y la Selva Central,* ed. J. V. Murra, Vol. 1, pp. 8–266, Vol. 2, pp. 1–269. Huánuco: Universidad Nacional Hermilio Valdizán.

Outwater, J. Ogden, Jr.
1978 "Edificación de la Fortaleza de Ollantaytambo." *Tecnología Andina,* ed. R. Ravines, pp. 581–589, Instituto de Estudios Peruanos and Instituto de Investigación Tecnológica, Industrial y de Normas Técnicas, Lima.

Pachacuti Yamqui, Joan de Santacruz
   1879   "Antigüedades deste reyno del Pirú." *Tres Relaciones de Antigüedades Peruanas,* [1613] pp. 230–328, Ministerio de Fomento. Madrid: Imprenta y Fundición de M. Tello.
   1968   Relación de antigüedades deste Reyno del Perú, *Biblioteca de Autores Españoles,* [1613] Vol. 209, pp. 279–319, Madrid: Atlas.
Paddock, Franklin K.
   1984   "The Great Wall of the Inca." *Archaeology,* Vol. 37, No. 4, pp. 62–63, 76.
Pardo, Luis A.
   1936   "Maquetas arquitectónicas en el Antiguo Perú." *Revista del Instituto Arqueológico del Cuzco,* No. 1, pp. 6–17.
   1957   *Historia y Arqueología del Cuzco,* 2 vols. Callao: Imprenta Colegio Militar Leoncio Prado.
Paredes Botoni, Ponciano
   1986   *Guia turística—Pachacamac,* drawings by Régulo Franco J., 3d ed., Lima.
Paredes Botoni, Ponciano, and Régulo Franco
   1987   "Pachacamac: las pirámides con rampa, cronología y función." *Gaceta Arqueológica Andina,* No. 13, pp. 5–7, Instituto Andino de Estudios Arqueológicos, Lima.
Paulotti, O.
   1958–1959   "Las Ruinas de los Nevados del Aconquija, Noticia Preliminar." *Runa,* Vol. 9, parts 1–2, pp. 125–135, Buenos Aires.
   1967   "Las Ruinas de los Nevados del Aconquija—Los Dos Grupos de Construcciones." *Runa,* Vol. 10, parts 1–2, pp. 354–370, Buenos Aires.
Pease G. Y., Franklin
   1978   *Del Tawantinsuyu a la Historia del Perú.* Lima: Instituto de Estudios Peruanos.
Pizarro, Hernando
   1959   Carta a la Audiencia de Santo Domingo, [1553] *Cartas del Perú,* ed. R. Porras Barrenechea, pp. 77–84. Lima: Ediciones de la Sociedad de Bibliófilos Peruanos.
Pizarro, Pedro
   1978   *Relación del descubrimiento y conquista del Perú,* [1571] Pontificia Universidad Católica del Peru, Lima.
Plaza Schuller, Fernando
   1976   La incursión Inca en el septentrional andino ecuatoriano, *Serie Arqueología,* No. 2, Instituto Otavaleño de Antropología, Otavalo.
   ca. 1980   "El complejo de fortalezas de Pambamarca." *Serie Arqueología,* No. 3, Instituto Otavaleño de Antropología, Otavalo.
Polo de Ondegardo, Juan
   1916a   "Supersticiones de los indios, sacadas del segundo Concilio Provincial de Lima," [1567] *Colección de Libros y Documentos Referentes a la Historia del Perú,* ed. Horacio H. Urteaga, Vol. 3, pp. 205–208. Lima: Sanmartí.

1916b   "Relación de los fundamentos acerca del notable daño que resulta de no guardar a los indios sus fueros," [1571] *Collección de Libros y Documentos Referentes a la Historia del Perú,* T. 3, ed. Horacio H. Urteaga, pp. 45–188. Lima: Sanmartí.

1916c   "De los errores y supersticiones de los indios, sacados del tratado y averiguación que hizo el Licenciado Polo," [1571] *Colección de Libros y Documentos Referentes a la Historia del Perú,* ed. Horacio H. Urteaga, Vol. 3, pp. 1–44. Lima: Sanmartí.

1917   "La Relación del linaje de los Incas y como extendieron ellos sus conquistas," [1571] *Colección de Libros y Documentos Referentes a la Historia del Perú,* ed. Horacio H. Urteaga, Vol. 4, pp. 45–94. Lima: Sanmartí.

1940   "Informe del Licenciado Juan Polo de Ondegardo al Licenciado Briviesca de Muñatones sobre la perpetuidad de las encomiendas en el Perú." [1561] *Revista Histórica,* Vol. 13, pp. 125–196, Lima.

Porras Barrenechea, Raúl

1986   *Los Cronistas del Perú (1528–1650) y Otros Ensayos,* ed. Franklin Pease G. Y., Biblioteca Clásicos del Perú 2, Banco de Crédito del Perú. Lima: Editorial e Imprenta DESA.

Porras Garcés, Pedro

1983   "Paramentos Incásicos en el casco colonial de Quito." *Publicación de la Sociedad Amigos de la Genealogía,* Año I, No. 2, pp. 5–27, Quito.

Portugal Z., Maks

1956   "Plano Arqueológico de la Ciudad de la Paz, La Antigua Chuki Apu Marka." *Revista Khana,* pp. 85–122, La Paz. (Also in *Arqueología Boliviana,* ed. C. Ponce S., pp. 340–401, La Paz: Biblioteca Paceña– Alcaldía Municipal, 1957.)

1977   "Estudio arqueológico de Copacabana." *Arqueología en Bolivia y Perú,* Vol. 2, pp. 285–323, Editorial Casa Municipal de la Cultura "Franz Tamayo," La Paz.

Portugal Z., Maks, and Dick Ibarra Grasso

1957   *Copacabana—El santuario y la arqueología de la península e islas del Sol y la Luna.* Cochabamba: Editorial Atlantic.

Protzen, Jean-Pierre

1980   "Inca Stonemasonry." *Scientific American,* Vol. 254, No. 2, pp. 94–103.

1983   "Inca Quarrying and Stonecutting." *Ñawpa Pacha,* No. 21, pp. 183– 214, Berkeley.

Pucher, Leo

1945   *Ensayo sobre el arte pre-histórico de Samaypata,* Museo Arqueológico de la Universidad de San Francisco Xavier, Sucre.

Puento, Gerónimo

1974   "Probanza de Don Hieronimo Puento, Cavique Principal del Pueblo de Cayambe, de Servicios." *Documentos para la historia militar,* pp. 11–50, Dirección de Historia y Geografía Militar del E.M.C. de las FF.AA., Casa de la Cultura Ecuatoriana, Quito.

Quiroga Ibarrola, César A.
1962   "Ensayo monográfico de la organización del ejército y armas em-
       pleadas por los soldados del Tahuantinsuyo y por los conquistadores
       españoles." *Actas y Trabajos de II Congreso Nacional de Historia
       del Perú*, Vol. 2, pp. 358–416. Lima: Centro de Estudios Histórico-
       Militares de Perú.

Raffino, Rodolfo
1983   *Los Inkas del Kollasuyu*, 2d ed., La Plata: Ramos Americana Editora.

Raffino, Rodolfo A.; R. J. Alvis; L. N. Baldini; D. E. Olivera; and M. G. Raviña
1983–1985   "Hualfín—El Shincal—Watungasta: Tres casos de urbanización
       inka en el N. O. Argentino." *Cuadernos del Instituto Nacional de
       Antropología*, Vol. 10, pp. 425–458, Buenos Aires.

Ramos Gavilán, Alonso
1976   *Historia de Nuestra Señora de Copacabana*, [1621] Academia Bolivi-
       ana de Historia, La Paz.

Ravines, Rogger
1976   "El Cuarto del Rescate de Atahualpa." *Revista del Museo Nacional*,
       Vol. 42, pp. 113–143, Lima.

Rawls, Joseph M.
1979   "An Analysis of Prehispanic Andean Warfare." Doctoral dissertation,
       University of California, Los Angeles, 1979.

Reinhard, Johan
1983   "Las montañas sagradas: un estudio etnoarqueológico de ruinas en
       las altas cumbres andinas." *Cuadernos de Historia*, Vol. 3, pp. 27–
       62, Departamento de Ciencias Históricas, Universidad de Chile,
       Santiago.

Reinoso H., Gustavo
1971   "Vestigios Arqueológicos en la Región Occidental del Nudo del
       Azuay." *Revista de Antropología*, Vol. 3, pp. 227–248, Sección de
       Antropología del Núcleo del Azuay de la Casa de la Cultura Ecua-
       toriana, Cuenca.

Relación francesa
1967   *Las Relaciones Primitivas de la Conquista del Perú*, [1534] ed. R. Po-
       rras Barrenechea, pp. 69–78. Lima: Instituto Raúl Porras Barrenechea.

Repartimiento de Tierras por el Inca Huayna Capac [1556]
1977   Nota y transcripción por Don Adolfo de Morales, Comentario de
       Dra. Geraldine Byrne de Caballero, Museo Arqueológico, Departa-
       mento de Arqueología, Universidad Boliviana Mayor de San Simón,
       Cochabamba.

Rivera Dorado, Miguel
1972   "La Cerámica Killke y la arqueología de Cusco (Perú)." *Revista Es-
       pañola de Antropología Americana*, Vol. 7, pp. 85–123, Universidad
       Complutense, Madrid.
1978   "Procesos de aculturación en el Tawantinsuyu." *Revista del Instituto
       de Antropología*, Vol. 6, pp. 105–110, Facultad de Filosofía y Humani-
       dades, Universidad Nacional de Córdoba, Córdoba.

Rivera Sundt, Oswaldo

1979 "El Complejo Arqueológico de Samaipata." *El Fuerte Preincaico de Samaipata*, pp. 41–144. La Paz–Cochabamba: Editorial Los Amigos del Libro.

1984 "La Horca del Inka." *Arqueología Boliviana*, No. 1, pp. 91–101, Instituto Nacional de Arqueología, La Paz.

Rostworowski de Diez Canseco, María

1953 *Pachacutec Inka Yupanqui*. Lima: Imprenta Torres Aguirre.

1969–1970 "Los Ayarmarca." *Revista del Museo Nacional*, Vol. 36, pp. 58–101, Lima.

1970 "El repartimiento de doña Beatriz Coya, en el valle de Yucay." *Historia y Cultura*, No. 4, pp. 153–267, Lima.

1972 "Breve Ensayo Sobre el Señorio de Ychma o Ychima." *Arqueología PUC*, No. 13, pp. 37–51, Seminario de Arqueología Instituto Riva Agüero, Pontificia Universidad Católica del Perú, Lima.

1977 *Etnía y sociedad*. Lima: Instituto de Estudios Peruanos.

1978–1980 "Guarco y Lunahuaná—dos señoríos prehispánicos de la costa sur central del Perú." *Revista del Museo Nacional*, Vol. 44, pp. 153–214, Lima.

1981 "Mediciones y cómputos en el antiguo Perú." *La Tecnología en el Mundo Andino*, ed. Heather Lechtman and Ana María Soldi, Vol. 1, pp. 379–405. Mexico City: Universidad Nacional Autónoma de México.

1983 *Estructuras de poder andino*. Lima: Instituto de Estudios Peruanos.

1988 *Historia del Tawantinsuyu*. Lima: Instituto de Estudios Peruanos.

Rowe, John H.

1942 "Sitios históricos en la región de Pucara, Puno." *Revista del Instituto Arqueológico*, Vol. 10–11, pp. 66–75, Universidad del Cuzco.

1944 An Introduction to the Archaeology of Cuzco. *Papers of the Peabody Museum of American Archaeology and Ethnology*, Vol. 27, No. 2, Harvard University, Cambridge.

1945 "Absolute Chronology in the Andean Area." *American Antiquity*, Vol. 10, pp. 265–284, Salt Lake City.

1946 "Inca Culture at the Time of the Spanish Conquest." *The Andean Civilizations*, pp. 183–330, *Handbook of South American Indians*, Julian H. Steward, gen. ed., Vol. 2, *Bulletin* 143, Bureau of American Ethnology, Smithsonian Institution, Washington, D.C.

1948 "The Kingdom of Chimor." *Acta Americana*, Vol. 6, pp. 26–59, Mexico City.

1967 "What Kind of a Settlement Was Inca Cuzco?" *Ñawpa Pacha*, No. 5, pp. 59–76, Berkeley.

1970 "La arqueología del Cuzco como historia cultural." *100 años de arqueología en el Perú*, ed. R. Ravines, pp. 490–563, Instituto de Estudios Peruanos and Petróleos del Perú, Lima.

1979 "An Account of the Shrines of Ancient Cuzco." *Ñawpa Pacha*, No. 17, pp. 2–80, Berkeley.

1982 "Inka Politics and Institutions Relating to the Cultural Unification of the Empire." *The Inca and Aztec States 1400–1800,* ed. George A. Collier, R. I. Rosaldo, and J. D. Wirth, pp. 93–118. New York: Academic Press.

1985 "Probanza de los Incas nietos de conquistadores." *Histórica,* Vol. 9, No. 2, pp. 193–245, Departamento de Humanidades, Pontificia Universidad Católica del Perú, Lima.

Ruiz de Arce, Juan

    1955 Adbertencia que hizo el fundador del bínculo y mayorazco, a los subsesores en el & . . . , [ca. 1545] *Boletín de la Academia Nacional de Historia,* Vol. 25, No. 86, pp. 179–200, Quito.

Rydén, Stig

    1947 *Archaeological Researches in the Highlands of Bolivia.* Göteborg: Elanders Boktryckeri Aktiebolag.

    1957 *Andean Excavations I—The Tiahuanaco Era East of Lake Titicaca. Publication of the Ethnographical Museum of Sweden,* No. 4, Stockholm.

Saignes, Thierry

    1985 *Los Andes Orientales: Historia de un Olvido.* Instituto Francés de Estudios Andinos and Centro de Estudios de la Realidad Económica y Social, Cochabamba, Bolivia.

Sancho de la Hoz, Pedro

    1917 Relación para S. M. de lo sucedido en la conquista . . . , [1534] *Colección de Libros y Documento Referentes a la Historia del Perú,* ed. Horacio H. Urteaga, Vol. 5, pp. 122–202. Lima: Sanmartí.

Santacruz Pachacuti Yamqui, Joan de. See Pachacuti Yamqui, Joan de Santacruz.

Santo Tomás, Domingo de

    1951 *Lexicon, o Vocabulario de la lengua general del Perú,* [1560] edición facsimilar, Instituto de Historia, Universidad Nacional Mayor de San Marcos, Lima.

Sanzetenea, Ramón

    1973 "Incallajta—Torreón." *El Diario,* August 5, La Paz.

    1975*a* "El sector arqueológico de Pocona Incaico." *Los Tiempos,* November 4, 1975, Cochabamba.

    1975*b* "Los establecimientos estatales incaicos en los valles de Cochabamba." *Los Tiempos,* August 17, Cochabamba.

Sarmiento de Gamboa, Pedro

    1965 "Historia de los Incas," [1572] *Biblioteca de Autores Españoles,* Vol. 135, pp. 193–279. Madrid: Atlas.

Schaedel, Richard P.

    1951 "Major Ceremonial and Population Centers in Northern Peru." *Proceedings of the 29th International Congress of Americanists,* Vol. 2, pp. 232–243, Chicago.

    1966 "Urban Growth and Ekistics on the Peruvian Coast." *Actas y Memorias del XXXVI Congreso Internacional de Americanistas,* Vol. 1, pp. 532–539, Seville.

Schjellerup, Inge

1979–1980 "Documents on Paper and in Stone. A Preliminary Report on the Inca Ruins in Cochabamba, Province of Chachapoyas, Peru." *Folk*, Vol. 21–22, pp. 299–311, Copenhagen.

1984 "Cochabamba—An Incaic Administrative Centre in the Rebellious Province of Chachapoyas." *Proceedings 44th International Congress of Americanists*, ed. Ann Kendall, pp. 161–187, *British Archaeological Reports*, International Series 210, Oxford, England.

Schmieder, Oskar

1924 "Condorhuasi—eine befestigte Siedlung der Inkas im südlichen Bolivien." *Mitteilungen aus Justus Perthes' Geographischer Anstalt*, Vol. 70, pp. 229–230, Gotha.

1926 "The East Bolivian Andes South of the Río Grande or Guapay." *University of California Publications in Geography*, Vol. 2, No. 5, pp. 85–210.

Schobinger, Juan, et al.

1966 *La "Momia" del Cerro el Toro*, supplement to vol. 21, *Anales de Arqueología y Etnología*, Universidad Nacional de Cuyo, Mendoza.

Segovia, Bartolomé de

1943 Relación de muchas cosas acaecidas en el Perú . . . , [1553] *Los Pequeños Grandes Libros de Historia Americana*, serie I, Vol. 4, first document. Lima: Librería e Imprenta D. Miranda. (Incorrectly attributed to Cristóbal de Molina [el Almagrista].)

Shea, Daniel

1966 "El Conjunto Arquitectónico Central en la Plaza de Huánuco Viejo." *Cuadernos de Investigación*, No. 1, pp. 108–116 and 3 figs., Universidad Nacional de Hermilio de Valdizán, Huánuco, Perú.

Sherbondy, Jeanette

1982a "The Canal Systems of Hanan Cuzco." Doctoral dissertation, Department of Anthropology, University of Illinois at Urbana-Champaign.

1982b "El regadío, los lagos y mitos de origen." *Allpanchis*, No. 20, pp. 3–32, Instituto de Pastoral Andina, Cuzco.

1986 "Los ceques: Código de canales en el Cusco Incaico." *Allpanchis*, No. 27, pp. 39–60, Instituto de Pastoral Andina, Cuzco.

Silva Galdames, Osvaldo

1977–1978 "Consideraciones Acerca del Período Inca en la Cuenca de Santiago (Chile Central)." *Boletín del Museo Arqueológico de La Serena, Chile*, No. 16 (edición homenaje a Dn. Jorge Iribarren Charlín), pp. 211–243, La Serena.

1983 "¿Detuvo la batalla del Maule la expansión Inca hacia el sur de Chile?" *Cuadernos de Historia*, No. 3, pp. 7–25, Departamento de Ciencias Históricas, Universidad de Chile, Santiago.

Spurling, Geoffrey

1982 "Inka Military Organization." Unpublished seminar paper, Department of Anthropology, Cornell University, Ithaca. Courtesy the author.

Squier, E. George
  1877   *Peru, Incidents of Travel and Exploration in the Land of the Incas.*
         New York: Harper and Brothers.
Stanish, Charles, and Irene Pritzker
  1983   "Archaeological Reconnaissance in Southern Peru." *Field Museum of
         Natural History Bulletin,* Vol. 54, pp. 6–17, Chicago.
Stanislawski, Dan
  1946   "The Origin and Spread of the Grid-Pattern Town." *Geographical Re-
         view,* Vol. 36, pp. 105–120, New York.
  1947   "Early Spanish Town Planning in the New World." *Geographical Re-
         view,* Vol. 37, pp. 94–105, New York.
Stehberg L., Rubén
  1975   Diccionario de sitios arqueológicos de Chile Central. Publicación
         Ocasional, No. 17, Museo Nacional de Historia Natural, Santiago
         de Chile.
  1976   La fortaleza de Chena y su relación con la occupación incaica de
         Chile Central. Publicación Ocasional del Museo Nacional de Historia
         Natural, No. 23, Santiago de Chile.
Strong, William Duncan, and Gordon R. Willey
  1943   "The Southern Survey." Archaeological Studies in Peru, 1941–1942,
         Columbia Studies in Archaeology and Ethnology, Vol. 1, pp. 18–25.
         New York: Columbia University Press.
Strube Erdmann, León
  1963   *Vialidad Imperial de los Incas.* Serie Histórica, No. 33, Instituto de
         Estudios Americanistas, Facultad de Filosofía y Humanidades, Uni-
         versidad Nacional de Córdoba, Argentina.
Sullivan, Walter
  1974   "Study of Andean Shrines Gives New History View." *New York
         Times,* p. 39, March 19 (report of Vescelius lecture).
Tapia Pineda, Félix
  1984   "Excavaciones arqueológicas en el sector habitacional de el Fuerte de
         Samaipata, Santa Cruz." *Arqueología Boliviana,* No. 1, pp. 49–62,
         Instituto Nacional de Arqueología, La Paz.
Tello, Julio C.
  1940   "Pachacamac." *El Comercio,* p. 13, August 4, Lima. (Courtesy R. E.
         Daggett.)
  1941   "La Ciudad Inkaica de Cajamarca." *Chaski,* Vol. 1, No. 3, pp. 2–7,
         Lima.
Thompson, Donald E.
  1967   "Investigaciones arqueológicas en las aldeas chupachu de Ichu y Au-
         quimarca." *Visita de la provincia de León de Huánuco en 1562,* ed.
         John V. Murra, Vol. 1, pp. 357–362, Universidad Nacional Hermilio
         Valdizán, Huánuco.
  1968   "Incaic Installations at Huánuco and Pumpu." *Actas y Memorias del
         XXXVII Congreso Internacional de Americanistas,* Vol. 1, pp. 67–74,

Mar del Plata. (Published separately in *El Proceso de Urbanización en America desde sus Orígenes hasta Nuestros Días*, ed. Jorge E. Hardoy and Richard P. Schaedel, Buenos Aires, 1968.)

Trimborn, Hermann

1959   Archäologische Studien in den Kordilleren Boliviens. *Baessler Archiv, Beiträge zur Völkerkunde*, n. F., Beiheft 2, Berlin.

1967   Archäologische Studien in den Kordilleren Boliviens. *Baessler Archiv, Beiträge zur Volkerkunde*, n. F., Beiheft 5, Berlin.

Trujillo, Diego de

1948   *Relación del Descubrimiento del Reyno del Perú*, [1571] ed. R. Porras Barrenechea. Seville: Imprenta de la Escuela de Estudios Hispano-Americanos.

Tschopik, Marion H.

1946   Some Notes on the Archaeology of the Department of Puno, Peru. *Papers of the Peabody Museum of American Archaeology and Ethnology*, Vol. 27, No. 3, Cambridge.

Ubbelohde-Doering, Heinrich

1966   *Kulturen Alt Perus*. Tübingen: Verlag Ernst Wasmuth (in English as *On the Royal Highway of the Inca*, trans. Margaret Brown. New York: Praeger, 1967).

Uhle, Max

1903   *Pachacamac—Report of the William Pepper, M.D., LL.D., Peruvian Expedition of 1896*, Department of Archaeology, University of Pennsylvania.

1912   "Los orígenes de los Incas." *Actas del XVII Congreso de Americanistas*, pp. 302–352, Buenos Aires.

1917   "Fortalezas incaicas: Incallacta-Machupichu." *Revista Chilena de Historia y Geografía*, Vol. 21, pp. 154–170, Sociedad Chilena de Historia y Geografía, Santiago.

1923   *Las Ruinas de Tomebamba*. Quito: Imprenta Julio Sáenz Rebolledo.

Urteaga, Horacio H.

1919–1920   "El ejército incaico." *Boletín de la Sociedad Geográfica de Lima*, Vols. 35–36, pp. 283–331, Lima.

1938–1939   "Tambo Colorado." *Boletín de la Sociedad Geográfica de Lima*, Vols. 40–41, pp. 86–94, Lima.

Urton, Gary

1978   "Orientation in Quechua and Incaic Astronomy." *Ethnology*, Vol. 17, No. 2, pp. 157–167.

1981   *At the Crossroads of the Earth and the Sky: An Andean Cosmology*. Austin: University of Texas Press.

Urton, Gary, and Anthony F. Aveni

1983   "Archaeoastronomical Fieldwork on the Coast of Peru." *Calendars in Mesoamerica and Peru—Native American Computations of Time*, ed. Anthony F. Aveni and G. Brotherston, BAR International Series 174, Oxford.

Valcárcel, Luis E.
1934–1935   "Sajsawaman Redescubierto." 3 parts, *Revista del Museo Nacional*, Vol. 3, No. 1–2, pp. 3–36; Vol. 3, No. 3, pp. 211–233; Vol. 4, No. 1, pp. 1–24, Lima.
1939   "Sobre el origen del Cuzco." *Revista del Museo Nacional*, Vol. 8, pp. 190–223, Lima.
Valencia E., Abraham
n.d.   *Pesas y medidas inkas.* Centro de Estudios Andinos, Cuzco.
Valencia Z., Alfredo
1977   "Excavaciones Arqueológicas en Machupijchu: Sector de la Roca Sagrada." 4 pages, 3 plates, Centro Regional Sur de Investigación y Restauración de Bienes Monumentales, Instituto Nacional de Cultura, Cuzco.
1984   "Arqueología de Qolqampata." *Revista del Museo e Instituto de Arqueología*, No. 23, pp. 47–62, Universidad Nacional de San Antonio Abad, Cuzco.
Van de Guchte, Maarten
1984   "El ciclo mítico andino de la piedra cansada." *Revista Andina*, Año 2, No. 2, pp. 539–556, Centro de Estudios Rurales Andinos "Bartolomé de Las Casas," Cuzco.
Vargas Ugarte, Ruben
1949   *Historia General del Perú, Virreinato (1551–1596)*, Vol. 2. Barcelona: Seix y Barral Hnos.
Wachtel, Nathan
1973   "Estructuralismo e historia: a propósito de la organización social del Cuzco." *Sociedad e ideología*, pp. 23–58. Lima: Instituto de Estudios Peruanos.
1980–1981   "Les Mitimas de la Vallée de Cochabamba, la politique de colonisation de Huayna Capac." *Journal de la Société des Américanistes*, Vol. 67, pp. 297–324, Paris.
Walter, Heinz
1959   "Die Ruine Pucara de Oroncota (Südost-Bolivien)." *Baessler Archiv*, n.F. Band 7, Heft 2, pp. 333–340, Berlin.
Wedin, Ake
1963   *La Cronología de la Historia Incaica.* Instituto Ibero-Americano Gotemburgo Suecia. Madrid: Insula.
Wiener, Charles
1880   *Perou et Bolivie.* Paris: Librarie Hachette.
Williams, Carlos
1985   "A Scheme for the Early Monumental Architecture of the Central Coast of Peru." *Early Ceremonial Architecture in the Andes*, ed. Christopher B. Donnan, pp. 227–240. Dumbarton Oaks, Washington, D.C.
Xérez, Francisco de
1970   "Verdadera Relación de la Conquista del Perú y Provincia del Cuzco, llamada Nueva Castilla," [1534] *Crónicas de la Conquista del Perú*, pp. 27–124. Mexico City: Editorial Nueva España.

Ziolkowski, Marius S., and Robert M. Sadowski
  1984 "Informe acerca de las investigaciones arqueoastronómicas en el área central de Ingapirca (Ecuador)." *Revista Española de Antropología Americana*, Vol. 14, pp. 103–125, Universidad Complutense, Madrid.

Zuidema, R. Tom
  1964 *The Ceque System of Cuzco*. International Archives of Ethnography, Supplement to Vol. 50, Leiden.

  1968 "La Relación entre el patrón de poblamento prehispánico y los principios derivados de la estructura social incaica." XXXVII Congreso de Americanistas, *Actas y Memorias*, Vol. 1, pp. 45–55, Buenos Aires.

  1977*a* "The Inca Calendar." *Native American Astronomy*, ed. Anthony F. Aveni, pp. 219–259. Austin: University of Texas Press.

  1977*b* "The Inca Kinship System: A New Theoretical View." *Andean Kinship and Marriage*, ed. Ralph Bolton and E. Mayer, pp. 240–292, American Anthropological Association, special publication 7.

  1978 "Shafttombs and the Inca Empire." *Journal of the Steward Anthropological Society*, Vol. 9, Nos. 1 and 2, pp. 133–177.

  1980 "El Ushnu." *Revista de la Universidad Complutense*, Vol. 28, No. 117, pp. 317–361, Madrid.

  1981*a* "Inka Observations of the Solar and Lunar Passages through Zenith and Anti-Zenith at Cuzco." *Archaeoastronomy in the Americas*, ed. Ray Williamson, pp. 316–342. Los Altos, Calif.: Ballena Press.

  1981*b* "Anthropology and Archaeology." *Archaeoastronomy in the Americas*, ed. Ray Williamson, pp. 29–31. Los Altos, Calif.: Ballena Press.

  1981*c* "Comment." *Latin American Research Review*, Vol. 16, No. 3, pp. 167–170.

  1982*a* "Catachillay—The Role of the Pleiades and of the Southern Cross and Alpha and Beta Centauri in the Calendar of the Incas." *Ethnoarchaeology and Archaeoastronomy in the American Tropics*, ed. Gary Urton and Anthony Aveni, *Annals of the New York Academy of Science*, Vol. 358, pp. 203–229, New York.

  1982*b* "The Siderial Lunar Calendar of the Incas." *Archaeoastronomy in the New World*, ed. Anthony F. Aveni, pp. 59 107. Cambridge: Cambridge University Press.

  1982*c* "Bureaucracy and Systematic Knowledge in Andean Civilization." *The Inka and Aztec States: 1400–1800*, ed. G. A. Collier, R. I. Rosaldo, and J. D. Wirth, pp. 419–458. New York and London: Academic Press.

  1983*a* "The Lion in the City: Royal Symbols of Transition in Cuzco." *Journal of Latin American Lore*, Vol. 9, No. 1, pp. 39–100.

  1983*b* "Hierarchy and Space in Incaic Social Organization." *Ethnohistory*, Vol. 30, pt. 2, pp. 49–75.

  1986*a* "Inka Dynasty and Irrigation: Another Look at Andean Concepts of History." *Anthropological History of Andean Polities*, ed. J. V. Murra, N. Wachtel, and J. Revel, pp. 177–200. Cambridge and London: Cambridge University Press, and Paris: Editions de la Maison des Sciences de l'Homme (originally in French in *Annales [ESC]*, Vol. 33, Nos. 5–6, Paris, 1978).

1986b *La Civilisation inca au Cuzco,* Essais et Conférences du Collège de France. Paris: Presses Universitaires de France.

Zuidema, R. Tom, and Deborah Poole
1982 "Los límites de los cuatro suyus incaicos en el Cuzco." *Boletín del Instituto Francés de Estudios Andinos,* Vol. 11, Nos. 1–2, pp. 83–89, Lima.

Index